Divine Play, Sacred Laughter, and Spiritual Understanding

This page intentionally left blank

DIVINE PLAY, SACRED LAUGHTER, AND SPIRITUAL UNDERSTANDING

Patrick Laude

DIVINE PLAY, SACRED LAUGHTER, AND SPIRITUAL UNDERSTANDING
© Patrick Laude, 2005.

First published in 2005 by
PALGRAVE MACMILLAN™
175 Fifth Avenue, New York, N.Y. 10010 and
Houndmills, Basingstoke, Hampshire, England RG21 6XS
Companies and representatives throughout the world.

PALGRAVE MACMILLAN is the global academic imprint of the Palgrave Macmillan division of St. Martin's Press, LLC and of Palgrave Macmillan Ltd. Macmillan® is a registered trademark in the United States, United Kingdom and other countries. Palgrave is a registered trademark in the European Union and other countries.

ISBN 978-1-4039-7015-2

Library of Congress Cataloging-in-Publication Data

Laude, Patrick, 1958–
    Divine play, sacred laughter, and spiritual understanding / by Patrick Laude.
        p. cm.
    Includes bibliographical references (p.) and index.
    ISBN 978-1-4039-7015-2
        1. Laughter—Religious aspects. 2. Wit and humor—Religious aspects. 3. Religion—Humor. I. Title.

BL65.L3L38 2005
202'.1—dc22   2005043189

A catalogue record for this book is available from the British Library.

Design by Newgen Imaging Systems (P) Ltd., Chennai, India.

First edition: October 2005

10 9 8 7 6 5 4 3 2 1

Table of Contents

Acknowledgments

I want to thank the Faculty of Languages and Linguistics at Georgetown University for providing me with a 2003 Research Summer Grant that allowed me to complete this manuscript. Thank you to Alireza Nurbakhsh for allowing me to reproduce a revised version of the article "*Malâmiyyah* Psycho-Spiritual Therapy" (*Sufi*, 54, summer 2002) as chapter 10 of this book. My deepest thanks to Christian Fitzpatrick for his liminal and catalytic insights, to Jason Steffen for his attentive and thorough assistance in establishing an extensive bibliography, to Clinton Minaar for his close editing of the manuscript, to André Gomez and Jean-Pierre Lafouge for their careful reading and precious suggestions, to Amira El-Zein and Jacquelyn Bralove for their perceptive enthusiasm in favor of this project, and to my wife Aun Ling for her loving support.

INTRODUCTION

The chapters that follow delve into a wide range of topics that may, at first sight, puzzle a prospective reader in search of a unity of purpose and an architectonic coherence. Nevertheless, the underlying principles and the general focus of this collection of studies will not escape, upon careful review, a reader's attention. The underlying concern of this book is the question of the relationship between the Absolute and the relative, the Necessary and the contingent, God and the created worlds. This question is both fundamentally simple and indefinitely complex depending upon the vantage point one adopts in order to approach it. This question is simple inasmuch as it may always be reduced to schematic metaphysical syntheses that can provide readers endowed with some intellectual intuition with all that they may need to penetrate the conceptual avenues that lead to transformative knowledge. A metaphysical idiom, whether it be highly conceptual like the Advaita Vedânta or simply allusive, symbolic, and nonsystematic like Chuang Tzu's, requires that it not be taken as a literal exhaustion of reality by means of representations. In fact, even its most sophisticated conceptual "constellations" are nothing but symbolic lights that only suggest the infinite vastness of the dark vault of the essential Night. In an ultimate sense, there is nothing more simple than the Absolute, since—as Henry Corbin reminds us[1]—the latter is *ab-solutum*, free in the most radical and integral sense. This supreme freedom from everything cannot but involve simplicity since it includes in its very definition a perfect independence, and since such an independence is incompatible with any kind of compositeness, the latter necessarily entailing the intrinsic constraint that would result from the relationship between its parts. Therefore, the Absolute could be defined as That which is perfectly free, unbound, and simple. In sharp contrast to this perfect simplicity, all that we may experience in our life and in the universe that is most familiar to us, is inextricably marked with compositeness. This compositeness is concomitant with the contingency and relativity of all that we can experience in this realm. In the current context, we understand contingency as the state of a being deprived of intrinsic necessity, and relativity—apart from its strictly technical reference of being exclusively relative to the human mind—as the state of being that is dependent upon something else for its existence, and also of being intrinsically involved in a relation with something other than itself.

The relationship between the Absolute and the relative is in itself a question, since it appears prima facie, contradictory. How can the Absolute, which is unbound, be seemingly bound by a relationship with something else? The very definition of the Absolute precludes Its being relative to, and *a fortiori* contingent upon, another reality. It follows that the Absolute as such does not, and cannot, enter into any "relation" with anything "other" than Itself. In fact, to posit any "other" besides the Absolute would be, *ipso facto*, self-contradictory since it would amount to limiting the field of the Absolute, thereby leaving something out of It, something that could not but be, therefore, "related" to It in one way or another. In other words, if the Absolute is to be what It is, then nothing else can *be* in a full sense. And this is, by the same token, the reason for Its being Infinite, since it can lack nothing that would remain "outside" of Itself, as it were. Any consistent doctrine of the Absolute is therefore by definition "unitarian," or better "non-dualistic": it excludes the very possibility of otherness while including any apparent otherness into the one and only Reality.

On the other hand, there is no doubting that relative beings do exist. We know it to be for being one of them, and for not doubting our existence for a single moment, whatever we may understand by "existence." So, the coincidence of the Absolute and the relative is already, as suggested above, a paradoxical possibility, or a paradoxical impossibility. How can the Absolute and the relative meet? And if they do, can the Absolute still be considered the Absolute? And how can the relative be "related" to what is, by definition, "unrelated" in a universal sense? This is the mystery par excellence, a mystery that we live every day, most often without even being conscious of it.[2] The two terms of this "necessary" and "impossible" relationship are both intrinsically close and infinitely distant. In a sense, all the diverse matters that we propose to discuss in this book provide allusive, enigmatic, and paradoxical answers to this coincidence of opposites. The phenomena that we study in the following pages are all situated at the critical intersection of two incommensurably disproportionate realms, the Absolute and the relative, whence emerge the unsettling, ambiguous, unbalanced, and puzzling aspects of reality that they oblige us to consider and confront, albeit reluctantly.

In a most general sense, the realm of the relative is an expression, or a manifestation, of the Absolute. In this respect, the relative reflects the perfections of the Absolute, and provides us, therefore, with a measure of order and balance that stems from these perfections. This, in a very concrete and immediate sense, is why we can and must go about being who we are and doing what we do in this world, while knowing that this world is not "the whole story," and certainly not the end of it. In another sense though, the Absolute manifests Itself, as a flash so to speak, in particular realities and phenomena that bear a more direct imprint of Its reality than the overall realm that proceeds from it. This is the privileged and sacred domain of symbols, theophanies, saints, prophets, and revelations. Now, these more direct manifestations of the Absolute, which are like vertical and powerful influxes of light, bring with them both a message of transcendence and a message of immanence, in a dual complementarity that, in a sense, replicates the two dimensions of distance and closeness within their theophanic array of influence. There is, first, a definite sense in which the Absolute cannot be manifested in the relative without cracking the shell of the latter. When these two incommensurable realities meet, there cannot but be "trouble in the kingdom," even though this trouble is ultimately the means of transcending the plane upon which the trouble appears to be real, and, therefore, the violent way of establishing a new and higher balance and peace on the ashes of a previous and precarious equilibrium. From this standpoint, the irruption of the Absolute within the relative is lightning-like, like the Lakota clown *heyoka*, as it shatters and destroys the fabric of this world, like Dionysus' maenads rip apart their garments in the ecstasy of their amorous rapture for the god, or like Shiva annihilating the present world in order to give rise to a new one. Considered from this vantage point the relative has ultimately no reality, and only the Absolute *is*.

From another standpoint, the relative also "includes" seeds of absoluteness, if one may say so, and these seeds may be grown into ladders leading up to heaven. This is the point of view of the world as a "natural" theophany. However, even these spiritual seeds, these metaphysical messages, involve a sacred element of "foreignness," "oddity," or "madness" when considered from the standpoint of ordinary consciousness, either in themselves, like the terrible and awesome aspect of nature and beauty, or as a kind of shadow, which is like the harsh ransom of transcendence within immanence. There is no beauty that does not testify to God's beauty, as many mystics have indicated, but there is also no beauty that does not entail limitation, and thereby point indirectly to a higher level than its own. A given perfection may be perfect on its level, but it excludes other perfections, while being condemned to imperfection by both space and time. One way or another, if the world of relativity shares in some reality it is because something, or some things, in it do not fit into its self-satisfied tendency to claim and pretend that it is "absolute" in its own right. Moreover, the dialectic of closeness and distance that lies at the core of the relationship between the Absolute and the relative accounts, in its own complex way, for the ambiguity of the realm of relativity, a realm in which God is both present and absent, infinitely far and "more intimate" to ourselves than our selves.

The prime objective of this book is to explore those turbulent and ambiguous zones where the Absolute destroys, shatters, unsettles, troubles, and tricks for the sake of an awakening and a rebirth, as well as to study the odd occurrences and phenomena that bear witness to the sacred, and thereby the "immeasurable measures" of the Absolute, from within the world of relativity. These zones are both "necessary" and "impossible" in the sense that they mediate realities that in a certain sense have no "*medium*." The domain of mediation is that of a third term, a term that must in the last analysis make us understand that there is only One. Oddity is the ransom of mediation, because that which mediates can never, by definition, be totally on one side or the other.[3] The goal of these studies is to explain and situate these phenomena within a meaningful metaphysical and mystical context, in order to demonstrate their crucial importance for a deepening of one's understanding of Reality, and one's understanding of oneself. These are neither picturesque and bizarre excesses, tricks and follies to enjoy as an entertaining therapy for worldly boredom; nor should they be dismissed as marginal and accidental, or even worse, rejected as dangerous and subversive. These cracks of light are, on the contrary, the unavoidable and fruitful manifestations of realities that one can ignore or despise only at one's own spiritual and psychic impoverishment. The relationship between the Absolute and the relative is ultimately predicated on the higher reality, perfection, and intrinsic equilibrium of the former as Supreme Principle; and yet it is also true, and it cannot be ignored, that the incommensurable disproportion that this relationship necessarily involves is not without its lot of paradoxes, compensatory excesses, and madness for real sanity's sake. In a world as fragmented and topsy-turvy as that in which we live today, it is particularly undeniable that contemporary mankind cannot but encounter the sacred "scandals," holy "shocks," and divine "surprises" that result from the coincidence of opposites and the meeting of extremes. To pretend that it can be otherwise would amount to not heeding Pascal's famous and ever-relevant statements: "What is man in nature? Nothing in relation to the infinite, all in relation to nothing, a mean between nothing and everything," and "Man is neither angel nor brute, and the unfortunate thing is that he who would act the angel acts the brute."[4] There is in the human condition, as if suspended between the Infinite and the finite, an unavoidable aspect of disequilibrium that cannot but be taken into account if one aims at finding a supreme balance in the Absolute. Man is like a drop of water carried away on the waves of the Infinite; he cannot pretend being what he is not, he can only realize that he is not. As a contemporary Sioux medicine man, in his plain and refreshing language, puts it:

> You can't be so stuck up, so inhuman that you want to be pure, your soul wrapped up in a plastic bag, all the time. [. . .] Being a good medicine man means being right in the midst of the turmoil, not shielding yourself from it. It means experiencing life in all its phases.[5]

Now, it might be a good way to define the chapters that follow as various explorations of what it means to remember the One in "the midst of the turmoil."

This being said, we have to add that one or another of the phenomena that are explored in the following pages may not speak to all readers with the same sense of need and urgency. We know by experience that the stories of Coyote, the tricks of Hermes, or the extreme pranks of holy fools are not, and need not, be to everybody's liking and profit, far from that. To some extent and *mutatis mutandis*, what is true of esoterism can also be said of "cracks of light." Both share the precariousness of their manifestations and the circumstantial relevance of their teachings. Moreover, esoteric doctrines and practices lend themselves to concealment and paradox given their profundity and subtlety. The kinds of phenomena that we propose to study thereby serve, not infrequently, as vehicles or masks for esoteric teachings. In acknowledging this relationship, however, we do not mean to equate "cracks of light" with esoterism as such. Be that as it may, although the phenomena that we examine in this book do not necessarily address an exclusive group of readers, there is still no doubt that they may speak "louder" to those who have a good ear for them—if one may be allowed this paradox, while discouraging, disturbing, or even irritating those who, for some reason or another, do not spontaneously enter into the "logic of their illogicality." It must be recognized that two readers with similar backgrounds and perspectives may react differently to, say, a reading of some of Rabelais' obscene stories, in which one may pluck a flower of hidden meaning from within the mud, while another will do away with the whole thing out of a sense of uselessness, and even perhaps disgust. Without implying that one of the readers is "right" and the other "wrong" for reacting in a certain way, we must certainly recognize that these stories may bear some lessons for one, while remaining more or less irrelevant for another. Differences of outlook on this matter no doubt stem from a complex network of sensibility, vocation, experiences, cultural determinations, and so forth. Moreover—and this is another important aspect of the parallel one can draw between esoterism and our phenomena—just as esoterism can be turned into fanciful elucubrations or dangerous errors, "cracks of light" can also be turned into "cracks of darkness." One needs to be aware that, when dealing with them, one is as it were dancing on a razor's edge. And this leads to a final question of ponderous import: why in the world deal with these de facto slippery and a priori disorienting facts when everything is already so perversely upside down in the world in which we live? We have already provided some answers to this question above, when quoting Pascal, but we would like to add two more interrelated answers inspired by a native American perspective. In the foreword to an edition of Black Elk's revelations to Joseph Epes Brown, we read that most contemporary Indian sages think that now the time has come to divulge what had been heretofore dangerous to reveal: the reason being that truth can defend itself by its own nature against any kind of profanation, and that it has never been so needed as it is today.[6] To radically abnormal situations, one must respond with radically atypical means. As a matter of fact, this eschatological perspective is already inscribed in Coyote's stories, as testified by these words of "Old Man"—God, or the Supreme Spirit:

> "Coyote and myself, we will not be seen again until Earth-woman is very old. Then we shall return to earth, for it will require a change by that time. Coyote will come along first, and when you see him you will know I am coming. When I come along, all the spirits of the dead will be with me. There will be no more Other Side Camp. All the people will live together. Earth-mother will go back to her first shape and live as a mother among her children. Then things will be made right." Now they are waiting for Coyote.[7]

Coyote prepares the ways of the One, but he often does so in a destructive and disorderly fashion, and there is no way around that paradox—although there is always a way above. Only the way above bears the hallmark of absolute necessity, but it also remains true that, in our world of indirection that ultimately "Heaven will direct," the zigzagging and puzzling path of Coyote may save us from falling from cliffs and banging into stone walls.

This page intentionally left blank

CHAPTER 1

MÂYÂ AND THE DIVINE TREASURE

Within the Islamic tradition, representatives of Sufi mysticism often refer to a prophetic tradition in which God declares, "I was a hidden treasure and I wanted to be known, therefore I created the world." This *hadîth qudsî* (a tradition transmitted by the Prophet of Islam in which the Divinity speaks in the first person) includes, in a way, the whole metaphysical doctrine of the relationship between the Absolute and the relative, and it may, as such, constitute a general introduction to the philosophical underpinnings of our present study. There are at least four levels to consider in this saying: (1) that of the I, the pure Subject, (2) that of the Divine Subject's perception of being a "Hidden Treasure," (3) that of the Divine Will ("I wanted"), and (4) that of the Divine as Object of knowledge.

God's utterance in the first person indicates, here, the primacy of Subjectivity within the Divine Order. God says "I" before anything else because he is "I" "before"[1] being anything else. God is pure Consciousness "before" He may become an Object for Other-than-Himself. Consciousness is prior to Being in the sense that it includes Being, there being no Consciousness without Being. This is the reason why Hinduism, particularly in the Advaita Vedânta school, considers the Divine primarily as a Subject, *Âtman*. *Âtman* is the underlying Self of all that is. At a second "stage," God's "awareness" of being a "Hidden Treasure" introduces a symbolic "distance" within Himself that is like the "invisible point" from which a divine "desire to be known" emerges. The "Hidden Treasure" is traditionally understood as referring to the Divine Essence in Its deeper dimension of unknowableness. The Innermost is a "Treasure" because It "contains" the most precious possibilities of being, and it is "Hidden" inasmuch as these possibilities are "buried" within It in an undifferentiated mode.

This essential dimension is unknowable inasmuch as It transcends any determination and any relation that would allow for a "comprehension," and thereby a delimitation, of Its infinite mystery. Christian mystical theology has sometimes referred to this essential realm, in the terms of Dionysus the Areopagite, as a "hyperluminous Darkness" or a "Darkness that is beyond light," a paradoxical image that can be better understood when one considers the implications of the symbolism of the "blinding sun." Along these symbolic lines, Dionysus refers to the Divine Essence as "the pure, absolute and immutable mysteries of heavenly Truth (that are) veiled in the dazzling obscurity of the secret Silence, outshining all brilliance with the intensity of their Darkness and surcharging our blinded intellects with the utterly impalpable and invisible fairness of glories surpassing all beauty." The supreme Essence is too luminous not to appear dark, by dint of Its pure and intense luminosity, from the point of view of that which lies below the domain of Its Light.

In addition to the dimensions of subjective consciousness and inexhaustibly blinding mystery that we have just highlighted, the *hadîth* of the "Hidden Treasure" symbolically alludes, moreover, to a manner of "lack" or "need," as it were, within the supreme plenitude of the Essence. This mysterious and paradoxical "lack" or "need" is expressed in various ways in different esoteric traditions: it may be referred to as a kind of "sadness" of the One in Its "Aloneness," as in Ibn 'Arabî's gnosis, an "emptiness" like the Christian *kenôsis*, or a "contraction" or "withdrawal" as conceptualized by some currents within Jewish Kabbalah by their notion of *tsimtsum*.[2]

The contradiction inherent in the notion of a divine Perfection that would "need" something lies at the core of the supreme metaphysical enigma. This perplexing enigma is none other than a symbolic expression of the roots of Relativity in the Divine, Relativity referring to all realities that are not absolute in the sense of being metaphysically "free" from any dependence upon another reality. The "unevenness" of Creation, the "imbalance" that is a direct result of manifestation and relativity, must be prefigured in some way within the Divine Order. The *hadîth* that we have quoted represents this prefiguration symbolically in the form of a consciousness of being "concealed." It has therefore the metaphysical advantage of not envisaging this prefiguration, literally or directly, as a lack that would inherently affect or contradict the Divine Plenitude and Infinity. The dimension of concealment, as with its parallels of "sadness" and "aloneness," still alludes to a manner of "singularity," and therefore in a certain sense to an "oddity" within the Oneness of God. The number one, being so to speak the archetypal source of all odd numbers, is intrinsically open to duality, as expressed through the manifestation of Otherness, or through Creation. "Concealment" can therefore be envisaged symbolically as the hidden principle of a rupture of balance within Unity, at least inasmuch as it becomes the object of an awareness on the part of Unity.

It goes without saying that this paradoxical manner of speaking is only symbolic and allusive, and should not be taken literally as referring to a fundamental disequilibrium within the Divine. Be that as it may, the awareness of concealment results in the emergence of a "desire to be known" within the Divine Unity. This "desire" points for the first time to a tendency toward "externalization" or a "going out of oneself," to the emergence of a dynamic, outward-leaning motion within the One. It is only when this "desire" has been satisfied that we can properly speak of an entrance into the domain of what has been called the "subject–object" mode of consciousness-without-an-object, a mode that is characterized by an intrinsic polarity between a subject that knows and an object that is known.

The Divine first conceives of Itself in an "objective" manner, as a Hidden Treasure, before "conceiving" the "objects" which will be endowed with "something" of Its Subjectivity in order for them to be able to perceive It in their turn as Supreme Object, or Treasure. The *hadîth qudsî* of the Hidden Treasure thereby points to an objectifying externalization (to become an object that is known by a subject) resulting from the innermost mystery of Subjectivity as "Consciousness-without-an object."[3] Multiplicity, as a consequence of the projection of the Hidden Treasure within the objective realm of duality, thus becomes the outermost counterpart of the "rupture of balance" resulting from the emerging awareness of "concealment." As a result, the polarity between subject and object, which is the very principle of relativity, entails a kind of reverse "concealment," a concealment that Sufism often characterizes symbolically as a "veil," *Hijâb*. The realm of the "subject–object consciousness" involves an illusory distance that opens the door to levels of perception and consciousness expressed by the Sufi notion of the "thousand veils," which both reveal and conceal the Divine Light. The polarity between subject and object also presupposes the reality of various perspectives of the same object, as well as a multiplicity of facets in the object as it may be experienced by the subject. The first consideration—that of a plurality of veils upon the Divine Reality—implies a kind of game of "hide and seek" on the part of the Divinity and is the highest paradigm of the tricking humor at work throughout Universal Reality.

In a sense any tricking "prestidigitation" is archetypically related to this Divine Play. As for the second characteristic, it archetypically accounts for the diversity of outlooks and aspects upon which the very ambiguity of relative reality is founded, and which is the source of all modes of humor, laughter, and demiurgic play with possibilities. This realm is, properly speaking, that of the Hindu *Mâyâ*, whose disequilibrium and ambivalence cannot be resolved upon its own plane since it has no meaning independently from the Higher Reality that "allowed" it to be. *Mâyâ* is in that sense the realm of absurdity, but an absurdity that can at any moment be reabsorbed into the Pure Meaning of *Âtman*.

The Hindu—and specifically Advaitin—notion of *Mâyâ* may be approached from a variety of perspectives that ultimately involve either an ontological, or an epistemological emphasis. It could be said that, in principle, the first approach pertains to a metaphysical description of reality, or the doctrinal dimension of Advaita, whereas the second is mostly relevant to the "subjective" realm of method, or the way of spiritual realization. But in fact, classical expositions of the doctrine of *Mâyâ* define the latter's ontological status on the basis of epistemological principles. From an ontological point of view *Mâyâ* is both a mystery and a necessity. It is a mystery because *Mâyâ* cannot be considered as either real or unreal. The "indetermination" of its ontological status stems from its being both the Absolute, *Brahman*, and not the Absolute at the same time. *Advaita* is by definition non-dualistic (*a-dvaita*), which means that it posits that only *Brahman* is, and that, therefore, everything is *Brahman*. The Upanishads express this non-duality by postulating an emanation of the universe from *Brahman*, but "despite this emanation *Brahman*' is still the same'—in which case it is evident, whatever else may be true, that the universe and *Brahman* are not identical; and it is precisely the identity of the two that the West understands by pantheism."[4] Therefore, in one sense the universe is *Brahman*, and in another sense it is not. According to the latter perspective the universe can be defined as *Mâyâ*. *Mâyâ* is the universe as distinct from *Brahman*; the idea of *Mâyâ* is therefore crucial to a proper understanding of the paradox of the dual nature of the Absolute as being both inclusive and exclusive.

Yet another correlative dimension of the concept of *Mâyâ* in relation to *Brahman* is that of the production of the universe. While *Brahman* is undoubtedly the principle of all that is, It cannot be considered as Creator of the universe since It stands beyond all dualities and oppositions, including that which relates creatures to a Creator. It follows from this that the Creator of the universe can only be considered at the level of *Mâyâ* This Creator is called *Iswara*. In Swami Prabhavananda's terms, "*Iswara* is *Brahman* united with *mâyâ*, the combination which creates, preserves, and dissolves the universe in an endless and beginningless process. *Iswara* is God personified, God with attributes."[5] From this definition of *Iswara* we may infer that *Mâyâ* pertains to the entire field of Relativity: *Mâyâ* is the Relative. A most important consequence of including *Iswara*, or God as a person, within that field lies in the fact that God and His Creation are no longer conceived as two "absolutes" standing apart from each other. The realm of the universe "as different from God" loses its ontological "density" and becomes porous, so to speak, to the universal immanence of *Brahman* as non-dual Principle.

Although we have begun by sketching a kind of metaphysical mapping out of *Mâyâ*, Advaita Vedânta tends to approach the latter from an epistemological point of view. In that sense, *Mâyâ* is none other than the rope, which is mistakenly taken to be a snake, to use one of the symbols consecrated by the Advaita tradition. She is the product or the effect of a superimposition (*adhyâsa*) upon the only Reality of *Brahman*, or *Âtman*, the latter term referring to the Absolute as Self. This superimposition, which is the bitter fruit of ignorance, results in a fundamental distinction between subject and object. *Mâyâ* is in this sense what Franklin Merrell-Wolff has proposed to call the field of the subject–object consciousness, as contrasted with the domain of Consciousness-without-an-object.[6] The latter refers to *Âtman* as such; it refers to Reality as perceived from the standpoint of Reality, therefore without any trace of objectification. As for the former, it results from *avidyâ*, that is, lack of knowledge or "vision." *Vidyâ* is ultimately identification with *Âtman*, whereas *avidyâ* is akin to a distinction between subject and object, a distinction that is congenitally entailed in individual cognition. It is highly instructive to note that *Mâyâ* is sometimes referred to as *lîlâ*, or play. The only significant distinction between the two concepts lies in that the term *lîlâ* tends to be reserved for *Mâyâ* as production of the Creator or *Iswara*. Inasmuch as *Mâyâ* might be equated with *Iswara* she would not be referred to as *lîlâ*. In the terms of Shankara, "the activity of the Lord [. . .] may be supposed to be mere sport (*lîlâ*), proceeding from his own nature, without reference to any purpose."[7] The manifestation of the Absolute is not purposeful, even though it is meaningful. It is purposeless to the extent that *Mâyâ* cannot be accounted for in terms that would be other than her mere being as superimposition on the Absolute, *Âtman*. It is meaningful inasmuch as she is ultimately none other than pure Meaning or pure Being, when perceived from the standpoint of

Âtman. Mâyâ is a projection, a "dream," and as such it is neither fully real nor fully unreal. *Mâyâ* is inexplicable in itself, and yet without her nothing can be "explained." Her appearance is without beginning, and without cause; her end is reached only through *moksha*, or deliverance from the illusion of separativeness, which stems from the superimposition of the relative upon the Absolute. The ontological and epistemological ambiguity of *Mâyâ* is the very key to a full understanding of the "seriousness" of the world while being also the door opening onto an awareness of its lack of "seriousness." That is why, as M. Conrad Hyers has insightfully argued, the sacred and the comic are so intimately dependent upon each other, "in both directions lie those demonic possibilities that may be realized by eliminating either side of the dialectic of the sacred and the comic."[8] The world is a serious matter because it is none other than *Âtman*, and because *Mâyâ* is its outer "weaving." But the world is also not to be taken too seriously because it is not *Âtman*; and it is so because *Mâyâ* cannot be seen as real when the error that results from superimposition has been corrected and the rope is recognized as being a rope and not a snake. To see *Mâyâ* as exclusively unreal amounts to frivolity or cynicism. To see *Mâyâ* as exclusively real amounts to idolatry, fanaticism, and a radical lack of sense of humor. Any phenomenon that reveals the lack of full reality of *Mâyâ* is a liberating way toward the Absolute, and such is the laughing playfulness that rips apart the close-knit textile of existential illusion.

Although *Mâyâ* is often associated with the realm of physical reality, it would be more accurate to consider her as particularly akin to the psychic realm. Strictly speaking of course, *Mâyâ* encompasses both of these domains. When referring to these two domains we are implicitly alluding to the widespread worldview of three hierarchically arranged levels of reality that is to be found in several metaphysical and mystical traditions. This tripartition is present in Plato in the form of the distinction between three layers of "subjective" reality, that is, *noûs*, *psyche*, and *soma*. The *noûs* is the spiritual principle of man "consubstantial" with the archetypes and may therefore know the Forms or Ideas. *Soma* is the physical reality, the most external and "unreal" fringe of reality. As for *psyche*, it encompasses the plastic and "humid" (Heraclitus) domain of the expanses of the soul, the latter referring not only to individualized animic substances but also, and above all, to the "ocean" of the animic forms and appearances that is the "milieu" within which individual souls live and move. Sufism presents us with the same layout in the "objective" realm, with its *'âlam al-jabârut*, *'âlam al-mithâl*, and *'âlam al-ajsâm* (world of omnipotence, world of the alike, world of bodies).[9] The "world of the alike" is none other than the psychic, animic, or intermediary realm in which spiritual realities "take form," as it were. It is a world of "imitations," "copies," analogies, and symbolic reverberations. This world is the domain of theater and representation, a realm that suggests the "unreal reality" of *Mâyâ* par excellence. The fact that this intermediary realm is also the field in which the art of magic—as the manipulation and use of psychic forces—is exercised, rings a particularly meaningful bell when related to the pervasive reference to *Mâyâ* as a "magic of God."[10]

Although it could be argued that the physical realm is more *Mâyâ*-bound than higher domains, precisely because it holds less "reality" than the latter, the case could also be made, and more satisfactorily, that the intermediary status of the psychic realm suggests an affinity between its level of manifestation and the nature of *Mâyâ*. If *Mâyâ* is to be understood as making the link between the Real and the unreal, while partaking of both, the same could be said analogically of the animic dimension, a dimension that relates the higher spiritual spheres to the physical shell of the universe, or vice versa. Eknath Easwaran has suggested the relevance of this analogy in defining *Mâyâ*—the third element that mediates between "Conscious spirit" and "unconscious matter"—as "the confusion of the other two, the mix-up of their roles."[11] On the spiritual and epistemological levels, *Mâyâ* is none other than the soul, or the ego, inasmuch as it fluctuates between its function of faithful reflection of spiritual realities and that of dispersion within the multiplicity of phenomena. On that level too, *Mâyâ* is both real and unreal. The individual locus of consciousness solidified in the form of an egoic substance is undoubtedly real insofar as it prolongs pure Consciousness, but it "becomes" unreal as soon as it posits itself as being independent of its source. This is the deepest root of all forms of egocentrism and egoism, thereby—directly or indirectly—the root of all evils. It could also be said that it is real only insofar as it knows itself to be unreal, and that it is unreal to the extent that it thinks of itself as fully real. The absence of a notion of *Mâyâ* at the level of subjective life amounts to an absolutization of the egoic consciousness.

Georges Vallin has argued that such is the generic definition of consciousness in the West, a definition that is the very source of the Western emphasis on the tragic dimension. In other words, the Western mind has been entrapped in a kind of absolutization of the ego as locus of individual consciousness, an absolutization that cannot but entail a profoundly dramatic and fateful battle against finitude with the very weapons of finitude. Even the best sapiential avenues of

Western philosophy, such as Plato's wisdom, do not provide as clear a recognition of the illusion of individual self-consciousness as does Hindu Advaita or Buddhism. By contrast, any spiritual context in which *Mâyâ* is taken into consideration so as to account for the ambiguities of the ego is *ipso facto* freed from this tragic obsession. In Vallin's terms, "Western man is essentially tragic because negativity is with him original and not only derivative. His belief in the reality of the ego seems to us to explain in what way he remains fundamentally distinguished from the traditional Asian man."[12] Tragic destiny is a result of an absolutization of the relative that amounts in fact to an ignorance of the realm of *Mâyâ*. By contrast, a metaphysical sense for the play or comedy of existence stems from the full consideration of the ontological ambiguity of *Mâyâ*. The notion of *Mâyâ*—or its equivalents outside of India—is thereby central to an understanding of the jokes and tricks that are integral parts of the metaphysical perspective and the esoteric outlook.

CHAPTER 2

AMBIGUITY OF THE DEMIURGE

In his important chapter on the "Demiurge in North American Mythology"[1] Frithjof Schuon has suggested a profound correlation between the notion of *Mâyâ* and that of the Demiurge. According to Schuon the "key to this doctrine is basically that by definition Infinitude demands the dimension of the finite."[2] *Mâyâ* can be considered as the extrinsic dimension of Infinitude. She is so inasmuch as she can be defined as the unfolding of the inexhaustible core of the infinite Reality. *Mâyâ* is like the projected mask of the faceless Infinite.[3] This unfolding results of necessity in the production of finite beings that may be considered as fragmented shells of the Divine Whole. Fragmentation and externalization are by the same token the very roots of what we call evil. Evil has nothing absolute, or even fully real, about it; it is only the extreme consequence of the inversion and fragmentation of Reality as *Mâyâ*. Now the Demiurge can be precisely defined as the ambiguous principle of the unfolding of *Mâyâ* as it manifests itself in the onto-cosmogonic process. Frithjof Schuon has remarkably encapsulated the metaphysical foundation of the doctrine of the Demiurge while distinguishing the various levels of manifestation of the creative Word on the level of Being and Existence:

> The creative Word can be understood at two levels, and it is this "fluctuation" that explains the all but general incomprehension, on the part of theologians, of the Platonic "demiurge." In the first place, the Word is situated at the degree of the ontological Principle, Being, of which it is the active pole, the Vedantic *Purusha*; it is the Divine Intellect which conceives the possibilities of manifestation or the archetypes. Next, at the very center of Universal Manifestation, there is the operative reflection of *Purusha*, namely *Buddhi*, the manifested and

acting Word; and this is the demiurge proper. This *Buddhi* is "the Spirit of God which moved upon the waters," while the divine *Purusha* remains immutable, since It pertains to Pure Being; but as we have said, Being is mirrored at the center of Existence—as *Buddhi*, precisely—in order to become efficient.[4]

In order to attain to a full understanding of the above passage, one must be aware that traditional metaphysical doctrines tend to distinguish three planes of Reality that may be represented by the open sky, the sun, and the world as illumined by the latter. These are (1) Non-Being or Beyond Being, the *Nirguna Brahman* (Non-Qualified Absolute) of Advaita, Meister Eckhart's Godhead, the *Ayin* (Nothing) of Kabbalah, and the *Ahadiyah* (Divine Unity) of Sufism, (2) Being or God as Creator, and (3) Existence or Universal Manifestation. Inasmuch as the Divine Word is the Principle of Creation, It does not explicitly appear on the level of Beyond-Being. This is why mystical theologies of the Essence, even in a monotheistic context, tend to transcend the level of God-as-Person in order to emphasize that the Divine Essence stands infinitely beyond any Creator as related to Creation, while the Creator is obviously "included" within this Divine Essence, and therefore not in any way "relative" in the sense in which a created reality is.

* * *

Even though some cosmological terminologies might seem to collapse the notion of God and that of the Demiurge—such as in *Timaeus*, where Plato refers at times to "the divinity" (*ho theos*), and at other times to the "demiurge" (*ho dêmiourgos*)—the Demiurge pertains, strictly speaking, to a lower level than that which is the purview of the Creator. The Demiurge does not create *ex nihilo*, but rather shapes the universe from disorderliness into order, from chaos into cosmos. As such, he may appear as a kind of subordinate "officer" working at the service of the Sovereign Good. This subordination is already implied by the fact that the Demiurge "makes" the world by gazing upon "patterns" (*paradeigmata*) that are transcendent in relation to him. The Demiurge does not draw creatures from his own non-manifested all-possibility, nor does he extract them from nothingness, but he is rather a divine "maker," an artificer, or a "constructor" who works an amorphous, recalcitrant, and disorderly matter into a harmonious cosmos. Matter is not only lacking in order and intelligibility, but it also tends to resist the informing influence of the Demiurge as he directs his gaze upon the paradigms in order to bring the world into conformity with them. This negative and subversive aspect, which is philosophically articulated in Aristotle's hylomorphic doctrine of matter (*hylê*), was highlighted by Philo of Alexandria, with whom it provided a philosophical argument in favor of Biblical theodicy.[5] In this context the matter upon which the demiurgic principle operates is the very source of evil, and God's goodness is thereby exempted from any responsibility for this evil. Accordingly, the demiurgic level, by including the source of evil within its fold, excludes the Biblical Creator from the realm of ambiguity: it works for the Sovereign Good while operating upon the principle of its negation, that is, "recalcitrant" matter. In keeping with the implications of the Demiurge's function as an agent of God and a "tamer" of matter, the Greek term *demiourgos* literally refers to the idea of a "public work," which in a way emphasizes both the laboring nature of the Demiurge and the relatively lower and external character of the realm within which he works for the sake of the whole. As such the Demiurge is the archetype of the craftsman or the artificer, and he is in fact often associated with the symbolism of the potter. He uses a preexisting reality, whether it be potential, infra-formal, or chaotic that he shapes along the lines of his design, a design that is in fact a reflection, albeit "from a distance," of the patterns "situated" in the "ever and forever" (*aei*) of the Supreme. This is the picture of the Demiurge that Plato proposes in his *Timaeus*:

> Wherefore also finding the whole visible sphere not at rest (*hesychia*), but moving in an irregular and disorderly fashion, out of disorder he brought order (*taxis*), considering that this was in every way better than the other. (30a)[6]

Plato's Demiurge orders and "pacifies," or "beautifies" the world, not only—as we have already mentioned—by referring his work to the models or the paradigms of the Good, a realm that transcends him and his work, but also out of a desire to make things in his own nature, as testified by Plato's indication that "He was good, and in him that is good no envy ariseth ever concerning anything; and being devoid of envy. He desired that all should be, so far as possible, like unto Himself" (29e).[7] Whence the ambiguity of the Divine in Plato, a notion that may refer either to the efficient cause of the cosmos, or—on a higher level—to its "formal" cause, that is, to the intelligible Prototype of Reality. This difficulty—which betrays in its own manner the very complexity of the onto-cosmological process—may account for Plato's allusion to the "hard work" (*ergon*) of "discovering" the "Maker and Father" (*poiêtênkai patera*) of all things, and the impossibility (*adunaton*) of "telling it" to all men (*eis pantas legein*) (28c). In other words, this passage may be interpreted as a hint at the multilayered structure of the Divine Reality and a correlative recognition of the esoteric nature of the teachings that can take into full account and make sense of this complexity.

Even though the order of exposition in the *Timaeus* begins with a description of the Demiurge's construction of the "Body of the World," which involves primarily a harmonic combination of the four cosmological elements (first fire and earth, and then air and water as "proportional" mediators) Plato instructs us that, chronologically and ontologically, the first work of the Demiurge was the production of the World Soul. It is only at the second stage that the Body is formed "within" the Soul and united to her "center to center" (*meson mesêi*) (36e). In a sense the Demiurge is separate from the World Soul since He "produces" and "informs" Her, in a way that is analogous to the process through which, in the Hindu Sâmkhya, *Purusha* "informs" *Prakrti*.[8] But in another sense the Potter and the Clay are indissociable; they are one and the same reality.[9] This "discrete unity" that defines the relationship between the Demiurge and the World Soul finds an extrinsic reflection in the very process through which the Demiurge "produces" the World Soul. While the duality of the Demiurge and the World Soul implicitly unfolds from a single Principle, as a move from unity to duality, the "formation" of the World Soul proceeds from a duality that is mediated by a third term in order to be brought back to unity. So it is that, for Plato, the Demiurge makes use of three elements in order to shape the World Soul: Sameness, pertaining to the indivisible and changeless; Otherness, the principle of divisibility, change, and multiplication; and Being or Essence (*ousia*), which is conceived as a reality commonly proportional to both Sameness and Otherness. There is, everywhere in the manifested universe, Identity and Difference, while Being is the "middle way" uniting these two distinct principles. It is "with the Essence" or "with the aid of Being" (*meta tês ousias*) that the Same and the Other are united, the latter being "forced" into this unity by reason of its tendency to introduce "alterity." This is a way of suggesting that when the Demiurge's work is considered from the standpoint of the element of Sameness, it reflects the changelessness and simplicity of Being; when his work is envisaged from the vantage point of Otherness it expresses the realities of division and change together with all that these principles entail.

The complex Platonic combination of the Same, the Other, and Being amounts to nothing else, in Hindu parlance, than a symbolically circumstantiated recognition of the cosmogonic reflection of the interplay of *Âtman* and *Mâyâ*. Considering this interplay on the metaphysical and onto-cosmological levels, it could be said that the Creator is *Mâyâ* in *Âtman* and the Demiurge is *Âtman* in *Mâyâ*. The Demiurge can be considered either from the point of view of *Âtman*, whence its intelligibility and its character of "Higher *Mâyâ*," or from the point of view of *Mâyâ*, in which case it is the lack of intelligibility that dominates, or "Lower *Mâyâ*." The Demiurge is the principle of production, and as such, he is also the principle of inversion. Any production, or any manifestation, involves the passage from nothing to something, but since "nothing can come out of nothing" it must mean that something is already *in potentia* in "No-Thing." Manifestation, being a kind of externalization, appears to be "nothing" when considered from the standpoint of the essences of manifested beings. Conversely, the essences seem to be "nothing" when they are envisaged from the vantage point of manifestation. One of the most suggestive expressions of this paradox is found in Chuang Tzu's reference to the archetypical "holes" through which the wind of existentiation blows. Holes are empty and so in a sense "nothing," but without them the music of wind and moving air could not be heard, or manifested. Just as a tree reflected in a pool keeps its shape and is at the same time inverted, what is innermost *in principio* appears outermost in manifestation. The Divine Treasure (the Infinite as "concealed") becomes the Universe (Infinity being the principle of outward multiplicity). The "good" aspect of the demiurgic work is a reflection of the archetypes. This aspect appears most clearly in Plato's Demiurge, since the latter shapes the world by imitating the Good, or the Ideas. As for the "bad" aspect, or let us say the ambiguous dimension, of the demiurgic principle, it results from the inversion that is involved in the process of manifestation, as it is expressed in Plato by the symbolic principle of Otherness. This principle of Otherness appears primarily on the level of Existence, since this level is the one most obviously related to the aforementioned inversion. But it may also appear on the level of Being, as is testified, among numerous examples, by the ambiguous function of Shiva in the indu *Trimurti*.[10] Shiva is both one of three supreme gods and the ambiguous principle of cosmogonic manifestation, sometimes bordering on what Semitic monotheism would define as "satanic."[11] This shows that demiurgic ambiguity is not only to be found at the Center of Existence, which is its primary domain of manifestation, but even somehow higher, on the level of Being.

The latter remark holds true also in the case of Semitic monotheism, as shown by the Quranic name of the "best of deceivers"

(*Khayr al-Mâkirîn*) that is paradoxically attributed to God. The *Qur'ân* often refers to God's works as tricks performed upon men, especially upon the unbelievers whose actions are "made (by God) to appear beautiful in their own eyes." Two occurrences of the term *Khayr al-Mâkirîn* are to be found in the Arabic *Qur'ân*. The first appears in the *Surah* of "The Family of 'Imrân" (3:54): "And (the unbelievers) plotted and planned, and Allâh too planned, and the best of planners is Allâh" (Yusuf Ali translation). The translation of *Khayr al-Mâkirîn* by "best of planners" alludes to the providential dimension of the demiurgic function of God, but it fails to render—probably by a kind of moralistic uneasiness with the concrete implications of the term—the element of cunning—and quasi-malevolence—that is part and parcel of the Arabic term.[12] Actually, from the standpoint of the demiurgic principle, which outwardly manifests the infinite Possibility of the Supreme, even errors must in fact be considered as "relative realities" since they proceed from the fragmentation that is necessarily entailed by the process of manifestation.[13] The Demiurge is the "prince of errors" inasmuch as errors proceed from the fragmentation that is part and parcel of Relativity. Considered from a "subjective" and epistemological point of view, it can even be said that the Demiurge is nothing but the projection or the superimposition of our own limited perspective upon reality, since "objectively" (or rather "subjectively" when considered for the standpoint of the only Subject) there is no absolute separation within Reality. This is why the Supreme Liberation from the realm of Relativity can also be considered as the only way to be liberated from "the Empire of the Demiurge."[14]

Christ's spiritual message of freedom from sin is, on a religious plane, an expression of that liberation from the demiurgic realm. And this fact explains why the Gospel's reference to the "prince of this world" is replete with implications that identify Satan with the Demiurge. The "otherworldliness" of Christ's message is parallel to an emphasis upon a consideration of the world of Creation from the point of view of the Fall, or within the perspective of a "separation" from the Divine. In other words, the world is squarely identified with the demiurgic domain as Satan's kingdom. Although this perspective may, as we see, lend itself to seemingly dualistic tendencies in the Christian spiritual outlook, it is important to stress that, strictly speaking, the negative connotations of the "world" result in fact from a perversion inherent in the postlapsarian way of envisaging reality—in a dualistic manner, precisely—rather than in the world as Creation. In the most profound sense, it is this perversion that "makes" the world an "empire" of the prince of darkness.

Still, it is also true that the corruption of the human perception of the world, being intimately connected to any apprehension of the latter, has tended to become objectified to the point of "contaminating" the world of nature per se. *Genesis* expresses this "contamination" symbolically when it describes the consequences of original sin not only in terms of human perception and destiny but also in terms of the terrestrial conditions of life and work following Adam's transgression: "[. . .] Cursed *is* the ground for thy sake, [. . .] thorns also and thistles shall it bring forth to thee" (*Gen.* 3:17–18).[15] On the one hand, the spiritual possibility expressed by works such as St. Francis' *Canticle of the Sun*, for instance, in keeping with a vision of God in and through his creatures, precludes a radical ontological dualism in Christian orthodoxy; on the other hand, the world *is* a "valley of tears" for Christians. In this respect, one of the most strikingly symbolic manifestations of the negative Christian apprehension of the demiurgic realm is to be found in Christ's admonition against ambiguity: "Let your communication be, Yea, yea; Nay, nay: for whatever is more than these cometh of evil" (*Matt.* 5:37). This admonition is a symbolic allusion to the "schizomorphic" dimension of the perspective of Christ, a perspective that entails an emphasis upon the distinction between the world of grace and that of nature, and that cannot take into account the ambiguous status of the demiurgic field on the spiritual level.

Again, this unambiguous emphasis should not, strictly speaking, confine Christianity to an irreducible metaphysical duality, but there is little doubt that it lends itself to be so used, albeit abusively, as a foundation for radical dualism. Most of the key concepts of Gnostic and Manichean dualism are indeed to be found in the New Testament, especially in St. Paul's Epistles and in the Gospel of Saint John. These implications have been developed and amplified by Gnosticism, which has been in a sense incapable of making sense of both the positive and the negative points of view of the demiurgic process, and has therefore hardened the bipolar aspect of the Demiurge into a dualistic ontology, thereby parting way from both orthodox Christianity and genuine gnosis. Losing sight of the unicity of the Essence and the grounding of all further determinations and manifestations in that Essence, Gnostic dualism tends to focus on the dimension of separation—as expressed par excellence in the realm of the Demiurge—in order to build its vision of two universal principles that would be at odds in the universe.

In order to try and bolster this "one-dimensional" form of metaphysics, traces of dualism have not only been unburied within the Gospels, but even in the Old Testament. It has been argued, for example, by Robert Ambelain,[16] that the dualistic distinction between a Creator and a Demiurge can be implied from the *Book of Genesis*, and that this distinction testifies to the Gnostic affinities of the latter. According to this thesis, and as is already plain upon a reading of the sacred text in its literality, Genesis clearly presents us with two different accounts of Creation. The first version runs from the first verse of chapter one ("In the beginning God created the heaven and the earth") to the third verse of chapter two ("And God blessed the seventh day . . ."); while the second begins with verse four in chapter two ("These are the generations of the heavens and of the earth . . .") and concludes with the end of the same chapter. These two narratives are moreover distinguished by the fact that God is referred to as *Elohim* ("God" in the King James version) in the first while being named *Yahweh Elohim* ("the Lord God" in the King James version) in the second.

The two stories of the creation of man are interesting to compare on account of those differences: the first story relates that on the sixth day, "God (*Elohim*) said, Let us make man in our image, after our likeness." The second narrative tells us that "the Lord God (*Yahweh Elohim*) formed man of the dust of the ground, and breathed into his nostrils the breath of life, and man became a living soul." Whatever one may think of the relationship between these two accounts, they appear to refer respectively to two different levels of the creation of man. It is plausible that the first story describes creation on the level of Being, or from the point of view of the archetypes, whereas the second one would illustrate the creation of man on the level of his "entry" into Existence, or, which amounts to the same in this case, from the standpoint of the Demiurge. This interpretation can be supported by two main factors, one having to do with the content of the narrative concerning the creative act as such, the other related to the Hebrew divine onomatology that is involved in these passages. First, one cannot but be struck by the difference between God's creation of man as a result of His Word ("And God said . . .") and His Will ("Let us make man . . .") on the one hand, and the shaping of man's form "of the dust" that is then animated by the "breath of life."

If one is to read these two verses without even taking into account their respective contexts one may readily admit to their alluding to two different stages in the same process of creation. Man is first an "Idea" or an archetype in God, and it is as such that he is subsequently "willed." On that level, he is in the "image" and "likeness" of God, which suggests a process of imaginal "ideation," rather than an actual physical "making." This stage, then, clearly corresponds to the ontological level of Being, the realm of archetypes. It is only at a second "stage" that man is shaped in his physical form and is "animated." The very notion of "forming" and the reference to the earth ("dust") places us squarely in the domain of the demiurgic work.

In parallel to the two terms of this distinction, the two Hebrew names that preside respectively over these different aspects of the creation of man appear to reflect two different levels in the creative process. The term *Elohim* is a plural and may therefore allude to the distinctiveness of archetypes such as they are conceived in God's intelligence. Furthermore, Jewish Kabbalah associates the Name *Elohim* with the three highest *Sefirot* that form the "Great Face" of God (*Arikh Anpin*), and it also more specifically refers to the third *Sefirah*, *Binah* or "Intelligence" as *Elohim*.[17] Now *Binah* has been defined as "the onto-cosmological 'Intelligence' [. . .] which determines the pure Quality, the particular divine Aspect, the proper Archetype."[18] *Binah* refers to "Ideas" as they are differentiated and still unified in God's Wisdom (*Hokhmah*). As for the name *Yahweh*, it implies by contrast the idea of a descending influx and appears, therefore, to correspond fittingly to the "formative" and efficient aspect of creation. Its final consonant, *H*, symbolizes the "receptive cosmological principle" [19] which is none other than the last *Sefirah*, *Malkhut*, the "Kingdom." This last *Sefirah*, *Malkhut*, is a kind of reverse analogy of the Supreme Crown, the first *Sefirah*, *Kether*, the latter referring to the Divine Essence in its transcendent dimension, the former to the Substance as Divine Immanence. While *Binah* is the "Divine Mother" that corresponds to the ontological level, or Being, *Malkhut* is the "Divine Daughter" that, while still situated *in divinis*, refers more particularly to the cosmological level of Existence. In this connection, it is instructive to note that thirteenth-century Kabbalistic speculations consider that the Divine "I" appears only on the level of *Malkhut*, whereas *Binah* (*Elohim*) corresponds to the grammatical function of object or third person ("He") and "Thou" to the "totality of the *Sefirot* in *Malkhut*.[20] In the Biblical narrative, the Divine "I" appears only in *Genesis* 1:29–30 and 2:18, but it is especially asserted at 3:15, where God curses the Serpent and chastises man and woman: "I will put enmity between thee and the woman, [. . .] I will greatly multiply thy sorrow and thy conception, [. . .] I commanded thee." God in the third person (1:1) precedes God as addressing a second Person (1:22, 28), which in His turn comes prior to God in the first person (1:29). Moreover, the repeated assertion of the Divine "I" in chapter three coincides with a third stage in the process of creation, following that of "ontological conception" and "cosmological formation," that is, the properly speaking "divisive" aspect of the demiurgic process. The two last stages correspond symbolically to *Malkhut*, the Principle of Divine Immanence that corresponds most closely to the Hindu *Mâyâ*. The first stage of those two coincides with *Malkhut* as synthesis of the other *Sefirot* while the second one manifests the final process of Divine manifestation. "Positively," it refers to the highest dimension of the Demiurge as "lower stage" in creation (it is the level of the "Thou," the shaping of man and breathing of a soul into his nostrils), while "negatively" it corresponds to the separation and chastisement that follows the transgression (the level of the "I"). What is clear, in both cases, is that *Malkhut* is only involved on levels that presuppose a duality as expressed by the relationship between an "I" and a "Thou."[21]

A third factor that intimates such a distinction between the level of Being and that of the Demiurge, or Existence, is that of the sexual definition of man following his creation. In chapter one of Genesis man is created "male and female." This passage strongly suggests the primacy of an androgynous nature. There is no suggestion whatsoever of a sexual partition, but rather that of a human "completeness" that is after all also "in the image" of God, since God cannot exclude any qualitative perfection, and therefore includes both essential masculinity and femininity within His nature. It bears stressing that this does not refer to a lesser "sexualization" as it were, but on the contrary points to a maximal integration of sexual polarity. Man is made "male and female" and not "neither male nor female." By contrast, chapter two presents us with an explicit "separation" between the male and the female. Adam is created alone first, and there is a clear sense that he is "in need" or that he is incomplete in some way: "but for Adam there was not found an help meet for him" (2:20). As woman proceeds from the "separation" of one of Adam's ribs, we are given to think that this stage in the creation of man corresponds to a lower step in the process that spans from God's archetypes to manifested forms. Still, this fragmentation is not as much in the mode of a division as it expresses, positively, a differentiation. At a further stage though, which is expressed by the curses upon woman and man following the transgression, differentiation is turned into a clear sense of division, lack, suffering, and evil. The three stages correspond, in a sense, respectively to (1) man *qua* man (both male and female) as dwelling in the Spirit, beyond all dualities; (2) man as male or female and as such a symbol of totality in their own right, being complementary archetypes "included" in the higher human archetype and projected into Existence from the level of Being, and finally (3) man as male or female lacking totality by virtue of their separation from each other, a separation that manifests itself on the level of Existence exclusively, thereby only relatively and provisionally.

The preceding distinction between ontological and cosmogonic stages within the Biblical narrative is a scriptural symbol of the subtle metaphysical distinction, developed by Frithjof Schuon, between the "Principle-Person" and the ambiguous realm of the "Principle-Demiurge":

> To the Principle-Essence belongs Possibility as such, thus universal Possibility; the Principle-Person is not responsible for the latter, because it merely crystallizes the fundamental consequences thereof, namely the archetypes or the "ideas." The Principle-Demiurge, in its turn, does not bear the responsibility for the archetypes; it merely transfers them to the universal substance, whose center it occupies, and which obliges it to differentiate and particularize them, as well as to contrast them, in conformity with the characteristic structure of this substance.[22]

Let us note that the distinction between the level of Being and that of the Demiurge is not to be considered in an absolute manner when it is envisaged from the standpoint of the existentiating projection. In the process of creation, there is on the one hand an aspect of onto-logical necessity—the Creator's will to create—and, on the other hand, an element of demiurgic initiative that appears more and more "arbitrary" as it gradually descends the various stages of existentiation. The unity of Being precludes a tight compartmentalization of these aspects, just as it forbids any exclusive perspective on their unfolding. This is illustrated by the aforementioned example from the Bible: the two narratives seem to refer to two different levels of the Divine work, and yet they cannot be construed as completely discrete without thereby compromising or jettisoning the unity of the Divine nature and purpose. The fact that the beginning of chapter two of Genesis does not fit with the actual articulation between the two narratives tends to indicate an intention to blur the distinction between the two depictions of creation. It may be that such is precisely the case so as to prevent a radically dualistic reading of the narrative. Given the exo-teric and religious tendency to fix provisional concepts into all too rigid dogmas and to confuse levels of metaphysical consideration, it may very well be that such an organization of the narrative has the merit of preserving and highlighting a clear sense of the Divine Unity above and beyond any subtle metaphysical distinction of ontological levels. This is all the more plausible when one considers how ancient

Gnosticism tended to read this distinction into an anthropological dualism. Thus, Robert Ambelain's reading of these passages in the wake of Gnostic speculations amounts to a radical distinction between "spiritual man" and "carnal man." Such a radical anthropological distinction runs parallel to a clear-cut separation between God and the Demiurge. Now the crux of the matter is that this distinction might be conceived as a clear subordination of the Demiurge to God, but it may ultimately lead to a sort of Manichean dualism. Jewish speculations have sometimes highlighted the first possibility, as "the notion of a demiurge under the command of Yahweh was familiar to some Jewish sects of the Saadia period."[23]

In this view of things, God is thought as having created by Himself but still through the intermediary work of a supreme demiurgic being sometimes identified as a supreme Angel. In Christian parlance, this being could also be considered as the Son or the Word. In Frithjof Schuon's view the latter perspective would amount to an understanding of the Trinity on the level of Existence, and therefore as comprised of the Essence of Existence (the Father), the "Personification of this Essence" (the Son), and, finally, "the Radiance of the Logos in the world and in the souls" (the Holy Spirit).[24] In conformity with this latter perspective, the historical mainstream of Christian theology has tended to identify Christ with a "Holy Demiurge" who is the Prototype of Creation. As a scriptural basis for such a conception, the prologue of St. John's Gospel testifies that "All things were made (*egeneto*: came into being) through the Word." Christ is in that sense the Logos that crystallizes the Essence at the center of Universal Existence, and who is at the same time, on the level of Being, the Prototype of Creation. From a slightly different standpoint, one can also see the Holy Spirit as participating in this supreme demiurgic function as a principle of radiating manifestation. This is, so to speak, the highest possible definition of the demiurgic domain per se.

On the other hand, several passages from the New Testament appear to indicate that the world is under the sway of another being whose function is primarily negative and subversive; and this being is also endowed with demiurgic characteristics. St. John's Gospel refers to the "prince of this world" (*o tou kosmou toutou archôn*) (14:30) as "having nothing in me (Christ)," and other passages strongly suggest that this *archôn* is none other than Satan having dominion over the world. Here the demiurgic aspect of Satan seems to be totally severed from the work of creation through the Word. The episode of the temptation in the desert constitutes a particularly striking illustration of this metaphysical severance. Christ's tempter (*diabolos*) took him to the top of a mountain, showed "him all the kingdoms of the world, and the glory of them; and saith unto him, All these things will I give thee, if thou will fall down and worship me" (*Matt.* 4:8). The devil is therefore not simply to be understood as a fallen angel who reigns over hell, and who would come upon earth to bring destruction and disorder, but he is in fact also to be considered as "the symbol, the action, the law, of the Universe."[25]

He is the "symbol" of the Universe because he epitomizes the "separation" from God that the Universe entails: the Greek word *diabolos* derives from the verb *diaballô*, "to throw away, or apart." That the *diabolos* might at the same time be conceived as *symbolon* of the Universe points to his supremely enigmatic and paradoxical nature when one considers that the function of the *symbolon* is to "bring together" (*symballô*), a function that is directly antithetic to that of the *diabolos.* The latter is moreover the "action" of the Universe in the sense that he embodies a dynamic energy that "makes" the world as a constant moving away from the divine Center. The aspect of constant "negation" that is associated with the devil can be better understood when considered in light of this ever-fragmenting motion that he embodies and fosters.

As for Satan's role as "law," it must be remembered that the law of the Universe expresses the rigorous aspect of Reality on the level of manifestation. This takes us to the outermost shores of Divine Rigor and judgment, as it were. In this connection, it might be helpful to recall that the *Book of Revelation* characterizes the Devil (*o satanás*) as "the accuser of our brethren, which accused them before our God day and night" (*Rev.* 12:10). This aspect of "accusation" appears to identify the function of the Devil with the lower strata of the dimension of Divine Justice. In this sense, several passages from the Old Testament could be conceived as bearing witness to Satan's role in the economy of Providence, such as *Psalm* 109: "Set thou a wicked man over him: and let Satan stand at his right hand, [. . .] when he shall be judged, let him be condemned: and let his prayer become sin" (6–7). In point of fact, the distinction between God's judgment and Satan's work is far from being obvious in many Biblical and Quranic narratives. This relative lack of a clearly observable line of demarcation explains why the Demiurge is sometimes identified to the Logos, or Christ, or an Archangel, while he is at other times envisaged as Satan, and, following a third intermediary scenario, occasionally considered as a Logos-Demiurge to whom Satan is subordinated as a kind of dark angel of Divine Wrath. In the latter case, which is perhaps the most satisfactory of the three metaphysical scenarios on account of its

finer and more subtle "attunement" to the ambiguities of the demiurgic unfolding of Creation, Satan might be seen as a personification,
on the psychic plane, of the negative and dispersing aspect of the
Demiurge.

One may, in this respect, raise the question why traditional
Christianity, among the various religions, is more disposed to considering the world as being entirely under the sway of the dark demiurgic legions of Satan. The most immediate answer to this question lies
in the observation that Christianity represents and fosters a perspective that focuses—to the point of "disequilibrium" and "madness"—
upon the chasm separating the Divine realm from the world of the
"flesh," or of Grace from nature. This chasm is "filled" by Christ and
by Redemption without being any less real on its level and in its "temporary" triumph. Christianity cannot but harden the cleavage between
the Divine realm and the demiurgic field since it is entirely predicated
on the "incredible," and "unheard of," fact of Incarnation, the most
dramatic and "unintelligible" sacrifice of God who accepts to descend
into the realm of that which is most adverse to Him. The "folly" of
Divine Redemption and the diabolic "darkening" of the world are in
this sense intimately interrelated. In this perspective, there seems to be
no middle ground between absorbing the whole of the demiurgic
function in Christ, or of identifying it with the somber plotting of
Satan. The intermediary perspective can only manifest itself incidentally, in an esoteric and precarious dimension, since it is much too subtle and paradoxical to be entrusted to a dogmatic theology for
collective spiritual consumption. The recognition of an "irreducible
dualism" on the level of Universal Relativity is unavoidable on the
level upon which it must occur, that of Relativity precisely, which does
not mean that it cannot be transcended on the level where *Mâyâ* dissolves into *Âtman*, the Non-Dual Self. While dualistic Gnosticism
stops at the irreducibility of duality on the demiurgic level of *Mâyâ*,
authentic gnosis steps beyond the latter to realize that there is none
other than That which transcends and integrates both I and Thou.

*   *   *

In the Abrahamic world, two characters can be read as interesting and
instructive illustrations of the monotheistic way of integrating the
demiurgic principle with the religion of the One God. These are the
Jewish Metatron and the Quranic al-Khidr. The ambivalent status of
these two characters is a first striking fact. In Judaism, Metatron is
introduced as an angel, but he is also identified with the prophet

Enoch, while the Islamic Khidr, or Khadir, is rather envisaged as a prophet, sometimes Elias, while also being considered as a celestial being. The eminence of Metatron is such that he is considered to be one of the angels who contemplate the Divine Face, thereby deserving the title of "Prince of the Countenance." He is, in fact, the Supreme Angel, who is like the divine Summit of Creation.[26] His "princely" status in relation to the Divine King already suggests that a sort of divine kinship is conferred upon him. There are additional factors that led some Jewish speculations to consider Metatron as a kind of "lesser God." Gershom Scholem mentions the Talmudic account of Elisha ben Avuyah's vision of a seated Metatron, a posture that suggests divine status.[27] Some rabbinical commentaries on *Exodus* 23:21–22 also suggest that Metatron is like a second Lord. Along these lines, the perplexing "Come up unto the Lord" (*Exodus* 24:1) uttered by God Himself has been interpreted as founded upon the fact that it is Metatron who is thus referred to by God Himself on account of his name being like His own. *Exodus* 23:21 already indicates, when referring to the Angel announced to Moses, that "my Name *is* in him." Talmudic rabbis were aware of the dangers that such a spiritual exaltation of Metatron might pose to the faithful preservation of a strict monotheism, and such a concern expresses in a sense the whole monotheistic predicament when dealing with the Demiurge. As for the association of Metatron with God's Name, it points both to his function in creation—since God creates through His Name, and also to his spiritual salvific power—God saving through His Name. The first of these aspects is involved in Metatron's role in the creation of the Heavens. When referring to the formation of the Kingdom of Heavens, Leo Schaya mentions Metatron as the active irradiation of the divine immanence or *Shekhinah*, which he also defines as the immanence of *Hokhmah*, the divine Wisdom.[28] Metatron can be characterized, in this respect, as the Holy Spirit reflected in creation. As such, Metatron is conceived as the prince of wisdom and the prince of understanding, and he appears as the primary intermediary between the divine and the human, having knowledge both of the celestial and terrestrial domains. This intermediary status is typical of demiurgic characters as it refers to the ambiguities of the dimension of divine immanence. Such ambiguities appear in full light when Jewish mysticism envisages Metatron as having two sides: a positive one that the *Zohar* equates to the *Sefirah Yesod*, the Foundation, from which proceeds the Kingdom (*Malkhuth*), or Divine Immanence, and a negative one that is envisaged as Lucifer, the angel of evil who carried the light (*Luci-fer*) before confiscating it for his own ambitious and rebellious purpose. While he is primarily a servant of the Supreme in the workings of Creation, Metatron becomes tenebrous when he is envisaged as isolated, or as severing himself, from his Divine Master. Lucifer is fallen precisely because he wanted to ascend and be like God: "How art thou fallen from heaven, O Lucifer, son of the morning! [. . .] For thou hast said in thine heart, I will ascend into heaven, I will exalt my throne above the stars of God. [. . .] I will ascend above the heights of the clouds; I will be like the most High" (Isaiah 14:12–14).

Metatron's double identity is reflected, in the *Zohar*, in the symbol of Moses' rod which is a helper on the one hand, but is also, when changed into a snake, a figure of evil.[29] Let us note, moreover, that Metatron is sometimes designated by the name *na'ar*, or "youth." This reference is probably not to be interpreted as a chronological allusion,[30] that is, to his posteriority, as has been occasionally suggested, but rather as an allusion both to his "lesser" being vis-à-vis God, and to his status of "servant" of God. More profoundly, this name may also refer to his higher identification with the Divine Intellect, the fountain of eternal youth. In that sense, Metatron may appear as the universal initiator who transmits the Divine Light to those he assists: one is "ever young in the Intellect," in Meister Eckhart's words.

The second aspect of Metatron, his prophetic and salvific identity, appears through his connection with the patriarch Enoch, with whom he is identified by some traditional data. This is related in the *Sefer Hekhalot*, also called *3 Enoch*, in which the patriarch declares that God called him " 'the lesser YHWH' in the presence of his whole household in the height, as it is written, 'My name is in him.' "[31] Enoch is one of the very few, together with Christ, the Virgin Mary, and Elias, that monotheistic traditions consider as having been taken directly to heaven, and having thereby reintegrated into their celestial prototype. More specifically, Enoch is said to have been transformed from a man into an angel. Thus, St. Paul teaches that "by faith Enoch was translated so that he should not see death, and was not found, because God had translated him; for before he was taken he had this testimony, that he pleased God" (Hebrews 11:5). Continuing this tradition, Islam refers to Enoch under the name of the prophet Idrîs, and the *Qur'ân* mentions him in several verses, including the following: "Verily! He (Enoch/Idrîs) was a man of truth (and) a prophet. We raised him to a high station" (19:56–57). His ascension to a celestial status is parallel to his appointment as "scribe" at the divine court, and his assigned duty of recording the good and bad actions of men.

By contrast, but not without analogy, some Jewish traditions present him as the angelic advocate of Israel in heaven's court.[32] It is interesting to note that the latter function appears to be the counterpart of the role of "accuser" that *Revelations* assigns to Satan. These are, so to speak, the two sides of the "recording" function of the demiurgic principle as it is envisaged through the figure of Metatron. The various myths and interpretations of Metatron provide us, therefore, with a dual spiritual motion of "descent" and "ascent." This dual aspect allows us to emphasize the intermediary, communicative, and also ambiguous, function of the demiurgic principle that is at work in the stories and views of Metatron. Gershom Scholem indicates that some Kabbalists reconciled these two aspects, the "human" and the "divine," by introducing a distinction between a higher Metatron and a lower Metatron. This distinction was based on the fact that the name Metatron can be written in two different Hebrew forms, one comprised of seven letters, the other of six.[33] The first form, which is also the oldest, includes the letter *yod* as second letter of the word, whereas the second form does not. *Yod* is the first letter of the Divine Tetragrammaton (YHWH). Thus, the seven-lettered version of the name of Metatron refers to the "divine" or archangelic aspect, which is the supreme and active manifestation of the *Shekhinah*, whereas the six-lettered form is understood to refer to the patriarch Enoch, who "possesses only some of the splendor and power of the primordial Metatron." This distinction accounts, in its own symbolic way, for the intermediary and ambivalent status of the demiurgic principle, and its reflection at different levels of creation.

The Quranic account of the mysterious guide of Moses in the *Surah* "The Cave" (18:65–82) offers other important avenues of exploration into the demiurgic dimension. It is important, first of all, to note that the character introduced in the *Qur'ân* is never named. The *Qur'ân* refers to him as "one of Our slaves": "Then found they one of Our slaves, unto whom We had given mercy from Us, and had taught him knowledge from Our presence" (18:65, Marmaduke Pickthall translation). This servant of God has directly received from Him a knowledge that is defined as "*min ladunnî*," or "coming from Us." The translation "Our presence" is particularly justified since it points to a participatory, gnostic, or mystical type of knowledge that cannot be reduced to rational or juridical learning. Moses, the prophet of the Law par excellence, requests of this unexpected acquaintance that he instruct him in the knowledge of God's ways. The only condition placed by the mysterious guide for accepting Moses' request is that the latter should not ask him any questions before he is given an explanation of the meaning of what might happen.

Three episodes present Moses with appearances of impropriety and transgression on the part of al-Khidr. First, al-Khidr opens a breach in the hull of a boat; Moses cannot prevent himself from expressing the suspicion that al-Khidr did so to drown the people who were on board, and strongly voices his moral outrage. Next, al-Khidr kills a young man, whom they had encountered on their way; Moses blames his companion for this action. Finally, after having been denied hospitality by the inhabitants of a certain city, al-Khidr rebuilds a wall that was about to crumble without asking a salary for it, as Moses had suggested he do. Upon parting from his companion, al-Khidr provides Moses with the answers for which he has not been able to wait: the boat was damaged because it would otherwise have been appropriated by a king, thereby ruining the poor people who owned it; the young man was going to impose rebellion and unfaithfulness upon his parents; as for the wall, it belonged to two young boys: their father had buried a treasury underneath, and al-Khidr did not want them to find it before they had become adults. As a conclusion to his explanation, al-Khidr unequivocally states that he has performed none of these seemingly bad actions "upon his own initiative" (*wa ma fa'altuhu 'an amrî*), thereby alluding to his serving and executing God's will. Upon each of al-Khidr's actions, Moses expresses his shock and indignation, in conformity with the moral and legal perspective that he embodies.

The *Qur'ân* particularly emphasizes his lack of "patience," and al-Khidr had actually prophesied from the outset that Moses would not be patient with him (*innaka lan tastatî'a ma'î sabran*, 18:67), founding this prediction on Moses' lack of knowledge. Al-Khidr's knowledge of God's way is direct, or inspired, whereas Moses' is indirect and legal; al-Khidr's point of view is synthetic: he is able to situate actions and events within the "greater picture" of God's Will, the All-Possibility that transcends purely moral apprehensions of the Divine, while Moses can only understand God's Will on the level of His injunctions and proscriptions. Moses' lack of patience is connected to his inability to consider reality beyond the level of phenomenal existence and literal meaning. Al-Khidr embodies the demiurgic unfolding of possibilities inasmuch as he actualizes these possibilities in conformity with the providential order, but on a level where the truth and justice of these manifestations may not be understood prima facie. Al-Khidr represents the amoral perspective of metaphysics, a perspective that is not accessible per se from the strict point of view of the Law.

It is interesting to note that al-Khidr's explanation of his own actions is expressed in three different grammatical ways, with three different subjects: in the first account, al-Khidr relates the intent of his action in the first person singular: "I wanted (*aradtu*) to damage (the boat)" (18:79); in the second instance, the subject of the verb is in the first person plural, "we wanted (*aradnâ*) that" (18:81); while in the third case, the subject is in the third person singular, "your Lord wanted" (*fa arâda rabbuka*) (18:82). This grammatical shift is highly illustrative of the various levels of Divine Will. The Divine Will is first considered from the standpoint of the "demiurge's" apparent initiative; it is then envisaged in the perspective of a fusion of the demiurgic and Divine Will *stricto sensu*; while it is finally presented as God's highest decree. This mobility of perspective, which takes place within the space of a few verses, is clearly indicative of a possible shift in the level of understanding of the onto-cosmological unfolding. Let us note, however, that al-Khidr embodies an "enlightened" demiurgic perspective, in the sense that he remains fully aware of God's will as it is manifested to him: he is a *servant* (*'abd*) in a full and direct sense, and not only a passive and unconscious instrument of God's will.

A few additional remarks are in order concerning the implications of the demiurgic process as illustrated in the *Surah* of the Cave. We should notice, first, that the narrative introduces Moses and his servant at the point where the former has just lost his fish at the meeting place of the two seas. These two seas have been traditionally interpreted, in the context of Sufi metaphysics, as the Lower and Higher Waters: their confluence is the *barzakh*, or isthmus, that lies between the animic and spiritual realms, the soul and the Spirit-Intellect. It is in this *barzakh* that is situated the "inversion," which makes it possible to pass to the other side of the mirror, that is, to change perspective in the sense of not taking the soul any longer as point of reference and identifying with the Intellect as center of consciousness. In this context, the fish represents the spiritual symbol, the "sacramental" and transcendent means that allows one to "swim" from one sea into the other. Al-Khidr is himself "at home" in both domains, and one of his functions is actually to "join" the two worlds of light and darkness.

From another standpoint, which is the metaphysical complement to the aforementioned spiritual point of view, the fish may point to the unity of being (*wahdât al-wujûd*) since it bears witness to a continuity between the two oceans. Be that as it may, having lost his fish, a symbol of the Spirit, Moses cannot progress any further and he finds himself obliged to retrace his steps, and perhaps even gets lost (18:64). It is precisely at this moment that he meets the mysterious traveler who will henceforth serve as his spiritual guide. In the verses that follow, Moses and al-Khidr are described as wanderers, as if their lack of a clear and intended direction alluded to the "providence" of

God's will over their path. Let us note that, by contrast, Moses' initial intent was particularly clear in terms of its goal: "And when Moses said unto his servant: I will not give up until I reach the point where the two rivers (seas) meet, though I march on for ages" (18:60, Pickthall trans.). On this mysterious and unsettling way, the patience demanded by al-Khidr of Moses is none other than the trust required from the soul on the spiritual path inasmuch, or as long as, it cannot reach the level of vision that is the purview of the Intellect. The soul's relative "darkness" prevents man from being totally transparent to the Intellect, and this is the reason why the soul must "wait" before being revealed the "full picture" of Reality. Moreover, the "separation" (*hadhâ firâqu baynî wa baynika*) (18:68) that puts an end to the association of al-Khidr with Moses, marks, in a certain sense, the failure of the soul to be totally trusting in the Spirit. The Law, and the Revelation that vehicles it, and which Moses "embodies," is required precisely because of the incapacity of man, or of the overwhelming majority of men, to remain "connected" to the Intellect, and to be, so to speak, transparent to it. Let us note, in addition, that Moses displays an unconscious presumption, similar to Peter's toward Jesus, when he declares that he will disobey none of al-Khidr's orders (18:69). This presumption is the narrative and psychological mark of man's disconnection from Intellection, thereby pointing to an inner contradiction and to a profound spiritual powerlessness.

The ill-inspired "impatience" of Moses and its spiritual correlates find an echo in the story of Alexander's quest for the Fountain of Life in various literary sources such as the *Shâh Nâmeh*. Ananda Coomaraswamy mentions that some versions of Alexander's quest describe the King on his way to find the Fountain of Life, which he discovers by chance, but which he is later unable to locate when trying to return to it. The Fountain is located in the "Land of Shadows" beyond the West.[34] In the *Shâh Nâmeh*, Alexander is guided by al-Khidr until they come to a bifurcation and part company. Al-Khidr is the only one to find the Fountain. In Nizâmî's *Iskender Nâmeh*, Alexander's failure to reach the Fountain is due to his impatience, whereas al-Khidr finds the Fountain without having to look for it. These various versions of the myth share an emphasis on the failure of impatience and deliberate intent, while highlighting the apparent gratuitousness and "randomness" of spiritual discovery. In all cases, al-Khidr is associated with the unexpectedness and freedom of grace: this mysterious character conveys a sense of the suddenness and unconstrained mobility of the Holy Spirit. The individual initiative of the seeker—whether Moses or Alexander—is consistently stained with an element of impurity. This bears witness to a key of the way of knowledge: only God can know Himself, and any motion toward Him is fundamentally none other than a motion of Himself toward Himself. Al-Khidr is the prophet of this Divine Knowledge, a knowledge that cannot be rigidly set in the language of formal prophecy. The reference of several sources to a "Land of Darkness" that lies beyond the West, where the Fountain is to be found, may refer to the realm of the Divine Essence that spreads beyond all terrestrial limitations. It is there that the secret of immortality can be found. This immortality is also characteristic of al-Khidr, whose green color and association with rainfalls is highlighted in many traditional sources. The *Iskender Nâmeh* associates the two symbols when mentioning that al-Khidr's steps leading to the Fountain of Life trace a wake of falling rain and growing grass.[35]

The anonymity of al-Khidr in the *Qur'ân* suggests that the function he embodies and symbolizes cannot be exclusively assigned to a single character. And, in point of fact, it must be underlined that the *Khâdiryah* function appears in a whole constellation of characters within the monotheistic world. This constellation includes the prophet Enoch, or Idrîs, Hermes, the prophet Elias, or Ilyâs, and St. George, among others. The prophet Elias is sometimes identified with al-Khidr or associated with him. A famous Persian painting of the sixteenth century, from the *Khamsa* of Nîzamî, represents the meeting of the two characters at the Fountain of Life. On this miniature, al-Khidr is depicted wearing a green garment, whereas Elias is clothed in a white garb. Whiteness plainly refers to the essence of all colors, a fact that may be interpreted as an allusion to the function of ultimate resolution and explication of theological differences that the Jewish tradition assigns to Elias. This function is in keeping with three major characteristics of Elias in the Jewish tradition: his tendency to reveal himself under various guises; his uncovering of divine and celestial secrets; and his eschatological role as the herald of the Messiah. As a scriptural example of Elias's ability to metamorphose, the *Midrash* teaches that, in the *Book of Esther*, he took the form of the chamberlain Harbonah to inform King Ahasuerus of Haman's intention to hang Mardocai (7:9–10). This ability clearly alludes to the spiritual affinity of Elias with the supra-formal dimension, an affinity that fosters the manifestation of the Spirit in many forms, colors, and through diverse human vehicles. Such a freedom from forms is undoubtedly connected to a privilege of direct inspiration.

Elias is the prophet of charisma, by contrast with the prophets of divine institutions, such as Moses. A rabbinical tradition is highly instructive in this respect, illustrating the very particular role played by Elias in the tension between spiritual charisma and institutional tradition.[36] It tells us of a protracted argument between Rabbi Eliezer and Rabbi Yoshua, two Jewish sages who lived in the early Christian era and who represent respectively the Chamai and Hillel schools. In the course of the argument, Rabbi Eliezer, who often finds himself in disagreement with the other rabbis because of his strict interpretation of Scripture, calls successively for a tree, a canal, and walls as witnesses to the truth of his point. As a response, the tree moves, the water of the canal starts running upstream, and the walls begin to lean. The other rabbis do not accept these prodigies as evidence in favor of Eliezer's reasoning on the grounds that, notwithstanding their spectacular character, they remain irrelevant to the core of the argument. Finally, Rabbi Eliezer says: "If I am right, may Heavens prove it!" At this moment, a celestial voice confirms the truth of Eliezer's claim. This is interpreted as Elias's voice, the voice of direct celestial inspiration, the "Revelation of the Prophet Elias" that is the counterpart of the Revelation to Moses. It is interesting to note that this celestial inspiration is no more accepted as criterion of truth by Rabbi Yoshua than the leaning of the walls. Yoshua reproaches the walls for getting involved in a disputation concerning the Law, which is why, according to the rabbinical tradition, the walls did not fall in spite of their leaning. The Rabbi also objects to the authority of the celestial voice on the grounds of *Deuteronomy* 30:12: "It (the Law) *is* not in heaven, that thou shouldest say, Who shall go up for us to heaven, and bring it unto us, that we may hear it, and do it?" This opinion clearly illustrates the tension, and even the conflict, between the two perspectives, the Mosaic and the Eliatic, the former pertaining to the formal Law, the latter to the Law from above.

This celestial dimension of Elias is also bound to the third aspect of his function, that is, the eschatological mission. The coming of Elias is referred to as the prelude to the Messianic era. Its scriptural basis appears in the very final section of the Old Testament, the two verses of the *Book of Malachi*: "Behold, I will send you Elijah (Elias) the prophet before the coming of the great and dreadful day of the Lord: And he shall turn the heart of the fathers to the children, and the heart of the children to their fathers, lest I come and smite the earth with a curse" (Mal.4: 5–6). Leo Schaya has commented profoundly upon this last verse of the Old Testament:

> The "heart of the fathers" is the inward, central, essential aspect of the traditions,—their esoteric, spiritual, universal kernel—as well as the

teachings, methods and influences that flow out from them. The "heart of the children" is their spiritual receptivity,—their inward acceptance and reception of what is given them by their "fathers" and their respective traditions.[37]

It must be noted that the "heart of the fathers" could be represented by the upper horizontal section of a semicircle, open below and thereby providing its "rain" of grace, whereas the "heart of the children" would then be symbolized by the lower horizontal section of the circle, indicating the receptive emptiness of the heart open to vertical grace: the two "hearts" taken together therefore form a perfect circle, which is a fitting image of the eschatological "completion" of the spiritual cycle. This eschatological coming into perfection, like the formal metamorphoses and the celestial unveilings of the prophet, is connected to Elias's greater charisma and mission: his conciliation of divergent doctrines and interpretations of Scriptures. In the Jewish tradition, this is highlighted by the Talmudic use of the word *Teiqu*, which is traditionally interpreted as referring to the four initials of *Tishbi Ietarets Qushioth Veyabaoth*, "the Tishbite (Elias) will solve the questions and difficulties." To use a specifically Kabbalistic image illustrating the need for a spiritual *tikkun*,[38] the Eliatic function is akin to a recollection of the sparks of divine wisdom disseminated, because of the fragmenting multiplicity of existence, within the various traditions and perspectives. The spiritually "demiurgic" role of Elias at the end of history is therefore the perfect complement and closure, on the level of the Spirit, to the demiurgic function of the archangelic Metatron that took place at the "dawn" of manifestation, and on the level of existence. The perspective that is involved within these various transformations is fundamentally circular, as it befits a type of spiritual reality that could be defined as a reoccurring allusion to the Center from within the ambiguous realm of the periphery.

This page intentionally left blank

CHAPTER 3

DIONYSUS, SHIVA, OSIRIS

The question of the relationship between Unity and multiplicity is one of the most central components of metaphysics. In a sense, it is a mystery and a paradox. As much as it may be so, an understanding that the One may "become" many and that the many may "reveal" the One is at the core of the metaphysical outlook. It must be admitted that the expressions of this understanding cannot but be, on some level, a challenge to the discursive faculty and to ordinary consciousness. The Christian Mystery of the Trinity is one of the most striking occurrences of this challenge, as it transcends the logic of exclusion by upholding both the unity and distinction of the Persons. In a sense, any divine manifestation constitutes a bridge between the world of above, that of the One, and the world of below, that of the many. In the general context of such theophanies some divine figures are endowed with a function that is particularly akin to the reconciliation of extremes. Such mediators present us with characteristics that tend to puzzle or disorient the analytical mind in search of human images of unambiguous divine integrity, as if these gods were taking it upon themselves to dress their celestial identity with the colorful mantle of terrestrial tribulations.

Dionysus is one of the most direct manifestations of the duality and ambiguity that characterizes the link between the divine and the human realms, the domain of absoluteness and unity and the domain of relative multiplicity. Duality is already inscribed in the very name of the god, as indicated by the prefix *di-*. The myth of Dionysus's birth illustrates this dual nature, together with his association with the domain of becoming.[1] Let us remember, in this context, that the myth is but the external shell of profound metaphysical and spiritual realities to which only ancient initiates had access. Along these lines of interpretation,

Plutarch warns his reader against the reduction of the myth to a mere historical reality:

> [...] when you will have heard what Egyptian mythology has to say on the gods: wandering, dismemberments and other misfortunes of this kind, you will need to remember of what I have just said (Their theology contains an enigmatic wisdom—*ainigmatodê sophia*) and keep yourself from thinking that it corresponds as such to an event or a real fact.[2]

Further on, Plutarch specifies that "the myth [...] is the image of some veridical tradition which refracts our thoughts toward realities of a higher order" (359a).

This methodological preamble having being laid out, let us turn to the myth. Dionysus's father was the supreme god, Zeus, while his mother was a mere mortal, Semele. The latter has been associated by some scholars (Kretschmer, Nilsson, Wilamowitz) to the Thracian cult of the Earth Goddess, a hypothesis that reinforces the function of Dionysus as the connecting mystery between polar opposites such as heaven and earth, the masculine and the feminine, unity and multiplicity. The myth emphasizes Zeus's celestial attributes of power and rigor, particularly lightning: Semele was struck by Zeus's lightning and consumed by flames while giving birth to Dionysus. She was later reborn and taken to Olympus, ascending among the gods, and becoming herself a goddess. As for Dionysus, it belonged to Zeus his father to save him from the fire and to nurture him by placing him in his own body, specifically his thigh, until his birth. The thigh may be taken to represent the "instinctive" and dynamic aspect of reality. Dionysus is thus a divine archetype of the "twice born" who experienced both a birth in the human flesh, and a second birth, proceeding directly from the divine realm. The spiritual analogy with Christ is striking, as has been noted by several commentators. Simone Weil, for example, went so far as to write in one of her letters that Dionysus (as also Osiris) is "in a certain sense Christ himself."[3] The instantaneity of the *fiat* in the Gospel, during the Annunciation, is also not without analogy to the lightning bolt of Zeus that consumed Semele. Moreover, the destinies of Semele and Mary show striking parallels as well, since they were both mere women on the one hand, while yet enjoying a sort of divination through their direct ascension to heaven. In Egypt, Isis plays an analogous, though distinct, role vis-à-vis Osiris. She is both sister and wife, and she also acquires a supreme divine status, even, according to Plutarch, becoming identified by the Greeks with the Divine Essence in Its infinity and inaccessibility: "I am all that has been, is and will be, and no mortal has ever lifted my veil" (Plutarch, 354c). One can perceive that Isis, like Semele in Greece and Mary in Christian theology, may be envisaged at different levels. She is a woman, a goddess, the prototype of the cosmogonic Substance informed by the Spirit, and—on the highest plane—the supreme Mystery of the Divine Essence.

It is evident that Dionysus embodies the principle of the spiritual reunification of the diversity that characterizes the realm of terrestrial immanence. Walter Otto has judiciously emphasized the god's function as a sort of bridge between the world of the Olympians and that of the vicissitudes of terrestrial existence.[4] The contrast that has been drawn, in the wake of Nietzsche's *Birth of Tragedy*, between Dionysus and Apollo, is in this respect enlightening and far-reaching. The Pythagorean interpretation of Apollo's name as a negation of multiplicity (*a-pollôn*), and his identification with the "monad," is a suggestive indication of the deepest layers of meaning within this contrast. In this context, Apollo is to be understood as a divine manifestation of the principles of transcendence and unity. In *Cratylus*, Socrates mentions, among other possible linguistic associations, the connection between his name and the idea of simplicity, akin to the Greek word *aploun*. In this same text, Socrates emphasizes four fundamental functions of Apollo: purification, conformation to simplicity, exactitude or the ability to reach the target, and harmonization (*Cratylus* XXII). All of those characteristics pertain, in one way or another, to transcendence, absoluteness, and unity. They "exclude" multiplicity and infinity. Inasmuch as he is a representative of these principles, Apollo is the Olympian god par excellence. By contrast, Dionysus's personality, life, and cult are characterized by elements of transgression, complexity, inebriation, and chaos. His perspective is not exclusive but inclusive of all realities on all levels of existence.

The meaningful contrast between Apollo and Dionysus must be understood as expressive of a complementarity of perspectives, not as an irreducible opposition. As Walter Otto has asserted: "The Olympian religion never repudiated or rejected the terrestrial but always acknowledged its sacredness. This is why the most important impulses to vitalize the Dionysiac cult issued from the Apollo of Delphi."[5] The Apollonian and Dionysiac perspectives were seen by ancient Greeks as two necessary components of an integral understanding of reality. Nothing would be more erroneous and more harmful spiritually, psychologically, and socially, than to reject the Dionysiac dimension and place it within a kind of "demonic" domain to be excluded from the field of "normative" spirituality.

The same dimension of duality and ambiguity highlighted by Dionysus also appears, in widely different ways, in the two mythological figures of Hermes and Pan, the latter being, significantly, the son of the former. In his *Cratylus*, Plato contends that both Hermes and Pan revel in their double nature inasmuch as they are closely connected with the invention and circulation of language and reality. In this regard, Socrates draws a profound link between the spoken word (which is the invention and the province of Hermes) and the sense of totality (*pan* in Greek): "You know that discourse expresses everything (*pan*) and that it circulates and moves everything constantly, and that it is double, both true and false." The connection between language, creation, motion, and ambiguity is the hallmark of Hermes. The realm of multiplicity, which results in a sense from the word, entails contrast and ambivalence. Plato associates this realm with the "tragic," referring thereby to the sacrificial "scapegoat" or *tragx* (*tragikos*) that lies at the sacred origin of the Greek tragedy. The metaphysical association between multiplicity and sacrifice is a crucial element in this vision of reality. On the highest level, it suggests a dismemberment of Unity that has to be reassembled through human and animal sacrifice. The sacramental communion of the Dionysiac cult, in the form of eating the flesh and drinking the blood of a young goat, highlights the spiritual significance of this dismemberment while also shedding light on the meaning of the later Christian mysteries. The sacrificial young goat is identified with Dionysus, as it is torn into pieces before being consummated by the devotees. The rite of *omophagia* (eating of the flesh) recapitulates the two phases of manifestation and reintegration: the suffering of the god amounts to an assumption of multiplicity, but this suffering also opens the way for an appropriation of the Dionysiac spiritual reality by its practitioners.

An analogous thematic emphasis is to be found in Osiris's death, dismemberment, and rememberment by his wife Isis and his son Horus. After Seth has torn Osiris's body into fourteen pieces, Isis, assisted by birds and four-legged animals, goes in search of her husband's parts. She finds them in different places and tricks Seth by making molds of these parts, which she gives to priests in these locations so as to institute her husband's worship. Only the god's sexual organ is not found, which prompts Isis to make a mold of it and introduce a worship of the phallus. Horus, aided by Anubis and Thoth, is finally able to reassemble the parts that had been collected by Isis. The rememberment of the god is therefore dependent upon the quest of the goddess for the separated parts of his body. This part of the myth is highly symbolic of the function of the feminine element in restoring the unity of the totality, this function being akin to the divine dimension of infinity that relates, includes, and unites.

The close association of Dionysus with violence, sexuality, and women is another important dimension of his myth and cult. Violence appears in his life story from the very beginning since it is an integral part of his birth. His conception is sudden and violent, and the way he enters the life of his devotees shares in the same lightning-like outburst. One knows Dionysus as the raging god, the mad god accompanied by frenzied maenads, or *bachai*, a troop of women who follow him after having rejected the order and conformity of social and marital life, for "he rips the ones he has affected out of their wifely decency and morality and mates them with the mysteries and madnesses of the chaos of night."[6] This association with women expresses the affinity of Dionysus with the infinite, which women embody through their beauty and grace. This also needs to be situated within the context of his relationship with Semele, his mother. The latter may be interpreted as symbolizing the utter receptivity of pure Substance. Her disappearance from this level of existence and her reintegration into the heavenly realm leaves Dionysus in the presence of "substitutes" who serve as "nurses": first Semele's three sisters and later, in another sense, the maenads. Some versions of the myth tell that the young Dionysus was nursed by the women attending him in a cave. The chthonian aspect of the latter probably alludes to the "instinctive" dimension of the Dionysiac inspiration. Shiva is also consistently associated with caves, and with telluric forces immanent in mountains and forests. This dimension is also implied, in a different way, in the episode of the second birth from Zeus's thigh, the latter member being associated with the dynamics of the instincts. Be that as it may, the substitution of "nurses" for the mother may account for a change of level in the sense that it confirms Dionysus's assumption of the domain of multiplicity. Even though the pure feminine Substance is not directly accessible on the plane of terrestrial existence, it is still present within the diverse manifestations of femininity that surrounds Dionysus throughout his life and in his cult.

We find, of course, an analogous association of Shiva with the feminine element and its immanent manifestations. The god is always paired with the goddess—Pârvatî, Durgâ, Gauri, or some other form—who is an incarnation of the *Shakti*, the dynamic life of the divine that is also "effective" and transformative. Actually, Shiva is not conceivable without his *Shakti*; the two of them form a syzygy, the two components of which cannot be dissociated. In this respect Shiva represents motionless Being, while Shakti pertains to dynamic production and becoming. The phallic *lingam* is a direct affirmation of that most central character of Shiva. From another standpoint, the god is the ever mobile transgressor of limits; as such, he negates any form that would fix becoming, and he destroys any misleading identification of static fragments with the infinite totality. Shiva is Being, and he is also, in a sense, the principle of freedom that prevents any confusion between becoming and What lies beyond it. Like love, Shiva is the great incendiary of forms. It is therefore not surprising to verify that, like Dionysus, Shiva is primarily the god of eroticism. However, in a distinctly more direct way than the Greek god, Shiva is also the ascetic par excellence. He is often presented, especially in scripture and folkloric and popular accounts, as a wild, roaming, and mad ascetic who lives as a hermit in the forest and threatens the order of society and the appropriate status, and behavior, of women. This dual, and prima facie perplexing, status, stems from the two-sided reality of the Absolute as affirmation and negation of the negation.

In the *Bhâgavata Purâna*, Shiva is married to Satî against the will of her father Daksha who curses Lord Shiva at the divine assembly.[7] This conflict is emblematic of an opposition between two understandings of religion: one that focuses on forms as a way to gain merits and preserve the social order, and another that aims at unveiling the non-duality of Reality. It is to be noted that this rejection of Shiva on purely social and unenlightened grounds is presented by the same *Purâna*, in Nandisvara's words, as representative of a formalistic and dualistic understanding of the Veda:

> Anyone who has accepted Daksa as the most important personality and neglected Lord Siva because of envy is less intelligent and, because of visualizing in duality, will be bereft of transcendental knowledge (*tattva*). Pretentiously religious householder life, in which one is attracted to material happiness and thus also attracted to the superficial explanation of the Vedas, robs one of all intelligence and attaches one to fruitive activities as all in all.[8]

Nandisvara does not claim the illegitimacy of Daksha's perspective; he merely, and vehemently, criticizes the setting of his very limited understanding above that of Shiva for reasons of jealousy. Shiva is misunderstood by Daksha because he does not fit the image of sanctity and decency upon which Daksha's religious life has been founded. The eminence and supreme purity of Shiva escape his understanding because the god appears in forms that *seem* to contradict them. The remainder of the narrative unambiguously reveals the equanimity and generous gentleness of Shiva vis-à-vis Satî when the god kindly explains to his wife the "mechanics" and pitfalls of spiritual jealousy. The fact that Shiva's defamation is developed within the context of his relationship with Satî, the divine archetype of female devotion and fidelity, is not fortuitous: Daksha's misunderstanding of Shiva stems from a conventional vision that cannot perceive the god as the agent of a conciliation between the most extreme levels of reality, life and death, ritual impurity and spiritual purity, and this conciliation is all the more foreign to the father-in-law when it touches the context of marital life and sexuality in general. The association of Shiva with emblems of death, nakedness, and wandering life cannot but conflict with the dualistic and somewhat horizontal perspective that is voiced by Daksha. Shiva's affinity with death and cemeteries is the hallmark of his ability to reduce manifestation to ashes. His lack of concern for physical cleanliness is an allusion to the lustral eminence of metaphysical knowledge over rites and external purifications. But the most striking element in Daksha's negative portrayal of Shiva—as far as our thematic focus is concerned—lies in his apparent madness and his ability to switch from one extreme emotional state to another. Crying and laughing are, in a sense, the same for Shiva: both are expressions of a violent crushing of solidified psychic forms, thereby functioning also as symptoms of the emergence of That which lies beneath the illusory stability of the soul.

The aforementioned references to an "instinctive" dimension that is an integral part of Dionysus's and Shiva's respective personalities and cults must be situated within the context of the spiritual connection of these two gods with the animal kingdom. Shiva is also called Rudra, and he is, as such, Pâshupati or the Lord of wild beasts. Dionysus's connection with the animal and vegetal kingdoms is also widely attested. This association can be considered from a variety of standpoints. In the *Shiva Purâna*, Shiva is said to have instructed the other gods about the need to acknowledge the reality of their animal nature; he thus invites them to reach a real understanding of the universal meaning of that nature, which is eminently present in them, as it is also, albeit differently, in men. In this context, the name Pashupati, as connected to the term *pâsha* or bond, emphasizes the fundamental connection between the divine and the animal, as exemplified in mankind. Pâshupati is the Lord of the unity of all beings, and Shiva's association with "instinct" must not be interpreted negatively as a rejection of reason, but rather as a symbolic, and no doubt even spiritual, emphasis on the immediacy of the esoteric knowledge that the Lord fosters and embodies. Now, the term *pâsha*, and *pâshu*—meaning the individual self, is also connected, negatively this time, to the bonds that weave relative existence, thereby impeding spiritual liberation. Shiva-Pâshupati is precisely He who liberates from these bonds.[9]

In the Shivaite traditions, which are in this respect akin to Tantric disciplines, this liberation is often associated with a spiritual transference of vital energy from the lower objects of desire to the Sole Reality. The partial identification and numerous associations and fusions of Shiva with Kâma, the god of pleasure, express this fundamental law. Like Kâma, Shiva is a god of eroticism, but this affinity does not exhaust their respective natures and functions. As Wendy O' Flaherty has rightly noted, "it is clear that whereas Kâma is merely one aspect of Shiva, the reverse is not true [...] Shiva is Kâma, but he is more as well, and it is this 'more' that opposes Kâma."[10] Shiva is desire, but the essence of this desire is actually turned against desire as a limitative "bond." The "bond" that binds everything to the One is that which unbinds from all bonds. This explains why Shiva is Pâshupati, but also why, according to Umâpati's Siddhânta perspective, "Shiva is of like nature of the self, the difference being the self is bound and Shiva-ness is unbound."[11] The correspondence between Shiva and the individual self is not simply a metaphysical indication of the Supreme Non-Duality, it also refers to the fundamental analogy between the unicity of the Self (*Âtman*) and the "uniqueness" of each *jîva*. When Shiva shows the way of a conversion of desire into unbound Desire, he does so not only as the Self of all selves but also as the supreme prototype, so to speak, of selfhood.

On a spiritual level, the principle of the use of desire to transcend desire may be expressed in a variety of methods, but all have in common the fact of taking the domain of immanence as a starting point for spiritual realization. The key is the control and the transmutation of the energy of desire. Shivaite Tantric disciplines may include all kinds of techniques that make this transmutation possible, as, for example, the retention of the seed. The fundamental idea presiding over this methodical orientation is that "ascetic fire" (*tapas*) and sexual fire (*kâma*) are not, in reality, antithetical forces but, in fact, two aspects of the same reality. *Tapas* includes as it were *kâma*, whence the possibility, for the Shivaite ascetic, of transmuting the latter into the former. Shiva is not a destroyer in the sense of denying or annihilating the existence of someone or something; rather, he is an agent of reintegration who reabsorbs a lesser reality into its apparent opposite.[12]

Another aspect of this use of immanence as a means toward spiritual progress, which is of particular interest with respect to one of the central themes in this book, is evidenced in some of the practices of the Pâshupata sect, a group that, as indicated by its name, is directly connected to the nature of Shiva as Lord of "animals." While most Tantric schools would associate *tapas*, or contemplative concentration or "fire," with a kind of "burning" of the fuel of desire at the flame of devotion, or meditation, Pâshupata practitioners base their sexual method on the idea of a transfer of *karma* from one individual to another. In other words the *karma*, good or bad, of a given person may be transferred to another in the context of sexual desire. The principle of this transfer is predicated on the fact that the total quantity of *karma* remains constant, the only variable being its share or allotment among individuals. In order to benefit from a transfer of *Karma*, the ascetic must make use of the *appearance* of lust and its slandering attribution to one by others. The *Pâshupata Sutra* describes one of the modalities method as follows:

> He (the Pâshupata) should take up his stand by a group of women. . . . Turning his attention to one of them that is young and pretty he should stare at her and act as though he were setting his desire upon her and honoring her. When . . . she looks at him, he should act out the symptoms of love such as straightening his hair, etc. Then everyone, women, men, and eunuchs, will say, "This is no man of chastity; this is a lecher." By this false accusation their merit comes to him and his bad *karma* goes to them.[13]

The symptoms of erotic attraction are said to be acted out by the practitioner in a way that replicates Shiva's erotic dancing in the Pine Forest, in the myth in which the god *appears* to seduce the wives of the *rishi*, the sages. In the myth, Shiva manifests the outward attitudes of love-making without actually engaging in any sexual activity. Being both highly erotic and chaste he calls upon himself the suspicion of others who, as a consequence, attracts negative *karma* upon themselves. What is an expression of his *nature for* the god becomes an intentional practice of imitation for the Pâshupata devotees. Analogically, as Shiva's dance is an intrinsically erotic expression that is only *extrinsically* understood as lust, it appears more than likely that the Pâshupata's acting out of erotic emotions amounts in reality to the conspicuously spectacular amplification of a "mood" that remains controlled within the psychic sphere, rather than being a mere pretense. In other words, the "magic" of simulation and the transmutation of actual eroticism are convergent. It could be said that such practices are founded on a kind of psycho-spiritual "exorcism" of the negative potentialities of sexuality through which the practitioner—in the image of Shiva's apparent lust but real chastity—proceeds to cure his desire by way of desire, as if through a kind of homeopathic treatment, thereby manifesting outwardly its symptoms in order to neutralize more effectively its possible spread. This neutralization, in itself a source of positive *karma*, is moreover parallel to the expulsion of the negative *karma* through the cultivation of an appearance of impropriety, appearance that becomes reality in the eyes of those who "see evil." As Shiva, the Pâshupata remains chaste; there is no physical contact between him and the women. The transfer of *karma* is played out on the basis of an awareness of the discontinuity, and at times inversion, between social appearances and inner realities. This method is not without evoking some aspects of the *mâlamiyyah* practices in the context of Sufism, as exemplified by the "people of blame," who worked at attracting upon themselves the censure of hypocritical and ignorant people in order to further their detachment from themselves.

All the aforementioned characteristics of Shiva point to the fact that his nature constantly "contradicts" the partial element of reality that prevents one from perceiving the whole of Reality. As Wendy O' Flaherty has indicated, this is why "among ascetics he is a libertine and among libertines an ascetic."[14] Shiva is the god that always says "no" in the name of a higher "yes." According to Abhinavagupta,

> The God, whose nature is a free consciousness, whose characteristic is the supreme light, due to his own intrinsic nature and as a result of his enjoyment of the sport of concealing his own nature, becomes the atomic, finite self, of which there are many. He himself, as a result of his own freedom, binds himself here by means of actions whose nature are composed of imagined differentiations. Such is the power of the God's freedom that, even though he has become the finite self, he once more truly attains his own true form in all its purity.[15]

The Shivaite negation is none other than that overflow of boundaries that is a synonym of supreme freedom. Shiva is not only the Unbound and That which unbinds; he is also the bound existence that responds to our tendency to "define" Shiva as "purely" unbound. Shiva is therefore constantly playing "hide-and-seek" between the bound and unbound reality. This is akin to his sacrifice, which is parallel to that of Dionysus and Osiris, since, in Abhinavagupta's terms once again,

> The Consciousness of the Self, as a result of its own intrinsic nature, is full of all things, and there is nothing whatsoever to be added to or subtracted form it. However, as a consequence of its capacity for action which is difficult to understand, and because of its unblemished freedom,

the highest Lord skillfully plays at the sport of hiding himself. In this respect *mâyâ* is nothing more than this self-concealment brought about by the Lord, even though his nature is unconcealed and manifestly clear.[16]

In a sense, Shiva is never what he appears to be, since he is beyond all appearances, while being indefinable in terms of the opposition reality appearance.

*   *   *

There is a paradox in Dionysus: his divine personality is both highly masculine and yet undoubtedly feminine. His masculinity is not only evidenced by his high deeds as a warrior; it is also clearly demonstrated by the almost irresistible charisma that leads women to flock around him. This affinity and proximity is not simply a wild sexual association, it is rather a spiritual devotion that extols sexuality to a level that reconciles the most ecstatic passion and the most virginal purity. The opposition of the maenads to the world of Hera, the world of marriage and the law, stems precisely from the fact that Dionysiac sexuality is to be identified essentially with a "natural" and primordial norm whose inner purity transcends the regime of the law. Maenads would not devote themselves to Dionysus if they did not perceive in him an element of feminine infinitude in which they recognize themselves. One could parallel, *mutatis mutandis,* the devotion of the maenads toward Dionysus with the group of holy women toward Jesus.

The double status of Isis vis-à-vis Osiris—as both sister and wife—points to an analogous symbolic mystery. There is, between the Egyptian god and goddess, both a kind of consubstantiality and a clear complementarity. Plutarch's version of the myth supports the copresence of these two dimensions when he tells us that Isis and Osiris already loved each other before they were born and were furtively united in the darkness of their mother's womb (Plutarch 356a). Similarly, women are drawn to Dionysus's nature not simply because it represents a spiritual "phallic pole" toward which they are irresistibly attracted, but also because it manifests the infinite of which they themselves partake. In his nature—most apparent in his sexuality—opposites are reconciled without being negated; the most ecstatic and erotic dances converge with immaculate love. This conciliation of opposites is symbolized by the Dionysiac attribute par excellence, the thyrsus. It consists of a staff surrounded by branches of ivy or vines. The staff manifests the phallic principle, whereas the branches that enwrap it stand for the curves of the feminine principle, a suggestion of the unending musicality of the infinite. Even though Dionysus represents the dynamic assumption of multiplicity and the ecstatic dance of spiritual inebriation, ultimately he cannot be identified with the tempestuous and destructive character of the male warrior spirit. The fact that the Egyptians identified Dionysus with Osiris, and not with the rebellious and destructive Typhon, Osiris's adversary, is in itself a confirmation of the rich, integral, and ultimately positive and constructive nature of Dionysus. According to Plutarch, the identification of Dionysus with Osiris is based primarily upon "the charm of his persuasive speech and all the resources of chant and music (*odês pases kai mousikês*)" (356b) that they share. It bears stressing that Plutarch's notation refers here to a "feminine" dimension of both Dionysus and Osiris, that is, their ability to melt the hardness of heart of their listeners through their inner attunement to the songs of the infinite. This characteristic is also highly representative of Shiva, since the Hindu god is equally characterized by a cult centered upon singing and dancing, *kirtana* and *nata*. As with Dionysus, Shiva is the "Lord of dance" (*Natarâja*) and he is in tune with the dynamic unfolding of creation as "cosmic dance." As Alain Daniélou has noted: "The parallels between the names and the legends of Shiva, Osiris, and Dionysus are so numerous that there is little doubt about their original identity."[17]

The "musical" aspect of Dionysus is also akin to another characteristic that he shares with Osiris: both are fundamentally connected to moisture. Dionysus is not only the god of wine; he is also the god of the "humidifying principle and power" (*hygropoion archê kai dynamis*) in general. As such, Dionysus and Osiris are associated with the generative principle that presides over the beneficent development of life. In this context, Plutarch reminds his readers of the etymological connection between the Greek words referring to sexual intercourse and ejaculation and the three words *hyios* (son), *hydôr* (water), and *hysai* (to rain) (364d). The first word alludes to the nature of Dionysus as son par excellence, since he was born twice—from his mother and from his father, from the flesh and from the spirit. As such, he is a central manifestation of divine theophany par excellence.

As for water it stands here for the principle of fusion and diffusion between all realities. Water is the most unitive of the elements inasmuch as it penetrates and dissolves everything; it is as such a symbol of immanence. Its purifying function is directly related to its property as being symbolically, or effectively, restorative of a primordial mode of existence. Rain refers us back to the double nature of Dionysus as both terrible and loving. It proceeds from lightning, but it is at the same time the great dispenser of life and joy. According to Plutarch, everything that is of a "humid nature" is considered to be "flowing from Osiris" (*Osiridos aporroen*) or an emanation of Osiris (365d). The connection of water with life is omnipresent in Egypt, within the context of a civilization closely bound to the spiritual meaning and beneficial influence of the Nile. This is so profoundly true that Egyptians conceived of water as the principle of the three other elements, earth, air, and fire. The Egyptian myth tells of the fight between Osiris and Typhon, the latter embodying all that is dry and "at war with the humid" (Plutarch 364b). Osiris is moreover associated with darkness, while Typhon is associated with paleness and whiteness. Black symbolizes the rich and powerful influx of life, the wealth of being, while white points, in this context, to a loss of color and energy that is associated with decay and death.

It bears mentioning that these considerations should in no way be construed as a kind of evolutionist interpretation of the gods in terms of purely natural phenomena, which supposedly became divinized at a later stage. The immanence of Osiris vis-à-vis the various natural elements does not in the least negate his divine transcendence vis-à-vis these same elements. As Plutarch puts it in his *Peri Isidos kai Osiridos*, "the essential is to keep oneself with a most extreme vigilance from unintentionally restricting the divine, from circumscribing it within the realm of the winds, waters, seeds, crops, the transformations of the earth and seasonal changes, thereby abolishing it" (377d).

* * *

Dionysus is described by tradition as being able to change water into wine, a miraculous ability that clearly associates him with certain aspects of the Christic reality. In this respect, wine symbolizes an awakening of illuminative consciousness through which the whole of reality is transfigured by spiritual insight. Wine is esoteric knowledge. It therefore comes as no surprise that, like Dionysus, Shiva is the god of inebriation and liquor. To Dionysus's famous affinity with wine answers Shiva's ritual association with *bhang*, a beverage that is prepared with crushed leaves of hemp. According to Alain Daniélou, every Shivaite must drink *bhang* at least once a year, and this beverage is also widely used to foster meditative practices. The ritual use of *bhang*, like that of wine in Christianity, is a symbolic union with the god. Its meditative use—which quite evidently presupposes the very antithesis of a hedonistic perspective, since it involves both rigorous ascetic training and proper guidance, and also requires inner qualifications and a traditional context that are very unlikely to be the appanage of contemporary Western men and women—far from leading to a passive state blurring the mind's faculties, aims at facilitating the emergence of a more acute spiritual discrimination, a kind of sober exaltation of consciousness. More generally, the association of the Dionysiac and Shivaite perspectives with intoxicating beverage, points to the particular function of these gods as bridging the gap between the realm of transcendence and that of immanence. The specificity of this perspective lies in an emphasis on the potential power of immanence, as expressed in the element *ânanda* or beatitude, to serve as a vehicle for reaching spiritual realization. The Tantric perspective, based on the spiritual transmutation of natural impulses and emotions, is akin to both the Dionysiac and Shivaite inspirations, since they are characterized by a dynamics of mystical interiorization that springs from a conscious and methodical integration of exteriority.

Madness, in Greek *mania*, is one of the fundamental characteristics of Dionysus. This madness is representative of the god himself, and it is also communicated to his devotees. For the ancient Greeks, as Plato testifies, *mania* was a divine dispensation and was associated with a sort of shamanistic possession. The Biblical tradition was not oblivious to this either, as testified by the Hebrew association between spiritual joy and madness.[18] In the case of Dionysus, this madness was manifested through wild dancing and roaming that emanated a strong charismatic power of attraction. In Euripides's *Bacchae*, the god is described as holding "the torch high, our leader, the Bacchic One, blazing flame of pine, sweet smoke like Syrian incense, trailing from his thyrsus. As he dances, he runs, here and there, rousing the stragglers, stirring them with his cries, thick hair rippling in the breeze" (vs. 186–195, Ian Johnston trans.). Mysterious obscurity, frenzied mobility, and powerful shouting are the hallmarks of a Dionysiac ambience. The darkness of the night suggests an abyssal unity that is the kingdom of the god. His is not a world of harmony and clear formal differentiation, but a magico-spiritual blend of forces and spirits rising from the depths of being. As for the shouting and cries, and all the sound and fury that resound in the wake of the god, they evoke a violent awakening of consciousness and energy. Dionysus has not come to bring peace, but—to paraphrase his mission in Christic terms—to bring war between father and son, husband and wife, and so on. His domain is that of the transcendent irruption of the Spirit that severs social bonds and regenerates the world by infusing a strong dose of raw reality within the realm of fossilizing forms. His maddening mobility is thus akin to Shiva's, he who wanders like a madman in the forest, and who is actually sometimes called the mad one (*Unmatta*). On the highest level this madness is an image and a manifestation of reality itself. In fact, the unending flow of existence does not respond to any imperative of propriety and logicality; it proceeds as a kind of raw, untamed, and violent unfolding that cannot easily be channeled along secure and protective boundaries. Dionysus is the god who constantly overflows the nicely disposed vases of provisionally fixed realities. It is so because of Dionysus's deep attunement to the mystery of divine existence, because of the "madness" in which the god "moves" and flourishes. Madness is connected to the unpredictability of the present moment in that it stems afresh from pure being. It is also bound to the constant transformation and ever-renewed self-transcending of reality. The infinite overflows with its possibilities and these possibilities manifest themselves against one other, as ever-moving waves that outreach each other. Dionysus represents the deepest spiritual attunement to this unending flow that no limited shore can contain. It goes without saying that this madness is not unrelated to a powerful sense of death, since both the vital inspiration of the moment and the transcending freedom of existence are in fact fundamentally inseparable from an acute sense of finitude, the background of which is none other than a consciousness of the infinite. Liberty, in all present "madness," flows from a death to the past and the future as characteristics of the realm of sequential causality and psychosocial continuity and coherence. As for the unending overflow of life, it is quite evidently tied to the disappearance of that which had just appeared, life and death being intimately intertwined as in a sacred embrace.

Dionysus's madness, as Shiva's, is also highly communicative, and even though Osiris himself might not be depicted by the Egyptians as being as "mad" as his Greek and Indian counterparts, there is no doubt that his devotees' behavior is no less wildly ecstatic than that of the maenads and Shivaites: "They envelop themselves in a nebrid, they wear thyrsus, they shout and indulge in transports that are identical to those of the possessed in bacchic orgies" (Plutarch 364e). It must be added that this maddening "epidemic" is particularly highlighted in the deportment of women, as if the god enjoyed a special relationship with them, and as if their own intuition of his true nature were more profound and intense than that of males. This, no doubt, is connected with Dionysus's humid nature, both as a principle of affinity with femininity and as a principle of sexual complementarity, as indicated earlier. Water is associated with the plastic domain of the substance and, on a lower level, that of the animic world. It is the generative principle from which everything flows. In a sense, Dionysus identifies with the substance of reality, of which the myriad of women who follow him are a manifestation on the level of multiplicity. If maenads spontaneously enter Dionysus's dance it is because they are already part of this dance, the substantial and informal core of their nature being suddenly freed from the relatively accidental and peripheral definition of womanhood according to social mores. The psychological "fixation" of femininity within social strictures is dissolved by the sudden catalytic surge of the god; whence the feeling of unity between Dionysus and the maenads, as if the latter had suddenly become a kind of prolongation of the former.

The myth of the unintentional and adulterous relationship between Osiris and Nephthys corresponds to one of the dimensions of this same mystery. It is said that Osiris was misled by the resemblance between Isis and her sister and that Nephthys used this resemblance as a way to unite with him in love.[19] Nephthys was the sister of Typhon (or Seth), but she was also his wife. She is as if the "dark" sister of Isis, in that she represents the lower feminine possibilities. Even though she is contrasted with Isis, she is, so to speak, redeemed by assisting her sister in her quest for the dead body of Osiris. At that point, she chooses the service of Osiris and Isis over her marriage with Typhon. Even though her union with Osiris is marked by an element of error, trickery, or transgression, it is also based on a resemblance that suggests the unity of the feminine principle whatever might be its level of manifestation, higher or lower. Her leaving Typhon to serve Osiris and Isis clearly illustrates that Egyptians did not conceive of a feminine duality in the same terms as they conceived of a masculine one. The fight between Osiris and Typhon is highlighted as a radical antagonism that can only be resolved through the ultimate victory of Osiris. There is only "one." Plutarch indicates that Osiris is associated with all that pertains to regularity and order within the phenomena and cycles of nature (Plutarch 371b). On the contrary, Typhon always introduces an element of disorder and excess. He disrupts the course of the universe in a negative and deadly fashion, by contrast with Dionysiac disruption, which is always fertile and positive. Typhon is actively engaged in a negation of life and the good: his evil-doing is substantial.

As for Nephthys, her negativity is not substantial but is, rather, the distant consequence of the unfolding of creation. According to Plutarch, Nephthys represents the realm of passive realities (*pathetikoi*) in which the divine archetypes are disseminated and subjected to gradual degeneration, desegregation, and death. Nephthys is "bad" to the extent that she remains the wife of Typhon, which amounts to saying that she passively negates the "forms" (*eide*) and "emanations" (*aporroai*) of the divine. But she is good inasmuch as she gives herself secretly to Osiris, that is, insofar as her underlying and "hidden" substance remains a vehicle of the archetypes. On the one hand, she subjects

herself to the principle of negation represented by her brother and
husband; on the other hand, she betrays him out of a more fundamental faithfulness to Osiris. Her final alliance and association with
Isis, the "legitimate" wife, is an image of the unity of the feminine
substance beyond the contrastive diversity of its aspects. It bears
stressing that Isis alone sometimes represents the different levels and
aspects of the feminine substance, independently from Nephthys,
since she "undergoes metamorphoses and puts on all kinds of forms
(*morphas*) and appearances (*ideas*)" (Plutarch 372e). As such she is
defined as "universal receptacle" and is designated as *myrionymos*
(with a thousand names).

In order to further our understanding of the mystery that is symbolized and enacted by the three gods whom we have been considering,
it is particularly rewarding to analyze the passages from Plutarch that
comment upon the identification between Dionysus and the Egyptian
Osiris. The elements that associate the two gods may allow us to gain
access to the most fundamental strata of meaning involved in both
myths. First, Plutarch alludes to a secret initiatic knowledge, which he
cannot divulge, and that is clearly related to the principle of the unity
between the two gods Osiris and Dionysus. This is, so to speak, the
hidden and inner side of the myth, beyond the formal differences that
delineate the respective identities of the Greek and Egyptian gods. It
pertains to the initiation into Mysteries, to which Plutarch was privy.
Second, ritual elements are mentioned, which may not be decisive
since they might also apply to a wide spectrum of religious practices
that have nothing to do with Dionysus or Osiris. Such is the case of
manifestations of spiritual inebriation and devotional exaltation. The
third element refers to a common theriomorphism, that of the bull.
This animal is associated with chthonian qualities that are also akin to
rites of fertilization and renewal. On a higher level, one must note that
Shiva is also depicted as riding a bull, Nandi. This is directly related to
the god's function as an agent of the transmutation of instinctive and
sexual impulses. More generally, the myth and rites pertaining to a
dismemberment and rememberment of the god presents, Plutarch
tells us, with a fourth major characteristic common to both Dionysus
and Osiris: both gods are clearly associated with the cycle of death and
rebirth. They are not "Olympian" gods of permanence; they pertain
to the realm of becoming inasmuch as it expresses the ever-present rise
and fall of reality. This is clearly expressed by the fact that they are
both human and divine. Their assumption of mortality is a direct
symbol of their clear affinity with the realm of becoming and immanence. Their spiritual odyssey retraces the destiny of mankind as being

subjected to death, but also called to immortality. Osiris undergoes two symbolic deaths: he is first suffocated within a chest into which he had been tricked by Typhon and the chest is abandoned to the stream of the Nile; second, Osiris is later on dismembered by the same Typhon, his body being torn into fourteen pieces. Isis will later find these parts and her son Horus will reassemble them with the assistance of Thoth. In R.T. Rundle Clark's words, Osiris is "the essential victim. [...] he is the sufferer with all mortality, but at the same time he is all the power of revival and fertility in the world."[20]

As A.K. Coomaraswamy has indicated, the passage from Divine Unity to cosmic multiplicity is often depicted in the form of a sacrificial dismemberment. The One has to be dismembered into many so that the many may "re-member" the One.[21] The dismemberment of Osiris and Dionysus, as opposed to certain other mythological occurrences, is effected by people other than themselves, thereby implying an emphasis on the dimension of suffering inherent in the sacrifice. Notwithstanding this emphasis, the sacrificer, the sacrificed, and the sacrifice are One.[22] In the case of Shiva, we have already mentioned the god's association with the *pâshu*, who is also the victim of sacrifice and, thereby, the sacrificer himself since the sacrifice is ultimately none other than that of the One. Whether appearances point to a voluntary sacrifice or not, it remains that the heroic dismemberment of the god must always be envisaged as an essential dimension of his nature, and not as an element that could be extrinsically imposed upon him. In that sense, Shiva, Dionysus, and Osiris represent the Abyss of divine infinitude and the ever-flowing manifestation of the possibilities that It includes. As an illustration of this principle, Shiva is known as "the fathomless abyss." [23] This suggests that the three gods are not gods of becoming as such; rather, they are gods who embody the transcendence of the Infinite vis-à-vis forms, whence their association with death and resurrection, but also transgression and renewal. This also accounts for the paradoxes of their nature, and the apparent amorality of many of their actions. With them, forms are not only constantly emerging from the inexhaustible fount of the Divine Mystery, but they are also constantly negated and transcended in the name of that Mystery.

At this juncture, it is important to recognize the role of the principle of cosmic dispensation that crystallizes and manifests this overflow within the world of forms. This principle, which could be defined as the cosmic dimension of the Logos—namely the demiurgic Logos at the center of existence— is envisaged in the form of a god of wisdom and language. This is the function imparted upon Thoth in Egypt,

Ganesha in Hinduism, and Hermes in Greece. All three gods are, in one way or another, closely akin to, or associated with, the god of supreme transcendence, whether it be a matter of filiation—according to some sources, Ganesha was born from Shiva's smile—or one of service and assistance—Thoth is instrumental in helping Isis in her "re-membering" of Osiris, and Hermes plays a crucial role in hiding the baby Dionysus from the jealous Hera and sewing him in Zeus's thigh. Thoth, Ganesha, and Hermes are all associated with wisdom, intelligence, invention, scholarship, and language. They personify the cosmic dimension of the Intellect in its demiurgic aspect. Their respective mythological associations with Osiris, Shiva, and Dionysus are highly significant when considered from the metaphysical stand-point. Subjectively, or spiritually speaking, Shiva is the Self, *Ātman*, whereas Ganesha is the cosmic aspect of the *Buddhi* or Intellect. As such, like Hermes and Thoth, Ganesha presides over the coming into being of existential realities; he is both a god of liminality, random-ness, and luck, as well as a god of logical invention and ordering. Plato tells, for example, that Thoth[24] was considered by the Egyptians as the god presiding over the invention of the arts, particularly those associ-ated with language. In his *Cratylus*, he further explains that the supreme god of creation, Thamus, did not always agree with Thoth's justifications for the arts. In other words, Thamus represents, in a cer-tain respect, Divine Being inasmuch as it brings into existence, through a process of selection as it were, the possibilities that are latent in the Infinite. As a kind of cosmic reflection of the Infinite, Thoth appears, by contrast, as the demiurgic producer of a myriad of realities that may or may not be brought into existence. Ganesha occupies an analogous position in relation to Shiva. Ganesha is son of Shiva; he is the "Hindu counterpart of Hermes"[25] insofar as he is the keeper of thresholds and inasmuch as he casts his blessings upon the initiation of new enterprises. His association with learning and matters of the mind is another "hermetic" signature. The ambiguous aspect of the demiurgic Logos appears symbolically in Hermes' amorality, in Thoth's[26] occasionally demoniacal character, and in Ganesha's "monstrous" compositeness. This prima facie unsettling composite-ness is also, on the deepest level, a symbol of the totality of the Supreme that reconciles all differences and oppositions. As John A. Grimes has eloquently shown, Ganesha is the Self, he is the Supreme Shiva, and he is also, as such, an incarnation of the supreme non-dualistic sentence, *Tat Tvam Asi* (That Thou Art).[27] The totality, of which Ganesha provides an incongruous image, is also reflected in the ambivalence and mobility of the demiurgic aspect of the cosmic Logos.

Its ambiguity stems from its being both receptive—thereby reflecting Divine Perfection—and productive and creative—thereby entering the world of imperfection. Conversely, the cosmic Logos being a reflection of the Divine Infinitude, may lead it or him —Ganesha—to transcend the limited perspective of the human good, while his productive side participates in the effulgence of the Good.[28] Ganesha, Hermes, and Thoth are in that sense representations, or rather manifestations, of the principle of polarization, that is, the process through which the rays of the Divine Light manifest different properties in different directions. Hermes was born in a cave removed from the world, "Ganapati's truth flows from the ice cave of the infinite," and Thoth is said to introduce Re's life into "the secret cave" in order to bring back to life Osiris's exhausted mystery.[29] The three "assisting" gods therefore embody the emergence of the defining light of manifestation from the supra-formal obscurity of the infinite.[30] They polarize this light in a way that brings both strife and harmony.[31]

CHAPTER 4

DIVINE TROUBLEMAKERS

The invention of culture and the arts is universally envisaged as a demiurgic irruption and effulgence that entails an element of ambiguity. Sometimes, the mythico-moral resolution of this cosmic ambiguity takes place on the basis of the staging of a competition between two brothers representing good and evil forces respectively. Among the Iroquois, for example, the cosmogonic process in its positive aspect is carried out by Yoskehâ', while his brother Tawîskarà presides over the negative force of death. The name Yoskehâ' implies the idea of spring, renewal, and rejuvenation, whereas Tawîskarà is associated with winter and the deadening effects of cold. In this particular mythology, the powers of life are akin to the powers of invention and production since Yoskehâ' has also taught men the use of fire, which he had received from the demiurgic tortoise.[1]

Instead of contrasting two figures representative of good and evil forces, other mythologies consider the principle of ambiguity as being embodied by a sacred personage whose character and actions can be envisaged from distinct points of view. Such is the case of Susano-no-Mikoto in Shinto. As with other forms of shamanism, Shinto does not strictly differentiate between the realm of good and the realm of evil. The invisible realm that it envisages cannot be defined in moral terms since it embraces the entire expanse of reality. The Divine encompasses all that is, and It may therefore be apprehended in all the aspects of reality, whether they be high or low. There is no trace of dualism in this vision since all *kami* realities are "different manifestations of the same spirit."[2] The apparent contradiction between good and evil must therefore enter the very reality and understanding of the Divine. It is important to note that within the realm of the Shinto distinction between Ara-Mitama (Rough Spirit) and Nigi-Mitama

(Gentle Spirit), it is the former that represents and actualizes the creative power in the universe. The demiurgic process is "rough" in the sense that it brings reality to a new stage of being through a kind of ontological violence without which the divine unfolding of the Spirit would be hindered, and would in fact be impossible. And this is precisely the function of Susano-no-Mikoto, a divine being whose moral ambiguity is like the mythological symbol of the demiurgic unfolding. Susano-no-Mikoto is the son of the first male Kami, Izana-gi-no-Kami, whose daughter is Amaterasu-omi-Kami. Both were born following Izanagi's failure to convince his deceased spouse Izanami to flee from the realm of death to join him. According to the Shinto scripture *Nihongi*, Susano, having been granted the earth as his king-dom by his father, wanted to see his mother a last time before assum-ing his new function. In the *Kojiki*, Susano is given the seas, and not the earth. Upon receiving the former from his father, he weeps and cries without end, so that he is finally expelled by his father. Amaterasu, who has been given the heavens as her province, becomes suspicious of her brother's intentions; she thinks that his departure might be a sign of his intention to rob her of her realm. They then agree that he should undergo an ordeal in the form of a contest with her: if Susano gives birth to sons he is to be cleared of suspicion; otherwise he is to be deemed guilty. The legend tells that Susano bred five sons while Amaterasu gave birth to three daughters.[3] However, Amaterasu con-tested the outcome by claiming that Susano's sons were a result of his chomping the jewels that belonged to her. A trial then takes place that vindicates Amaterasu. Indignant at the outcome of the judgment, Susano involves himself in all kinds of mean and mischievous acts against his sister.[4] Among the latter, he "strewed excrements in the palace" of Amaterasu, thereby involving the basest elements of terres-trial reality in the alchemy of the world process, a fact that echoes the integration of "gross matter" in the Tantric worldview and ascesis.

It bears stressing that even though Susano is presented in the myth as a tempestuous and disorderly character, it can hardly be denied that he did not commit any action that would have justifiably accounted for his fate. In a sense, he was himself the victim of the universal "trickery" of the world. His being right and wronged is a manifesta-tion of the amoral dimension of the demiurgic process, and a sure sign of the distance separating the good as such from the terrestrial realm of ambivalence. And it should be noted in passing that Amaterasu displayed a less-than-candid attitude in her dealing with her brother. The somewhat amoral outcome of the story is less important though, at least in cosmogonic terms, than the apparent rebellion of Susano.

Shinto does not reproach Susano with being either wrong or evil; rather, it reproaches him for having indulged in excessive reactions when he understood that he had been cheated. As J.W.T. Mason has rightfully contended, it is highly instructive to see how shamanistic Shinto refuses to turn Susano into a kind of devilish character:

> Had analytical ecclesiastics been at work on the Susano myth, Susano would have been turned into a Devil, thrown from Heaven to Hell for trying to gain control of divine spirit with evil intent.[5]

The fact is that the perspective of shamanism in general is not inclined to reject evil as a kind of separate province of Reality. Shamanism considers reality as unitary, and the sharp contrasts that appear in its unfolding are nothing but the externalizations of the ambiguity of the cosmogonic process. Dualism is fundamentally foreign to shamanism, even though the fight against evil spirits is part and parcel of the function of the shaman. The passional and tenebrous element that of necessity enters into the economy of the Real is not conceived as intrinsically foreign to the course of the good. It is, on the contrary, integrated within the story of the latter. Frithjof Schuon has expressed this point of view by indicating that even though the final victory of Amaterasu amounts to a recognition of an eminence of the celestial over the passional, the latter remains necessary to the unfolding of reality and must therefore be conceived, in a sense, as a good as well:

> Susano-o is banished to the earth, which indicates the final victory of "the Sun" over "the Tempest" or, more precisely, of Knowledge over the passional element; but the latter in its capacity of "productive energy" is necessary to the cosmic economy, and this is why Susano-o, without losing his celestial dignity, had earthly issue.[6]

Everything that enters into the economy of Reality needs, in a sense, to be integrated and assimilated into that Reality. "Evil" is not conceived here as an absolute antithesis to the good, but as a subordinate dimension of the latter. Such an apprehension of universal opposites and alternations makes it impossible to fix discrete realities into rigid patterns of contradiction, which would lead to radical dualism and obstruct the metaphysical and natural fluidity of the whole.

Nearly all shamanistic and mythological traditions envisage the realities to which we have just referred in an analogous pattern of integration through fluid ambiguity that borders both on beneficial contribution and evil part. In Ancient Scandinavian religion and folklore, the character of Loki embodies and enacts some of the same traits characteristic of Susano. The two most immediate enigmas that are presented by Loki lie in his ambiguous nature—is he really divine or not?—and, correlatively, in his relationship with the gods—is he their friend or their enemy? The fact is that although considered as being a god, Loki has remained without any cult and without any precise function in the economy of divine life. He is a marginal god, as illustrated by the fact that he is the last Aesir to be listed in the *Skaldskaparmal*.[7] Moreover, his frequent assistance to the gods cannot dispel the fact that he is the agent of the destruction of the world. A third more general enigma has to do with his moral status: is he good or is he bad, and what is his role in the economy of the world? Here again, the benefits of his clever intelligence are ultimately outweighed by his harmful treason. In order to explain away these fundamental ambiguities, or contradictions, the temptation is strong, for contemporary scholars, to rely upon an historical and chronological study of the figure of Loki. The relationship between the two sides of Loki is then accounted for in terms of an evolution that would see the "bad Loki" gradually eclipse the "good Loki." Georges Dumézil has called for critical caution against this historicist interpretation on the basis of the many amputations that it entails; he has also raised questions about theories that would see exclusively Christian influences as means of accounting for a kind of demonization of Loki. For Dumézil, "the apories and antinomies [...] far from veiling or diluting Loki's personality or from proving a 'historical evolution' which would have diverted or even inverted its meaning, defines it constitutively as complex and contradictory."[8] Any attempt at doing away with the intrinsic ambiguity of the character condemns us to missing the deepest metaphysical and spiritual meaning of Loki.

As with many other trickster figures, Loki reconciles opposites without in the least confusing them: actually there seems to be, in him, such a maximal extension of opposites that only a complex inherent ambivalence can make them coincide in the same character. As noted by Dumézil, there is in Loki an extreme distance between the category of the small that is assigned to him and the cosmic expansion of his role, especially in eschatological matter. Among the Aesir family of the supreme gods, Loki is identified as very small in height, and he has no kinship with any other of the gods. He is one of a kind, as well as diminutive in his external aspect. The absence of a clear lineage in his divine ancestry makes it plain that his nature is marginal: he is a kind of outcast among the gods. His father is said to be a giant. This is important in the sense that the war between gods and giants, like that between *devas* and *asuras* in India, is central to Scandinavian myths. Within this schizomorphic structure that clearly delineates opposite realms, Loki's identity is somewhat hybrid, as he bears the influence of a titanic heritage while being associated with the gods. Moreover, his primary role seems to consist in serving as a companion to the latter, almost as a servant. He is a messenger, a scout, a kind of valet, and a buffoon.[9] His small size, which he shares with many a trickster, is suggestively indicative of his status as an exception, as an atypical phenomenon comparable to a small gray dot within a white surface. However, as the drama of history unfolds, it appears that Loki's role becomes more and more comparable to that of an increasingly black and large spot. From a function of semidivine helper of the gods, he ends up incarnating the final eschatological fury and revenge of the forces of evil gathered for the *Ragnarök* (the Doom of the Gods or Powers). He will become the helmsman of the nave of inhabitants of hell who invade the earth together with the giants during the final cosmic episodes of the *Gotterdammerung*. It is highly instructive to note the parallel between the darkening of times and the increasing role of Loki in the historical unfolding of the cycle. It is as if cyclical conditions presented us with a different understanding of the role of demiurgic ambiguity. In the early phases, Loki is like a servant of the gods who helps them bring forth the world, as it were. The characteristics that are highlighted are very similar to Hermes' in that respect. He is not only a messenger and a scout—making it possible for communication to occur between discrete domains, and exploring the realm of possibilities— he also displays, as Hermes, a mesmerizing ability to escape, flee, and disappear, as if in smoke. This ability to disappear, which is symbolically related to his association with the wind, is akin to his expertise in metamorphoses.

In the later phases of history, by contrast, Loki appears under his aspect of wickedness, revenge, and ability to promote discord among gods and men. Like the Irish Bricriu, Loki is the prince of discord, and this obviously connects him to the diabolic.[10] He takes pleasure in sowing division and it goes without saying that this pleasure is increased exponentially in times of crisis and dissolution. By providing opportunities for conflicts, Loki opens the wounds of relativity and differentiation; and because of his association with impulsiveness, curiosity, and greed, his role cannot but lead to a kind of pulverization of reality, which is also for him a sort of revenge against the order of things to which he never fully belonged. He assists the gods in making the world what it is, but he is never in charge, being merely a kind of energetic technician working toward the actualization of possibilities. Once his passion and cleverness have rejected the yoke of a higher wisdom he becomes free to indulge the lower strata of his nature. It is to be noted that this indulgence makes him oblivious of his own interest, unleashing consequences that are ultimately self-destructive. This is fundamentally related to the cosmogonic process as it strives to assert itself up to the extreme limits of existence, opening onto nothingness. Loki's increased and self-destructive independence from and opposition to the gods, parallel to his ever-growing subversive role, cannot but result in a sort of self-explosion.

One of the enigmas of Loki is that, like Hermes and Thoth, he is also clearly associated with intelligence. He is the most clever and cunning of all gods. This practical intelligence is the hallmark of his role as helper of the gods; it is akin to the Greeks' *metis*, as exemplified in Ulysses' skills. In Snorri Sturluson's *Edda*, a surprising connection is established between Loki and Ulysses: it is stated that "the Turks told tales about Ulysses and that they gave him the name Loki, for the Turks were especially hostile to him." [11] *Metis* is also a form of political intelligence, in the sense that it thrives in the context of human relations of power. This intelligence cannot, however, be equated with that of Odin. Dumézil has contrasted these two types of intelligence by proposing to refer to them as "impulsive intelligence" and "recollected intelligence" respectively.[12] In other words, it could be said that Odin represents the highest wisdom, while Loki embodies the demiurgic and productive dimension of intelligence. This intelligence of Loki is also probably akin to Lodurr's—the hypothesis of an identification between the two characters having been proposed by scholars such as de Vries and Dumézil— who, in the *Edda*, endows men with the "instinctive" and "bodily" intelligence that is associated with their physical envelope. The superficiality and immediacy of this intelligence— which is perfectly akin to the impulsiveness emphasized by Dumézil—clearly indicates its relatively peripheral and external character. Loki's intelligence is, as it were, the extrinsic limit of cosmic intelligence, which is itself only a reflection of divine wisdom. This type of intelligence is especially useful and effective when dealing with the dimension of absurdity, that is, with the domain of exceptions and shadows that characterizes relativity. When Loki hears that the good Baldr has been protected from his apprehension of an impending death by the oath that his mother, Frigg, Odin's wife, has obtained from the whole mineral, vegetal, and animal kingdoms, he swiftly cozens Frigg, under the form of a woman, by having her disclose that the young mistletoe has been the only plant not to be asked to swear, having been deemed to be too green to inflict any harm. Later on, after having plucked a branch of mistletoe, Loki convinces Hodr to participate in the mock archery and fencing party during which the gods play at pretending to harm Baldr while knowing full well that none of their weapons can inflict any damage on him. Loki gives the mistletoe to Hodr as an arrow, and advises him to aim at Baldr. Baldr is killed and all the gods lament the loss of Baldr.[13] This episode is highly indicative of the two foremost aspects of Loki's intelligence. First is his glibness and his ability to elicit secrets from others by taking a variety of forms. His ability to change into a woman is particularly striking in several instances, suggesting not only the fluid ambiguity of his nature, but also—in the warrior societies of the Scandinavians—his lack of virile courage and his identification with the plastic and moving substance of the world.[14] The second aspect of his intelligence highlighted in this passage lies in his rare capacity to take advantage of the fissures and imperfections of existence. Frigg's protection of Baldr appeared to be without cracks, expressing a perfect necessity, but there was indeed an element of imperfection—symbol of the ambiguity of the relative—and Loki was characteristically able to take advantage of it. The intellectual superiority of Loki vis-à-vis other gods is therefore only a paradox if one does not take into account that it applies almost exclusively to a domain that is most distant from the supreme intelligibility of the realm of wisdom. Loki is all the more clever to the extent that he is most "ex-centric" to the world of the gods. This is, moreover, confirmed by the fact that his intelligence is rarely without an element of stupidity or ridicule; and these ridiculous situations are more often than not the unintended consequences of his cleverness.

Hermes presents numerous analogies with Loki, while opening more directly the realm of the trickster to the horizon of wisdom. In fact, the historical "development" of the figure of Hermes leads us from the cosmology of shamanism to the gnosis of Hermeticism and Monotheism; from the world of nature as theophanic unfolding to that of the Logos as principle of divine knowledge. In the oldest myths, Hermes' conception and birth already present us with a somewhat atypical character: the child Hermes is the offspring of Zeus, the supreme god, and Maia, who lives in seclusion in the remote Arcadia. It is said that Zeus fecundated Maia in the darkest part of the night while all other gods were sound asleep. Maia is the most beautiful of the seven daughters of Atlas and Pleione, the Pleiades. Despite, or perhaps rather because of, her beauty, she lives quite a withdrawn life in a cave on Mount Cyllene. It is interesting to note that Hermes is the fruit of the union of the highest and the deepest, the most evident and the most hidden, light and night, splendor and mystery, the god of Mount Olympus and the goddess of the remote cave. This double origin already suggests the dual, communicative, and ambivalent nature of Hermes, two characteristics that will be confirmed in his offspring, particularly in the figures of his two sons Pan and Hermaphroditus. Pan represents the most unmitigated expression of pure virility, while Hermaphroditus is, on the contrary, the mythological archetype of the androgyne. Paradoxically, these two seemingly divergent filiations are in fact reconciled in the figure of Hermes, since the son of Zeus is both associated with sexual seduction and the phallus, on the one hand, and ever-changing ambivalence on the other hand. One must also note that the "career" of Hermes takes him from the hidden recesses of the mountainous and wild Arcadia to the bustling activity of the urban marketplace. This wide range of location spans the entire field of reality, from the mystery of the divine essence, as symbolized by the secret darkness of the motherly cave, to the furthest shores of cosmic manifestation, where the wheel of becoming spins the quickest, in the busy world of human interactions and commerce. This is also indicative of the function of Hermes as mediator between the most diametrically opposed dimensions of reality, a function of reconciliation of polarities. By taking the hidden secret of the divine to the most visible degrees of the human realm Hermes fulfills his role as messenger of the gods. He can thereby be identified with the flash of light of the divine Logos which exteriorizes, or reveals, the innermost core of Reality. The Egyptians identified Hermes with their god Thoth; the latter, like Hermes, was regarded as a kind of helper, messenger, and recorder, of the supreme solar god, Amun. He was also considered as the god of the moon on account both of his association with cyclical changes and qualitative time divisions, and his reflecting the central light of the sun.[15] In his first capacity, Hermes-Thoth is, at it were, the divider of eternity and the multiplier of time. He is the instrument, or the catalyst, of the transition from the eternal present to the flow of time, including its host of measures and allotments to mankind. Fragmentation, segmentation, and limitation pertain, in his sphere of activity, to the manifestation and production of this world, and to the innumerable distinctions that its coming into existence entail. The world of series, records, lists, and classifications may be seen as a hermetic inventory of the myriad existential manifestations as reflected in the separative "gaze" of the demiurgic production. As a lunar reflection of the divine sun, Hermes-Thoth also fulfills a properly "speculative" function of interpreter and intermediary between the world of the gods and that of man. His Egyptian, and Greek, association with wisdom, *logos*, and hermeneutic and mantic practices derive from his capacity to transmit and translate divine messages to mankind through oracular crystallizations and the deciphering of cryptic formulae from beyond. In this respect, Hermes' ambivalence is akin to his nature of "mirror" with respect to divine realities: the images reflected in the mirror are not only faithful copies of the originals but also inverted versions of them.

It is said that, at his birth, Maia wrapped the infant in swaddling bandages. As she fell asleep, Hermes was able to free himself from this swaddle, thereby inaugurating his ability to untie knots by spells, the art of magic over which he would henceforth preside being characterized by this skill. In this perspective, magic can be defined as a "solving" of the coagulated psychic forms that "freeze," so to speak, their ability to circulate and interact in fluid motions. This art is moreover prefigured in the cosmogonic production that calls phenomena into existence through the spoken word. In this process, as in the lower realm of magic, the sound of the voice plays a determining and demiurgic role with respect to phenomenal appearances. It literally "evokes" realities, an ability that moreover accounts for Hermes' patronage over poetry. The mythological tale of Hermes' invention of the lyre converges with his mastery over verbal magic by presenting him as both highly ingenious and powerfully seductive. Upon fleeing from his mother's cave in search of adventure, Hermes chances to find a tortoise. His coming to realize into what he could turn her was immediate. In Lewis Hyde's elegant translation of the Homeric Hymn: "just a swift thought can fly through the heart of a person haunted with care, just as bright glances spin from the eyes, so, in one instant, Hermes knew what to do and did it."[16] He fastens reeds to the shell, and in other versions he uses the intestines of one of the cows he has stolen from Apollo—a more interesting account from the standpoint of his ability to turn transgressions into blessings—and thus was the lyre invented. The Homeric Hymn tells us that he was able to enchant Apollo by using this newly invented instrument. At that juncture, Hermes is staged as a bard who sings the high deeds of each and every member of the divine lineage. His ability to charm Apollo with sounds and words is not only a hallmark of his cunning and expertise in flattery; it is also, and above all, a clear indication of his attunement to the "music" and the "magic" of the world. Hermes is able to "transmute" the heart of those who listen to him through his skill at "arranging" sounds and words within a wholesome unity that suggests intelligibility and delight. This is also a part and parcel of his panoply as a demiurge.

The most ancient Greek descriptions of Hermes present him as the god of theft, and more generally of secret and cunning action, as exemplified in magic. As Norman O. Brown has emphasized, the stress does not lie as much on the action of stealing as it does on the modalities of the action.[17] After all, there are modes of stealing that do not involve secrecy, or manipulation, as for example robbery by force. The actions of a genuine thief are characterized by ingenuity and secretiveness. In the Homeric Hymn to Hermes, the latter is more specifically related to an ability to deceive by manipulating the words of an oath. This ability is primarily made possible by the fact that, to ancient Greeks, an oath was binding only when understood literally. In the Hymn narrative, when asked by Apollo where the cattle are to be found that Hermes has stolen from him, the god of stealth answers by saying that he, Hermes, does not look like a cattle-raider and that he is too young—a new born baby—to be interested in such things. When taken into his father's presence, that is, before Zeus, Hermes swears that he has never driven Apollo's cattle to his house, and has never stepped across its threshold. The fact is that he has led the cattle backward so that the animals' hoofprints might take the tracker to the place where he had stolen them; he has also made magical sandals for himself, thereby covering his own traces. In an ancient culture such as that of archaic Greece an oath is the most sacred and binding of things; it carries with it the awe of an absolute power. Hermes' skills, however, consist in telling the truth while yet not telling it. He is able to do so by taking advantage of the levels of meaning that are involved, or rather by playing on appearances. He does not *appear* to have crossed the threshold: because of his magic the cattle do not *appear* to come from where they come; and he certainly does not *look like* a cattle-raider. On all accounts, he takes truth at the most literal level, a literalness that, in fact, denies reality and truth. He is a master at dissociating language from reality. Truth is not for him an ontological matter, it is a verbal one. Hermes reigns over the world of representations. This mastery over language makes him the god of magic and the god of sexual seduction. Both arts pertain to a use of external forms for the sake of appropriating and making use of power.

Hermes appears in many guises and is often considered in conflicting ways throughout the history of Greek civilization. Equating Hermes with the universal figure of the trickster, Norman O. Brown has encapsulated the main aspects of the god in relation to the various historical contexts in which he manifests himself:

> Depending on the historical circumstances, the trickster may evolve
> into any one of such contrasting figures as a benevolent culture hero

nearly indistinguishable from the Supreme God, a demiurge in strong opposition to the heavenly powers, a kind of devil counteracting the creator in every possible way, a messenger and mediator between gods and men, or merely a Puckish figure, the hero of comical stories.[18]

For Brown, following Malinowski, it is the variations in economic, social, and political contexts that explain the diversity of the trickster's panoply, as is eminently exemplified by Hermes' various "characters." These modifications, or evolutions, in the myth are conceived of as a necessity, justifying as they do reflections of changes in socioeconomic modes of exchange. Brown reads the various images of Hermes, from the earliest mythological literature to Classical Greece, as an outcome of the tensions between the institution of kingship and the emergence of a class of professional workmen initially subordinate to royal power; at a later date, they are envisaged as the result of the contrast "between the established authority of the aristocracy and the native intelligence of the rising lower classes," as well as stemming from the passage from a communitarian and agrarian society to the reign of "acquisitive individualism."[19] Brown goes so far this way that he accounts for the Homeric emphasis on Hermes being able to steal Apollo's cattle on the very first day of his life as "the symbol of the birth of a new world in which, [. . .] the lower classes come into their own."[20] Now, the association of a trickster figure like Hermes with subordinate classes is undoubtedly a reoccurring theme in most mythologies. This association can be, and has been, interpreted on a variety of levels that are not necessarily contradictory, or could even be conceived as a manifestation of the same reality on a variety of onto-logical levels. The affinity between the trickster, who is a transformer and not a creator as such, with the working classes is related to quali-ties such as practical ingenuity and creativeness, qualities that are akin to *technê*, which is the ability to make use of cunning intelligence in dealing with nature, whether it be in agriculture or commerce. The demiurgic intelligence of a trickster like Hermes may be read as the archetype of such abilities. The social relationship between the King and his servant is indeed often reflected in the mythological relation-ship between God and the Demiurge, such as in the case of Zeus and Hermes. The modern critical outlook tends to account for this corre-spondence in terms of socioeconomic infrastructures being mani-fested in cultural superstructures, while the traditional perspective sees this same correspondence as being part of an ontologically grounded network of analogies. There is no reason to think that a penetrating understanding of the latter would be utterly exclusive to a recognition of the former. However, to reduce Hermes, or the trickster in general, to a kind of ideological superstructure that would reveal, by reflection, in a "transparent" and quasi-mechanical fashion, the evolution of the socioeconomic conditions of ancient Greece, or any other land, would amount to missing the profound coherence that defines, beyond meaningful variations in emphasis or aspects, the figure of the god of magic and commerce. In other words, the modifications, or evolution, of the myth and the figure of the god himself, can simply be understood as the result of the adoption of various circumstantial points of view that manifest the diversity of aspects that are included, explicitly or implicitly, within the religious and magic function of Hermes. The various aspects of Hermes that Brown enumerates are fundamentally inscribed in the function of the god. This function can be summarized as one of communication and mediation, hence ultimately of transformation. The aspect of communication, which appears most clearly in the ultimate role of Hermes as messenger of Zeus, is profoundly connected to the notions of the threshold and the boundary, which seem to be the original root of the very name of Hermes (*herma*: stone-heap or boundary-stone). It is also related, as a mode of sacred mediation, to the god's close association with magic. In traditional worlds the interaction with members of foreign groups was ritualized through specific greetings, sacred boundary stones, and magical practices: the point of contact and communication between discrete cultures and tribes was the site of a qualitative difference in the nature of space. Magic was a form of protective and facilitating practice in view of communication, whence its association with Hermes. All of these interrelated functions involve a mastery over subtle relationships between domains that are, a priori, separate. Hermes presides over the negotiation of an ever-precarious unity or continuity between these domains while being keenly aware of their distance or distinction: he is the master of continuity in discontinuity, and discontinuity in continuity. The ambivalence or tension that is inscribed in this function cannot but give rise to a variety of aspects and reputations. This is nowhere truer than in the two parallel phenomena of *techné* and magic. These two kinds of activity were in fact thought of as connected in ancient Greece, and it can even be said that technique was a kind of magic, or manipulation of forces, whereas magic undeniably involved specific technical skills. As a manipulation of psychic forces magic is the ambiguous art par excellence, since its reputation is utterly dependent upon its finality. The ordinary distinction between white and black magic does not refer to the modes of operation of the "magician" but to the goals that he pursues. This fundamental ambiguity of the art of magic is replicated in *techné* since the latter bears no spiritual or moral attribution in itself. The ambivalence of *techné* is in a sense parallel to that of the trickster. As such, Hermes can be presented either as an initiator who transmits practical knowledge to mankind, like Prometheus, or as a seductive cozener, as in Hesiod's account of Hermes' tempting of Pandora. In the latter narrative, Hermes is significantly associated with the female character of Pandora: she was the first woman on earth, and presents a meaningful analogy with the Biblical Eve. However, she is not only a representation of the female sex, or a misogynistic symbol of women's unhealthy and disastrous curiosity, she had also, and above all, received from the gods all the possible gifts of intelligence, beauty, and talents, as indicated by her name *pan-dora*, gifted in all. Notwithstanding these gifts, it is made plain by the myth that she was given not only as a blessing to mortals, but also as a source of sorrow. The ambivalence of her character is epitomized in her association with a jar containing good things, according to the account of Theognis, bad things, according to the account of Hesiod, and—according to both—Hope, only the latter having remained in the jar following her opening and sealing of it. The ambivalence of the contents of the jar is not necessarily, or exclusively, to be taken as indicative of specific historical concerns on the part of the various storytellers: more fundamentally, they point to the very ambiguity of the world of manifestation as such, as exemplified by human abilities and skills. In fact, it is not so much the content as such that is at stake as it is the way in which it is envisaged and made use of. Jane Harrison has correlated Hesiod's version of the myth with the Dionysiac rite of the opening of the jars that involved a new wine considered to be sacred and capable of inducing both good and bad effects.[21] One is also reminded of Baudelaire's reflection concerning the potentially antithetic consequences of the consumption of wine and drugs, namely their capacity to make gods out of some and human beasts out of others.

The shifts in the archaic Greek view of Hermes from a benevolent and beneficent god of magic and technique to a trickster conceived as the master of invention and mischief—indeed the catalyst and initiator of the Dark Age or *Kali Yuga*—in Hesiod's account of the conflict between old agrarian communitarianism on the one hand, and economic individualism on the other hand, is indicative of the fact that the same principle, that of demiurgic unfolding, may be considered "upstream" or "downstream," as it were. In other words, the possible socioeconomic correlations that may be highlighted in the evolution of the religious concept and cult of Hermes can be related, corroborated, and ultimately founded upon metaphysical, cosmological, and eschatological principles that are, at bottom, so many expressions of the ambivalence of the ontological and cosmological unfolding of possibilities. For example, Hermes can be considered as a beneficent god inasmuch as he helps bring into existence techniques and practices that enhance the skills of mankind in its dealings with nature, thereby actualizing the potentialities of synthetic knowledge on a lower plane of existence; but he can also be seen, later on, or from another point of view, as introducing a new mode of life that may be equated to a period of deviation and degeneracy. In other words, his myth is a way of describing chronologically, or diachronically, what is, in essence, a cosmogonic phenomenon. Lewis Hyde's reading of Hermes, in the Homeric Hymn, as one who shows the way of a "method through which an outsider penetrates a group and alters hierarchy" is a valid universalization of the substance of Brown's thesis. It recognizes the function of the trickster as one of playing at the "joints of the cultural web," that is, at all points where cultural distinctions and polarities are highlighted. The story of the way in which Hermes stole Apollo's cattle refers to such a play by its confusing of the distinction between truth and lies, as well as its bringing change, that is, becoming and ultimately death, into the realm of intemporal presence and truth.[22] Hermes is, in that sense, the "prince of this world," hence his not-so-surprising affinities with the devil of monotheism, as suggested by his association with sexual seduction, in Hesiod's myth of Pandora, and his reputation as a "whisperer" like the Quranic Satan. The trickster may thereby "evolve" into a devil.

It is interesting to take note of the fact that the evolution that Norman O. Brown has traced in his classic *Hermes the Thief* is also manifested in the evolution of Hermes' iconography:

> In early archaic art Hermes is a bearded, muscular, and rather comical figure [...] In the sixth century Hermes begins to lose his beard, and becomes, as Apollo had been before him, the image of the perfect young gentleman, the ideal ephebe, the flower of physical and mental culture, refined by the leisure arts and music and gymnastic—the concept immortalized in the Hermes of Praxiteles.[23]

This evolution manifests not only the elevation of Hermes' stature to that of an equal of Apollo, as reflecting, presumably, a shift in the socioeconomic *rapport de forces*, but also, undoubtedly, a sort of "erasure" of the archaic, most profound implications of the original Hermes. The virtual absence of a comical dimension in the later character—and, perhaps, the reduction of this aspect to one of mere ingenious, and socially acceptable, wit—is in particular highly indicative of a gradual moving away from the concept of Hermes as a trickster that could be set in the category of Loki or Amerindian animal demiurges.

The association of Hermes with lottery in Classical Greece, and particularly in Athenian democracy, is a relatively low but meaningful manifestation of the demiurgic nature of the god. Chance happenings correspond to the lowest level of divine manifestation, those in which the intelligibility of divine operations are, as it were, minimal, or even quasi-inexistent, or rather humanly imperceptible. This is highlighted by the qualitative difference between Apollo's "prophetic" function and Hermes' mastery over lottery. At Delphi, the two kinds of divination were considered unequal given the higher status of Apollo as "prophet of Zeus," by contrast with Hermes' relatively external function of manifesting Zeus' will. However, quite paradoxically, the inferiority of Hermes as a messenger, and the "imperceptibility" of the divine will in the domain of lottery over which he presides, is at the same time a reflection of the highest level of divine meaning, as indicated by the role of chance in Greek mantic devices such as the casting of dice. One cannot simply dismiss this phenomenon as pertaining to the level of lower skills, or of identifying its abuses: chance happenings and lottery refer, in a sense, to higher realms of the divine will, those precisely that are the most foreign to any human mastery. Thus, the lack of skills deemed to have characterized practitioners of mantic lottery, although criticized by Delphic priests, testifies also to a higher level of "prophetic" reality, not with respect to human abilities to interpret signs, but in terms of a most direct "interference" of divine liberty within the domain of terrestrial necessity. Manifestations of this interference are both the least meaningful of phenomena, in the sense that they defy immediate intelligibility, and the most significant occurrences of the transcendence and infinitude of the divine will. Accordingly, Hermes' function as "pure messenger" or herald of the divine is in a definite sense manifested through his association with lottery.

In the Homeric Hymn, Zeus' reactions to the news of his son's theft are seemingly contradictory: he laughs at his son's nimbleness at claiming his innocence, but he also orders Hermes to give back the cattle to Apollo. This is a most profound illustration of the two aspects of Divine Reality: on the one hand, Zeus is somewhat amused by his son's ability to make good of his own transgression, which implies that he cannot consider it as serious, to the point of fundamentally undermining the order of his realm; on the other hand, Zeus' will is expressed by his insistence that Hermes give back the cattle to their legitimate owner, thereby restoring the world to its state of original order. The first reaction is akin to a knowledge of Reality in all its scope; the second to a will of the good as opposed to evil. In this connection, it could be said that Zeus' laughter is more "essential" than his order, in the sense that it expresses his immediate and intimate reaction to the theft, his order being more "peripheral" since it does not so much express his godly nature as his external and extrinsic justice within the range of his "courtly" order. The divine nature is not "affected" by the tricks of Hermes, whereas the divine "institution" is undoubtedly desecrated. It bears stressing that these two aspects are in fact indissociable in Zeus, or that the distinction does not imply a kind of schizomorphic duality in Zeus. It must be noted, moreover, that Hermes is completely obedient to Zeus' order, although he is quick to go back to "no good" when preventing Apollo from taking away his cattle. This is, on the one hand, an illustration of the constantly changing nature of Hermes, his demiurgic mobility, but it also points, on the other hand, to the paradox of his submission to the supreme god's will being "parallel" to the relative "independence" of his own will from the latter, as soon as Zeus' will is not expressed directly and, as it were, by and through his authoritative presence. In other words, Hermes both expresses and derails the divine will, thereby bearing witness to the indirection of the cosmogonic process.

CHAPTER 5

COYOTE AND KIN

$\mathbf{C}$oyote is probably the most famous Amerindian trickster. Tales and anecdotes about his tricks and misadventures abound in the folklore of Native Americans. It is important to beware, at the outset, that this folklore is oral, which means that it is subject not only to personal transmission and transformation, but also to rules and traditions that define its domain of manifestation and application. In other words, Coyote's stories are neither a rigid canon, nor a set of stories that can be told and applied in every condition and in all contexts. For example, among the Navajo, Coyote stories are told exclusively in the winter time, following the first frost and preceding the first thunderstorm.[1] This is highly indicative of the psycho-spiritual and cosmic implications of these tales. It is likely that Coyote's tales perform a subtle compensatory function within the community at that time, bringing laughter at a time of cosmic and human contraction. They therefore fulfill a very specific role while teaching us that Coyote's stories are not *for all times*. Like all good things they have an organic meaning; their comical and transgressive value cannot be put into motion in an indiscriminate manner. Moreover, Coyote's stories need a specific human and social context. As with all traditional folklore and "literature," they involve a storyteller and an audience, the latter being an essential participant in the process of narration. This participation integrates all the emotional and physical aspects of mankind, not only the deciphering mind. In traditional lore, stories and poems do not belong exclusively to an "author"; they express a collective wisdom that reflects, in its turn, the divine archetypes. The ritual and linguistic context is also an essential element in these stories: their telling is subject to specific taboos and takes on a life of its own when performed in the aboriginal language of the community. In the absence of these contexts, Coyote's stories can be dangerous, as Barre Toelken notes in his preface to Barry Lopez' anthology. And their spread in print is, in our times, another manifestation of the "necessary anomaly" of our contemporary culture. Nevertheless, these stories are better printed than lost, better profaned than forgotten, since for all practical purposes the sacred core of the stories protects itself by itself.

As with most North American tricksters, Coyote's identity is neither exclusively animal, nor exclusively human. On the one hand, traditional stories consistently depict him with the characteristics of a scavenger animal: most Coyote narratives begin with his roaming around in search of food. Tricksters are scavengers, whether they are crows or coyotes, as the function of these types of animals is both repugnant and useful, or even necessary. In an insight into one of the mysterious workings of providence, Swami Ramdas noted that "in the economy of nature, crows play the part of scavengers" so that, thanks to them, places are "swept clean."[2] In this function abjection and purification converge. But Coyote is not only a scavenger; he is also a mobile and noisy animal who may appear as a kind of caricature when compared with his cousin the wolf. There is nearly always something imitative about him: he tries to reproduce what he is not, or create a fantasy out of reality. In this connection, it is notable that one of the hunting strategies of the coyote is to make it sound to their prey as if there were dozens of coyotes with them, where in fact there might be only two or three. A confusing concert of sorts is played out as a trick, and this cunning technique points not only to the skills of deception possessed by the trickster, but also to its ability to make something out of nothing, or rather to "make believe" things that are not. Now, even though Coyote undoubtedly takes after the animal that bears his name, he is also depicted as sharing in the life of man: he likes to boast that he is a brave warrior, or a skilled craftsman, that he has a wife and a mother-in-law, that he likes to sleep in a teepee, preferably with one, or several, beautiful maidens, and enjoys good food. So, perspectives on his real nature, animal or human, are constantly confused or mingled. Does it mean that he represents the animal part of mankind, its appetitive and concupiscent nature, with all its tendencies to excess and ridicule? Certainly, for one would not laugh so much at his tricks and adventures if one did not recognize something of oneself in him. Moreover, the shamanistic outlook from which Coyote's stories emerge is not prone to draw absolute boundaries between different domains of reality. Notwithstanding this confusion of sorts, does it also mean that Coyote functions as a sort of objectification of these traits precisely because he is not quite human? Yes, indeed, for his being exclusively human would not allow so easily for the purifying catharsis of laughter. His ridiculous "monstrosity" has to be ours, and yet not ours; it must provide us with a sufficient degree of identification, while yet sheltering us at a critical distance. As such, one may say, as Barre Toelken has conceded, that "Coyote is the exponent of all possibilities through whose antics and actions we see ourselves and the moral ramifications of our thoughts."[3] There is, however, more to Coyote's double or uncertain nature than a mere pedagogic strategy. Coyote's undifferentiated status between man and animal is also bound to his role as an ancestor and initiator of mankind, an "embodiment of a native world view of relationships between mankind and nature."[4] For Native Americans, even today, ants are not ants, they are "ant people." Coyote, like other tricksters, precedes mankind on earth; he is actually sometimes the shaper of the earth, even the "creator" of man—although not *ex nihilo*—or at least the discoverer of cosmic goods, such as the sun and moon. His preceding man on earth gives him a quasi-divine status, and refers to a time, before history, when the only beings on earth were animals.[5] Coyote's magic is a heritage from that time before time, from that space that preceded the fragmented space that is now ours.[6] It allows him to know and sense things before everybody else, and to travel anywhere in no time. He knew, for example, that white men had landed in the East before any tribe of the West had even heard of these strange newcomers.[7] He conserved this ability from the era when animals were alone on earth. However, these animals were not "like" animals such as we know them today; they were "like" human people. Many Amerindian myths speak of how animals made the world.[8] This often happens out of water, when a clump of earth emerges from the flood; sometimes it has to be sought at the bottom of the ocean, and brought back, a task that is Coyote's function. At other times it involves the slaying of a gigantic monster and many stories tell of Coyote's fight with the latter. If Coyote is not, strictly speaking, the creator of earth, he is often the "shaper" of mankind. A myth of the Miwok from central California tells how Coyote and his companion Falcon made humans out of a kind of magic, using crow and buzzard's feathers as "prime substances" that Coyote planted on hills, and to which he gave names. Each and every one of these animal feathers was like a malleable "matter" upon which a name was "deposited" as a gift of soul. Once humans appeared out of them they were exact replicas of Coyote and Falcon. So both had to take a different shape in order to remain distinct from men, and all other original people were also changed into animals, to each of which Coyote gave a name.[9] The shamanistic mind is familiar with these transformations, as it is not so much centered on the essences than on the unity of the existentiating flow that manifests them and constantly modifies these manifestations. In keeping with the ups and downs and compensatory paradoxes of this onto-cosmogonic flow, the trickster Coyote is like a god, and at any rate certainly a demiurge—a kind of archetypical human who "precedes" mankind, testing man's possibilities for better or worse. It is to be noted that, in the Miwok myth, Coyote and Falcon are clearly of a different "kind" to the crows and buzzards that they pluck. Can we simply take this to be a "naïve" narrative inconsistency, or an unimportant detail not to concern ourselves with? Perhaps, but what it does suggest is that the boundaries between terrestrial kingdoms are fluid, and that divine intelligence may, and in fact does, manifest itself throughout all of these kingdoms. What it also indicates is that Coyote is not just an animal, nor even a humanized animal, but a "spirit" that presides over the unfolding of reality. He is endowed with a cosmogonic function that is inseparable from the very shortcomings of his nature. The latter frequently accounts for the appearance of space, time, and cosmic alternations. Coyote is the great "fragmenter" and disperser, if one may say so. This plainly appears in the Zuni myth of the coming to being of the seasons. In the beginning, Kachinas—who are angels, or messengers and intermediaries between the heavens and mankind on earth—kept the sun and moon in a box that reminds one of the Pandora myth. They were in full command of the alternation between day and night, opening the box to let either the sun or the moon leap out. Coyote suggested to Eagle that they steal the box; Eagle accepted on condition that they would not open it, but Coyote's curiosity was finally too strong: he opened the box, and as the sun flew to the edge of the sky, as did the moon, it was the first winter. Alternations were no longer controllable; they became a necessity as harsh as that of the first winter.[10] A similar story presents Coyote's stealing of the sun and moon from the bag of the chief of the Village of Light, who lived on the other side of the mountain, as a blessing to mankind: "He goes where nobody else dares to go."[11] But this blessing, interestingly, is not considered as such by all: the chief of the Village of Darkness, from which Coyote originates, is fully aware that the sun and the moon are "mixed blessings." In his mind, the sun can be blinding, and the light of the moon can encourage love-making instead of sleeping, man becoming thereby lazy when hunting. But still, the inhabitants of the village see the benefits of the theft rather than its negative outcome, and they make Coyote their chief. This story is highly instructive with respect to the ambivalence of the demiurgic manifestation. One is free to side with the chief of the Village of Darkness, or with Coyote and his fellow villagers. Manifestation, as symbolized by the appearance of the sun and moon, does not happen without its share of inconveniences and damages, and still, it is applauded by most as an "enrichment" of reality, while being ultimately a metaphysical necessity. Coyote brings out the ambivalence of the "whatever more" there is to reality, while making us run the risk of losing sight, albeit temporarily, of the essential. In a sense, the trickster embodies the outer reaches of the onto-cosmological realm, or the outermost dynamics of the cosmogonic process. As such he leads us either to the limit beyond which there is only nothingness, or on a catapulted return to Being. Coyote is the extreme limit of manifestation that borders on nothingness, whence his exploration of the confines; but this limit is also the point of necessary return: Coyote spins the wheel that brings us back to the One. As Lame Deer puts it, "sinning makes the world go round,"[12] and this is exactly what Coyote is all about. For Indians, as for Taoists *mutatis mutandis*, reality is a circle, and it works in circles.

In the Miwok myth, Coyote is not a priori interested in creating man. It is only because he is induced to do so by Falcon that he finally goes along with it. The supreme argument of Falcon is that he *must* do it because he *can* do it.[13] The question, therefore, is set in terms of possibility rather than necessity; or let us say that necessity only results from possibility. Mankind is just a possibility; from a strictly demiurgic standpoint it has no special privilege. Let us note that two "sacrifices" occur for mankind to enter into existence: one is a simulacrum of sacrifices, where Coyote plays dead; the second is a real sacrifice, crows and buzzards are entrapped in Coyote's body following his apparent death. More specifically, they are entrapped in his left buttock. In a sense, this trick is a demiurgic and comical substitution for the usual cosmogonic sacrifice in which a primal being, whether it be a monster or a snake, is either cut into pieces or delivered from its inner parts to give rise to creatures. Here, not only is Coyote's self-immolation merely apparent, but also the creation of man begins from one of the lowest parts of his body. The whole narrative context, the involvement of scavenger birds, and the association with the buttocks, highlights both the transmutational nature of the process and the ambivalence of the product, that is, mankind. This phase of the creative process is only the elementary foundation though: there follows a ceremonial phase that suggests the more positive or elevated aspects of mankind. The components of this ceremony are three in number: first, the plucking of the features of the birds that have been entrapped in Coyote's buttocks; second, the planting of these feathers on hills along the four directions; and third, the magic "transformation" of these feathers into men, crow feathers becoming men in general, buzzard feathers becoming chiefs. All of these elements take us into a symbolic context that points to the spiritual nature of man, but a spiritual nature that has been "incubated" in the demiurge's lower realms, and which thereby participates in matter as the extreme limit of the onto-cosmogonic process.

Following the appearance of men, Coyote indicates to Falcon that they, and all other animals, must henceforth change form in order to remain distinct from mankind. In this myth, therefore, ancestor animals did not look like animals, but they looked like men, even though their nature was not like that of men. Animals were more than men, in the sense that they were beings endowed with an immediate sense of the divine presence—men before men, so to speak. Even though Coyote, Falcon, and others lost their human form, abandoning their preeminence in the terrestrial existence to mankind, as it were, they retained a certain superiority vis-à-vis men, for they remained faithful to their nature, being unable to go astray from it; and this characteristic they share with the gods.

Coyote is constantly on the move, ever looking for trouble. The troublemaker is he who unblocks sterile stases, and also unleashes a hell of sorts. One does not go without the other. As such, Coyote is an embodiment of the randomness of adventure, and the adventure is nothing other than what "happens" without being planned or intended. It is not only that he is always depicted as looking for food, or for sexual gratification; there also seems to be in him a profound need for having things turned upside-down, for breaking boundaries, and thereby changing the way things have been going. He is a catalyst for modification; he comes across events and people, and his first reaction to them is either one of desire, or one of imitation. As for desire, it is first of all related to food. Coyote will eat almost anything; he will even eat his own roasted anus and find it delicious. It seems that he can ingest and assimilate all that he wants, provided that he *wants* it badly enough. His association with excrement is not accidental: it fulfills a variety of important functions. For one thing, the scatological dimension of the character corresponds to the breaking of a taboo. Coyote, as with most other tricksters, is the only one to be able to erase the limit between the pure and the impure. On another level of consideration, the passage from food to excrement, and the assimilation that it makes possible, without forgetting the return to food through fertilization, is an immediate image of the cycle of transformation. When Coyote wants to raise an army of warriors to march on

Wolferine's village, he "spent one whole day defecating around the shore," and from all of this he made warriors and canoes.[14] His is an alchemical attitude that can put everything to a good use, even, and especially, that for which nobody has any use.

Besides food, there is obviously a strong urge for sexuality. He often chances to meet women on his way, some young and beautiful, but also some older and decrepit, and some who are even members of his own family, not to mention himself when he admires a reflection of his face adorned with antlers in the water. His impulse to possess them is immediate and irresistible. Here again, the reoccurring figure of the mother-in-law is the hallmark of the breaking of a taboo, since among Indians the latter could often not even be spoken to by her son-in-law. Be that as it may, the outcome of Coyote's encounters with women is rarely, if ever, a success. Women seem to consider him with a blend of interest, attraction, amusement, and disgust. He is not attractive to them in any pleasing sense of the term; in fact he is plain ugly. He occasionally tricks them, but he is also more often than not tricked by them. The effects of his concupiscent nature are ambivalent: his wanderlust makes him alive and seductive to women, as if he were "awakening" them to pleasure and happiness; but it is also amusing by its excess and inconsistency, and not infrequently repugnant by its frequent crudeness and downright obscenity. It could be said that he awakens a whole spectrum of reactions from within women, as if he were actualizing, sometimes at his own expense, the whole gamut of feminine modes of sensibility and experience. In this respect, he is undoubtedly the demiurge of female sexuality, and more generally of woman as a symbol, and a concrete occurrence, of universal manifestation. This is most obviously suggested in traditional tales in which he is staged as a welcome male visitor in a village of women who have never before seen a man. On such an occasion he easily becomes a strong pole of attraction, while being ultimately incapable of satisfying all needs, and thereby being changed, as is often the case, from a hero into a villain. His erotic presumptions come to no good. It goes without saying that, aside from his spirit of adventure and his daring ways, his seductiveness is also akin to transformation, and even to magic. This ability to change forms, which is related to his primordial function as a demiurge, is illustrated in many ways, including through his appearance as an animal, a younger man, his transvestite behavior, and change of sex. Coyote is not bound by any distinction, as he seems to embody a life force that inhabits and animates many forms. He is even able to give wolf puppies as children to a brave young warrior. A particular case of Coyote's sexual transformation is that of dissociation with some parts of his body, most often his sexual member, but also other "shameful" organs such as the intestine or the anus. In some stories he is able to send his penis away from the rest of his body to satisfy his desires, as when he sends it through the bottom of a pool of water in which young ladies are playing.[15] In some other stories, he cuts off his legs and pulls out his intestines, but he is also able to put them together again. One can argue that this ability suggests an undifferentiated state that is primitive and inorganic, and that is undoubtedly true. But one can also understand it as an allusion to a primordial way of being in which parts of the body were endowed with enough "intelligence" to be able to function by themselves, or even to be reassembled or grown again when need be. Sometimes, this fragmentation of the body entails a humanization of a given physical organ. So it is particularly with his penis, which is in a sense the center of Coyote's "personality." He talks to his member as if there were two subjectivities within himself.[16] And his member talks to him as well; it says, for example, "I won't quit (yelling) until you sleep with your mother-in-law."[17] His member can even escape his control, and flee away from him, as a kind of independent entity. One can say without the least doubt that this implies a dissipated mode of consciousness: Coyote does not master himself because he has no center, and this is comically illustrated by his physical organs occasionally roaming away. But that is only one half of the story, for his separation from his sexual parts, and his ability to talk to them, may also point to a sort of de-identification from his physical functions. It depicts in a burlesque manner the human conflict between appetites and duties, desires and rules. It also shows the divine and universal energy working through the veil of the concupiscent individual.

The perspective of the Coyote trickster has sometimes been summarized as follows: at the beginning nothing is sacred; at the end everything is sacred. The first phase, that during which "nothing is sacred," is one during which the trickster, by his wanderings and transgressions, breaks normative rules of behavior that are held to be sacrosanct by men. This stage corresponds to a kind of systematic antithesis that "negates" the circumstantial status quo and explores the confines of possibility. Spiritually, this state of affairs that Coyote transgresses, may be taken to represent a perspective that tends to reduce reality to the level of a commonsensical and conventional horizontality. Epistemologically, it is akin to a perception of reality "outside of" the transcendent principle that is its raison d'être. This is the ordinary vision that is purely passive and limited to a set of social representations. By transgressing these representations Coyote reduces the world to a state of disorderly fluidity, a kind of plastic indifferentiation, and that, in a sense, is what he himself is. He is like a primal and "natural" substance in which all qualities are blended and blurred. This is, on some level, the chaotic original state that most forms of shamanism envision at the beginning of this world. The Taoist *Huntun*, which means Chaos, the Emperor of the Middle, also corresponds to this original state. In the Chinese myth the two characters *Shu* and *Hu*, who live at two extremities of the world and whose conjunction forms the word lightning, "quickens" the appearance of the world—as befits their respective names, "short" and "sudden"— by opening seven holes into *Huntun*. As a result of this "sacrifice," *Huntun* dies; and this death is the beginning of the world as we know it. This stage, following the primordial sacrifice, opens onto a situation in which the world is subjected to becoming. Similarly, when Coyote deprives things of their conventional fixity, he reduces pure existence to its original plasticity. The first paradox is that he does so in the name of his own contingency and absurdity. It is as if Coyote were breaking the solidified contents of existence by pitting them against the hardened stupidity of his own greed and lust. Through a combination of imitation and transgression, he breaks the ice of "ways as they are," revealing the waters that lie underneath, not without often getting cold or drowned in the process. The second paradox is that Coyote may come to inform this fluid *materia* with the intelligence of the spirit. This pertains, properly speaking, to the end of his mission, that which consists in pointing out the sacredness of all things. In her collection of myths about Coyote, Mourning Dove tells the story of God assigning this mission to Coyote:

> God tells him: "They (the monsters) must be stopped. It is for you to conquer them. For doing that, for all the good things you do, you will be honored and praised by the people that are here now and that come afterward. But, for the foolish and mean things you do, you will be laughed at and despised. That you cannot help. It is your way."[18]

Coyote cannot escape his *dharma* as an ambivalent creature of light and darkness: that is what God asked him to be. His "doing good things" consists in carrying over the orders of God, bringing the light of intelligence into the darkness of matter. He is not God, however, and he sometimes goes astray from this mission; or as Mourning Dove puts it, "there were times [...] when Coyote was not busy for the Spirit Chief. Then he amused himself by getting into mischief and stirring up trouble."[19] This duality of the trickster figure is at times expressed in a mythological bifurcation of his identity. From one ambiguous figure two brothers, or twins, issue forth: one takes upon himself the "evil" of the cosmogonic process, the other its "good" aspect. This can also mean, in other cases, that the "good" twin may be more or less identified with the higher god, whereas the "evil" twin will be left to his own destructive devices.[20] The diversity of the language of myth does not exclude the unity of reality.

By his transgressions, Coyote restores everything to the state of a primal undifferentiated substance—below good and evil, so to speak—that is the distant and inverted reflection of the Higher Mystery situated beyond good and evil. This is why Coyote's transgression is both "good" and "bad," depending upon the point of view. Coyote sometimes does the will of God: through intelligence he carries on the work of the promotion of the good within the world, as a true demiurge and culture hero, thereby tending to actualize the work of the Spirit through a negation of darkness and ignorance. But he sometimes does his own will: he works on his own behalf or for himself, and it is thus that he creates the world, the existence that tends toward nothingness. He therefore reconciles the extremes, and builds a bridge between spirit and matter. He is identified with a prolongation of the Divine Will as it wants to assert the good within existence; but he is also identified with the indirect—and ultimately subversive in its furthest consequences—projection of the Divine Will as infinite All-Possibility. There is actually a reverse analogy, or a chiasma, between the lowest will of Coyote, which manifests the highest Will of God, and his highest will that reflects God's lowest will. The outer confines of his most random actions ultimately "translate" the infinite possibility of the Higher Mystery, whereas the most constructive and inventive aspects of his mission seem to flow from the Divine Intellect.

For Coyote, it is said that "nothing is sacred in the beginning" because transgression and subversion is a way to distinguish good from evil, the lawful from the unlawful, and, in point of fact, the sacred from the profane. Such distinctions are delimitations that are comparable, in a sense, to the "multiplying" of men and tribes and the "naming" of creatures, which is Coyote's prerogative. But ultimately everything is made sacred: by transgressing the good Coyote bears the responsibility of evil, thereby indirectly relating all that is, including the privative and the negative, to the Divine Source. It is not for nothing that Coyote is both a servant of God and a troublemaker. One cannot let go of one aspect or the other without missing the point of his delicate and thankless function. He is like the shadow of God: he takes upon himself the "dirty work" of creation, and this is why he is both praised and mocked or vilified. In his perspective, the only way to make everything sacred is to start by treating nothing as sacred. But in an ultimate sense, for Coyote these two attitudes are one and the same since the exhaustion of the possibilities of manifestation is both a constant transgression and a constant sacralization: a transgression in the etymological meaning of passing beyond limits; a sacralization in the sense of "sacrificing" or "murdering" Unity to reach the very limits of indefinite multiplicity, thereby paradoxically and ultimately bringing the latter within the fold of the former. The dual aspect of Coyote appears in full light in the following conversation between Old Man— God—and the trickster, which takes place at the time when Old Man realizes that Coyote "has done everything he is capable of doing." At this point, God wants to take Coyote back where he started from, an illustration of the fact that Coyote can only work in circles. When Old Man descends to earth to tell Coyote that his work is finished, Coyote pretends not to know him, and he flatly denies that he has been working at God's behest. At this stage, he even challenges Old Man's authority by asking him to prove that he is God by means of moving a lake close to a mountain. Outsmarting the trickster, God does nothing but revert the challenge by asking Coyote to prove that he is indeed Coyote by moving the lake, which Coyote does. Then, God asks Coyote to move it back, but Coyote is unable to do so in spite of all his efforts. Not only is Coyote's subordination to Old Man thus evidenced, but it is also plain that Coyote can only "move" things away, and not "move" them back by himself. Only Old Man can move them back and Coyote must finally concur with this fact.[21]

The Promethean aspect of Coyote is therefore only partial: it may involve a kind of "competition" with God, but never a rebellion. That is what distinguishes the demiurgic from the satanic. The "competition" of Coyote with God stems both from the power that he has received from above to carry out his work, and from his tendency to forget that he is only a subordinate. It is in the second element that resides the comical aspect of Coyote, a comic aspect that pertains primarily to a sense of disproportion. For Coyote, to compete with God means to exhaust the possibilities that he has received from above. He is thereby ultimately put back in his right place, his original starting point. The end is like the beginning: Coyote spans the whole range of the illusion of separativeness, scouting the vast horizon of the illusory—while not unreal—possibilities before returning home to his master, albeit somewhat reluctantly.

As mentioned earlier, Coyote is the prince of imitation. Imitation is the realm of the demiurge, because the demiurgic realm is not fully real; it is only a copy of the archetypical original, as it were. Coyote often meets people whom he sees performing actions that strike his curiosity or fancy, and he ends up outdoing these actions for the sake of his self-defeating and inordinate impulses. The story of Coyote and the man who was throwing his eyes up in the cottonwood tree is particularly telling in this respect. Seeing the man throwing his eyes on the tree and getting them back later, Coyote cannot but be interested in doing the same. He is kindly taught to do so by the man, but is warned that he can only do it up to four times. Having thrown his eyes four times in a row, Coyote thought to himself: "That man's rule is made for his country [...] I don't think it applies here [...] This is my country."[22] Of course, the result of his not heeding to the man's warning is that, when thrown away a fifth time, the eyes do not come back. This episode is typical of the trickster's ambivalent sense of relativity: this sense is based on a mode of intelligence, an intuition of the limitation and relativity of prescriptions and proscriptions, but it is also fundamentally self-seeking and flawed. At bottom, it depicts the ability of human intelligence to undercut itself, through its own excesses and detours. Coyote's intelligence is mimetic and transgressive; it reproduces what it perceives but it cannot stop short at a given limit. Many stories present us with a situation where Coyote is taught to perform a trick, or a magic feat, but on condition that he not repeat it beyond a certain amount, most often four times, a sacred number for many Amerindians. Each and every time, Coyote is unable to keep his promise, and he "transgresses" this number out of unconsciousness and passion.

Edshu, the trickster-god of the Yoruba, is an African cousin of Coyote in that he exemplifies some of the fundamental traits of the demiurgic function. In one story,[23] he is told to give to an old man a hat with four sides of different colors: red, white, green, and black. He does so in order to play a trick on two peasants whom he has seen working in adjacent fields on each side of the road. When one of the peasants claims that he has seen the old man wearing an odd red hat, the second one retorts that the hat is in fact white. There ensues an argument that turns into a bitter quarrel, which becomes so violent that the two men have to be brought to justice to settle the case. Since the judge is quite unable to render a fair judgment and to come to a verdict, Edshu reveals his subterfuge and he asserts that his intention had been indeed, from the start, to provoke a fight between the two men: "I wanted it that way. Spreading strife is my great joy."[24] This African tale is particularly interesting in several respects. First of all, as Joseph Campbell has noted, the correspondence of the four colors

with the four directions of space indicates that Edshu's perspective is
to be identified with the *axis mundi*, the center of the cosmos that lies
at the center of the four colors, the top of the hat so to speak. One
finds similar axial symbols pertaining to the trickster in other African
myths such as Legba, a trickster figure from Benin. The latter is often
associated with a human counterpart called Fa: "Fa lives on a palm
tree in the sky. From this height, Fa can see all that goes on in the
world. [...] Every morning, Legba climbs the palm tree to open Fa's
(sixteen) eyes."[25] Let us note that the tension between the axial eminence of the trickster Legba and his rambunctious pranks is resolved
and synthesized in his being appointed as the messenger of the
supreme God, Mawu. Legba's oddity makes him unable to govern
one of Mawu's kingdom, but Mawu still delegates him to visit his six
brothers' kingdom as a messenger of his father. As a messenger, he
becomes the embodiment of the communication between the world
of the Divine and the world of terrestrial imperfection. One may,
prima facie, be surprised, or even shocked, by the association of the
trickster figure—that is the most mobile and inconstant of mythological heroes—with the very polar axis of existence, the symbol of the
motionlessness of the Principle. The key to this enigma lies in the fact
that extremes meet, and that the respective perspectives of mobility
and motionlessness converge in their being independent from the formal fixity of limited outlooks. In other words, the ability of the trickster to play with the multiplicity of points of view stems from his
identification with the transcendence of all limited perspectives, which
is none other than the axial position. The most central and the most
peripheral meet, as it were. It goes without saying that this convergence entails an indifference to the moral laws of society, since Edshu
makes fun not only of both peasants and their "certainties," but also
of society's incapacity to resolve their differences. What could be
called "the point of view of colors" is of course the point of view of
relativity, and this point of view is by definition unable to give access
to the "full picture" of reality. The intentional character of the "trouble"
and conflict introduced by the trickster figure opens the way to a further dimension. In this particular story, trouble and conflict result
from an incapacity to "imagine" other points of view, and to acknowledge them as legitimate. This lack of imagination and acceptance is a
source of conflict insofar as a relative point of view is absolutized and,
becoming a matter of moral and spiritual identification, provides the
characters with a feeling of certainty that is all the more violent in that
their understanding is limited to the side of the hat that they have
been able to see. Let us note that Edshu is in fact responsible for this

state of affairs, a fact that can be interpreted both on a spiritual and a cosmological level. Spiritually, the revelation of the ridiculous and obstinate presumption of the peasants points to a lesson that may or may not be understood by most men, but which is crucial in gaining access to the full measure of truth. On a cosmological level, the trickster must be considered as a demiurge who brings possibilities into existence through strife. This is the essence of the Heraclitean *polemos,* the "war" through which realities are brought into being. Possibilities are at odds with each other, as it were, and it belongs to the principle of immanent existentiation to bring them to existence through a kind of competition. The coming to being of possibilities is neither a moral nor a "serious" matter. It is not moral because it has less directly to do with the Good as such than with the Infinite that must of necessity manifest itself through the myriad of possibilities. It may even shock the moral sense of men when they are unable to reach an understanding of Reality in its most transcendent dimension. It is not "serious" because, in parallel to the Hindu metaphysical "play" of creation— *lilâ,* it involves an element of apparent randomness and arbitrariness. Moreover, on the highest level, strife and conflict point to the need to integrate opposites.

In the wake of the consideration of the Hindu notion of *lilâ,* it is highly instructive to consider the relationship between the various spiritual tendencies or vocations of mankind, as encapsulated in the traditional "castes" or "orders," and the function of the trickster and clown. What appears first of all, in this respect, is that all categories of vocation can be related in one way to the demiurgic type. This comes as no surprise, in a sense, since this function is by definition polymorphic and omnipresent throughout the whole spectrum of reality. If one considers the most elaborate and rigorous delineation of functions such as it is expressed, on a sociological level, by the Hindu system of the *varna*—the various psycho-spiritual "colors" that refer to the four fundamental goals of life—one will see that all of the four categories, *brâhmana* (priest), *kshatriya* (warrior), *vaishya* (farmer and trader), and *shûdra* (servant), evince an affinity with a given aspect of the demiurgic function of clowns and tricksters. This is apparent when one considers the brahmanic caste, one that perhaps a priori is the most "foreign" to the aforementioned phenomena. As centered upon the finality of *moksha,* or spiritual deliverance, this *varna* is in a sense the most akin to a recognition of the aspect of *lilâ* that is inherent to *Mâyâ.* The brahmanical outlook is particularly given to perceive existence, including the various human roles, as a myriad of masks upon the one and only Self. In that sense, the *brâhmana* is particularly given to recognize the comically fictitious dimension of universal existence, and to be thereby spontaneously attuned to the function of the clown as "revealer" of that aspect of reality. Although the priestly function generally entails a character of gravity that derives from the centrality of the priest in the sacrificial economy of the tradition, it is no less true to say that the fundamental goal of this vocation is the most susceptible of reflecting the highest meaning of laughter. For his part, the warrior is perhaps no less able to recognize this aspect, but he may do so in a way that may be more subjective and dramatic in its modes. In fact, the type of the "holy fool" or "fool for Christ's sake" is undoubtedly akin to a combative spiritual vocation. If one is to admit, with Frithjof Schuon, that the perspective of the *kshatriya* consists in being "subjectively objective," or to aim at the highest realities in a more "individualized" manner than the priest, one may readily recognize that the "holy fool's" point of view shares much affinity with this outlook since it derives its dynamic vigor from a highly particularized and vocational manner of "colliding" with the "horizontal objectivity" of social conventions. The "individualistic" tendencies of the warrior, which, for example, are highlighted in the warring traditions of the North American Indians of the plains, finds a spiritual expression in the dynamic antagonism of the holy fool toward the world of tepid indifference and mediocrity. Another aspect of the warrior caste that avers a kinship with the spirit of the clown is the emphasis on action, or rather the act, that it involves. The clown is not only direct in his acting; it could also be said that acting is his way. There is an "extremism" of action with the clown that makes him particularly close to the way of the warrior. The instantaneity and totality of the act is what defines the vocation in concrete terms. Tom Boyd cogently encapsulates this martial dimension of the clown when he emphasizes his love of "decisive action":

> To speak of extremes as the way through chaos and pretense, we best reflect upon the nature of decisive action. Clowns always act deliberately and decisively. This ensures both their trouble and its resolution.[26]

This is indeed the heroic thrust of the clown, his subjective extremism at the service of higher principles. The latter remarks may lead us to think that the *vaishya* category—the producer, merchant, or farmer—might be the most impermeable to the perspective of "holy folly." This is true only up to a point, for this outlook may also participate in the demiurgic function in ways that differ from the priest and warrior while being none the less characteristic of certain essential elements of this function. The domain of production, crafts and commerce, which is the purview of the *vaishya*, is after all highly conducive to a recognition of the communicative and inventive aspect of the demiurgic function. The figure of Hermes, for example, has sometimes been associated by historians with the emergence of a mercantile class and the fostering of its values. In a sense, Hermes among the gods is very much like a merchant among high priests and heroes. His practical intelligence and craftiness is akin to the demiurgic contribution of the trickster. The commonsensical intelligence of the trickster provides a sense of horizontal objectivity that may sometimes balance, through the comic, the warrior's propensity to self-aggrandizement and the priest's potential immersion in formalism or hypocrisy. The priorities of the *vaishya* may thereby provide an opening into the world of the clown and trickster through his tendency to mock the occasionally ridiculous pretensions of the higher castes. In a sense, a higher caste may laugh at a lower caste on account of their gross identification with matter and their inability to see "beyond their nose," while a lower caste may mock, in the higher castes, the confusion between a sense of self-importance and the real dignity that stems from their transcendent goals. Such can be the burlesque role of the *shûdra*, the servant, a character who lacks a center, and whose peripheral aspect presents us with two possible, and opposing, functions. On the one hand, the *shûdra* can become the grotesque embodiment of man's engrossment with his illusory and constraining limits. On the other hand, he may function as a "puppet" of the gods, thereby illustrating a mystical utter loss of self that takes him within the realm of the "holy fool's" imbalance as a pure instrument of divine grace. These are also, incidentally, the two faces of the dog: oft-disgusting slave of his basest appetites, and a selfless servant of the Lord (*Domini canes*). If the clown or the fool is one who is totally possessed by the dynamic of his function, then he is akin to the servant's perfect submission to his Lord. Besides the four regular castes of India, it must moreover be emphasized that the clown, the fool, and the trickster reveal undeniable affinities with the various types of outcast. The main reason for this relationship lies in their heterogeneous nature, their ability to reconcile the most uneven and extreme levels of reality. The demiurgic character often manifests a somewhat protean nature that makes him analogous to the outcast, the latter being by definition a mixture of various tendencies. Through a sort of reverse analogy, this reconciliation of extremes, which is a hallmark of the clown and the trickster, can also be related to the *hamsa*, the "primordial man" who antecedes the diversification of castes. The difference between the two types lies in that the "reconciliation" over which they preside appears as "chaotic" and somewhat "random" in the former case, and harmonious, integrated, and synthetic in the latter.

In one of his pilgrimage notebooks, Swami Ramdas tells of his gratitude at having been taught by a *sadhu,* through a specific occurrence, how "man is God playing the fool."[27] This statement is wonderfully suggestive of the higher meaning of man's destiny, a destiny that highlights the paradoxical ontological status of our terrestrial adventure. It is interesting to note that, in Ramdas's narrative, this lesson follows the episode of the Hindu *bhakta*'s vision of Christ, as if the Pauline doctrine of the "foolishness" of the Incarnation were, so to speak, illustrated by this striking statement. Of course, the idea of a divine play is, as we have seen, far from being foreign to the Hindu world. The interesting point here, however, is that God is not only playing, but specifically, playing the fool, moreover, doing so through man's agency. Man is God's playground, a playground in which He plays hide and seek with Himself. Man "is" God, and he is, at the same time and so to speak consequently, a "fool." He has to be a "fool" in order to be "God" and man at the same time: the meeting of extremes cannot but involve a measure of disequilibrium and the "blind spot" of terrestrial relativity, the inverted reflection of God's infinite unfathomableness. God had to play the fool for, in, and through man so that man might become God's perfect fool in Him.

This page intentionally left blank

CHAPTER 6

READING THE TRICKSTER'S FOOTSTEPS

The trickster demiurge has been interpreted by anthropologists in three main ways. The first interpretation, which is perhaps the most common, sees the phenomenon as a grotesque release from the pressures and structures of normative society. Along this line of interpretation, the fact is highlighted that American Indian societies are characterized by very strong and stern social and psychological imperatives that make it necessary to integrate a kind of "safety valve" in order to ease the functioning of the group. This sociological approach accounts for the pervasive presence of the trickster as a beneficial and cherished character that brings laughter, joy, and freedom. This view of things may be bolstered, to a point, by reference to the parallel institution of the sacred clown in Amerindian and other traditional societies. The testimony of some Native American witnesses would tend to buttress such a psychosocial approach, as illustrated by Black Elk's account in John G. Neihardt's book. Commenting on the *heyoka* ceremony, which is characterized by absurd and foolish antics on the part of the *heyokas*, Black Elk remarks on the compensatory function of clowns when he mentions that "when people are already in despair, maybe the laughing face is better for them."[1]

A second interpretative tendency is, within the same "positive" vein, to see the grotesque adventures of the self-seeking and often ridiculous trickster as a symbolic allusion to the very nature of man. Characters such as Iktomi and Coyote would thus reflect the limitations and potentialities of mankind. As representative of this kind of understanding of the trickster, MacLinscott Ricketts argues that the latter is none other than "man, muddling through some of life's problems, discovering his own powers of mind and body, and using them, sometimes wisely, sometimes foolishly, but always enthusiastically."[2] Such an understanding of the trickster's nature and function is parallel to the position of a kind of "pre-humanism" within the perspective of traditional American Indians. This "godless way of humanism" (Ricketts) would be embodied in the instinctive, ingenious, and rebellious traits of the trickster, all eminently characteristic of mankind. Trickster stories would then spell out a kind of ritual religion of laughter without the gods, a purely human exorcism of suffering and failure that would be virtually subversive of the transcendent order, as testified to by the trickster's difficult relationship with the gods. Whether they situate the trickster in the context of a divine, cosmic, or purely human order, the two aforementioned interpretations share a highly positive view of the trickster in his own right as a principle of freedom vis-à-vis external norms and limitative reality.

Countering such visions of the trickster as a somewhat subversive figure in relation to institutionalized forms, some analysts have argued that the trickster should primarily be understood as a counter-exemplar whose function is less to extol the powers of the transgressive comic than to teach moral and social lessons *a contrario*. In an article entitled "Living Sideways: Social Themes and Social Relationships in Native Trickster Tales,"[3] Franchot Ballinger has pointed out the need to take into consideration the "socially didactic function that he (trickster) serves in Native American conscience." In this context, the trickster is not so much a hero as he is a "warning." Without rejecting the view of the trickster as a playful and disrespectful catalyst for transformation and increased freedom, Ballinger argues that "the one boundary Trickster does not cross, cannot cross, is the boundary of himself, a 'transgression' necessary for community. [...] In spite of himself, Trickster encourages us to see the world through the collective social eye and thus to see beyond the individual self."[4] This understanding of the trickster takes stock of the paradox of his inability to transcend personal appetites while ultimately playing a positive role in the life and destiny of the community.

The three interpretations that we have just sketched are in fact far from being exclusive of one another. A phenomenon as manifold and subtle as the trickster is necessarily multidimensional, and its various facets may give rise to paradoxical occurrences and lessons. It may very well be that the failure of sociopsychological interpretations to provide us with a full account of the meaning of this phenomenon lies in their underestimating, or even ignoring, the metaphysical vision that underpins and supports trickster myths and stories. Only

such a metaphysical vantage point can allow us to reach a full understanding of the seemingly antithetic aspects of the phenomenon. It
bears stressing that traditional and archaic cultures, such as those of
the Native American Indians, do not separate the psychological and
social dimensions from a sacred understanding of reality at large, and
that this understanding is predicated on a much wider comprehension of the latter than contemporary critics might be inclined to
acknowledge. In this very context, Joseph Epes Brown reminds us
that "Black Elk used to say (that) this world is a shadow of another,
more real world."[5] To say that the trickster fosters inner and outer
freedom through his wandering antics, that he brings out a new
world of inventions and discoveries through his haphazard foolishness, that he embodies the process of trial and error that presides over
manifestation and the ambiguities of mankind's endeavors, and that
his shameful or ridiculous acts teach us about the dangers and consequences of remaining enclosed within the circle of our self-centered
desires—all this is perfectly plausible and compatible when one considers the metaphysical *weltanschauung* that presides over his stories
and that form the background of all the seemingly unintelligible
chaos that he carries in his wake. The world of the trickster is a world
of "shadows." The very lack of "seriousness" and sense of responsibility displayed by the trickster figure is an allusion to this basic truth.
The pervasiveness of trickster stories in myths and folklore, and the
absence of any indignant sermonizing at his pranks, is in itself an evidence of the fact that the trickster phenomenon must be considered
as a pointer to the "not-so-real" nature of terrestrial experience. This
does not mean that such a pointer amounts to a dismissal of social
and moral norms on the level upon which they may have a meaning
and a necessity; but it certainly means that the story does not end
there, and that any fixation of these norms as a kind of absolute
misses the point of the full reality. The fact is that any human being
or society that can laugh at and with the trickster cannot perceive the
existential narrative as an end in itself, or as an independent realm.
The "heroic" dimension of the trickster—his ability to free mankind
from its shackles—is not only to be read as a kind of psychological
"trick," or as a mere social gain; but it is also and above all to be
understood as an infusion of reality from a vaster and higher world
into the relative strictures of horizontal and mundane endeavors. The
sacred and religious character of trickster is not at all, therefore, an
anticipation of the "humanist" claim to "make it" without the gods;
it is rather a paradoxical intimation of the primacy of the world above
and beyond, a world that may manifest itself in ways that are completely

unsuspected and unsettling. It follows from such an understanding of the trickster that Ricketts's identification of the latter with man is both undeniable and lacking. The trickster is situated between two worlds that he articulates together in a most inarticulate fashion. He is man, and he is more—and less—than man. He displays the weaknesses of mankind in a caricatured manner while being the agent of a divine plan that he carries out backwards, so to speak. As a kind of indirect and ambiguous messenger from another plane of reality, he fulfills a function of intermediary between vastly different realms. Ballinger's point about his not transgressing the realm of the ego is in no way at odds with the latter. While it is true that the modus operandi of his function is almost entirely contingent upon a self-seeking perspective—he is a creature of lust and greed—it must be stressed that this self-seeking mode is less the expression of a wicked and rebellious standing than the manifestation of desires and passions that are almost candid and "innocent" in their passional impetus. This is, so to speak, the raw substance of energy and life. The trickster's psychology is nearly always attuned to the whims of childhood, often combined with the messy tricks of adolescence, but never with the "mature" malevolence of "serious" adulthood. By not transcending the realm of "natural egoism" he paradoxically shows us the way in which nature can transcend itself through a kind of ruse with its own limitations. His message is in some respect alchemical in suggesting how evil can in some cases be a cure for evil. So, while it is true that the trickster figure does not overcome or transcend his own ego, it is also true that he may suggest the very limitations and illusions of the "mature" ego in his attempts at organizing and mastering the world, and his illusions of masterminding God's plans. Most of what is characterized as reality is a result of unintended and often chaotic *bricolage*, an odd game of more or less arbitrary causes and consequences that defies the psychological and social coherence of man as a seeming "master and maker of his own destiny." Moreover, it is not so much the ego as such that is at work in the trickster's ways, as it is the raw forces of instincts and appetites, as they express themselves inordinately in gluttony and lust. When the trickster abandons himself to the flow of his desires, he lets himself be carried away by the animal drives of his nature in a way that is like a distant and reverse reflection of the guiding inspiration of divine energy. Although he is, in a sense, the epitome of human ambivalence, he is in another sense not "human," but rather both animal and divine. Whence the zoomorphic wealth of his manifestations and transformations. Those who have focused on interpreting the trickster as a "liberator" of man, as a culture hero who helps him do away with his conventional complexes and impediments, tend to forget that he also expresses and defines—at least temporarily—a sacred order, even though the latter outstretches the confines of normative hierarchy. What Joseph Epes Brown has written about the clown could also be applied *verbatim* to the trickster:

> the role of the clown serves an enormously important purpose in that it opens a door, in a very subtle and effective way, into a realm of greater reality than the realm of the ebb and flow of everyday life.[6]

This realm is not characterized by an absence of meaning and order— quite to the contrary; it is immensely more meaningful and orderly than the ordinary world of man. Recent interpretations of trickster myths and stories along the lines of a deconstructionist outlook precisely miss this crucial point. Gerald Vizenor's understanding of the trickster as a kind of epitome of "no-meaning" is predicated upon such an utterly relativistic assumption and a purely "subversive" interpretation of this phenomenon. Basing himself on the chaotic and plural dimension of trickster narratives, Vizenor argues that "the trickster is a comic sign with no histories, no political, or economic signification, and no being, or presence in the narrative." For him, "the trickster is 'nothingness' in a narrative voice, an 'encounter' that centers imagination in *holotropes*, a communal being; 'nothingness' in consciousness and comic discourse."[7] Thus, not only does the trickster's function consist in opening the field of representational and cultural reality, but the very "hollowness" of the trickster character also situates him as the "de-centering" element in a purely syntagmatic system. While one cannot but agree with Vizenor when he remarks that the trickster has no definite "center," and that this lack of a center is precisely, and perhaps paradoxically, the foundation of his zigzagging creativity, one may argue that the trickster's lack of a center is less a negation of "centeredness" as such than a refusal to "fix" the center within any point on the circumference. The transformational genius of the trickster, perhaps above all when it is not intentional, stems from an ability to "roam" on the surface of reality and explore the field of possibilities, thereby bearing witness to the omnipresence of the creative center within everything. The trickster is like an awkward adventurer in search of a treasure, who, by digging holes left and right in an attempt at unburying and enjoying the objects of his desire, makes it possible for the waters of life to spring afresh from the depth of the earth. In fact the treasure is certainly not what the trickster thinks or desires: it is the underlying water that keeps everything alive.

If the trickster may appear as a "hollowness" or a "void" in the narrative discourse, it is because as the embodiment of a function, he is not an individual but a type. If he were an individual, he would be able to change, something he is quite unable to do. When Iktomi is caught by his wife trying to cheat on her with a younger lady, he promises her that he won't do it again, while the narrative voice tells us that he will. The world of the trickster is not a world of moral lessons; it is a world of metaphysical and cosmological designs. He is "nothingness" because he does not act with an individual purpose; he is not a subjective entity endowed with a specific identity: all he does is act out impulses that come "from nowhere," but this nowhere is in fact everywhere since it is the very source of the making of the universe of forms. This being said, the aspect of "meaningless" narrative play that Vizenor unveils in trickster stories might be interestingly related to the realm of *Mâyâ*, since *Mâyâ* is indeed, strictly speaking, meaningless when considered from her own limited standpoint. The "communal creation" that is at the heart of the trickster's narrative process, the endless vagaries of the story itself, its absence of moral resolution, certainly points to the dangers of a "monologic" or "absolutist" interpretation of trickster stories. As with any real myth, the trickster's myths are polysemic. This does not preclude the narratives from being centered on a search for meaning, nor from accounting for things as they are. So the trickster story is not only a more or less arbitrary and gratuitously creative language game; it is also, and above all, an instrument of knowledge and recognition. Now, Vizenor's point is well taken when he argues against the interpretative illusions of the social sciences when dealing with the trickster, but these illusions may only result from a truncated understanding of what knowledge and interpretation truly are. The stories of the trickster should not be deciphered as "primitive" and pre-rational attempts at "representing" the world in narrative forms, as if a conceptual translation was all that was needed to penetrate them. There are undoubtedly elements of pure enjoyment, free imagination, and creative renewal in trickster narratives, but these participate in modes of understanding and elucidation predicated on a certain way of *knowing as being* in the world. In other words, one must *know* that the light of true knowing cannot but entail shades of "unknowing" that are like the traces of the divine play of the Absolute within relativity.

CHAPTER 7

THUNDERING CLOWNS

The contemporary Western concept of the clown is situated, at least partially, within the continuity of a traditional Christian heritage that accounts for some of its highest meanings and manifestations, while bearing witness to an undeniable impoverishment of the sacred dimension upon which this foundation was laid. For one thing, the clown has been reduced to a mere source of amusement and the essence and the intrinsic necessity of this entertaining function has most often been lost sight of along the way. Another revealing factor of this impoverishment lies in the quasi-exclusive association of the clown with children, as if adults could only participate tangentially or marginally in his feats, or as if the clown were not "for them."[1] Moreover, this reduction runs parallel with the confinement of the clown within the circle of the circus, that is, in a domain of fantasy and dream that remains foreign to the actual "business" of life. Like the sacred and death, with which—as we see—he bears profound affinities, the clown has been expelled to the outskirts of life, so much so that he has become *persona non grata* within the range of "real life." At best, he is deemed to be an instrument of temporary relief, a kind of psychosocial luxury that one may enjoy once in a while. This was not the way among Native American societies, as also in many other traditional contexts. Here the clown was not just a pleasant entertainer; he embodied and acted out a vital spiritual and psychic function.[2]

In Native American tribes, the function of clown had a very direct relationship with the world above. At his highest level of manifestation, the clown was one of the most feared and respected of men; one most susceptible to enter into relationship with the supernatural, while doing so in an ambiguous manner that distinguished him clearly from other "experts" in sacred matters. Given his frequent association with

the domain of the holy, the hierarchical status of the clown was
generally quite eminent. Among the Pueblo Tewa, for example, the
two kinds of clowns, *Kossa* and *Kwirana*, were classified among the
Made People, that is, the highest category of Tewa people, which
means that they were situated above the Dry Food People, or common folk, as well as above the *Towa é*, the middle level people who
serve as "officials."[3] Notwithstanding such eminence, the pervasive
recognition of the sacredness of the clown was not without involving
an element of ambivalence. This ambivalence was connected to the
clown's ability to symbolically reconcile opposites, or for his tendency
to "gush forth" at the critical point of simultaneous contact between
different levels of realities or different perspectives. As a symbolic
manifestation of this spiritual vocation, the supernatural election of
sacred clowns was, in several tribes of the American Plains, highlighted and inaugurated by visions of lightning, or simply by a religious fear of lightning. Considered from a sacred standpoint,
lightning is a symbol, and a manifestation, of the awesome and dazzling rigor of the holy. In this perspective, the sacred is both frightfully
arresting and tremendously energizing. Lame Deer explains that the
graphic depiction of lightning among Sioux "as a zigzag line with a
forked end [...] and tufted feathers at the tips of the fork" expresses
the dual nature of *heyoka* power—the clown's power, good and bad,
and its spiritual source as "winged power."[4] The two parts of the fork
manifest the "good" and "bad" aspects of the vocation, as well as the
duality of lightning both as a cosmic power and a spiritual archetype.
These two aspects refer fundamentally to enlightenment and destruction: in many shamanistic cultures being struck by lightning was
understood not so much as a punishment from the gods but as a con-
secration from above. Among Siberian shamanistic cultures, a place
struck by lightning became endowed with sacred power. In this view
of things, the sudden descent of lightning is a source of death, but this
death is also, and more importantly, consecrated by an irruption of the
divine. Accordingly, the *heyoka* stood at the juncture where the irradiation of divine light coincided with the bursting into ashes of its
human receptacle, the latter disappearing thereby into the abyss of the
Void. In an altogether different Amerindian context, this aspect was
made manifest in the fact that Hopi clowns only appeared during ceremonies in the afternoon, when the sun begins to set and shows signs
of disappearance into the Void that lies beyond the horizon of forms.[5]
The "Void" referred to in this context can be taken in two senses:
metaphysically it refers to the Highest Mystery and its unfathomable
depth, situated beyond all determinations and images, a source of

infinite "surprises" and "shocks" that the clown stages in a burlesque manner; spiritually, the void of the clown means inner emptiness, humility found in being the object of a derisive reputation, and in perfect obedience to the call of the Spirit. The clown's function is one of death for the sake of life, and one of mediation between the Center and the periphery.

Given its very demanding and rigorous character, the function of sacred clown always involved obligations and charisma of a very special kind. As far as the Plains Indians were concerned, the main requirement—among Lakota *heyoka*,[6] Pawnee *iruska*, Arapaho *ha hawkan*, and other Indian clowns—pertained to contrary and antinatural behavior. *Heyoka* clowns would shudder at the peak of summer, and take their clothes off in the midst of winter. They would move backward, pretend to swim or wash in a puddle, and speak by contraries, referring to realities by means of their opposites. Now these kinds of attitudes were not freely chosen; they were rather imposed upon the person by the spirits presiding over these vocations. There was nothing fanciful or glorious about them, and they actually entailed a great deal of discomfort, danger, and suffering. The clown's relatives and those who closely interacted with him had also their burden of troubles to share: the way of the clown is to rush headway into troubles, shame, and crisis and to bring this trouble to the fore within his very own cosmic milieu. On the other hand, they were often considered as some of the most powerful *medicine men*.[7] Among Lakota people, for example, the spirit Heyoka could demand from his "devotee" that he perform feats that would put his life at risk. In fact, many related vocations implied that the clown court death by behaving in a foolishly bold manner, especially in battle. A sense of death and an affinity with the terrible and impending forces of nature was the mandatory background of the clownish function. The vocation was already in itself a kind of "social death" since, as we see, it frequently entailed a de facto isolation from the rest of the group. In fact, it would be misleading to think of the clown as a naturally humorous and happy person; far from it. The pleasant and amusing aspect of the clown should rather be understood as hiding a frightening side. The clown is shocking, disturbing, and even terrible, or else he is not a clown. His actions often bring disruption into the group, or into the ceremony. During Navaho night dances, clowns systematically disrupt the good order and composure of other dancers; they move out of synchronization with others, stop in the middle of a dance, and remain on the ground after others have left.[8] The negative reactions that the clown's behavior may cause in other men are more often than not accurate symptoms of the latter's own animic knots and disharmonies. His function is not only to bring relief in times of crisis, but also to annoy and unsettle in times of comfort and, in fact, at any unexpected time, since his thrust is to keep people awake by all means necessary. In California, some clowns would splash people with water or throw burning coal on their back to keep them alert.[9] The clown is a reminder that life is precarious and short. In that sense, he is the opposite of the contemporary popular entertainer, who tends to comfort his spectators in their worldly sleep.

Natural characteristics were at best only secondarily relevant to the vocation, since the clown was chosen by the spirits. If one wished to sketch a clownish predisposition, a susceptible terrain for the spiritual election that makes the clown, a better approach would consist in highlighting the unusually high and quasi-mediumistic sensitivity of a potential or future clown. In fact, a "clown in the making" may very well appear a priori as the opposite of a clown in the conventional sense of a "good time Harry," all the more so when one considers that the whole vocation can be in some respects defined as a reversal of nature.[10] It was not rare for a clownish predisposition to be linked to traumatic experiences of one sort or another. Abuse and suffering tend to open psychic and spiritual windows on the world beyond. The fear of lightning that is mentioned earlier is highly and symbolically characteristic of this kind of extreme psycho-spiritual sensitivity that involves an acute, almost unbearable, contraction in the face of the Absolute and the aspects and manifestations of rigor and majesty that it entails. It must be underlined in this connection that the *heyoka* phenomenon is akin to the violent clash of opposites that enters into the most turbulent zones of cosmic existence. As thunder and lightning result from the contact between extreme atmospheric zones, the clown is the human locus of an electrifying meeting of opposites. These extremes may be situated on the same level of existence, such as hot and cold, sad and funny, gentle and violent, feminine and masculine. But they may also be vertically connected, as the highest and the lowest, the noblest and the vilest. This vertical junction is best exemplified by the Hopi *kochare* clowns' entrance into the ceremony from the roof, often upside down and tumbling over each other. The clown is a celestial being who reflects the heavens in a reverse way, as if in a grotesque mirror, and his falling from the sky entails an element of ridicule since it expresses a fundamental exile from the world of "serious men." The clown is not at home in this world, and this is one of the reasons for his "contrary" ways. Among Hopi Indians the clown embodies the mystery of reversal between distinct cosmic or ontological sectors of reality: what is fine here is awful there, what is discomforting below is pleasant above, and so forth.[11] Clowns manifest these polar oppositions by acting here as if they were there, in a way that is neither here nor there. On an essential level, this funny, paradoxical, and often violent junction of opposites and disparate realities is nothing less than an esoteric allusion to the confrontation of the individual limitations entailed by the human state with the Absolute. In its illusion of "full" and independent reality, individual existence, because of its radical distinction from "nothing," tends to vest itself with a sense of absoluteness. Nearly every human falls into the trap of usurping the throne of the One in thinking "I am that I am." As a consequence, this absolutization of the relative produces the most terrifying fright when the individual most concretely faces his own finitude and is confronted with the transcendent. In this encounter, the individual reaches the limits of contraction, or he is as if thunderstruck by the only Reality. As such, he can only submit to the latter by losing all "sanity," a process that the *heyoka* initiation symbolizes, and act out ceremonially. Acting as a clown, because one has been constrained to do so, is not particularly enjoyable, to say the least, since it amounts to facing and overcoming the fear of being looked at as ridiculous or crazy.[12] It means inhabiting a world of desolate solitude. It is like looking constantly at one's deformities in a mirror; it also means looking at others' ugliness since the clown is one of the main catalysts of the manifestation of evil from within. This is another reason why the clown is often endowed with an extremely acute sensibility, he "feels" evil more than an average person does. The clown's ways, including mimicry, caricature, and threatening pranks, invite a painful self-awareness on the part of those who interact with him: he reveals blind spots and all the ugly unconscious elements that may suddenly come to the surface of the soul. As such, he plays an important, albeit somewhat extrinsic, role as keeper of normative ways and values since he threatens to reveal in others the elements of transgression and evil that almost everybody tries to conceal out of a sense of social self-protection.[13] This is one of the reasons why parodic imitation is often part and parcel of Amerindian clowns' behavior. It is not only that the sacred clown repeats what others are saying or replicates their gestures like a child: but by doing so he also suggests the ridicules of the soul and the human predicament, and he may even allude, consciously or unconsciously—for his perspective is not conceptual—to the nature of relativity as a faint and somewhat distorted "echo" of the Absolute. Imitating the powerful is particularly eloquent in this respect since it implies that one deflates their actual, or potential, presumption. To that end, the Cree and Ojibway clowns tended to parodically imitate the attitudes and gestures of members of powerful warrior societies.[14]

While the clown introduces discomfort and trouble among those whom he revels in annoying, it is to the clown himself that is reserved the ambiguous privilege of suffering most. He has to face his fear and shame, as it befits his heroic way, that is, one centered upon a subjective approach to the objective realm of the Spirit. The fear and the shame is moreover likely to be concentrated on precisely *that* which is most susceptible to arouse them in a given person; the medicine is never quite the same from individual to individual. Needless to say, such a fear, and its painful domination through clowning, presupposes that society—and the individual— still has enough norms and taboos to induce and register the apprehensions, tensions, and shame that it involves. On the one hand, it is true that every society has rules and conventions, thereby making room for the clown's behavior; on the other hand it is a question of degree, and the more normative and traditional the society, the more heroic the "fooling around" with its rules and ways of behaving is likely to be. The modern world has, in a sense, destroyed the sacredness of the clown by making it impossible for him to be what he really is, namely, a figure who draws his energy and makes his impact on others through the heroic tension that is entailed by the transgressive parody of normative realities.

As was suggested earlier, the importance of death in this vocation is highlighted by the association of clowns among Lakota and other tribes with thunder and lightning. It has been said that the clown's behavior was a way of averting lightning from striking both himself and the tribe, as well as from other misfortunes.[15] The role of the clown is in that respect apotropaic, or sacrificial—as if he were taking upon himself the charge of lightning. This is symbolically the case in so far as the function of the clown is one of balancing out imbalances. As Black Elk puts it: "when people are already in despair, maybe the laughing face is better for them; and when they feel too good or are too sure of being safe, then maybe the weeping face is better for them to see. And so I think that is what the *heyoka* ceremony is for."[16] Since lightning is associated with the rigor of the spirits—their ability to strike down—the clown may be said to prevent this chastisement by balancing out, through exteriorization, what might otherwise be "inwardly" imbalanced in the group. In other words, the comically obvious "transgression" of normative ways was a manner of making up for the hidden transgression of the group, thereby protecting the latter from the cosmic retribution that the collective disorder would otherwise bring about. The clown brings disharmony into the open so that it can be dispelled. However, the "transgression" of the clown is not only antisocial, it is also antinatural. In other words, his function is not confined to serving the group; it is also relevant to the cosmic order as a whole, and even, on the highest level, to the metaphysical realm. The idea behind the contrariness, backwardness, and absurdity is, therefore, twofold: first, the therapeutic exteriorization of human fears and disorders, and second—probably magical in scope—the symbolic counteraction and neutralization of nature's rigorous and destructive phenomena. In that sense, contrariness is a way of symbolically and magically going against the grain of the cosmic concatenation of effects and retributions, a shamanistic challenge to regular causality. Metaphysically speaking, contrariness thereby amounts to an unmaking of the world of manifestation, a kind of mystical "decreation" (to use Simone Weil's phrase) that opens onto the Absolute. At such a metaphysical level, it is likely that "contrary" behavior also constitutes an allusion to the intrinsically relative nature of opposites, thereby opening onto the non-dual root of all things. In other words, to refer to hot weather as cold is not only "absurd" or "senseless," it is also an implicit recognition of the fact that extremes meet, as is perceptible in the common experience of the blurring of hot and cold in extreme sensory perceptions, or in that of the mingling of pleasure and pain in some particular instances of human experience. This sense of relativity is, for example, highlighted in the typical feat in which *heyoka* performers pretend to get drowned in a puddle. The function of the clown also involves a particular charisma, especially in the context of specific ceremonies that highlight a transcending of normative, and relative, sensations. Among them is the ability to handle boiling water and fire. The Lakota *heyoka* ceremony included, for example, the boiling of a dog whose pieces of meat were taken from the hot pot by the clowns while they complained about the coldness of the water.[17] Walking on fire by clowns is also attested among the Cheyenne and Arapaho. Among the Pawnee, the clowns were even thrown into fire. According to some anthropologists, this ability to handle fire may be seen under two different aspects: either as an antinatural and contrary instance, as among the Lakota; or as symbolic of an ability to extinguish other powers, that is, external fire, through one's own power, or inner fire.[18] This appears to indicate a spiritual perspective characterized by a reabsorption of the manifested levels into their higher archetypes. In the same vein some Cheyenne shamans were characterized by their association with fire and their performance of supra-normal feats, such as walking through fire and eating coals, another point that is shared with the Lakota *heyoka*. They were also involved in contrary behavior and displayed the ceremonial behavior of sacred clowns. According to Karl Schlesier, a third group seemed to have been expert in the sacred knowledge of stellar motions, and a fourth category was associated with the near sky and was also characterized by contrary behavior such as inverted language. This group seems to have been akin to the Lakota *heyoka*, as indicated by their spiritual connection with Thunder, *Nonoma*. These kinds of shamans lived in isolation from the rest of the group because of their spiritual characteristics, and on account of the exceptional powers that were theirs, especially their mastery over the spirit of lightning. As a consequence of these awesome powers, one of the reoccurring aspects of the Indian contrary clowns was their not being allowed to marry, and their usual operation on the margin of society. This is no doubt related to the "high dosage" of their *medicine* and the dangers that it involves. It must be highlighted that the specifically contrary vocation of Plain Indians clowns was not necessarily related to clownish behavior as such. In point of fact, some of these vocations were quite exclusive of any "fun" in the usual sense of the word. The comic feats of clowns nearly always involved contrary behavior, but the latter is not to be thought of as being obligatorily related to comical elements. Among the Cheyennes, for example, contrary behavior may be parallel to a rule of life that emphasizes physical courage, dignity of deportment, and chastity. It is actually to be considered as an *ascetic*—and virtually penitential—vocation in the most exact sense of this term.[19]

The vocation of the clown is often connected with supernatural beings, or mythological entities that provide an archetypical basis or inspiration. It is interesting, for example, to note that among the Dakota, the *heyoka* is instructed by a god bearing the same name. This god is an enemy of Oanktahee who is the supreme god of the Dakota pantheon. He is, therefore, situated in a position of antagonism vis-à-vis the norms of nature that have been created by Oanktahee. E.O. Neill defines Heyoka as a polymorphic god in whom unity and multiplicity are reconciled: he is one and many at the same time. He is said to appear in four forms, that of a "tall and slender man with two faces," a "little old man with a cocked hat and enormous ears," "a man with a flute suspended from his neck," and "the gentle zephyr which moves the grass and causes the ripple of the water." These four appearances are prima facie disorienting in their diversity, although the characteristically polymorphic nature of the god may have prepared us to anticipate such a surprising combination. These forms suggest, moreover, revealing associations and symbolic affinities on the part of the Heyoka spirit. The "two faces" obviously refer to the ambivalent nature of the Heyoka spirit, good and bad, and the balancing demiurgic role that he fulfills. The Apache clown "Two Faces" corresponds to the same reality. He is the point of junction between polar opposites, particularly the serious and the funny. His "funny" work is a "serious" matter inasmuch as it is vital to the life of the group. In another sense, "seriousness" can be "funny" by its incongruous rigidity. The passage from one of the poles to the other is nothing other than the essence of "lived" metaphysics. It means perceiving, and acting out, the divine within and beyond the world, in a constant and unending shift. In that sense, the clownish "mask" reveals and conceals at the same time the profundity of this function. As for the grotesque and caricatural shape of Heyoka, it refers to clownish disproportions and to a sense of worrisome ugliness. Heyoka is an "ab-normal" and antinatural god, which is why those who are under his inspiration use addresses by which they mock and revile him. Some of his shapes must bear witness to the awesome and terrifying dimensions of the divine. As for his appearance in the form of a man with a flute, it may allude to his very strong magical powers, by means of which he is able to "charm" those who come under his spell. Suggestively, the fourth mode of appearance is formless and invisible, akin to the gentle wind of the Spirit that was manifested to Elijah in the Bible. In several ceremonies, especially among the Pueblos, the sacred clown derives his comical power from his pretending to be invisible, thereby expressing in a parodic, and ironic, mode an essential dimension of his vocation. The clown is like a "ghost" among humans. This last, and probably highest, mode of manifestation is a sure sign of the esoteric and hidden nature of the *heyoka* vocation.

In Oglala cosmology, Heyoka is also associated with the West Wind, which bears a privilege of anteriority among the four winds. As a point of fact, this wind holds the first direction in cosmogonic and ritual orientation. The myth tells us that the place of the West Wind was fixed first, even though it had been initially intended that this would be reserved for the North Wind. This change in order was either the consequence of the unfriendliness of the North, or the result of a deceit on the part of Wazi, the titanic wizard of the underworld.[20] The West Wind was endowed with bringing thunder and rain; it was also more generally connected with moisture. Moreover, it corresponds to the color black, which confirms the strong destructive and transformational aspect of this reality. Concomitant associations with the West Wind are the Thunderbird and the Rock, both divine symbols implying respectively terrifying rigor and merciful grace.[21]

And let us note in passing that Iktomi, the trickster spider who is in a sense a kind of ancestor of the sacred clown, is said to be born from the Rock. This association might be surprising prima facie given the sharp contrast between the irrefrangible and stable nature of the Rock and the extreme mobility of Iktomi. The paradox actually avers a profound complementarity in the sense that it could be said that Iktomi corresponds to the demiurge, whereas the Rock refers to the Higher God.

In the Oglala myth, relating how the West Wind became the companion of the Winged God, it is clearly implied that the latter is to be identified, or at least associated, with the god Heyoka.[22] It is said that Tate—the first shaman—had five sons: Yata, Yanpa, Eya, Okaga, and Yumni, and that they were enjoined to fix the directions of the winds. On the edge of the world, they encountered a cloudy mountain from which a frightful noise was heard: it came from the Winged God and his gigantic egg. The Winged God was terrifying, and reminiscent of Saturn since, like the ancient god, he was devouring his offspring; he is described as having a beak like an eagle with four rows of sharp teeth; its glance was like lightning and its voice like thunder [...] it had four jointed wings but no leg or feet, and eight toes bearing the talons of an eagle, each talon as long as an eagle's wing. It seized the egg and shook it, and the noise was like the rolling thunder.[23]

The aspect of terror that is associated with the Winged God is profoundly connected to the *heyoka* vocation. The *heyoka* can be said to experience and reproduce, in a symbolic manner, the West Wind's, or Eya's, heroic deed when, climbing up through the lodge, the tree and very nest of the god, he asks to see the latter himself. A swallow answers that should he do so, he will have to become *heyoka*, and behave in an antinatural manner. He is then rewarded for his bravery, both by becoming one of the companions of the Winged God (who also appears to him in the form of a giant) and by being first among the directions. Being associated with the Winged God, the West Wind fulfills a rigorous function of purification. After having become the companion of the Winged God, Eya is said to have been endowed with the role of "helping cleanse the world of filthy and evil things."[24] This function entails a certain ambivalence since it is both destructive and recreative, or at any rate transformational. The clown takes upon himself the ridicule and the abjection of the world of relativity, thereby "cleaning it up," so to speak. He is constrained to deal with all that needs to be evacuated from the social body. This is also illustrated, among the Lakota, by the fact that the animals that are generally associated with Heyoka are characterized by a somewhat marginal or subordinate status. They may express both the aspect of obedience and "dirtiness," like the dog, or they may relate separate domains like water and earth, or air and water, such as the frog and the dragonfly; or again, their motions and actions may be whirling and unpredictable like the swallow, the nighthawk, and the dragonfly.

The principle of exceptional spiritual power combined with some kind of social or psychological marginality and role reversal was widely known in the world of the North American Indians. In many tribes we can find types of shaman who are nonnormative socially, but all the more powerful spiritually speaking. Among the Cheyennes, there was a category of shamans associated with the blue sky who were characterized by a transcendence of polarities and opposites. In this context, the blue sky is akin to space and to the transcending of all contrastive determinations. The open space of the high sky is a totality that has no opposite, no part, and no end. It is only on the level of the near sky that the complementary dichotomy between sky and earth can be introduced. As for the blue sky, it corresponds to the Highest Reality, to Beyond-Being or Non-Being.

In *The Wolves of Heaven*[25] Karl Schlesier mentions three subcategories of shamans associated with the blue sky that are relevant to our current purpose. The first kind was called *hemaneh* ("half-man, half-woman") and they lived as transvestites, recapitulating in their being and behavior the qualities of both sexes. The *hemaneh* lived as a marginal figure, socially speaking, and as with most Lakota *heyoka*, he could not engage in sexual relations and marriage, a point that is important to note in order to stress the spiritual character of his vocation, by contrast with the contemporary phenomenon of mere sexual transgression. There seems to have been a recognition that such a sexual possibility was purely spiritual and could not be manifested on the concrete level of sexual mores and societal institutions. Although it is not directly related to contrary behavior as such, this kind of reversal may be related to the general principle of clowning as a manifestation of life "as it should not be." This aspect appears, perhaps, most clearly among some Southwest Indian cultures. As Alfonso Ortiz has demonstrated in his study of the Tewa *weltanschauung*, there exists a kind of universal polarity that runs throughout the range of cultural representations, as a reflection of ontological and cosmic realities: this chain of pairs include such elements as the gods and the world, the *kachina* ("angel") and the clown, the priest and the trickster, sky and earth, and so on.[26] Man stands in the middle zone of interplay between these two chains of analogical correspondences that span along the horizon of being. The "as it should not be" phenomena, eminently manifested in the form of the clown, involve both a manipulation of the terms of the system and its transcendence. This transcendence by and through opposition is not without analogy to the anthropological model of the hierarchical structure propounded by Louis Dumont in his seminal *Homo Hierarchicus.*[27] His theoretical model involves a vision of hierarchy as "inclusion (*englobement*) of the contrary." In other words, contrary to conventional opinion, genuinely hierarchical structures are never hermetically closed upon themselves; rather, they are open from within, as it were, because the higher hierarchical term not only "negates" the lower ones but also "includes" them within its own field. So, the exclusionary aspect of the system is only extrinsic, while its intrinsic dimension is eminently inclusive. Now the types of phenomena involved in clowning and "contrary" behavior are analogous in the sense that they amount to a negation that nevertheless still fundamentally opens onto an affirmation of what it negates. Clowning is in this sense a "hierarchically" oriented phenomenon, that is, a phenomenon that includes both a negation and the ultimate integration of that which is negated on a higher level of reality. There is, however, a difference between the generic hierarchical structure described by Dumont and the clown function. The hierarchical inclusion of the contrary can be illustrated, for example, by the inclusion within the *brâhmana* caste of the defining characteristics of the lower groups such as the *kshatriya* and *vaishya*. The caste system of India constitutes, in that sense, an intrinsically hierarchical structure characterized by an ultimate all-inclusiveness that transcends polarities and differences. The *brâhmana* is not only the "negation" of the *kshatriya*, he also includes the latter within his own fold. From one standpoint there is distinction and opposition between the two castes; but from a higher standpoint the contradiction is absorbed into the higher caste, which eminently contains the lower one. By contrast, the clown subverts the order of the structure, but in doing so he also opens the way to a transcending of polarities. The clown function does not, properly speaking, include the realities that it "negates," but it includes the very principle of negativity as a means of integration. This also accounts for the fact that the clown cannot be "located," as it were, in a particular, fixed place in the system. He is certainly a part of the system, but he is an ex-centric part that is both within and without. It must be added that the situation of the clown within the structure could be equated to that of both the *sannyâsin* and the *pariah* in the caste system. Like the clown, the *pariah* is marginal and, as it were, "residual" within the system, insofar as he is not integrated within the fold of its normative structure. Both figures are, in that sense, excluded from the system because they do not fit within its qualitative economy. However, the marginality of the clown is also akin to the renunciate, the *sannyâsin*, who abandons society from above. This affinity is predicated on the fact that, in spite of their obvious differences, the clown and the *sannyâsin* identify with the supernatural and sacred core of the system and, as such, embody the very motion of transcending the limitations that the latter entails.

An analogous situation presents itself with the *hemaneh*, who undoubtedly reconciled the opposites, in the form of the masculine and the feminine, and it was from this reconciliation that stemmed his extraordinary power. In a sense he could be identified with the archetype of the androgyne, or integral humanity, such as it was described, for example, in Plato's myth. In another sense, on a lower level, he manifested the principle of infinity, or the mystery of sexuality as a reflection of this principle, on a level that transcends the bounds of earthly limitations, whence his dangerously powerful possibilities, and therefore his exclusion from normative society. Sex reversal was seen as all the more powerful as it was conceived as antinatural. Inasmuch as social and sexual roles constitute a means of controlling magical and spiritual forces, their inversion involves ipso facto an opening onto the world of the supernatural: it liberates an invisible power that may prove to be constructive or destructive. One should not be surprised, therefore, that similar phenomena of transvestite shamans were also present in Siberia among various indigenous groups. Joan Halifax relates that this type of shaman is considered as the most powerful among the Koryaks.[28] Among Navajo Indians, phenomena of transvestitism are also well known. According to Alfonso Ortiz, these phenomena are bound to ritual practices that occur at the time of changes of season, particularly at the vernal equinox.[29] They may involve parodying of dress by women, or parodying of female behavior by men. These instances of role reversal through rituals "represent extreme instances of what occurs when the Tewa wish to mark an interruption in the normal flow of time."[30] Equinoxes and solstices correspond to moments of cosmic shifts, and consequently these times of "crisis" are acted out symbolically by clownish performances of role reversals, which is a clear indication of the transformative and catalytic function of the clown and related phenomena. It is very widely documented that role reversal and clowning are traditionally associated with fertility and renewal.[31] This function is also highlighted by the part played by the sacred clown, the Gray One, during the central Apache ceremony of the Changing Woman. She is the incarnation of the circle of becoming, as expressed through the change of seasons: she is Nature, or rather the Divine Immanence and Life within Nature. During the ceremony marking the menstruation of the Changing Woman, her symbolic birth, she is accompanied, among other characters, by a clown who is constantly whirling a kind of slingshot as a wheel, thereby acting out symbolically the cycle of becoming. More generally this function can be characterized as a kind of shamanistic mediation since it involves a constant shift between levels of realities, like man and nature, the spirits and men, which is akin to a breathing in and breathing out, a contraction and expansion, the moving relationship between the two terms being precisely recapitulated by the clown.

Having reviewed the various kinds of clown vocations, ceremonies, and performances that have been documented in North America, Julian Haynes Steward[32] has proposed a general theory of clowning upon which we pause for the purpose of discussion, and as a general conclusion to this chapter. The theoretical model proposed by Steward is, to our knowledge, the only one that is founded on a collection of data extending over all the main areas of North American tribal diversity, from California and the Plains to Central America. Steward does not even hesitate to bring in anthropological information from Africa and other non-American zones to buttress his theory and provide it with universal underpinnings. His model delineates four fundamental types of "objects" for sacred clowning. The first one, which may be deemed in fact to contain the essence of all the others, is directed at sacred, religious, and taboo realities that are first and foremost in the life of the group.[33] The more sacred the object that is derided by the clown, the more intense and "central" is his laughter. The clown is the only one to enjoy the privilege of not being situated under the jurisdiction of the sacred taboo; in Steward's words, "he is held accountable for nothing."[34] On one level, this infinite freedom is a manifestation of the supreme and boundless activity of the Spirit that cannot be contained within a single sacred form. On another level, the main sociopsychological interpretation of this surprising privilege has often been couched in terms of a need for periodical collective release in the context of highly structured collectivities in which the demands imposed by sacred ceremonies, practices, and taboos are extremely exacting. In most cases, the presence of burlesque or parodic laughter is adventitious in relation to the sacred phenomenon, such as when— in a ceremony—clown dancers mimic the ways of other dancers with the intention of making fun of them. In other, rarer, cases the explosion of burlesque laughter and mischief is situated at the heart of the ritual or ceremonial practice. It is intuitively understood that the manifestation of the sacred involves the creation of a zone of high tension. The emergence of this zone of high tension can produce a fatal imbalance and trauma if it is not accompanied by a kind of symbolic and psychic discharge that makes it easier for the individual and the group to integrate what has been received. This is undoubtedly the meaning of the reoccurring association between the sacred and clowning. It must be added that the psycho-spiritual "conflagration" that may be brought about by the sacred may also be akin to the very modalities of clowning. In that sense, which may correspond to the most central manifestations of clownish elements within the ceremonial precinct, the clown feats are in a sense the direct symbolic and operative manifestation of the emergence of the sacred.

Steward's classification includes sex and obscenity as the second component of the clown's performance. It is widely known that phallicism is particularly prominent among clowns. It appears obvious, prima facie, that the importance of the sexual element is related to its frequent association to the sacred as such. It is in the domain of sexuality that religious taboos are the most frequently concentrated. Sexuality is a divine power that must obey laws and traditionally involves sacralization. In that sense, everything that has been mentioned concerning the parodic disruption of the sacred could be similarly said of sexuality. Another characteristic that relates the two domains lies in the frequent association between sexuality and supernatural powers, especially in the context of clowning. It must be remembered, for example, that "the Heyoka were believed to have great supernatural power which enabled them, among other things, to satisfy their libido."[35] The concentration of power that is entailed by the clownish "shock" translates into an intense sexuality, although this sexuality is more likely to be manifested on a primarily psycho-spiritual level. As for the phallicism as such, as evidenced in the frequent exhibition of phalluses in clown ceremonies and antics, let us mention in this connection that the ithyphallic nature of many trickster figures corresponds to a cosmological reality. The main characteristic of the *Candomblé* statues of Exú, for example, is an immense phallus.[36] It may be said that the potentialities of the Logos brought out by the Demiurge—as expressed through the sexual symbol—are in this case envisaged in their "blind" and grotesque aspect. The North American Indian *heyoka*'s clown power is similarly associated with the generative and sexual energy. The *heyoka* "bomb effect" has to do, on the psycho-spiritual level, with sexuality as the most intense repository of energy and the manifestation of the infinite on the terrestrial level. Sexuality involves the manifestation of a numinous power that transcends the individual, irrupting in social life with a frightening violence that may rend the fabric of social bonds. Sexual clowning is like a taming of this uncontrollable power, a striking literary image of which is provided by Petrucchio's "coarse" and burlesquing treatment of Katarina's temper in Shakespeare's *Taming of the Shrew*. In fact, the frequent phallicism of clowning is a clear indication of the affinity between male sexuality and the burlesque. The trickster is almost always a male character. Lewis Hyde has raised the interesting question as to why this is so. He ultimately attributes this situation to the fact that the trickster figure epitomizes an "on-the-road opportunistic sexuality" and a "non-procreative creativity," which are both akin to masculine psychology.[37] Without questioning the plausibility of this explanation on a certain level, it could be added that it is their way of being "active in passive mode" that accounts for the fact that tricksters and clowns almost unanimously enjoy male characteristics.[38] These characters outwardly manifest an utter passivity with respect to what comes their way—such as objects of desire, opportunities for mischief, or psycho-spiritual impulses—but this apparent passivity is the modus operandi of a dazzling and zigzagging display of activity through feats, discoveries, voyages, and so on. In this sense, paraphrasing Lewis Hyde's title, it could be said that they actively "make the world" by being—passively—"fooled" by it.

The third category with which the American Indian clown is frequently associated is that of "sickness, sorrow, misfortune and need,"[39] to which death should most likely be added. There is perhaps no more illustrative occurrence of this aspect of clowning than the universal gag of the ridiculous fall. As M. Willson Disher has rightly noted, "all the comic aspects of misfortune are typified by the joke of falls."[40] The fall is the epitome of the dramatic actualization of the lack of balance inherent in the human condition. Any other misfortune happens, one way or another, in the mode of a fall, as is already implied by the etymological root of the word "accident." The "accidental" nature of man is never better highlighted than by a risible loss of equilibrium. In a sense, the clown takes upon himself the task of embodying and manifesting all the appearances of weakness, imbalance, and misery that he can: this is a way of "cleaning up" the psychic atmosphere of the group from the residual negative components that stem from actual encounters with these misfortunes. Laughing at human miseries seems to be a constant element in the history of mankind. In order to account for this reoccurring phenomenon there is no need to presuppose a kind of "temporary suspension of sensibility," to use Bergson's phrase, since it is more likely that the ability of men to laugh at such unhappy and unpleasant occurrences flows from an intuitive perception of a possible dissociation between man's physio-psychological makeup and his intelligence. Man can recognize his own misery in the clown, but he does so in an objectified manner, in such a way that he feels virtually liberated from the pain that he would normally experience in such a context. In this framework, the sacred clown is a catalyst of intelligence in the sense that he makes it possible for men to de-identify from themselves, and from the self-pitying tendencies that are entailed in the ego.

The fourth category of clownish pranks is related to a comical treatment of foreigners. Although such a treatment appears to have been present in many cultures, it is apparent that, among Native Americans, it has become increasingly important in direct proportion to the extent of their exposure to European peoples. The general model of clowning directed at foreigners amounts to a kind of "exorcism" of the odd: it is a sacred negotiation of the acceptance of others as human beings. By laughing at the "other," one may both neutralize the threat that he represents and integrate his reality into one's own view of the world. In the case of the more recent interactions with Europeans, this general pattern is altered by an ambivalent relationship that involves a measure of hostility given the realities of oppression. In such a context, clowning readily takes the form of a mocking parody of the oppressor. It bears stressing that this type of clowning is generally more secular than sacred. Among the Hopi, for example, the Piptuyakyamu, who are non-sacred clowns, specialize in the parodying of white people. They tend to dress as Anglo-Americans while caricaturing some of their ways or speeches.[41] A different, but parallel, modality consists in including symbols of the predicament of contemporary Native Americans in the treatment of the foreign character. This, no doubt, is a way of alluding to the sense of alienation that has resulted from the contact with white men. Along these lines, the *heyoka* clown Kermit Bear Shield may dance "in a modernistic costume replete with false nose, derby, hobo clothes, and a whiskey bottle with a nipple but containing no whiskey."[42] In such cases, the clownish parody belongs as much to Steward's third category as it does to the fourth, as the ridiculous imitation of white ways also betrays an allusion to the infantilizing effect of alcohol upon Native Americans (whiskey with a nipple). The Indian has become a "foreigner" to himself, and it is as such that he can become a target for the native clown.

The four themes around which American Indian clowning gravitates all appear to be connected, in one way or another, to the experience of a tremendous "otherness" that has to be reconciled with identity. It is plain that these various modes of alterity can ultimately be subsumed under the general category of the sacred. In traditional cultures, sexuality, sickness, death, destiny, and the encounter with foreignness—all these experiences involve a contact with powerful, supernatural, or transcendent forces. The sacred is par excellence the domain of a fascinating otherness with which men must familiarize themselves through rites, taboos, and ceremonial life. Sexuality is strongly connected to the holy as a force in its own right; it is a force that may command human individuals and make irruptions in their life in the form of the mystery of the other sex, and also in the experience of procreation. Misfortunes, sicknesses, and death are also closely connected to the idea of an intervention of other forces issuing from the divine world. To be struck by sickness, bad fortune, or death means encountering the force of an irreducible otherness that can constrain mankind. On a purely human level, the foreigner is par excellence the representative of this dimension of otherness. Louis Massignon has emphasized the way in which traditional worlds are characterized by an understanding of the foreigner as a portentous presence, the foreign host being the human embodiment of the divine visitation.[43]

It stems from all of the previous comments in this chapter that the various forms of clowning, or their various objects, constitute ways of integrating the realm of otherness into one's own identity and being. The encounter with otherness—whether it be in the form of the sacred, death, destiny, sexuality, or native differences—amounts prima facie to an experience of fear, the fear of the unknown. Clowns operate in such a way as to reconcile us with these fears by means of a burlesque desecration. In doing so they help individuals and communities deflate the threat that these phenomena may a priori entail, not so much with a view to debasing or annihilating their existence, but rather with the intention of neutralizing the subjective compression or anxiety that is raised by their encounter. In so doing, the clown facilitates the process through which some of our "shells" may fall and make us able to break away from the ego's hold on our perception of reality, thereby opening us to a sense of participative unity.

CHAPTER 8

SPIRITUAL LAUGHTER

When the Shinto goddess Amaterasu leaves the cave in which she has hidden in order to escape her brother Susano's tempestuous behavior, she does so because she has been enticed by Uzume's dancing,[1] her curiosity having being aroused by the other gods' laughing at the dance. This is an archetypical example of laughter as "divine mirth," a mirth that is also readily expressed by Uzume's merry dance. It is worth noting that some versions of the myth define Uzume's dance as obscene, which is highly symbolic of the transgressive dimension of the demiurgic process that prompts the actualization of ontological possibilities. This element is also in consonance with the obscene, popular mask of wisdom that expresses the highest metaphysical and cosmological truths in the garb of trivial or socially repulsive phenomena. The function of this transgressive dimension is connected with a transcending of limits that suggests the unity of all that is, whether it be morally commendable or not. This episode expresses both a cosmogonic event, since Amaterasu has in a sense produced the world through being lured by dance, and a spiritual archetype, given that the gods' laughter is a particularly direct manifestation of inner relief.[2]

The relationship between laughter, metaphysics, and mysticism is a rich and fascinating domain that has been little studied. One of the reasons for this situation lies in the fact that religious phenomena are most often considered as a "serious matter" while laughter is often thought to be mere entertainment and is not usually envisaged by the majority as bearing any relationship to religion. Laughter smacks of profanity, and even profanation. Now, this conventional understanding of the matter is, as has already been indicated, highly partial. As with all other human phenomena, and in fact more than most, laughter opens onto the realm of spirituality. When Rabelais reminded his readers that *"rire est le propre de l'homme"* (laughter is man's privilege), he was no doubt alluding to the potentially divine dimension of human laughter, since no privilege of this kind can presumably be unrelated to what Semitic religions consider as the theomorphic nature of man.

John Morreall, in his interesting book on the philosophy of laughter entitled *Taking Laughter Seriously*,[3] has categorized the contributions of Western philosophical theories of laughter under three rubrics: the superiority theory, the incongruity theory, and the relief theory. These generic theories encompass, in fact, a variety of subtheories that present relatively significant differences among themselves, but the fundamentals underpinning these subcategories remain the same. The first type of understanding of laughter goes back to ancient Greek philosophy, particularly Plato and Aristotle, and is later on exemplified by Hobbes's theory. The substance of this theory of laughter lies in the hypothesis, or the recognition, that laughter involves a sense of superiority on the part of those who laugh. This feeling of superiority also entails a sense of distance that accounts for the "insensibility" detected by Bergson in laughter.[4] It also accounts for the definition of laughter as a "mixed emotion" in Plato's *Philebus*, and for the tension between the demands of Christian charity and the eruption of the comic.[5] This sense of superiority may not always be expressed by laughing *at* others but it must, according to this theory, in all cases imply a sense of victory and eminence, and it is herein that the virtues and the pitfalls of laughter lie. In comedy, the classical *castigat ridendo mores* ("comedy chastises ill deportment by laughing") highlights the positive function of this "superior" laughter. Through laughter, vices can be pointed out and corrected, thereby contributing to the moral health of the individual and the community. Genuine comedy is, in that sense, a purification through comical objectification. However, the implicitly aggressive and polemical aspect that this theory attaches to laughter may easily give rise to excesses that entail arrogance and insolence. It may also involve a loss of control, a possibility that Plato envisaged, in his *Republic*, as the primary reason why the guardians of the city, the class of warriors, should not be allowed to indulge in intense laughter. Such is also one of the main reasons why, for Aristotle, the social priority in dealing with humor and laughter is to draw limits and promote a sense of moderation and propriety, which would keep them from transgressing the realm of the law. Joking must manifest itself within the "middle state" (the *ariston metron*), for otherwise it runs the risk of erupting abusively. Indeed, for the Stagirite, "a joke is a kind of abuse."[6] Society and the Law cannot leave the

potentially transgressive nature of laughter unchecked.[7] Thomas
Hobbes, within the context of his pessimistic view of man as being a
wolf for man, takes this point of view a step further, and cannot but
reduce laughter to the status of an effective but dangerous weapon in
the struggle for life. This leads him to write, in chapter VI of his
Leviathan:

> Sudden glory is the passion which maketh those grimaces called laughter;
> and is caused either by some sudden act of their own that pleaseth
> them; or by the apprehension of some deformed thing in another, by
> comparison whereof they suddenly applaud themselves. And it is inci-
> dent most to them that are conscious of the fewest abilities in them-
> selves; who are forced to keep themselves in their own favor by observing
> the imperfections of other men. And therefore much laughter at the
> defects of others is a sign of pusillanimity. For of great minds one of the
> proper works is to help and free others from scorn, and compare them-
> selves only with the most able.

Hobbes's conception of laughter is therefore purely negative: laughter,
as he understands it, stems exclusively from a blend of self-consciousness
and subjectively advantageous comparison with others. In this view,
laughter is never indicative of joy as such, and it never manifests as an
ability to "poke fun at" oneself. Laughter is substantially egocentric
and malevolent. Now, this is obviously a very incomplete picture of
the phenomenon: too many dimensions and aspects of laughter are
left out of account because they do not fit with the Hobbesian theory
of man. However, this is not a point that we would like to pursue
here. It appears rather more interesting to develop an examination of
the ways in which Hobbes's analysis points to a profound truth of
which it remains, however, ultimately unaware. There is little doubt
that laughter can, and often does, involve a sense of superiority. In a
way, joy or any other mode of happiness, also involves a feeling of
overcoming odds or misfortunes; a state of elation is a symbolic victory over death and unhappiness, while suggesting a state of completeness. Joy has often been defined as the feeling of being one with,
and connected to, everything; a feeling of being what one must be,
and ultimately what one is. In this context, joyous laughter expresses a
sense of superiority over the lower realms of one's ordinary self, as also
over the lower shores of reality.

On the "negative" side of this feeling of superiority, it is no less true
that laughter may specifically serve as a weapon in a kind of moral and
spiritual warfare. The devil can laugh at those whom he misleads, and

the saint, too, may laugh in return at the devil's final discomfiture. Now the fundamental question lies in understanding why this is so; why is laughter often associated with the comparison of two realities, one of which appears to be suddenly sub-rated through laughter? Metaphysically, such a possibility cannot be without connection to a hierarchy of the states of being, either normatively or abusively. The matter at stake amounts to knowing, in the last analysis, *who* is laughing, and at *what*. The ego may laugh when thinking that it is superior to, or victorious over, other egos, or simply over adverse circumstances. But does it mean that all laughter arising out of a "sense of superiority" stems from the ego? The not-so-rare phenomenon of people laughing at themselves implies that it cannot be so. In other words, there is a type of laughter that is associated with the hopes and fears of the ego, and therefore thrives upon an abusive sense of superiority, and there is another type of laughter that proceeds from a sudden consideration of the ego, or aspects of the ego, as "laughable"; this ego can be our own, or it can be the "ego as such" as manifested in others. In the latter sense, laughter may be a spiritual door by opening onto a level of reality that shatters the illusions of egoic self-importance. When considered in light of the non-dualistic doctrine of the Self—the Substance that is immanent to all realities, or the true universal Subject that "grounds" and yet still transcends all limited subjectivities—the question of laughter as a mode of superiority takes on a much more profound and interesting turn. In this light, the possibility of laughing at oneself and at others is predicated on the ability to transcend oneself, and the latter can, in fact, only be accounted for in terms of the immanence of the Self. In other words, the capacity to be able to laugh at oneself presupposes at least a minimal degree of dissociation from the ego, and this dissociation must presumably involve a self-transcendence of some kind.[8] At its height, a fundamentally spiritual laughter engages a subjective change of level through which the ordinary locus of consciousness is relativized. But this process of dissociation and relativization is not restricted to the subject alone; it may also take place in relation to objects. Laughter, in a spiritual context, occurs when the realm of relativity, the veil of *Mâyâ*, is pierced through and "exposed." As Ramana Maharshi has said, in the context of spiritual inquiry, "A day will dawn when you will yourself laugh at your effort (to seek to gain Reality). That which is on the day of laughter is also now."[9] The "effort" gives credence to the reality of the *jîva*, the individual, as well as to the reality of the obstacles, and ultimately to that of *Mâyâ*; it therefore entails an element of tension that can only be transcended in the Self, for tension cannot but be the result, or the symptom, of an egoic contraction, whether it be for the sake of the good that is being aimed at, or on account of the bad that is being rejected. However, the "day of laughter" has already come since the Self already *is*. Thus, a sudden shift to this *now* can cause an "explosion" of laughter, or else coincide with laughter or be accompanied by it. To the proponent of the "superiority theory," Ramana Maharshi would most likely put the question—a paraphrase of his favorite "Who am I?"—: "Who laughs?" Inasmuch as it is truly spiritual, laughter is divine: laughter is the trilling, or thundering, of the Self. Its nonmental, nondiscursive character pertains, on one level or another, to the immediacy of the Self. From that standpoint, the "aggressiveness" of laughter is none other than the shattering of subjective illusions. It is an aspect of spiritual warfare. However, spiritual laughter is fundamentally benevolent, even though it may still be perceived as malevolent by those who strongly identify with their defining and "serious" limitations. Such an understanding of laughter is apparent both in Hinduism and in Buddhism, particularly in Zen where illumination is not infrequently connected with laughter.

To the question of knowing whether laughter should be conceived as the cause, the consequence, or the coincidental occurrence of spiritual illumination, it could be answered that all three might be true, depending on the context. Laughter as a dissociative phenomenon may certainly open the way to a recognition of a higher level of consciousness by clearing the ground, as it were, from under man's psychic clutter. In this context, the role of comedy, and the variety of moods (*rasa*) that it involves, can be conceived as a spiritual preparation, or method, conducive to a detachment from oneself, and ultimately a breakthrough into the domain of the Self. Laughter involves a breaking down of the hardened egoic substance through a kind of "grinding" of the soul. However, it is no less true that laughter can be the consequence of a shift of consciousness, in which case it will be conceived as a "criterion" of illumination, or the hallmark of a higher awareness. The abruptness of laughter may, in this sense, reflect the sharp contrast between two states of consciousness.

In this same order of ideas, the Zen tradition shows how spiritual practice may result in thundering laughter. If one were to doubt that powerful laughter may be a legitimate spiritual expression one could refer to this passage from the autobiography of Zen Master Hakuin: "As for sitting, sitting is something that should include fits of ecstatic laughter—brayings that make you slump to the ground clutching your belly."[10] On this level, laughter might be associated with psychophysical postures, particularly in terms of centering upon the *hara*, or the lower center of gravity that plays such an important role in Japanese culture and spirituality. However, this is only the most elementary aspect of the phenomenon. Although laughter may be understood both as a cause and a consequence of a change in one's mode of consciousness, there is probably no higher recognition of the spiritual dimension of laughter than that which associates it with a coincidence between the outburst of laughter and the shift in consciousness itself. In this context, Zen laughter is thus often related to a loss of balance that *immediately* coincides with a different outlook on oneself and the world. In this particular view of things, equilibrium will be defined as a stasis, or a status quo, that precludes a deepening of one's spiritual consciousness. Because of a shift in the usual "balance" of consciousness, laughter may erupt simultaneously with the springing forth of an insight into one's relativity, and into the ridiculousness of one's ordinary existential "posturing." In this connection, the experience of *satori* is often associated with a loss of equilibrium that is akin to burlesque and bursting laughter through its destabilizing directness and vigor. Let us mention for example the *satori* of this Rinzai Master who twice reached the illumination on the occasion of a fall:

> Suddenly the temple bell struck the second hour, time of the first morning service, which we were expected to attend. I tried to get up, but my feet were so numb with cold that I fell to the snow. At that very instant it happened, my *satori*. It was an enrapturing experience, one I could not hope to describe adequately. [. . .] One day on my way back from *sanzen* (presenting one's view of a *koan* to the master) and while descending the temple steps, I tripped and fell. As I fell I had my second *satori*, a consummate one.[11]

This is no doubt the clearest indication of the *immediacy* of the experience of spiritual laughter, an immediacy that involves a sudden "overlooking" of the ordinary arrangement of things and a liberation from the usual grip of the self. If laughter, any laughter, implies a loss of self-control, the negative connotation that is most often associated with this loss is actually extolled and valued by the Zen perspective, precisely because it allows for a "letting go"[12] of the egoic crispations that have defined the walls of our inner prison. In that sense, laughter is in itself a spiritual awakening. The modality of this awakening is akin to the absoluteness of Reality that appears in all its pristine freshness and "violence." While spiritual tears have often been compared with a melting of the heart's hardened state by the consuming fire of divine love and mercy, spiritual laughter coincides with an abrupt shift that breaks up the shell of ordinary consciousness.[13] The verb "to burst," a symbolic expression common to both experiences, implies an "explosion" and disappearance of self, the source of which cannot be found in the self-reflectiveness and self-control of the individual. Another interesting example of this bursting that coincides with illumination is provided in the story of Shui-lao's enlightenment. It is said that when Shui-lao put to his Master, Ma-tsu, the famous question, "Why did Bodhidharma come from the West?" the latter, instead of answering him, had him bow down and then crushed him to the ground.[14] Shui-lao reached enlightenment and is said to have declared that since receiving his Master's shock therapy he had never stopped laughing. In this case, it is quite clear that laughter coincides with a realization of the disproportion between one's conceptual and verbal utterances and the reality of one's being. It is likely that when Shui-lao was made to taste the presumption of his posture, in putting the question to his Master, he could not but laugh at his previous *appearance* of learning and wisdom. This laughter proceeds indeed from a sense of superiority; but the fact is that there is nobody to appropriate this superiority: it can only explode in laughter. Laughter can coincide, therefore, with an openness to the unlimited. What laughs is That which transcends all limitations by its utter superiority.

This aspect of "opening" is obviously related to the second set of theories of laughter, in which the function of release is highlighted. This release has been given many interpretations, primarily on physical and psychological levels. Psychoanalytic theories, beginning with Freud, have been the most prominent in describing laughter as a release of psychic energy discharged because it has been "saved" for a purpose that it can no longer meet. In this overall view, jokes, as a particular instance of laughter, fulfill the function of manifesting freely, albeit unconsciously, within the realm of consciousness that which has been hitherto repressed because of social pressures and conditioning. In other words, jokes allow one to save the inner energy that would normally have been used to suppress tendencies. This unused psychic energy is then released in laughter. Independent of any evaluation of the partial validity, and the clear limits, of such a thesis on the psychological level, it is interesting to note that the terms in which Freud set the question of laughter, that is, as a release mechanism stemming from unconscious tensions, can be readily transferred from the realm of the subconscious to that of the supraconscious. In other words, the release that occurs on the occasion of laughter is a response to what Churchill and Grene denote as the "unanswerableness" of the situation.[15] Laughter is a positive and affirmative response to the experience of insurmountable limits and unanswerable questions. Metaphysically, these limits are nothing but the expression of the disproportion between our potential infinitude and our actual finitude. The "unconscious," or rather "supraconscious," is the infinite that we bear within ourselves, below—or above—the shell of our limited identity. This infinite subjectivity is most often veiled, or if one wishes "repressed," by what Advaitins define as a superimposition: it consists in mistaking the snake of the limited ego for the rope of the universal Self. The individual identity is, in that respect, nothing other than a complex network of negative tendencies that obstruct the infinite life that lies below the surface. In some situations, however, this limited identity is as it were caught in the net of its own "impossibility" and absurdity, and confronted with the riddle of its contradictory status as a being that is both real and unreal, infinite and finite, divine and human. When confronted with the apparent nonsensical aspect of our existence, through concrete occurrences that defy efficacious rational and practical responses on our part, we can only react with a manifestation of ourselves in which the commanding coherence and autonomy of our individuality engages in its own collapse—and that manifestation is laughter, an explosion of the boundaries of possibility. This is laughter as death. Laughter is like the last ineffable but sonorous word of relativity before its reabsorption into the Absolute. Thus, on its highest spiritual level, laughter allows one to escape upward, as if we were flying up and through the confining net of *Mâyâ*, both subjectively and objectively. In his *Mathnawî*, Rûmî tells the story of a lover who, when asked by his beloved to take his love back to its roots in God, "lay back on the ground laughing, and died laughing; [. . .] that laughter was his freedom and his gift to the Eternal."[16] Rûmî's story tells us of a disproportionate analogy that can only be resolved through the sudden "disappearing appearance" of the source of the disproportion. This resolution is therefore a meeting of extremes through which the limited self both asserts itself and lets go of itself, or rather asserts its true nature by letting go of itself. Through this example, we are given to highlight the deep connection between laughter and death. In a sense, laughter is nothing other than a victory over death and over the fear of death, as is also clearly indicated by the phenomenon of ritual laughter during the *Hilaria* and the *Lupercalia*[17] in Rome.[18] These festivals highlighted rituals that symbolically enacted the function of laughter as an exorcism of death in its negative aspect. Through its immediacy laughter shatters the obsession of time as a relative continuum leading to death: laughter explodes this oppressive limitation by engaging us totally, here and now, in an affirmation of being that transcends our thoughts, anticipations, and fears.

The paradox of laughter that we have just sketched can also be approached from the standpoint of "incongruity" theories. In the West, Pascal, Kant, Schopenhauer, Bergson, and others, have argued that laughter results from the perception of a disproportion, inappropriateness, disharmony, or abrupt contrast between expectations and results, or perceptions and reality. The incongruousness between the terms or phenomena must however be of a specific kind and manifest in a particular context in order to be a source of laughter, for all incongruities do not lead to laughter. Generally speaking, comic incongruity stems from the disproportion between a subjective feeling or inner concept and an objective occurrence or phenomenon, in a context where this disproportion disrupts the anticipation or perception in a way that underlies the latter's precariousness or relativity. In Bergson's theory of laughter, incongruity results from the perception of a mechanical, unconscious process within the course of life. In his view of things, laughter stems from an incongruity between the moving flexibility of life and the stiffness of the actions or thoughts of those at whom we laugh.[19] Fundamentally, comic incongruity presupposes that an inaccurate or partial perception of reality has been corrected, and laughter results from the liberation that this correction carries in its wake. Metaphysically speaking, the supreme incongruity is none other than the coincidence of the real and the unreal in *Mâyâ*. Laughter results from the perception of this metaphysical incongruity on the occasion of an experience or perception that suddenly shifts one's subjective focus by revealing the lack of reality of what had been hitherto been apprehended as real. This metaphysical laughter will most likely take place when the disproportion between the terms involved is maximal, or when the extreme distance between perception and reality is suddenly manifested. The Advaitin example of a man looking for a necklace that he is wearing around his neck presents a clear affinity with the world of laughter, and the realization of his mistake is presumed to produce a hearty laughter.

Along such metaphysical lines, Abhinavagupta's theory of laughter constitutes one of the most profound traditional doctrines of the comic. In Abhinavagupta's view, laughter (*hâsya*) is predicated upon the notion of perceived incongruity, or the subjective coincidence of two opposite or contrasted reactions. Commenting upon Abhinavagupta's view of laughter, Sunthar Visuvalingam states,

> In the case of bisociative laughter, the twin opposing reactions cancel
> each other out at their very inception and, whatever be their specific
> nature and qualities, we are immediately aware only of our impulse to
> laugh [. . .], which merely signals the presence of bisociation without
> elucidating its exact nature and components.[20]

Two distinct, and in fact often opposite, reactions meet in us, and the
outcome of this disharmonic contact is laughter. In the introduction
to his study of Abhinavagupta's theory, Sunthar Visuvalingam devel-
ops the idea that this concept of laughter has been theorized on the
basis of the role of the clown (vidūsaka) in Hindu drama. The clown
must induce a bisociative response among his audience: a sympathetic,
albeit unconscious, identification with the clown on the one hand,
and a feeling of disgust, shame, or indignation at the breaking of
taboos on the other hand. It is important to note that the unconscious
core of the sympathetic identification does not result in a resolution of
the incongruity on the conceptual level, nor does it reveal its proper
nature in any direct fashion. It corresponds, in this sense, to an
"instinctive" perception of that which lies below the surface of the
formal, exoteric structure of the tradition. Laughter is therefore
indicative, or symptomatic of the sudden encounter between the esoteric and exoteric dimensions of the religious universe. On the one
hand, there is "un-conscious" unity of the two, which can only be
accessed in the nonconceptual, nonformal intuition of presence—the
presence that, precisely, animates and "legitimates" the breaking of
forms and taboos—on the other hand there is a "conscious," reflexive,
and formal discontinuity in the mode of a dogmatic rejection of
the esoteric. Laughter, on the part of the audience, is the outcome of
the impossibility of identifying with one or the other dimension of the
subjective response. Laughter expels, so to speak, the tension brought
about by the bisociative response. In doing so, it makes it possible to
passively and "unconsciously" integrate the esoteric within the collective
context.

Analogically, spiritual laughter may be deemed to result from an
incongruous encounter between two different levels of subjectivity,
the divine and the human. The divine necessarily remains nonconscious
for the human qua human. However, given the ultimate unity of the
subjective realm, the realization of the Self does not obliterate individual consciousness. One can infer from this observation that a kind
of bisociation may occur with respect to the incongruousness of the

subjective coincidence of two levels of subjectivity. We would like to mention, in this context, the following anecdote: several Hindu disciples receive the *darshan* of a renowned *guru*. Suddenly the *guru* erupts with an explosive laughter. Everybody is unsettled, and the disciples are at a loss to identify the cause of this masterful laughter. The *guru* later explains that he laughed because his soul—the *jîva*, or individual portion of consciousness, had left "him" for a few seconds. The bisociative incongruousness that lies at the source of this outburst of laughter is undoubtedly connected to a situation in which subjective consciousness finds itself situated, as it were, on two planes, simultaneously. In such an exceptional instance, one does not know who one is anymore. In the context of our story, this unknowing cannot have any other resolution than laughter. It is as if the impossibility of reconciling two incommensurable aspects of one's reality could only be transcended in a release of energy that bears witness both to the limits of the individuality—without which the "breaking up" involved by laughter would be unthinkable—and to the shattering power of a Reality lying beneath the surface of individual consciousness. Mâ Ananda Mayî's *attahâsi* (divine laughter) expresses this sense of divine shattering by evoking the power of thunder that embraces, according to Swami Gitananda, all the levels of manifestation and leads him to state that "no human being can laugh like this."[21] In such heightened occurrences of laughter, it could be said that man is, as it were, "laughed away" by God.

This page intentionally left blank

CHAPTER 9

FOOLS FOR CHRIST'S SAKE

The figure of the "holy fool" is a quasi-universal phenomenon that manifests itself, in one form or another, in virtually every spiritual quarter of the world. Methodologically, it must, first of all, be highlighted that this type of phenomenon can be divided into subcategories that refer to widely different spiritual outlooks and vocations. The primary question is, in this respect, that of the reality or authenticity of foolishness. In other words, is the holy fool pretending to be a fool, or is he a fool for good? As we see, this distinction is meaningful when trying to circumscribe the phenomenon of holy folly, but is still in some ways problematic. Were it not problematic, the very meaning of the holy fool would be unthinkable, since this spiritual phenomenon is predicated on a kind of prestidigitation with this world and the other, normalcy and deviance, wisdom and folly.[1] It bears stressing, moreover, that the basic meaning of the word "fool" carries in its semantic wake the double implication of lack of sense and ridicule. The nonsensical dimension of the fool may be related either to a lack of wits, a deficiency of the rational faculty, or else to sheer madness, and mere psychic imbalance. Even though phenomena of holy foolishness are virtually to be found in every spiritual climate, it is undoubtedly in Christianity that this very particular vocation manifested itself in accordance with a religious outlook that provided it with both a sound scriptural grounding and a conducive spiritual climate and perspective. This is likely due to two primary factors: on the one hand, the general Christian perspective, although not necessarily adverse to intellectual speculation in the theological field, has categorically affirmed itself in opposition to a "wisdom of the flesh" that was by and large identified by early Christians with Pagan philosophy. The Christian perspective is grounded in the Mysteries, starting with the Mystery of God both One and Triune, and such Mysteries transcend, by definition, the realm of horizontal, rational intelligibility. From the start, Christianity has been defined as a spiritual humbling of human intelligence that calls forth a mode of knowledge associated with the fusional presence of Love rather than with intellectual perception.

Second, such an outlook is parallel to an inversion of terrestrial priorities and hierarchies. The meek have precedence over the powerful, the last over the first, the simple over the worldly wise, children over adults, and the like. Although the figure of the holy fool has been highlighted in nearly all spiritual traditions, it can be argued that it bears a particular affinity with the Christian spiritual perspective on the basis of the inversion of values that is at the core of the Christic teachings. While holy fools appear no less frequently in the Islamic tradition than they do in the Christian world their status in Islam is arguably less central, at least with respect to the spiritual "organicity" of the tradition, than is the case in Christianity. The reason for this difference lies in the respective spiritual economies of the two religions. Islam emphasizes that the terrestrial domain, particularly the social dimension of human life, can and must be an adequate reflection of the Divine Will. Man himself, as representative or vice-gerent (*khalîfah*) of God on earth, is the best example of this direct reflection. The whole legal network of the *sharî'ah* bears witness to a divine ordering of the horizontal plane of existence by the vertical axis of the Quranic revelation. Symbolically speaking, it could be said that when considering terrestrial realities as reflections of divine archetypes, Islam places the emphasis on the similarity between the reflections and the objects reflected rather than laying stress upon the inversion that all reflections necessarily entail. This also accounts for the historical legitimacy, from an Islamic standpoint, of a Muslim political order. The Prophet Muhammad was also a political leader in his own right. This is not to say that the Prophet could not be put forward as a model for Sufi "holy fools," as we see when dealing with the *Malâmati* tradition, but he would do so on the basis of factors that are only tangentially, or extrinsically, relevant to his mission. By contrast, the very figure of Christ is emblematic of a reversal of values that involves, implicitly or explicitly, both a "mocking" of the world by Christians and a "mocking" of Christians by the world. Christianity looks at the terrestrial reflection of God by focusing on the inversion that it entails. This tendency is already inscribed in the role of God's laughter in the Bible, since the latter is, first of all, a laughing *at* mankind before being a laughter *with* mankind, as John E. Benson has argued.[2] There is a divine laughter that sub-verts as a prelude to a divine laughter that re-verts. The Psalms, a part of scripture that one would not usually associate with a sense of the comic,[3] express most directly the former aspect in verses such as the following (2:2–4):

> The kings of the earth set themselves, and the rulers take counsel
>   together, against the Lord, and against his anointed, saying,
> Let us break their bands asunder, and cast away their cords from us.
> He that sitteth in the heavens shall laugh: the Lord shall have them in
>   derision.

Verses from Psalms 37, 52, and 59 include similar expressions. This mode of triumphant laughter expresses the "destructive" transcendence of the Divine, as also suggested by God's supereminent position of "sitting in the heavens." On this level, God's laughter is, as it were, reactive, and therefore relatively extrinsic, while being involved in the drama of mankind's tragicomic miseries. This is a laughter of victory, the terrible laughter that affirms power and annihilates. The second aspect, however, the "laughing with us," is also exemplified in the Psalms:

> Then was our mouth filled with laughter, and our tongue with singing:
> then said they among the heathen, The Lord hath done great things for
> them. The Lord hath done great things for us; whereof we are glad.
> (126:2–3)

Here, laughter is not as directly reactive; it is rather a kind of inebriation with God's presence and immanent mercy. It is as if God's intrinsic laughter, as overflowing joy, were communicated to those whom He protects and loves. It is also a laughter of relief, of reassurance following trials and dangers, since these verses refer to the return of the holy people of Israel from their captivity in Babylon. Laughter therefore manifests in the wake of a "reversal" of fortune, from captivity to freedom, from exile to homeland, from death to life.

In the Gospel, the whole of the Beatitudes, which arguably express the essence of the Christian spiritual ethos, almost exclusively focus on this spiritual reversal, "Blessed are the poor in spirit: for theirs is the kingdom of heaven, blessed are they that mourn: for they shall be comforted, blessed are the meek: for they shall inherit the earth" (Matt. 5:3–5). This aspect of inversion of terrestrial values and "wisdom according to the flesh" is eminently highlighted by St. Paul's admonition concerning the "foolishness" of the world and the "foolishness of the Cross": "If any man among you seemeth to be wise in this world, let him become a fool, that he may be wise [. . .] for the wisdom of this world is foolishness with God" (1 Cor. 3:18–19). The wisdom according to the world is nothing but "self-deception" because it is based upon an illusory identity, that of the "old man," an identity that is constructed out of the nothingness of the world. Christian "foolishness" is the first phase of a therapeutic treatment that aims at the restoration of true wisdom. There is no continuity between a "worldly wisdom" founded upon the sense of moral and social responsibilities and the wisdom of Christ. "Natural" or "rational" wisdom is not to be a propaedeutics to spiritual wisdom; in fact it is an obstacle to the latter. In the spiritual reciprocity between the Divine and the human, the divine "folly" of the Cross—that is, God's allowing Himself to be humiliated and persecuted for the sake of men—is to be responded to by the human "folly" of Christian life. Man must "debase" himself in order to find his true dignity in God, and he is to do so by imitating the divine "humiliation." The true Christian must wear the "purple livery" of Christ, be mocked, despised, and must be considered to be a fool. There is undoubtedly a contradiction, or at least an extreme tension, between a human sense of social respectability and self-esteem and the Christian call for heroism. One of the highest expressions of this is found in Saint Francis of Assisi's path. Franciscan spirituality is entirely founded on a sense of social shamelessness that castigates all human presumptions of order and truth. The *Imitatio Christi* of early Franciscans manifests itself in the most brazen manner in the clothing and daily behavior of the Friars. As the *Fioretti* expresses it: "because they preferred to bear shames and insults for the love of Christ over the honors of the world and the respect and praise of men—indeed being reviled, they rejoiced, and at honors they were afflicted—and so they went through the world as pilgrims and strangers, bearing nothing with them save Christ Crucified."[4] The very image of Christ entering Jerusalem on a donkey is the spiritual exemplar of such a humiliation. Following this divine exemplar, the holy fool enters the same apotropaic mold as his Master. As an apotropaic saint he takes upon himself the sins and suffering of the world; he becomes, as it were, a spiritual lightning rod for the sake of others. He "subverts" the subversive order of the world to save others from its hypnosis and illusion.

Now, the principle of the Christian "subversion" of social and earthly values was very early manifested by the existence of Christian "fools" who would make a mockery of the "old man" and his concomitant human conventions.[5] We find literary traces of the type of the holy fool as early as the fifth century,[6] but there is little doubt that this type must have been in existence earlier since it corresponds so acutely to a Christian spiritual possibility. Two of the first accounts of holy folly, Palladius's *Historia Lausiaca* and John Rufus's *Plerophoriae*, present us with types of seeming "madmen," thereby introducing two major aspects of the phenomenon of holy folly, namely hidden pretense and loss of wits. John Rufus's account is particularly interesting in this respect since it highlights both the feigned madness and the scandalizing strategies of an Egyptian monk. The monk begins to laugh incongruously every time somebody comes close to him. He is also involved in seemingly senseless activities such as the perpetual gathering of pebbles in two baskets.[7] The laughing habit seems to be a means of keeping men away; he thereby protects the holy precinct of his secret before God. When asked questions, the monk responds by laughing at the questioner; he thereby refuses to enter the "logic" of discursive and conversational coherence, taking refuge in the "idiocy" of his spiritual state so as to shield himself from the strictures of the world of profane language and dialectical pretensions. As for the endless gathering of pebbles it pertains to a type of behavior that involves utilizing spiritual riddles as symbols of the illusory and ambiguous character of human existence. This does not mean, however, that all sense is absent from this enigmatic behavior. On the contrary, the Egyptian monk explains to one of his interlocutors that he had "picked up each pebble and placed it in the basket on the right or the one on the left depending on whether it prompted him to think a good thought or a bad one."[8] The monk would eat each evening only if the right basket was fuller than the left one. Here, a seemingly senseless action points to a moral and spiritual teaching, but it does so in a way that suggests the little weight of mankind, and the lack of substance of most of its concerns and endeavors. The whole spiritual economy of human existence is reduced to the derisive size of a childlike game.

These spiritual orientations are developed and brought to a height in the *Life of Symeon the Fool*, a hagiography written in the seventh century by Leontius, the bishop of Neapolis on the island of Cyprus. This text is essential in helping us reach an understanding of the fundamentals of the early Christian holy fool's perspective.[9] Let us note at the outset that the narrative specifies that Symeon began to act as a fool past a period of time of twenty-nine years during which he practiced asceticism in the desert in the company of his friend John. It is important to note that Symeon's decision to leave the desert was prompted by a meditation on St. Paul's admonition to Christians not to be content with their own salvation only, but to work diligently toward saving others as well: "Let no one seek his own good, but rather the good of his neighbor" (1 Cor. 10:24) and "All things to all men, that I might save all" (1 Cor. 9:22). The fool's vocation is therefore a charitable and sacrificial one. This sacrificial dimension is moreover confirmed by the symbolic migration from the silence of nature to the bustling activity and noise of the city. As Jesus entering Jerusalem, Symeon enters Emesa in order to save souls, and he explicitly states that he will do so by "mocking the world." So it is quite clear from the outset that the fool's perspective bears a profound kinship with that of spiritual warfare. In this respect, the fool may perhaps not be a perfectly contemplative figure given his tendency to share in the spiritual combativeness of the warrior for Christ. Like his Master, he has not come to bring peace but war to the world of "well-behaved" men. His intention is to take on worldliness and sin within its own stronghold, so to speak. Indeed, the urban environment is organically connected to the fool's vocation for a variety of converging reasons: it offers the highest concentration of human souls; it tends to be the nest of all kinds of human evils and vices (theft, prostitution and fornication, drunkenness and gluttony, dishonest commercial activities, political abuse, etc.), it provides the fool with the most numerous opportunities for becoming a figure of social opprobrium. Even though this aspect is not explicitly mentioned in the spiritual "program" of Symeon, one may assume that this opprobrium results from an intentional letting go of all instincts of self-preservation and self-interested prudence. Symeon is thereby able to work toward his own sanctification while awakening a desire for salvation within others. It is in the city, the seat of urbane civilization and highly codified interactions, that this transcending of prudential reflexiveness may take place in the most drastic and effective way. The city is, for all practical purposes, the battlefield par excellence in the fight between good and evil, spirituality and worldliness. It is also the very manifestation of the "madness" of the world, a world of chaotic impulses and unintegrated psychic tendencies.[10] However, following Symeon's decision to make good on his vocation of "foolish" spiritual presence within the city, his spiritual companion John cautions the would-be fool against the appropriateness of his choice by highlighting the need for an unshaking spiritual foundation: "Beware, be on your guard, brother Symeon, unless as the desert gathered together, the world disperses; and as silence helped, commotion hinders."[11] The crux of the matter lies in the original inspiration of the desire to become a fool in the city. Such an inspiration must come from God and cannot be the result of a mere individual whim. Contrasting a true vocation with spiritual presumption or mere imagination, John stresses the benefits of city life for those who are firmly rooted in the nourishing ground of divine grace. Such a rooting involves a state of grace that is characterized by a perception of all forms—even those that are qualitatively disharmonious and contrary to the Good—within the context of Divine Love and Divine Presence.[12] Symeon's entering into the city is characterized by actions that immediately precipitate his cathartic function within Emesa. He enters the city walls with a dead dog attached to his belt, and on his first public appearance the next day throws nuts at women attending mass from the pulpit, puts out candles in the church, and overturns the tables of pastry dealers. Derek Krueger has rightfully stressed the way in which Symeon's behavior on these occasions can be read as a spiritual exercise in the imitation of Christ.[13] The episode of the entrance into Emesa recalls Jesus' entrance into Jerusalem on a donkey, while Symeon's angry treatment of the pastry chefs echoes Christ's chasing the merchants out of the Temple. There is, however, a profoundly enigmatic language, or teaching, in all these seemingly outrageous actions. In this respect also, Symeon's actions can be deemed to be an "imitation of Christ," in the sense that they may be read as "acted out" parables. Nuts tend to be associated, in mystical language, with the distinction between the essential core and the accidental shell, thus corresponding to the Gospel's differentiation between the spirit and the letter. It is remarkable that Symeon would throw these nuts at women attending church, thereby alluding to the potentially "hypocritical" and formalistic dimension of outward practices. It is all the more remarkable that he would do so "from the pulpit," as if indicating the didactic nature of his prank. The "putting out" of the candles might also be a kind of ironic allusion to the dialectic of *lux* and *tenebrae*. Symeon's "language" might appear "obscure" to the women but the real "darkness" is actually on the side of the latter. One cannot but think, in this connection, of Christ's advice "not to put a light under a bushel," a symbolic action that can be associated with those who bury the spirit under the letter, spiritual awakening under formalistic and social practices. The aforementioned actions appear to imply, on Symeon's part, both a desire to save souls "whether through afflictions which he sent them in ludicrous and methodical ways, or through miracles which he performed while seeming not to understand, or through maxims which he said to them while playing the fool."[14] These various strategies amount to a twofold priority: to subvert the order of the world, and to provide men with a symbolic teaching. It bears stressing that these two goals do not presumably address the same spiritual and moral ills or the same human beings. The first aspect, undoubtedly the most scandalizing to most, functions as a way of placing the world of social conventions "on its head." In a sense, it is a kind of alchemical transmutation of the "holy anger" felt by the saint when he comes in contact with the evils and presumptions of the world. This most important element of transmutation has been judiciously suggested by M. Conrad Hyers when he highlights the role of humor as a "ritualization of aggressive impulses in substitution for the most violent and destructive expressions."[15] This "ritualization" is by definition connected to the grotesque since the latter functions as a form of caricature that reveals the ugliness of evil in a graphic and striking way. In that sense the fool performs an eminently apotropaic task, by taking upon himself, as it were, the chaos that results from the worldly perspective. One may note in passing that, by contrast with the holy fool's behavior, Christ's indignant reactions vis-à-vis the Pharisees or merchants at the temple do not display any "slapstick," grotesque, or even simply comical aspect. The fact is that Christ does not "need" to engage into this ritualized transmutation, precisely because of his divine status. Christ does not "joke" about human ills, even though he can at times manifest a kind of ironic humor toward them. His divine status and his redemptive function preclude a burlesque mode, at least within the general spiritual economy of Christianity. Even John the Baptist, who can be taken in some ways as a model for Christian holy fools, is not at all characterized by humorous traits, quite to the contrary. The Baptist is undoubtedly a marginal and shocking figure by the standards of worldly propriety, but his "mad raging" against the world is of a much more dramatic, not to say tragic, kind than burlesque in any way. It appears, therefore, that by adopting, or being inspired by, a "foolish" mode of predication and presence, Symeon and other holy fools take upon themselves a redemptive role, but they do so in a mode that is of necessity "distinct" from that of their divine and prophetic models. In a sense, the holy fool's pranks represent a further stage, or a further development on a lower level, in the Christian history of redemption. The light of redemption must enter all the layers of reality, including the most ambiguous, if not the vilest. From a given standpoint Symeon's feats of grotesque behavior could almost be understood as a "sacred caricature" of Jesus' own teachings and actions. But the "caricatural" work does not imply here a dismissive parody of its model, as is usually the case; it is rather to be seen as a kind of grotesque "mirror" of human pettiness and misery that makes the light, as it were, accessible to the remotest zones of darkness. The concealment of sanctity that is at the core of Symeon's attitude, and of most holy fools in general, is therefore not only the methodic support of an extreme humility that aims at preventing one from giving way to the complacency of social recognition, it is also a spiritual phenomenon analogous to the coming of the "Light into the darkness that comprehendeth it not." Holy madness lies at the junction of a necessity and an impossibility. It responds to the need of truth to communicate itself to the outermost zones of reality, where an almost completely dark night reigns; but it also heeds to the extreme difficulty, not to say quasi-impossibility, of the darkness accepting and receiving this light. Whence the character of extreme paradoxical possibility that can be assigned to the phenomenon of the holy fool. Whence also the extreme sacrificial tension that the holy fool's function entails. The razor's edge of his function is predicated on the acute tension of opposites that must, however, be sacrificially reconciled.

The question of the integration of laughter or humor into Christianity is instructive in that respect since it pits two divergent visions against each other, both of which may be ultimately incomplete. On one side, M. Conrad Hyers and Elton Trueblood have defended the view that, despite what most analysts would readily concede prima facie, Christ's teachings are indeed imbued with a sense of humor that permeates the entire worldview that he imparted to his disciples. In his essay "The Humor of Christ," Elton Trueblood argues for the humorous thrust of Christ's teachings. The main foundation of his argumentation lies in stressing the nonliteral character of many, if not most, of the Christic teachings.[16] This nonliteral and parabolic mode of expression is consonant with certain modalities of humor, and this holds particularly true with respect to the sense of mobility and relativity that is most often involved in humor. Christ's way of understanding the world and expressing spiritual truths presupposes a radical distancing from immediate, conventional, and literal perception. Now this is precisely the hallmark of a comic apprehension of reality that is in conformity with a sacred perspective. However, it remains doubtful whether this overall approach itself provides sufficient grounds for establishing Christ's sense of humor, since there exist other types of expression, besides humor, that are based on a nonliteral apprehension of reality and discourse. To add that gravity, and even the tragic, bears a paradoxically intimate relationship with laughter will not take us very far either in trying to provide evidence for Christ's comic dimension. Analyses that attempt to reveal this aspect of Christ's personality and teachings have also tried to capitalize on the presence of spiritual traits that are most often contiguous to some aspects of the comic, such as Christ's emotional responses like anger, or his associating with socially disreputable people. However,

Christ's anger against the merchants in the Temple is not particularly comical in itself; there is not even a hint of humor in Christ's words on that occasion, and the violent intensity of the scene ("the zeal of thine house hath eaten me up," John 2:17) would rather evoke the pathos of tragedy than that of laughter. As for Jesus' association with prostitutes and tax collectors, which Elton Trueblood defines as a "gay crowd," it may tangentially be connected to the comic on account of the presumably colorful and jovial ambience that may have emanated from such a group. But even in this context Christ's words do not seem to depart from an instructional solemnity, and he is never shown in the Gospels as portraying himself in any way that could be attributed to the "many bad characters" whom he haunts. As such, these authors do not make a sufficient case for considering Jesus' behavior and teachings as primarily imbued with sacrificial gravity. More specifically, the type of examples borrowed from Christ's sayings that are put forward by Trueblood to bolster his thesis do not seem to pertain to the domain of the comic as such. Let us note, to start with, that they are very few in number. To collect an anthology of Christ's humorous comments and jokes would be a very difficult task indeed. Let us add that the mildly humorous character of some of Christ's parables cannot compensate for the overall solemnity and seriousness of his teachings. Indeed, a rhetorical question such as, "Is a lamp brought in to be put under a bushel, or under a bed, and not on a stand?" (Mark 4:21) wittily suggests the spiritual absurdity of those who "hide the keys of the kingdom"; but it hardly calls for hearty laughter. We may also smile at Christ's observation that "if the householder had known at what hour the thief was coming, he would have been awake and would not have left his house to be broken into" (Luke 12:39); but we are still quite far from the exhilarating feats of Zen masters, or the outrageous pranks of Taoist sages. The mild and subtle sense of humor that may be detected in some of Christ's statements conveys a discrete critique of the folly of worldly ways, but it does so in a way that never departs from a holy gravity centered on a divine sense of absoluteness. The best assessment of this subtly distancing effect of Christ's mode of expression might be found in Harry Emerson Fosdick's reflection that Christ "never jests as Socrates does, but He often lets the ripple of a happy breeze play over the surface of His mighty deep."[17] The fact that such teachings might give rise, a posteriori, to the kind of way illustrated by Symeon's naughty behavior does not in the least contradict their essential gravity. Symeon's ways are directly inspired by Christ's reversal of values, but they do not derive as much from Christ's witty statements as they do from the spiritual principles that animate those statements. Outrageous and caricatural slapstick pertains to a different genre, and fulfills a different function than smiling wit. The holy fool's way is no more in tune with subtle humor than it contradicts the absoluteness, urgency, and solemnity of Christian teachings. The difference in style of expression between Symeon and his divine model lies most probably, as was suggested earlier, in the fact that the former epitomizes the terrestrial realm of ambiguity in its most extreme extension, engaging the human in domains that imply a maximally hyperbolic distance from the divine, at least outwardly, whereas Christ, although incarnate and thereby participating in the drama of human existence, remains fundamentally divine in transcending the realm of heterogeneity from which the specifically human sense of laughter and comedy stems. In other words, inasmuch as the Christ takes flesh, he must be witness to the ambiguities of the human condition and thereby indulge, albeit moderately, in the humor of terrestrial existence. However, insofar as he remains divine, his nature cannot enter into the ambiguous realm of pettiness, sin, and misery from which a specifically human sense of the comic, and particularly of the burlesque or the grotesque, flows. If humor and laughter stem from a sense of relativity and the psychic shifts that it entails, then the absoluteness of the divine vantage point would seem to deny any possibility of humor and laughter on the part of Christ.[18] As Baudelaire puts it, "the Incarnate Word was never known to laugh [. . .] for Him who knows all things, whose powers are infinite, the comic does not exist."[19] In this view of humor, for which John Morreall argues,[20] a sense for the comedy in existence is incompatible with the seriousness that results from the position of the Absolute and the spiritual urgency that it involves.[21] This understanding of humor and laughter takes stock of the idea that the indivisible simplicity of the Divine Nature renders impossible the very process of dissociation that is at the core of humor and laughter. This is no doubt what Reinhold Niebuhr has in mind when he associates Christian humor and laughter exclusively with the surface of reality: "we laugh cheerfully at the incongruities on the surface of life,"[22] thereby acknowledging the healthiness of laughter "in the outer courts of religion" while insisting that there be "no laughter in the holy of holies." Niebuhr's distinction is founded on the wide gap between the ability of religion to acknowledge and play with the incongruencies that are part of natural life, and the spiritual incongruousness of taking humor into a domain, that of the sacred, in which "laughter is swallowed up in prayer and humor is fulfilled by faith." There is no distance and no disorder within the holy of holies, and only multiplicity and duality can give rise to humor and laughter. The latter are fundamentally connected to a sense of disorder and unexpectedness that cannot have any room in the Absolute or within a system of thought based upon the Absolute. In addition, and by way of consequence, the Christian perspective enunciated by the Gospels, and predicated on Christ's teachings, is so intimately focused on the idea of original sin that the latter becomes a kind of "spiritual absolute" that allows for no levity and no distance. Man is intrinsically and quasi-tragically enmeshed in the nets of sin, and there is nothing laughable about this predicament. We find this spiritual point of view expressed again and again in Christian mystical literature; such, for example, is the evaluation of the dangers of laughter according to the Orthodox teachings of Nicodemus of the Holy Mountain:

> When we take into account that our responsible and sinful life is carried on in a valley of sorrows, then even our laughter must be turned to mourning and our smile and joy to grief, as St. James the Brother of the Lord has said: "Let your laughter be turned to mourning and your joy to dejection."[23]

Any attempt at humor would seem to be a distraction from that serious stricture, and it would even possibly be harmful in that it would tend to alleviate the suffering that is the very fuel of the Christian spiritual strife. This is why Nicodemus quotes St. Basil's remark that "Christ never once demonstrated laughter, as far as the evangelical history is concerned."

Now, it appears that this philosophical point of view on the intrinsic lack of humor within Christianity might, in its turn, fail to account for the full range of Christian possibilities by absolutizing its own postulates and, more generally, failing to recognize the potential for laughter that paradoxically enters the very definition of the Absolute. A perspective that sees humor as intrinsically connected to radical philosophical relativism does not take into account the fact that a recognition of the Absolute can indeed produce an inimitable sense of humor, and that God himself, inasmuch as He is identified with the Absolute, is not tied to "seriousness" because of His own providential and all-encompassing outlook. What we would like to suggest here is that only a relatively exoteric understanding of the God of Christianity and His relationship with His Creation can be associated with a lack of humor and a rejection of laughter. If, and only if, God is posited and understood exclusively as a Supreme Being before whom the whole of Creation stands as a kind of absolute reality in its own right, then the Christian outlook, as any other monotheistic outlook for that matter, might preclude a profound sense of the comic of reality. This tends to be the case when theology is reduced to a rational exercise of the human mind exclusively focused upon the immediate and literal data of Scripture. In this perspective the world, and the ego as principle of spiritual "independence" and potential for actual rebellion against the only One who may rightfully say "I am that I am," are endowed with a kind of fundamentally autonomous reality that results in the onto-logical and moral "seriousness" of terrestrial endeavors. But such is not the case in the rich tradition of Christian mystical theology in which the mystical intuition or experience of the Divine involves an intimation of the radical "nothingness" of Creation, including mankind, before God as supreme and sole Reality. It is probably in Meister Eckhart's *Sermons* that one can find some of the most direct expressions of this reduction of all that is not God to pure naught. From the point of view of God's Essence, and the Intellect inasmuch as it is the *locus* of the Godhead, the various components of Creation are leveled down in such a way that "the very worst and the very best thing are exactly the same for this power, which receives everything from a position above the here and now."[24] It goes without saying that such a leveling down involves a greater ability to perceive the inversions, incongruities, and shifts of perspective that are part and parcel of the "laughing" way. Transcendence is not at all synonymous with "seriousness" in all respects, as is clearly indicated by Eckhart's reference to the Supreme, whose immanence within the human soul is referred to as "a power in the soul" lying beyond any human determi-nations and concepts, a power that "mocks such reverence (in word-ing such as 'refuge of the spirit,' 'light of the spirit') and the manner and is far above them."[25] This "mocking," which could very well be defined as "divine humor" consists in an ever-transcending of the limitations that human reason tries to impose upon the Divine. "Seriousness" is here on the side of the human, because man is tempted to fix and solidify the provisional outcomes of God's play. By recognizing the Godhead as transcending everything and everyone, including God as a Creator,[26] Meister Eckhart underlines the "absoluteness," therefore the supreme and unlimited freedom, of the Divine.[27] The Absolute is that which is not bound, not limited, but perfectly independent and thereby able to engage in the most mobile, unexpected, and dazzling game, a wellspring of infinite "humor." By contrast with this infinite freedom of God who, according to Eckhart, is ever "green," we could refer to trade, that most "gray" and "serious" of human activities. Alluding to Christ's chasing the merchants out of the Temple of Jerusalem, Eckhart deciphers the deeper meaning of this episode as bearing witness to the "foolishness" of those who "wish to barter with God."[28] Trade and commerce are by definition binding and predicated upon a reciprocity that precludes freedom on the part of either side in the transaction. To deal with God "seriously," humanly speaking, amounts to falling under the illusion that one can somehow deprive Him of His Freedom. Only "pure Love" is akin to this freedom because it is not founded on any expectation on the part of God. "Pure love" amounts for Eckhart to a full understanding of one's nothingness vis-à-vis God. This understanding is not only a recognition of God's Freedom, it is also, and by the same token, a participation into that Freedom.[29] The illusion of "separativeness" and egoic autonomy now collapsed, man finds himself completely unfettered by the "deadly seriousness" that it imposed upon him under the spell of an illusory freedom. His "joking" claim to independence, understood by the relativistic concept of humor as stemming from the absence of a constraining absolute frame of reference, can only end up in a tragic seriousness since it is bound to be enmeshed within the limits of his own finitude. Even though he may enjoy a sense of humor and laughter by being aware of the "interstices of absurdity" that result indirectly from God's infinite freedom, these brief glimpses in between the thread of the precarious fabric of relative existence are not enough to lift him above the realm of inescapable tragedy. By contrast, if humor and laughter can be defined as the "awareness that nothing is important in an absolute way,"[30] the man who recognizes that the Absolute, or God, is "no-thing" is in the best possible metaphysical situation to smile with sparkling wit and to engage in hearty laughter at the foolishness of earthly "trade." This mystical, or metaphysical perspective, as epitomized in Eckhart's work, might not be representative of the whole of Christianity in its historical development, but it undoubtedly corresponds to its highest spiritual possibility or its most consistent reading of Christ's teachings on the "naughting" of self and the comedy of the world. Aside from their mystical and metaphysical expressions as exemplified above, these teachings can also find some interesting echoes in other more familiar sectors of Christian scriptures and life. There is definitely a way in which Christian laughter may result from a sense of victory over evil and sin. One day, Basil the Blessed, a sixteenth-century Russian "fool," attends an edifying scene in a tavern: the owner of the place, always swearing and invoking the devil, curses a poor drunkard who has asked for drink. Upon hearing the curse of the man who sends him to the devil, the drunkard makes the sign of the cross. Basil laughs heartily, and is asked why. He answers that upon hearing the owner's curse, the devil had entered the drunkard's cup, but when the drunkard made the sign of the cross, the devil left running. Laughter consecrates the expulsion of evil because it revels in the ridiculous pretensions of the latter. There is, moreover, something deeply laughable in a situation in which even the most humble gesture in the direction of Divine Mercy on the part of an imperfect man, one who is condemned by social standards of good, can have evil run away so swiftly. This is an example of purifying laughter, the laughter of the truth to which the last word belongs, not only eschatologically but ontologically as well. As Michael Screech has rightly noted in his discussion of Erasmus' concept of Christian laughter, "The Christian (for Erasmus) is touched by the Infinite and will not only have the last laugh at the end of time: even now he laughs more insanely than the worldlings."[31] The laughing reversal of spiritual fortune that is staged by Basil's story is echoed in scriptural and spiritual sources. Commenting upon St. John Klimakos's *Ladder of Divine Ascent*, St. Gregory Palamas refers to laughter as the outcome of an inner experience of victory over sin through fear and trembling:

"Thirst and vigil afflict the heart, and when the heart is afflicted, tears spring up . . . He who has found this by experience will laugh"—he will laugh with that blessed joyousness which springs from the solace that the Lord promised.[32]

The profound link between tears and laughter highlighted by Palamas is directly derived from the Beatitudes: "Blessed ye who weep now, for ye shall laugh (*gelasete*)" (Luke 6:21), which is followed by its complementary warning, "Woe unto you that laugh now! for ye shall mourn and weep" (Luke 6:25). The metaphysical discrimination between the Divine Absolute and human relativities finds an eschatological reflection in the spiritual reversal described by Christ. In this respect, Christian laughter does not stem as much from a dualism that would allow for an inner dissociation as it actually results from a transcending of the tension introduced by sin within the soul, a healthy restoration of unity in joy.

Another instructive manifestation of laughter within the world of the Bible is the oft-commented passage of the Book of Genesis concerning Sarah and Abraham's laughter. Upon hearing that she will be given a child while she is very old, Sarah cannot but laugh. This can be interpreted as a kind of incredulous laughter, the laughter of human powerlessness and lack of faith. When reproached by God for laughing, Sarah denies that she has laughed, out of fear of God (Gen. 18:15).

Later, Sarah will understand this laughter in a completely different light, as if it were converted into another kind of emotion, when she gives birth to a son: "God hath made me to laugh, so that all that hear will laugh with me" (Gen. 21:6). The "human" laughter is no longer denied; it is transmuted into a "divine" laughter: all men are associated in this laughter because all may partake of God's mercy. What was an ambiguous laughter is turned into a full recognition of God's promise. Now, Sarah's laughter had been preceded by Abraham's: upon hearing from God that he will be given a son, Abraham "fell upon his face, and laughed" (Gen. 17:17). This laughter can be understood as manifesting emotions as diverse as joy, surprise, or relief. What is sure is that its power is clearly implied by the fall and prostration that accompany it. Abraham literally "explodes" upon hearing God's words. Louis Massignon considered Abraham's laughter as an "axial" experience, that is, a mode of direct awareness of God's transcendence, a laughter quenched at the very source of the divine. This laughter is akin to a swift removal of limitations: Abraham's laughter at his hearing God's promise of a son should be understood as a sudden understanding of the disproportion between "human impossibility" and "Divine All-Possibility," so to speak. Such laughter involves an abrupt shift of metaphysical level, and it is as such akin to the holy fool's loss of balance.

The analogies, but also the clear demarcation, between the Christic model and its imitation by the holy fool appear no less clearly with regard to the theme of the concealment of sanctity. This theme is one of the primary aspects of the holy fool's ethics, as exemplified by Symeon, since it is essential to his functioning under the mask of folly. This is a feature that is by no means exclusively Christian and it can in fact be found in other spiritual climates, such as *Malâmiyyah* spirituality in Islam. However, the extreme obscurity and precariousness of Christ's birth, his humble life, and his association with simple folk are already indicative of a particular Christian emphasis on the Divine being hidden in the eyes of the world. Moreover, from the standpoint of spiritual anthropology, it is not surprising that the aspect of concealment should be particularly highlighted in the Christian perspective since it is centered upon the need for a divine redemption as a response to the radical impotence of the human will. The affinity of Christianity and the way of outrageous "concealment" is all the more obvious when one considers Frithjof Schuon's assessment of the way of "blame" and "concealment" as being centered on the will rather than on intelligence, or as addressing primarily passional men rather than predominantly contemplative individuals. In other words, the need to conceal one's good actions or one's high spiritual state may be deemed to be predicated on an obsession with the obfuscating power of the egoic soul at the expense of a serene consideration of the objectifying function of the Spirit, or intelligence, as a divine dispensation. Criticizing the behavioral excesses of certain mystical schools and individuals, Schuon contends that such excesses do not conform to the norm of mankind; they are simply exaggerations that result from a disproportionately acute sense of the Fall, and a de facto ignorance of the sacramental virtuality of intelligence. Schuon's perspective on the matter is clearly normative, which does not mean that it excludes perspectives and occurrences situated outside of that norm as illegitimate in certain spiritual, psychological, and social contexts. Let us note, in addition, that Schuon himself is prompted to suggest that no absolute line should be drawn between the type of the "passional man" and "man as passional." In other words, to think that one can exempt oneself from the ambiguous predicament as a human being and remain immune from the measure of compensatory "excess" or "imbalance" that it entails would be tantamount to an underestimation of human limitations as such. On the other hand, it goes without saying that these limitations are, from a higher point of view, a pure naught, and that divine grace can liberate us from them at any instant.

Be that as it may, it remains that the Christian outlook is particularly given to emphasizing the seductive power of the soul and the impotence of the will, and that, being itself a kind of divine "excess" or "folly" responding to the disequilibrium introduced by the Fall, it can easily give rise to spiritual attitudes of "concealment" for the sake of humility or self-humiliation. These attitudes were not unknown to pre-Christian wisdom, especially in Greece, but Christianity gave a particular color to them. In this connection, Derek Krueger has developed an interesting parallel, and contrast, between the type of the Christian holy fool, as exemplified in Leontius's Symeon, and that of the Cynic philosopher, as epitomized by Diogenes of Sinope.[33] The analogies between these two types, and the likely influence that the latter had in helping define and describe the former, are little doubted. One finds in both the Cynics and Christian fools the same rejection of social conventions in the name of a higher type of consciousness. Now, it is quite clear that the latter is defined in a very distinct way in each case. The divergence of opinion, among Church Fathers, concerning Diogenes and the Cynics, is in itself highly indicative of the extent and limits of the parallel. All in all the positive evaluation of Diogenes by Christian writers focuses on his asceticism and rejection of luxury and earthly values, whereas negative reactions—sometimes from the very same writers—emphasize the extravagance, uselessness, and ostentation of his behavior.[34] In itself, the discordant aspect of these reactions highlights the ambiguity of the Christian conscience as it finds itself summoned to choose between the absoluteness of its claims and worldview and the need to accommodate these to the realm of social life. From a Christian standpoint, the latter concern is not necessarily to be depreciated since a Christian society cannot de facto function without a measure of horizontal equilibrium. Aside from this particular evaluation of conflicting concerns, the central tenet of Christian critics of philosophical "social ascesis" lies in a consideration of the subjective roots of outer manifestations. On the one hand, Christian apologists such as St. Basil of Caesarea applaud Diogenes' ridiculing of the world and its illusions;[35] on the other hand they chastise him for his own vanity and glory in taking an opposite stand to the vanity and glory of the world. Along these lines, St. John Chrysostom draws a contrast between Diogenes' astonishing ostentation and Saint Paul's inconspicuous decency. The fact is, still, that the same arguments could be directed at St. John the Baptist, and even at Christ to some extent. The crux of the matter lies no doubt in the Christian apologists' view that no human virtue or attitude can bear real spiritual fruits outside of the Spirit, and that Diogenes' asceticism cannot but fall, therefore, into a kind of *doxa* of its own making. The same external attitudes can proceed from radically different principles and intentions. Diogenes, and the Cynics in general, founded their outrageous behavior upon an understanding of nature (*physis*) that they felt had been betrayed, or lost sight of, by human civilization. *Physis* is in that sense constantly masked and repressed by *doxa*, the social "opinion" that Socrates also considered as a fundamental obstacle to the recognition of truth. The Greek word *doxa* is itself akin to a verb (*dokein*) that refers to appearances, or illusions. Diogenes' philosophical position consists in conveying a sense of reality by shattering the veils of *doxa*, the reaching of such a goal entailing a measure of emotional violence and disturbing oddity. Most of Diogenes' spectacular pranks[36] were connected to natural needs and suggested how civilized life was hypocritically and illusorily trying to suppress these needs, or at least hide them under a veneer of "civil" behavior. The famous story of Diogenes going through the city with a lamp in full daylight in quest of a "man" is also suggestive, as an existential riddle, of the same concern for a primordial "authenticity" that is more often than not excluded by urbanization and its negative consequences. Now it is quite clear that Christian holy fools are not as much interested in such a restoration of nature as they are intent on subverting both the "cultural" and "natural" dimensions of human life. Nature is not exempted, to say the least, from the corruption resulting from the Fall; it actually bears the imprint of that Fall. It is for that matter quite telling that even actions that might externally appear to be similar to that of Diogenes are, in Symeon's case, prompted by motivations that run contrary to a concern for a recognition of nature. It is so that, when finding himself in need of performing a "call to nature," "he squatted in the market place, wherever he found himself, in front of everyone, wishing to persuade (others) by this that he did this because he had lost his natural sense."[37] It is not, therefore, a sense of nature that is sought, but rather a suggestion of madness predicated upon a desire to hide one's sanctity and to produce a shock. This is also obvious when the saint is led to perform a miracle, a quite "unnatural" feat in itself, since his first reaction following such a performance consists in running elsewhere to behave in an inappropriate or incongruous fashion. Let us note that this spiritual "strategy" is not only, as it may seem, founded upon a consciousness of man's fallen nature and the ego's tendency to glorify itself, but more generally by a desire to underline the purely divine origin of miraculous events. The scandalous behavior of Symeon is in other words a way of suggesting, in a most graphic way, that every good proceeds from the only Good and not from human merits or gifts as such. The fact that a miraculous event may take place through the agency of a human receptacle seemingly full of miseries is a clear indication of the transcendent power of the Divine. By erasing the "human traces" of the Divine Good, as it were, Symeon might prevent a shortsighted worship of the human receptacle at the expense of a full consciousness of the freedom of Grace. This raises the more general question of the effectiveness of the fool's "strategy"[38] since we must remember that his sacrificial path is entirely founded on an intention to save others. In this context one can obviously object that the very disconcerting, at times disgusting, deportment of the saint is both too sibylline to be understood by most people, and possibly counterproductive in that his excesses might discredit religion in the eyes of some. In other words, well-meaning and pious citizens may be rightfully scandalized and unsettled by his eccentric comportment. A passage from Leontius's text might help us address these objections; it indicates that "some of his deeds the righteous one did out of compassion for the salvation of humans, and others he did to hide his way of life."[39] The former refer to miracles and secret charitable deeds; the latter are related to his naughty pranks. Now one must note that the two are profoundly associated. Symeon's methodical vocation consists in penetrating the lowest realms of urban life in order to bring the light of Christ into the most sinful and dark places of the city. He could presumably not have done so had not his external deportment clearly made him an outcast and a marginal figure in society. By being a fool he is free to associate with prostitutes, shady dealers, and the riffraff of society. Those who lack a spiritual intuition of the meaning of his behavior, and who are primarily scandalized by the latter to the point of being shaken in their beliefs, reveal in consequence the superficial formalism of their religious perspective. It may even be argued that Christ would have scandalized them as much as he did the Pharisees when he associated with individuals of bad repute. On the other hand, one has a sense that Symeon has indeed transcended the realm of self-consciousness out of a state of spiritual elevation that appears to border on ecstatic inebriation. After having rushed into a female's bath one day, arousing a storm of indignant violence toward him on the part of women, he explained that he was able to bear with the blows and the shame and remained perfectly indifferent because he "felt neither that (he) had a body nor that (he) had entered among bodies, but the whole of (his) mind was on God's work, and (he) did not part from Him."[40]

In a sense Symeon's whole personality is an enigma, or a paradox, and his life bears witness in that way to the paradox of faith. This enigmatic character is akin to a kind of muddling of human coherence and language. It bears stressing that Leontius's remark that "he played all sorts of roles foolish and indecent, but language is not sufficient to paint a portrait of his doings"[41] alludes to a way of humbling purely human means of ascertainment. When adding that "sometimes also he pretended to babble, for he said that of all semblances, this one is most fitting and most useful to those who simulate folly"[42] Leontius also suggests a deliberate "spiritual practice" of pitiless jumbling of rational and linguistic coherence that can be read as a symbolic subversion of the domain of the human *logos* and wisdom according to the flesh. Reason and language are not considered here as distant but valid reflections of the Spirit, or the Intellect: the dimension of discontinuity between the former and the latter is, on the contrary, emphasized to the point of apparent absurdity. This does not exhaust, nor necessarily define, the Christian outlook as such, but it certainly bears witness to one of its fundamental aspects, *credo quia absurdum est.* Set on making use of this absurdity for the sake of the only meaning that matters, Symeon builds by destroying, and he affirms by negating; but both his destruction and negation are predicated on a higher realm and a true word. As such, he embodies the very spirit of sacred humor, and he illustrates the point that—in

M. Conrad Hyers' words—the,

> same humor that profanes the sacred is also a prophetic voice raised in
> the wilderness, a comic figure or "holy fool" dressed like John the
> Baptist in camel's skin and eating locust and wild honey, making
> straight the way, [. . .] in its own outrageous manner it is an agent of
> redemption, [. . .] or in its very opening up of the sacred cosmos to the
> profane chaos, it bears witness to a faith in the ontological priority of
> cosmos over chaos.[43]

This utter paradox is expressed most acutely in Leontius's remark
according to which "the gestures which caused some to believe that
Symeon led an irredeemable life were often those through which he
displayed his miracles."[44] Several instances of the narrative present us
with a situation in which Symeon's deeds bring about divergent opin-
ions among different people.[45] The clown's deportment is thus a kind
of discriminating or catalytic phenomenon. Confronted with the disconcerting aspects of his behavior some people are taken closer to
God while others are on the contrary taken away from His mysteries
and ways. The symbolic language of the fool is therefore a kind of protection against the "swine" who would be all too ready to "consume
the pearls." Or it simply alludes to, and makes manifest, different
degrees of understanding of the Kingdom of Heaven.

Symeon's ways are fundamentally regenerative, especially when
making use of all that death entails in terms of transformative power.
In that sense, Harvey Cox's remark that "clowns personify the hope
for rebirth in a dying civilization"[46] strikes a particularly meaningful
chord when situated in the context of Symeon's spiritual work, and it
applies fittingly to the more general function of Christianity within
the ancient world, as represented by the figure of the "Christ clown."
This remark is also indicative of the overall spiritual meaning of laughter
as a victory over death and decay. Conversely, the derisiveness of the
clown bears witness to this very decay and the impending death that
it announces. There is something carnival-like about decadent and
decaying worlds: they are like an expression of the exhaustion of all
possibilities, particularly those that had until then been left aside, marginalized, or repressed. In his *Feast of Fools*, Cox argues that, although
this function is particularly relevant today, what he calls the "Christ
clown" had antecedents and roots in the past. This held true in
the very early stages of Christian history rather than during the
"Constantinian" age, for reasons that have to do with the liminality
and marginality of the age of catacombs and persecutions. In this

context, mention must be made, in the art of the age of catacombs, of representations of Christ in the form of a man with the head of an ass. In a sense, this unexpected representation is a suggestive image of the incarnation, God's assumption of even the lowest terrestrial form. Be it a symbolic allusion or caustic parody, there is no question that such representations imply an ambivalence highly representative of the situation of Christians "in the world" but "not of this world." The theriomorphic aspect of this depiction of Christ, as some critics have noted, is also in keeping with the semi-animal representations of gods in ancient worlds, especially in Egypt. In other words, the animal might not as much refer to a terrestrial creature as it does to a divine archetype, and the universal qualities that shine forth through it. Be that as it may, the parallels that Cox and others have drawn between Christ and the figure of the clown, as manifested respectively in ridiculing authorities, a wandering life, mingling with lowly or ill-reputed social classes, and the final parodic crucifixion, would also point to this vision of the "Christ clown." In paralleling the earliest and the latest phases of the history of Christianity with respect to the role and manifestations of the "Christ clown," Cox argues that both periods, albeit in different ways, suggest the same problematic relationship between Christians and the world. He claims that when the "established Church" reigned, during most of Christian history, the "comic Christ" went "underground" and manifested only very episodically.[47] In other words, when the Church is "underground" the Christ clown appears in full light; when the Church manifests itself in full "glory," in the world, then the comic Christ goes underground. There is a spiritual reversal that highlights two different dimensions of Christianity, the "comic" side being like an emblem of the inner dimension of the religion. Now, while the Christians of the catacombs were able to symbolize their social "folly" by the figure of the Christ donkey, does it mean that contemporary signs of Christian affinities with the Christ clown—in modern theology and the arts, for example—should be recognized as indicative of a same, or at least analogous, predicament? In order to be able to answer this question affirmatively, Cox encapsulates the contemporary view of the Christ clown as follows: "so we clothe Christ in a clownsuit, and that way we express many things at once: our doubts, our disillusionment, our fascination, our ironic hope."[48] On the basis of this statement, it appears that the contemporary "Christian comic" stems from an increased inner distance from faith and religion itself, and not, as in the catacombs, from a sense of being "ridiculous" and "foolish" in the eyes of the world and according to worldly measures. "Christ the harlequin" as understood by Harvey

Cox, and other modernist commentators, is not so much a figure of "mystical foolishness," as one suggesting spiritual deficiencies and fissures on the part of contemporary Christians. It is like the grotesque symbol of a self-reflexive unease with one's own Christian "being." In fact, along the same lines, theological references to Christ the clown can even become a way of subtly distancing oneself from the object of one's faith out of the incapacity to hold fast to it, a failure to identify to it as a martyr would. If and when it is so, Christian comic "levity" is on the verge of amounting to a symbolic denial of Christ. It does not replicate Peter's request to be crucified upside down out of a sense of unworthiness, but betrays, rather, a means of avoiding the "crucifixion" by adopting a "flexible" and "moving" standpoint that espouses the subversive fragmentation of the world, and saves one from the testing hardship of a conflict with worldly contemporary values. This problematic aspect of Cox's thesis appears in full light in the context of his concept of "prayer as play." Drawing a parallel between the two phenomena, he argues for a common definition of both as "disciplined fantasy."[49] Even though there is no argument that both prayer—at least in its vocal and formal modalities—and play both involve a kind of "imaginal" suspension of ordinary reality, it must be acknowledged that this suspension is of quite a different order in each case. Play cannot but involve a measure of distance, precisely because it is just "play"—a kind of parallel reality that we recreate at will. We may play with a deadly seriousness but we are all the more serious that we know it is just play, and thereby need to keep the reality of play alive in all its credible necessity. By contrast, prayer—and this holds true for any kind of prayer—involves a complete identification with its reality, an identification that excludes the least self-reflexive gap lest the very act of prayer be tinted with hypocrisy. Spiritual sincerity involves a totality that does not allow for any distance: and this is all the more true in proportion to the fact that it is the "Spirit who prays in us." This is completely independent from the fact that prayer may be carefree and joyful, or that it may be one with actions that involve a playful mood, like dancing, singing, or "playing" a part in a dramatic play.[50] But even so, the best dancers and the best actors are those who do not even allow for the minutest gap or distance within what they do: they have to be "all there." In that sense, prayer is no play at all. Now, this is only one side of the story, and we do not intend to claim that the "comic language" of Christianity cannot give access to a legitimate and effective way of challenging the modern world by making fun of it. However, this presupposes that the substance of what is presented, or alluded to, in jest, remain undiluted in the process, and that it not flow from the polluted source of a schizomorphic religious consciousness.

*   *   *

In the wake of early Byzantine hagiography of the holy fool, the world of the Russian Orthodox Church presents us with a spiritual context that shares a particular affinity with such types. The Greek *môros* is succeeded by the *yurodivy*, the extravagant and "mad" holy man that appears throughout the history of Russian spirituality. It bears mentioning, first, that notwithstanding the sporadic ubiquity of the type of the holy fool in the Christian world, the spiritual emphasis on the role of the *yurodivy* appears to be a distinctive feature of Russian Christianity. The *yurodivy* is a well-known and popular type in Russian lore and literature, and his central function is nowhere else more recurrent than in Russian hagiography. The Russian people have always cherished the *yurodivy*, and their narrative presentation of his manifestations sharply contrasts with that of Western outsiders visiting Russia. The latter, whether they be German like Taube and Kruze or English like Fletcher in the late sixteenth century, tend to describe the *yurodivy* as an exotic oddity that conjures up images of arrogance, indecency, and even diabolic manipulation.[51] This difference in treatment is most likely indicative of a certain divergence between Western and Eastern Christianity with respect to the understanding of the relationship between the limitative aspects of the social dimension and the stringent demands of spiritual ideals. One can hardly avoid the impression that the weakening of spiritual tension between these two opposite poles was not as much, or as early, welcomed as a "comforting" *fait accompli* in Russia as it was in the West. In Western Europe, at least after the medieval period, a certain erosion of Christian spiritual principles and practices may have translated into a more conformist approach to religion. This worldly leaning and formalistic conventionalism probably accounts for the lack of imagination and spiritual sensibility on the part of Western witnesses when it comes to validating the holy fools' nature and function. The spiritual impoverishment attached to such a decline in the spiritual "intelligence" of the oddly asocial ways of some of the saints, finds an interesting confirmation in the profane domain with the early disappearance of the fool in Western courts.[52] It seems that a certain spiritual sensibility to modes of presence that are not easily aligned to "ordinary" rational and societal categories has become more and more rarefied in the Christian West. It may also be that the Russian, and generally Orthodox, affinity with holy fools stems from a form of Christianity that was preserved from the pitfalls of the Western Church as a Roman "Empire," with its strict organizational centralization, and—later on—from the bourgeois and moralistic inclinations of not a few sectors of Northern European Reformed Christianity. As such, the world of Russia—and more generally the Christian East—could be deemed to bear striking affinities with the spring-like and sprightly world of Irish primitive Christianity.[53] This more satisfactory integration of an important dimension of the Christian sensibility, which joins the Christian Far-East and Far-West together in a "wild" embrace, is not without relation to the rustic and archaic popular identity of a majority of Russians: holy fools often issued from the peasantry, with which they shared a "coarse" and spontaneous—and in some ways paradoxical— sense for the otherwordly and the material at the same time.[54] The rough and primitive simplicity of Russian peasants is undoubtedly conducive to a naïve and refreshing sense of the sacred that does not shun the brutally odd either. This is also akin to the childlikeness of the *yurodivy*, his lack of mature sophistication. For if the holy fool is on the one hand like an adolescent who plays a role, or successive roles, in order to fool adults, he is in another sense a child whose inner purity is expressed through a disarming and revelatory spontaneity.[55] This childlikeness appears in the ability to rejoice at the smallest things and to consider even trivial objects as a source of wonderment and gratitude. Thus, the *yurodivy* Ivan Grigorievich Bosoj would collect wood chips, twigs, bits of glass, and pebbles and offer them to those he would meet, together with a few sayings of his own.[56] By contrast, the present hypertrophy of the mind and the hypnosis of "serious" terrestrial endeavors has made it more and more difficult for most Western people, whether they remain Christian or not, to assent to the unsettling message of divine "imbalance" when it manifests itself obtrusively "in the flesh." This is too unbearably shocking for the mental habits and the bourgeois system of values that has become almost inextricably woven into Christian practice. Any such kind of "madness" is thereby relegated to the domain of monstrous threat, expelled out of the bounds of society, if not out of reality, whereas traditional mentalities always tended to integrate psychic imbalance and "transgressive" anomalies within the fold of the world of men, since nothing real can be without its meaning and function. In John Saward's judicious words: "during the Middle Ages, the fool, whether sacred or secular, whether feigning or real, *belonged*."[57] There is, there-fore, nothing surprising in the fact that Peter the First's "emancipation" of Russia along Western lines was characterized by a ferocious rooting out of beggars, "hysterical" women, and other marginal figures. This was an attempt at "sterilizing orthodoxy" to use Irina Goraïnoff's apt phrase: an "asepticizing" of the archaic vigor and totality of Christianity in the name of Western postmedieval values. The seeds of these tendencies were already to be found, as suggested earlier, in the Western European lack of understanding of *yurodivye*, as early as the sixteenth century. Commenting on this, Irina Goraïnoff has rightfully noted:

> It is curious that none of the learned foreigners perceived the prophetic side of Nicholas (the Fool) [. . .] As Protestants, and thereby assiduous readers of the Bible, it did not come to these Englishmen's mind, imbued with their sense of superiority, that the Isaiah, Amos, and Jeremiah of the Old Testament were probably no less shocking to their own contemporaries than the Russian *yurodivy*.[58]

Such a lack of spiritual sensibility to the "spirit that bloweth where it listeth" is a result of a more and more abstract, literal, and rational understanding of scripture, which freezes its spiritual implications into reassuring and "marketable" formulae. It also characterizes a certain Puritanical understanding of Christianity that smacks of *bourgeois* narrowness and moralistic flatness.[59] In other words, the type of the holy fool has seemed more and more out of place in a theological and religious context that tends both to rationalize and socialize Christian ideas and practices. At the same time, political and social norms have tended to be increasingly divorced from spiritual principles. The figure of the Christian king lost much of its mystical aura as early as the late Middle Ages. The spiritual tension that presides over the everprecarious integration of the world of society into Christianity has rapidly lost much of its acuteness. In Russia, by contrast, this tension between temporal reality and spiritual ideal was all the more exacerbated that the figure of the *tsar* has long remained imbued with a sense of sacredness. In that sense, the pervasiveness of the figure of the *yurodivy* is historically intertwined with that of the *tsar*. The climate of mystical autocracy that permeates centuries of Russian history involves a fascination with a spiritual type that most antagonizes the central authority of the monarch while yet sharing a paradoxical proximity, if not occasional analogy, with it. The Russian autocracy found, in a sense, no other external limit and control than that of the *yurodivye*. Analogous phenomena could obviously be found in the West with the King's fool, as also in Islam with the irreverent and chastising attitudes of some Sufi mystics vis-à-vis the Sultan; but nowhere was such a complementary tension more recurrently and acutely staged than in Russia. The bond between the *tsar* and the holy fool is not only characterized by the "admonishing" function of the fool; it also hints at a mystical correspondence between the first and the last in the kingdom. This correspondence may even border on an identification. Irina Goraïnoff tells a most revealing episode of Prince Gregory and the *yurodivy* Procopius: as the prince was busy administering justice, the naked fool erupted into the room and abruptly placed the prince's *chapka* upon his own head. As a response, Gregory left his seat and set the *yurodivy* in his own place. This story, as meaningless, ridiculous, or shocking as it may be for a "rational" mind, is actually rich in meaning and refreshingly "realistic." First, it conveys a symbolic anticipation, in this very world, of the priorities and justice of the hereafter. By accepting that Procopius substitute him, Gregory demonstrated the depth of his understanding of Christian principles. Beyond this symbolic teaching, the episode also expresses the sacrificial dimension of both the kingly and clownish functions. Both the king and the fool are marginal figures in relation to the ordinary world of men; both serve the latter in a way that entails an appearance of "privilege" and "enjoyment," but which can in reality consist of pain and suffering for the sake of others. The king and the fool wear "masks": the king's mask has to do with the impersonal dignity of a function that transcends the individual. There is a latent duality between the king as a mere person and the king as hieratic embodiment of *auctoritas*. This duality is a heavy and sacrificial destiny for the individual to bear. As far as the *yurodivy* is concerned, the sense of duality is no less present, albeit quite different in its modalities. The duality of the *yurodivy* is like a symbolic dramatization of the tension inherent in man in general in his relationship with God. Meister Eckhart's distinction between the "outer man" and the "inner man"—a "synchronic" distinction that is at bottom parallel to St. Paul's "diachronic" contrast between the "old man" and the "new man"—is brought to an extreme degree of expressiveness by the *yurodivy*. His "outer man" is a spectacle for the world: he is literally a "monster," a portent of divine wrath, but in a way that is the reverse of what most people would expect, since the real "monster" is in the "respectable" beholder's eye. This is the realm of worldly "visibility," the judgment of society and of the other, whereas the true Self is invisible to worldly eyes. This invisible aspect, this anonymous reality, the "inner man," is only known by God. Symbolically, this is enacted by the binary rhythm of the typical day in a *yurodivy's* life: during daytime, he is "acting" within the world of men. This world is like a stage upon which he is aware, more than any other man, of playing a role. At night, the *yurodivy* retreats to his cell or his cabin, or under his bridge, where he prays. In a sense, "laughing John" and "weeping John" are but the two faces of the same spiritual reality. It is evident, moreover, that this binary structure is more symbolic than actual since the "spectacle" that takes place during the daytime is only the visible side of a life of permanent, and inner, prayer, day and night. Outwardly, the *yurodivy* consistently acts as a comedian; inwardly, he is constantly in orison, he is constantly "himself" before God, without any trace of "comedy." He thereby brings to the fore, in a most dramatic and caricatural fashion, the duality of the human experience in relation to God.

In the tradition of the raging predications of St. John the Baptist against Herod, the *yurodivy* is often staged in a context that endows him with the function of instrument of God's reminder and wrath. In the late sixteenth century, foreign observers noted that the *yurodivye* could accuse a prince with an uncompromising boldness that nobody else could match. Ivan the Terrible could thus be insulted with the utmost intensity by a "fool" like Nicholas the Saint. More subtly and allusively, a Russian account tells us how Nicholas, upon being invited by Ivan to share his banquet, strongly encouraged the *tsar* to eat the piece of raw meat he had served him. To the *tsar's* protestation that he could not, as a Christian, eat meat during Lent, Nicholas fulminated that being a Christian did not prevent Ivan from "drinking the blood of Christians," a daring allusion to his pillaging and murdering. The holy fool thereby embodies divine justice, or rather, he becomes its impersonal "spokesman." As a messenger of the Divine he is often clothed (if clothed at all) in the garb of a pilgrim, or a foreigner.

The association between the tradition of the holy fool and that of wandering eremitism has often been highlighted. John Saward has convincingly argued for its presence among the Irish wandering saints, like St. Columba or St. Brendan, a type that is undoubtedly related—if not historically, then at least "in the spirit"—with the Eastern *salos* and *yurodivy*. St. Symeon wandered from Edessa to Jerusalem and Emesa. He was an "outsider" in the eyes of the inhabitants of the city. One of the early Russian *yurodivye*, who was the first to be canonized specifically for foolishness, was the fourteenth-century Procopius, a German, at least as far as his reputation goes since there does not seem to be any historical evidence of his actual lineage. Being a wanderer, and sometimes a foreigner, the holy fool may appear as an embodiment of both the sacredness and strangeness of the "other world." Moreover, he is also "subjectively" a "foreigner" since he feels totally exiled in this world, which explains his oddity and his affinities with all those—beggars, prostitutes, drunkards, and simpletons—who are kept on the margin of social life. Like them, he is looked upon with suspicion, often rejected and humiliated, or even persecuted, for not sharing in the ordinary and parochial way of life of the collectivity. His whole existence is actually a scandal to society as a symbol of terrestrial complacency and perversion. In the words of Peter Brown, "the holy man [. . .] was thought of as a man who owed nothing to society. He fled women and bishops, not because he would have found the society of either particularly attractive, but because both threatened to rivet him to a distinct place in society."[60] And this "independence" from social ties, a purely "vertical" identity that is most particularly claimed by the holy fool and that situates him in the spiritual imitation of Christ's otherworldly lineage, is also the hallmark of his "prophetic" status, since there is actually a strong eschatological component in him.[61] This is why his function is particularly needed in times of spiritual decay, and also in times of political and social "tranquility," when the sharp edges of existence have been smoothed by times of relative peace and prosperity; and when Christian principles have been "conformed" to a comfortable and horizontal functioning of society. Inasmuch as human history may be defined as a gradual increase in "madness," that is, forgetfulness of what matters, the holy fool must appear as a compensatory presence and as a biting reminder of the Essential. An apothegm tells us that "a time will come when men will become mad, so that when they meet somebody who is not mad, they will turn to him and say: you are out of your mind! Because he does not resemble them."[62] This eschatological aspect is also related to the prophetic dimension of the *yurodivy*: like the Prophets of the Old Testament the holy fool prophesies in the desert—the spiritual desert of men. He warns that the end is close, standing as he does on the edge of time and terrestrial reality, deprived of the illusory support of social recognition and propriety. There is something both ridiculous and frightening about his behavior and his words. He weeps upon the state of spiritual dereliction of Christian society, and he complains about the lack of true Christians. In a sense, his function still presupposes a modicum of religious presence in society, without which there would not be any need for his admonitions and allusive riddles. But in another sense, any society, be it secular or not, could be "mocked" by the holy fool for being entrapped in its self-idolatry.

What strikes us in the accounts of clownish and "mad" behavior on the part of *yurodivye* is the extreme diversity of their ways, words, and pranks. They range from the fourteenth-century Nicholas and Theodore's boxing antics on Novgorod's bridge to the Blessed Basil's (*Nagokhodetz*) jovial laughter and walking on water in the sixteenth century, from allusive caricature to plain joy. Nicholas and Theodore were making fun of men's absurd and cruel quarreling and warring by reflecting these human evils in their grotesque mirror: only those who had eyes to see could see. There is a fresh genuineness about everything the *yurodivy* does: the holy fool is "himself" without concession. Even though some particular tricks and features might reoccur, like stuttering, roaming around half-naked, and shouting at powerful men, there is in a sense nothing more different from a *yurodivy* than another *yurodivy*. Being themselves in God, *yurodivye* cannot be "reproduced" by the social machine. Being free in Christ and only in Christ, the *yurodivy* is the most unhampered of men when it comes to the social and psychological comedy of manners. The *yurodivy* knows that in order to please God and be as God wants us to be, one has often to displease men, a truth that is expressed in the most uncompromising way by the fool Nil of the Sora:

> The good does not reside in a desire to please everybody. One must choose: to love truth to the point of dying for it and live eternally, or else do what is pleasant to men, to be loved by them but hated by God.[63]

The holy fool is an "original" in a sense that reconciles both the etymological meaning and the derived meanings of the word: his oddity directly flows from the spiritual "origin" or root of his being in God. But the diversity of the *yurodivy's* ways is not only due to the fool's utter spiritual sincerity: the wide expanse of the holy fools' behavior, from feats of asceticism like living half-naked in the midst of the freezing Russian winter to appearances of sexual impropriety, is also a way of stretching the world of human possibilities to their most extreme limits. By so doing, the *yurodivy* opens up the imagination of men beyond the confines of worldly conditioning; he opens a crack in the system of self-satisfied order and balance that is subtly built "on the margin" of God, as it were.

The marginal and ambiguous nature of the *yurodivye* may easily give rise to deviations or perversions that sometimes make it difficult to distinguish the grain from the chaff, the reality from the parody. The history of Russia is full of accounts of *yurodivye's* pranks, but it is often impossible, from the outside, to clearly differentiate the original from the copy. On the one hand, all kinds of illusions and individualistic excesses can hide behind the mask of the holy fool; on the other hand, the phenomenon itself is almost impossible to define by universal and clear-cut criteria. Still, because of the very high esteem in which they held this spiritual phenomenon, some Orthodox spiritual authorities did not hesitate to place very strict requirements and qualifications on the function of the holy fool. These conditions have been summarized by St. Seraphim of Sarov when he emphasized that a true *yurodivy* must respond to a "particular calling of God," and that he must be able to "resist the temptations of the devil."[64] The status of the *yurodivy* can only be a vocation, for only God can protect the holy fool from the multiple dangers and deviations that his slippery role entails. One cannot decide to be a fool, any more than one can decide to be anything that one is or is not substantially. What is, by definition, a kind of spiritual "hide and seek" can readily be abused by those who want to "hide" behind it, the hypocrites who play the part of cynics. This is no doubt the reason why the history of Russian spirituality is filled with ambiguous figures of disconcerting "temporary" *yurodivye* like Gregory Potemkin or General Souvorov, or pseudo-*yurodivye*, like the infamous Rasputin, whose role sometimes borders on the Satanic. From the standpoint of a spiritual criteriology, the difficulty lies, of course, in the fact that an inner call—being a "secret" between God and a given soul—cannot be easily, if at all, "verified" from outside, while—to refer to Seraphim's second criterion—the very behavior of the holy fool often makes it difficult to differentiate "temptations" from the spiritually spontaneous "breaking" of sociopsychological boundaries. This is all the more true in that the *yurodivy* takes sin upon himself, as it were, through his grotesque, shocking, and sometimes disgusting behavior. This pertains to his cathartic function vis-à-vis conformist and pharisaical concepts of good and evil, as well as pretentious illusions of psychosocial righteousness. By presenting to the world the "faces" of sin he purifies men not only from the dark attraction of evil but also from the righteous usurpation of God's judgment of good and evil. By seemingly blending good with evil, beauty with ugliness, he provides the faithful with an image of their own spiritual ambiguity, thereby preventing them from falling into presumption. The *yurodivy* "hides" his true nature in order to be able to denounce and unmask worldly "hiding," hypocrisy, and presumption. His "hiding" protects him, in a sense, but it is also, more profoundly, a mode of sincerity. "The Kingdom of Heaven is within you," which means here that inwardness cannot be reached without piercing through the surface of worldly appearances. In truth, genuine inwardness can only be perceived by God, any "exterior" recognition being, in fact, ambiguous and precarious. One must note, moreover, that the *yurodivy* does not always play the fool with everyone, precisely because not everybody is completely "fooled" by worldly appearances. Ivan Grigorievitch Bosoj, the nineteenth-century *yurodivy* from Kiev, left all his mad pranks at the door when conferring with his friend, the monk Ilarion.[65] What good would there be to play the fool with a man who has fully unveiled the foolishness of the world and his own ego? Still, in spite of occasionally confiding in certain rare individuals, his inner truth remains for the most part a mystery to others. This is true to such an extent that John Saward has even suggested that "there is hardly anyone, perhaps only his spiritual guide, who knows the truth about him."[66] Already in his lifetime, some people may have a vague sense that his "madness" is not without its share of mystery or blessings, but it is only after his death, and sometimes probably not even then, that his person might be surrounded with an aura of sanctity. Like the mystic in general, he is not in rebellion against institutions as such, but against the measure of spiritual *mediocritas* that institutions entail. Against social sobriety and propriety he "gets drunk" on spiritual sincerity. The same sincerity that manifests itself in playing the fool is also expressed, analogically, in one of the most striking features of *yurodivye*, that is, their nudity or seminudity, which are both, quite paradoxically, a "mask" and a way of "unmasking."[67] As a "mask," nudity is a way of attracting the blame of conventional people: it may thus function as a way of purifying oneself from a worldly "self-consciousness." In the Bible, the shame of one's nudity is a result of the original transgression of man, and more specifically flows from his eating of the fruit of the tree of knowledge of good and evil, "and they knew that they were naked" (Gen. 3:7). The sense of separation from God that results in shame must be, as it were, reverted so that man may not "know" himself anymore as separated and conscious of his body as a shameful trace and symbol of this separation. The "shame" before the world is a catalytic way of bringing out the "scandal" of standing outside of God's grace, so to speak. Nudity thus becomes a symbol of one's nothingness and a way of becoming reintegrated into the fullness with God. Nudity reveals to the eye the human condition in all its primordial simplicity: it hints at what lies beyond the realm of concupiscence. For many *yurodivye*, the state of nakedness amounted to a symbolic or real restoration of the prelapsarian state. Russian hagiographies also suggest two further dimensions of the phenomenon: asceticism, and spiritual consciousness. The first aspect pertains to an ideal of sanctification through penance and a rejection of all bodily comfort. This orientation goes back to the extreme modes of asceticism that the early Desert Fathers, stylites, gyrovagues, and others imposed upon themselves as mortification.[68] The example of Ivan

Grigorievitch Bosoj, who walked bare feet in the snow, is only one among many instances. The indifference of some *yurodivye* to the needs of the body can defy the imagination: it is an extreme, sometimes extravagant, kind of behavior that responds to and compensates for the worldly mediocrity that easily befalls a Christian society. This is the way nakedness is most often perceived from the standpoint of the world, namely, as an excessive asceticism confining to madness. When St. Francis and Brother Ruffino preached naked, people made fun of them because they took mortification to such extremes that they could, in their view, only be mad or naïve. The world is skilled at rationalizing and contextualizing the absoluteness of spiritual demands, so much so that whoever takes the Gospel too seriously can only be mad.

But this vision of nakedness is in fact the most exterior, and it does not do justice to the full meaning of spiritual nudity. On a deeper level, nudity can also be the sign, or the outer criterion, of a transformation of consciousness, that may be considered either as a high form of spiritual indifference or a state of mystical inebriation. The *yurodivy* does not know that he is naked in the sense that he does not know himself as being separated from God. We have mentioned an occurrence of spiritual *apatheia* and transcending the sense of the body in the anecdote about Symeon's entering the women's bath. In another sense, this indifference can be considered as a state in which the "normal" or conventional order of things becomes suspended, either temporarily or permanently. So, paradoxically, the nudity of *yurodivye* can be apprehended both as a testimony to the Fall, the need for shame and asceticism, or as an allusion to the transcending of the Fall, a recovery of primordial innocence.

The fool is an open question, a living paradox, an unresolved ambiguity. It is true that he sometimes reminds us of the "contrary" behavior of the North American Indian sacred clown. Ivan Bosoj wore boots in the summer and went barefoot in the winter.[69] It is in the space that is opened by his ambiguities and paradoxes that divine grace may enter his soul's dwelling, or that of others. The *yurodivy* does not close the door to grace through an illusion of human understanding or control. He is literally like a child. When asked questions by his visitors, Michael of Klopsk could do nothing but repeat the same questions *verbatim*, like a naughty boy.[70] Beyond the slapstick effect of such a trick, one may wonder whether the fool does not allude, in this childlike way, to the illegitimacy of most questions and the need to leave them open to God's answer. The acceptance not to be able to know is sometimes an evidence of wisdom.

Although we have insisted on the Orthodox and Russian specificity of the holy fool, we must also acknowledge, as befits our early remark about the affinity between this phenomenon and Christianity at large, that aspects and manifestations of the holy fool may be found in Western Christianity as well. In fact, John Saward's classic *Perfect Fools* is in a sense an attempt to unbury the treasury of "folly for Christ's sake" in the Western, and particularly Catholic, tradition. This can be achieved primarily by two means: an attempt at highlighting either the presence of explicit references to folly for Christ's sake in the life and works of great saints, such as St. Bernard, St. Thomas Aquinas, or St. Theresa of Avila, or of describing the general type of the holy fool in the Roman Church. The first enterprise cannot but be successful inasmuch as Christianity remains genuine Christianity: any Christian who takes his religion "seriously" will show and cherish aspects of spiritual folly, simply because "my kingdom is not of this world." The second aspect is more problematic because the type of the "holy fool" is clearly less visible, and also less recognizably "typified" in the Roman Church than it is in the Christian East. Russian Christians know what a *yurodivy* is, but how many Catholics have heard of the holy fool? There are, of course, historical figures of saints who have displayed characteristics clearly identifiable as pertaining to the vocation of the holy fool. The two most famous are undoubtedly St. Philip Neri and St. Benoît Labre. It is interesting, and revealing, to note that these two figures, as distinct as one may have been from the other, are situated at historical junctures that are critical in terms of the headways of humanistic and secular ideas and practices. Philip and Benoît may appear to epitomize, in that context, the Christian principle of subversion of worldly wisdom in the name of holy madness. In a context of human aggrandizement and delusions of mastery over one's own destiny, the theocentric and Christocentric perspective that these two saints embodied could not but find a powerful and appropriate mode of reminding society of the "one thing needful" in the humiliation of man's pretensions through folly and childlikeness. Philip Neri, born in Florence and sometimes nicknamed "the good Pippo," was a sixteenth-century Italian priest-saint and founder of the Oratory, a group gathered around his predication at the Church of the Holy Trinity. He was well known for his playful and irreverent jokes. In a period replete with self-aggrandizing worldly discoveries and realizations, St. Philip Neri incarnated a spiritually healthy sense of proportions that ridiculed humanistic and Promethean presumptions by drawing from the outrageously childlike and the downright foolish.

As Meriol Trevor underlines in his biography of the saint:[71]

> Of all the saints, Philip Neri is one most difficult to turn into a divinity or a plaster statue. [. . .] In an age of dignity and self-esteem Philip's unceremonious ways, his jokes, his habit of deflating the pompous and eloquent seemed quite extraordinary to the earnest, and even shocking to the conventional.

That he may have had such a function in the context of the Rome of the Renaissance was most likely not fortuitous. In fact, at the time that he was considering retiring as a hermit, in 1550, he received visions that told him his mission was in Rome. There was probably no time and place in the history of Western Christendom that gave rise to more blatant imperial excesses and worldly tendencies as the Papal court of the sixteenth century. Within the context of an ambience as problematic and potentially idolatrous as this, St. Philip's reported *facetiae*, such as his dancing before cardinals, are like symbols of a re-equilibriating function through foolishness, which is sometimes demanded from spiritual figures of a very particular calling. It is interesting to note that even though Pope Gregory XIV wanted to make him a cardinal, Philip declined, and that he became known, instead, as the head of the Congregation of the Oratory that was involved with both preachers and laymen. His function of presence remained therefore marginal to the ecclesial institution, and he was in fact accused by some of heresy and of trying to create his own sectarian group. In addition to his life of prayer, meditation, active charity, and predication, Neri's function was expressed in what Italians denote as *festività*, "the power of treating as a joke what one cannot really enjoy."[72] This cathartic attitude is like an alchemical transmutation of the poisons of terrestrial imperfections and evils: it consists not only in treating all tribulations with lightheartedness and joyful trust in God, but also in extracting the element of ridicule or absurdity that is buried under the immediate unpleasantness of misfortunes and breakdowns. As such, St. Philip's *festività* is essential to an integral psycho-spiritual health because it pricks the bubbles of dreams and illusions that congest the soul with their inflated nothingness. This re-equilibriating function through jest was also particularly manifested in relation to the faithful, their sins, their presumptions, and their dramatic self-importance. We know, for example, that the saint often behaved in an incongruous way with people who had a high opinion of themselves, not hesitating to pull their hair or hold their beard and chin.[73] Some of his most spectacular modes of deportment were also reminiscent of clownish and "contrary" ways, like wearing big white boots and clothes inside out, or else smelling dirty brooms in the streets.[74] These attitudes pertain to a spiritual language that is, by definition, given to a variety of levels of interpretation; but there is little doubt that it was more than the expression of a good sense of humor, or an eccentric and joyful natural disposition. Its underlying meaning was spiritual, and its manifestations could not be reduced to childish whims. As far as his teachings were concerned, his way of dealing with the ego also echoes the radical methods of some Sufis, like the *malâmiyyah*: as a priest, he would, on extreme occasions, require from some of his penitents who were particularly imbued with their "self-image" that they undress and walk out through the streets stark naked.[75] Ascetic attitudes of concealment were moreover reported on numerous occasions, although they seem to have occurred primarily during the latter part of his life, when Philip's reputation of sanctity was already established. As such, these penitential tricks were often connected to the need to hide spiritual charismata. In his mature years, because of a tendency to become entranced during his celebration of the mass, and concomitant manifestations such as trembling, inflating of his body, and levitation, he would read collections of jokes or would play with his dog before performing the holy sacrifice, in order to keep his mind distracted from these charismata and remain as inconspicuous as possible to others. The aforementioned remarks and anecdotes are enough to suggest that St. Philip Neri comes closer, within the Roman Church, to the spiritual type of the *salos* and *yurodivy*.

St. Benoît Labre's case appears to pertain to an altogether different type, which may present only partial or marginal affinities with the typological holy fool. As with St. Philip, Labre's historical and geocultural context is undoubtedly of great significance. Born in eighteenth-century France, he was a contemporary of the deist, agnostic, and atheistic *philosophes*, and he was actually destined to foresee the tragic events that marked the French Revolution.[76] In this context, "he could not [. . .]," in John Saward's words, "be more unrepresentative of his times."[77] Pope Pius IX's decree of beatification, which led to the canonization of Benoît Labre in 1883, specifically mentions the saint's virtues of humility and poverty as a spiritual antidote to, and a spiritual protestation against, the "impious sensualism that has invaded modern society."[78] St. Benoît's holy folly is closer to the childlike simplicity and obedience of the "naïve" fool than to the facetious and disruptive behavior of the "radical" fool for Christ's sake. One of the features that clearly associates Labre with the holy fool tradition lies in his attempt to attract upon himself the disgust of others so as to avoid the pitfalls of vanity and pride. This was particularly evident in his wearing of dirty and worn-out rags that kept many people away from him out of sheer physical repugnance; it was also evident in the lack of care he showed for his body and his incredible indifference to the teeming lice that were eating both his body and clothes. It is said that, at his death, six people had to work at cleaning and purifying the body of the saint from these insects that were to be found even in the beads of the rosary that he wore around his neck.[79] The outer barrier that Labre was constantly trying to build between himself and his fellow human beings also appears in his systematic fleeing of those who would show kindness and hospitality toward him.[80] Even though charity would require him to be grateful toward his benefactors, his subjective focus on a feeling of personal unworthiness as a sinner would have the last word, and he would kindly avoid any situation that could flatter and give some sense of comfort to his ego. By contrast, it is related that when children would throw trash at him and call him a madman he would slow down his pace and even stop to fully enjoy the benefits of this mortification.[81] To a lady who wanted to protect him from the humiliating vexations of a group of naughty boys, he said: "let them do, if you knew who I am, you would act even worse against me."[82] As in Philip Neri's case, but in a different way, Benoît's vocation could not be found in the context of a religious institution: his attempts at joining monastic orders, both Cistercian and Carthusian, failed.[83] Instead, he became known as a poor wanderer and pilgrim, in the tradition of the contemplative gyrovagues. His presence in the world was henceforth to be that of a foreigner and a pilgrim, a mode of sanctity that is both manifested in this world while yet not being of this world. Actually, this is not simply correct in a general sense, as it should be for all Christians, but it also holds true symbolically and vocationally in the sense that a life of vagrancy involves both a physical presence in the world and a constant "departure" from it.[84] His vocation was to be a hermit among men. Significantly, this life of wandering was not quite disconnected from a symbolic geographic center, that is, Rome, the holy city that was to become the home base of his peregrinations throughout Europe. This, no doubt, is symbolic of the Catholic specificity of his vocation, at the same time that it confirms, as in Symeon and Philip Neri's case, the particular function fulfilled by the holy fool in an urban setting. On the one hand, Benoît chose Rome—or Rome chose Benoît— because he could better preserve his anonymity among urban crowds, thereby "disappearing," so to speak, among them; on the other hand, it was for him a way of mingling with the poor and the outcast, sharing in the humble life of those who have nothing and are nothing.[85] He liked to be forgotten in the mass of coarse and simple people, he who could have claimed the spiritual knowledge of mystical doctor, in order to attend catechism.[86] Another aspect of his holy madness had to do with his distrust of language, and his occasional refusal to submit to its social usage. As with other holy fools, language became for him a riddle pointing to God, and God only. Asked by nuns on three successive occasions about a priest of their acquaintance that he had met on one of his previous stays, he answered each time: "he loves God." This is a clear example of the fool's rejection of the world-centered function of conversation and human cares, when the sharp focus of spiritual attention is abruptly placed upon the essential without any concession to the unconscious limitations of well-intentioned social and affective concerns. In keeping with the holy fool's cultivation of a bad reputation, and his tendency to attract worldly and "religious" blame upon himself, Labre seemed to relish the idea of appearing not only abject in the eyes and ears of people, but also suspicious to their minds. Once, when invited by his hosts, following dinner, to be taken to his room, he wanted to make sure that the room had a lock: "I am poor, I am a foreigner, you do not know me, you should lock me in."[87] He wanted to enjoy the humiliation of being a suspect. While the aforementioned characteristics of Labre's presence in the world undoubtedly echo some central elements of the typology of the holy fool of the Christian East, it is instructive to note that one salient aspect of the *salos* or *yurodivy* remains conspicuously absent from Benoît Labre's deportment, that is, the cultivation of social and psychological attitudes of manic disruption, seeming arrogance, and downright shocking behavior. Actually, testimonies and hagiographies present the saint as an amiable, soft-spoken, and reserved individual who would barely talk to women and would keep his eyes piously lowered to the ground. As for his devotion, it was silent and recollected, and he much disliked spiritual ostentation and outward "mystical" manifestations. On these points, one may of course attribute Labre's divergence from the expected "norm" of the holy fool to the "spiritual idiosyncrasy" of the saint. But it may also be that the emphases of his way were more particularly akin to the spiritual needs of eighteenth-century European Catholicism. The stress was on humility and poverty more than holy madness as such. It may be that modern Europe, in the prerevolution period that witnessed the onslaught on what remained of a traditional Christian ambience, was already not spiritually homogeneous enough to provide a framework for a "pure" type of holy foolishness, that which presupposes, precisely, a psycho-spiritual context in which "holy disruption" may play a beneficial role as an integrating part of Christian society. Moreover, Louis Cognet has argued that the end of the seventeenth century and early eighteenth century saw, with the theological quarrels over quietism, marked the "twilight of mysticism" in the West. This virtual disappearance of mysticism from the religious scene is no doubt symptomatic of a shift in emphasis that translates into a lessened receptivity to the disconcerting ways of the Spirit. After all, mysticism and folly for Christ's sake are most often intertwined in the history of Christian spirituality. Both phenomena place the emphasis on the spiritual dimension in an uncompromising, and quasi-absolute, manner. All mystics are "fools" par excellence in the eyes of the world, since they give themselves up to the invisible while disdaining the visible. As for fools for Christ's sake, they all bear the marks of a mystical vocation since they have turned their back on worldly ways and priorities, and have worked on turning the profane world upside down. A world deprived of mysticism is also a world without holy fools. However, when a Christian society is being clearly penetrated and alienated by elements of militant deism, agnosticism, and atheism, and not only by "natural" worldliness as in earlier centuries, the relative lack of cohesiveness that it experiences must affect the way in which holy folly manifests. Symbolic and spiritual disruption of an already profoundly disrupted Christendom is not the order of the day. Or rather, the modes of folly for Christ's sake that can and must manifest themselves do not as much pertain to a shocking breaking of the letter in the name of the Spirit, as they involve an insistence on an expression of the Spirit through a "mad" intensification of the letter. In a world that seeks to brush aside or accommodate Christianity to a purely horizontal perspective determined by a humanistic and rationalistic outlook, the fool is he who reminds people of the absolute and integral demands of religious life. Lukewarmness requires quite another treatment than hypocrisy, formalism, or self-satisfaction. The spirit of obedience, humility, and poverty that was embodied by Benoît Labre does indeed correspond to such a need. Labre's holy folly was not one of rambunctious joviality and playful tricks, perhaps precisely because such attitudes could not have drawn a clear contrast, and might possibly have be confused with the witty frivolity and disorderly transgressions of prerevolutionary France. Furthermore, Benoît was a layman and not a priest as was St. Philip Neri; the kinds of vices and faults he had to address—or he was made to address—were probably representative of society at large, that is, the effects of an increasingly secular outlook. His was not so much a function of presence within the Church as an institution, as it was for Philip Neri, but one of reminding all of the essence of evangelical virtues. In a sense, the differences between Neri and Labre can be referred to two levels of holy folly, as John Saward has proposed in his *Perfect Fools*, namely, the primary and general folly that is incumbent upon Christians in relation to the world—a mode of folly that Labre took to its extreme and most consistent form of manifestation, and the "dramatic and symbolic" folly, which, in addition to its function vis-à-vis the world, is often directed at the Church.

John Saward has argued for the existence of a Western tradition of Christian holy foolishness that he practically places on the same level as the Eastern one. Aside from eminent occurrences such as those of St. Philip Neri and St. Benoît Labre, Saward substantiates these claims of a Western tradition of holy folly by making reference to the foundational teachings of St. Paul on the matter in mainstream spirituality, as well as the persistence of regional manifestations of folly for Christ's sake, particularly in the Celtic world, including Ireland and Brittany. Notwithstanding the undeniable relevance and spiritual significance of these currents, such traditions and occurrences may be deemed insufficient to validate the claim of a Western tradition of holy folly that would be on par with its eastern counterpart. The fact that, by contrast with the situation that has prevailed in the Roman Church, the holy fool constitutes a well-defined type in the Orthodox martyrology that has involved specific instances of canonization,[88] bears witness to the limits of this claim. For one thing, the extension of this concept can be so wide that it almost loses a distinctive specificity; as Saward himself acknowledges, the "primary, Pauline form of folly is incumbent upon all who seek perfection."[89] As for the Celtic tradition of medieval Ireland, it appears, on the whole, to be characterized by an emphasis on good-hearted gaiety rather than on the specific, quasi-"technical," characteristics of the *salos* or the *yurodivy*. Finally, the "pathological" and "ascetic" madness of post-Reformation mystics such as Father Surin or Louise du Néant, another type of folly into which we have not here delved, does not seem to fit quite accurately into the patterns that are known in the Orthodox world—actual psychotic disorders entering, at least temporarily, into the definition of this kind of Western holy madness—the eastern type being more clearly reducible to phenomena of feigned psychic disorders. So, if one is to admit that the tradition of folly for Christ's sake—notwithstanding its relevance to understanding a wealth of Western European spiritual phenomena—is far from being as clearly recognizable and validated in the Catholic Church as it was—and is—in eastern Christianity, one is entitled to raise the question of the reasons for such a difference. A first line of answer might have to do with the Roman Church's imperial centralization, administration, and quasi-military organization: such a monolithic structure might not allow for marginal types of spiritual transgressions such as were common in the East. There was not enough "space," so to speak, within the hierarchy to allow for the phenomenon of the holy fool to develop fully. On the other hand, it could be argued that the Pope, inasmuch as he enjoys preeminent prerogatives of spiritual authority, would precisely require the re-equilibriating function of the "holy fool" so as to keep in balance the tension between the infallibility of his function and the unavoidable limitations of his individuality. The holy fool would, by the same token, be a reminder of the imperatives of evangelical poverty and humility in the midst of the imperial decorum of the papacy. And it could be said that such was, to some extent, the function of a few great saints like St. Francis or St. Philip Neri. Notwithstanding these important occurrences, the function of the holy fool was apparently never fully validated in the Roman Church. In fact, however, the transgressive and turbulent presence of the fool seems to have been reserved, in the West, for the periodical carnival that would place the whole Christian society, including the Church, upside down. But these fools were not holy fools; they were profane caricatures of the sacred. In other words, the principle of equilibriating transgression seems to have been, in the West, of a relatively more external and less directly spiritual nature than it was in the East where the charismatic presence and recognition of holy fools within the Church itself was consistently recognized and, ultimately, hailed.

The phenomenon of the Carnival of Fools was, in the Middle Ages, a way of releasing the tension brought about by the distance between the sacred and the profane, the spiritual and the secular. There were primarily two kinds of such periodical folly, at least in France: the New Year Feast of Asses and the pre-Lent Carnival.[90] Members of the lower clergy were involved in many of these carnivals, but there was no sense in which they could be interpreted, at least directly, as spiritual phenomena or teachings. These manifestations actually evolved into secular societies that were primarily involved in the staging of plays such as *farces*, *sotties*, and *moralités*. There is, moreover, ample evidence that the Church only tolerated them as lesser evils and that there was considerable effort, on the part of bishops, to limit and restrain the participation of priests in these events. Such manifestations seem to have corresponded to a problematic and precarious junction of the profane and the sacred, a way of integrating phenomena that were a priori discrete and incompatible. Now the fact that this integration could take place either on the margins of the Church or outside of it, but not within its sacred precinct, is a clear indication of its wide difference from Eastern models of holy folly. Here, in the West, the problem is not so much that of the tension between principles and realities within the Church, as it was in the East: it is rather one of conciliation, or articulation, of two spheres of reality that were fundamentally at odds.[91]

The problems of integration to which such phenomena point could, in a sense, be related to an interesting and penetrating hypothesis presented by John Saward. In the final pages of his book, Saward contends that Rome, or the Church of Peter, is entirely defined under the auspices of holy folly. Peter is the holy fool par excellence, as confirmed by his rendering in Native and Latino-American folklore,[92] in that he represents and manifests the imperfections, vices, arrogance, and ridicule of mankind. The stone upon which Christ is to build his Church is none other, in that sense at least, than the stone that had been cast away. The denial of Peter is both saddening and comical; it stands for man relying on his own strength and power, man without grace and without redemption. Now, such a man is ridiculous because of his pretense and vanity. There is a sense in which the Roman Church continues the pattern of St. Peter as holy fool. She is humiliated by her own shortcomings, and the Pope may become the symbol of these imperfections, and the humiliations that they entail. As the fool, the Sovereign Pontiff is both the supreme servant and supreme scapegoat: he "represents" in a most direct and concrete way the sins of the Church, and the sins of the world.[93] On the one hand, he shares in the redemptive passion of Christ as apostle of the truth; on the other hand, he does so almost "in spite of himself" or "against his will" since he does not measure up to the spiritual fullness of this function. He thereby fulfills a most crucial function of purification; for, in Urs von Balthasar's words, "Woe indeed to us if there is not a point where our common sins are concentrated and become visible, just as the poison circulating in an organism is concentrated at one point and breaks out as an abscess."[94] As was seen earlier, the fool is both a caricature and a spectacle: concentration and visibility are the means of an objectification that may prick the bubble of egoic and worldly illusions. Analogically, the blatant insufficiencies of the Church have borne witness to the Redemption by making it plain that man, and above all religious man left to his own devices, is a fool. But this purifying process of the expulsion of the poison presupposes that the organism be still in good health; or, in other words, the holy fool's function in relation to the Church presupposes a sufficient intensity in the tension between the forces of good and those of evil; or else it presupposes that the fallen nature of men and their understanding of, aspiration to, and familiarity with, theological virtues be sufficient to testify to their higher destiny while revealing the human weaknesses that stand in the way of the realization of that destiny. Such a function also presupposes, objectively speaking, that the redemptive power of the sacraments instituted by Christ be still a vector of grace that reveals the tension of man striving toward God, and by contact with which fallen human nature may appear in the "tragic" ridicule of its miseries. In order to be the supreme holy fool, the Pope and the Church need to appear in sharp contrast, nay in clear opposition, to a world that recognizes them as different, as the adversary, and thereby as the sacrificial victim of its mockeries and insults. When everybody is a fool there is no need for a fool; when a body is full of poison there is no need to make this poison "concentrated" and "visible" since its presence is evidently visible everywhere. The function of the holy fool is organic: it has a meaning only as an "odd part" of the whole. The blurring of virtually all spiritual tensions and differences within the Church, and between the Church and the world, makes the fool, in a sense, irrelevant. Before the state of the Church reaches such a final form of sickness, this irrelevance is subject to degrees, in proportion, precisely, to the loss of spiritual tension in such and such a cultural and historical context.

In suggesting a contrast between the Eastern and Western Christian treatment of holy folly, and its stronger presence and influence in the former than in the latter, we would like to delve deeper into the Western phenomena of inverted and topsy-turvy collective "folly" in the Western Church, and in Western Christendom in general. These phenomena did not simply pertain to individuals, but engaged the entire urban society while affecting the sacrosanct institutions of the Church. From the Middle Ages until the sixteenth and seventeenth centuries, the Christian West was the theater of festive parodies and subversions of the holy. First among these phenomena, the Christian Middle Ages saw the persistence of a kind of Christian version of the Roman *Saturnalia*, the Feast of Fools, which took place around Christmas at the time of the winter solstice. The Roman *Saturnalia*, which began on the sixteenth day of the calendar of January (that is, around December 17) were marked by a wild and rambunctious upheaval of all social norms. This "freedom of December" was chiefly characterized by an utter disruption of normal hierarchical relationships. Masters became the servants of their slaves, and the whole festival was like a symbolic restoration of the Golden Age, or age of Saturn, in which equality and freedom prevailed.[95] This is the era that the Hindus consider to have preceded the fragmentation of mankind into castes. It was a kind of "time out of time" that took the Romans back to a stage that preceded becoming and history, so to speak. The association of these festivals with Saturn and the winter solstice was obviously not fortuitous since this time of the year was considered a "door of the year," a time of "cosmic contraction" which, by a typical reversal, was also the time of a new beginning, thereby a period of joy and license. Beginning on the day of the winter solstice, days grow longer, and light increasingly fills the world. The coincidence of this cosmic moment with Christmas was highly significant to a Christian symbolic consciousness, since it associated the darkest moment of winter with the coming of the Light into this world. In this new context, the Feast of Fools seems to have reproduced and "christianized" the Roman *Saturnalia*, but the most interesting, and puzzling, fact lies in its involving a complete profanation of the most sacred institutions of the Church. This profanation seems to have been characterized by the convergence of two factors: on the one hand the need to give some release to the demands of religious solemnity and duties upon society, and on the other hand the desire to express, no doubt most often unconsciously, some of the most profound mysteries of Christianity within a symbolic language based on the Christian reversal of worldly values. The first aspect was manifested in the fact that these events were primarily a popular phenomenon, and that its instigators and organizers within the Church were members of the lower clergy. The part of the clergy that took part in these burlesque events was for the most part issued from the lower classes of society and it actually shared their life and cultural ambience. Since a whole society cannot be on par with the highest teachings of a spiritual discipline as demanding and exclusive as that of Christianity, it was recognized, albeit often begrudgingly, that "wine barrels would crack if one did not open them from time to time to give them some air."[96] This realistic wisdom was far from being universally accepted within the Church, though, as is testified by the fact that bishops repeatedly censured the excesses to which these festivals gave rise. However, there seems to have been a constant leeway between the official condemnation and the de facto toleration, as if a dogmatic rejection were not incompatible with a psycho-spiritual integration. This distinction between what was "taught" and what was "lived" was, in a certain way, the paradoxical trace of a wisdom that transcends the purely exoteric and puritanical understanding of reality. Let us note that the profanation to which we referred was far from being limited to relatively peripheral elements of the tradition. In fact there was even a "mass of fools," which was performed not only in cathedrals, but also in some monasteries. We have evidence of such parodies as late as the seventeenth century in Provence. On these occasions, the holy office was performed by lay members of the monastery wearing rags and chasubles worn inside out; they also held holy books upside down, pretended to read them with glasses covered with orange peels, and blew out the ashes contained in the incense-holder before covering their faces with them. Instead of reading the adequate texts, they whispered confused words and shouted in a discordant and disruptive manner. These kinds of masses were, so to speak, situated halfway between the sacred liturgy and its Satanic inversions in black magic; their therapeutic role acted as a kind of "homeopathic" treatment, serving thereby as a neutralizing factor of dangerous and negative manifestations by strengthening the socio-spiritual "immune system" of society. Beyond this aspect of "safety-valve," some parodies involved in the Festival of Fools were connected to intrinsic Christian symbolism. This symbolism is manifest in one of the variations of this Festival, called the Feast of the Ass. A whole Missal of the Ass was in fact composed in the thirteenth century: it describes in much detail the liturgical procession in which the Ass becomes the center of the cult in the form of a kind of *alter Christus*. The subversive parody is, therefore, associated with an allusion to the affinity of Christianity with this animal, which bears a cross on its back, and is at the same time emblematic of Christian "imbecility" or humiliation of human intelligence, as well as of enduring patience.[97] Another example of symbolic parody was highlighted during the election of the Bishop of Fools among the outcast or the innocents. This bishop was sometimes mounted on a donkey, and he always presided over burlesque versions of the liturgy. He blessed crowds during a mock procession. On the one hand, the Bishop of Fools was like an image of Christ humiliated in and by the world; on the other hand he was the source of a festive joy that not only released the populace from the tensions of the religious cadre, but also promoted a sense of joy and a liberation of energy prone to benefit religious life in general. In a sense, the attested association of the Feast of Fools with religious theatrical representations such as the Mysteries also demonstrates that the phenomenon was an illustration of the drama of Redemption, the drama of the Word incarnate penetrating down to the lowest strata of human reality. In addition, on a "liturgical" level, it bore witness to the profound fact that the sacred involves an entrance into a different kind of reality, and that this entrance is also part and parcel of the burlesque representation. The grotesque and parodic may appear on the verge of normative reality at the time precisely when this reality is rendered precarious by the irruption of the sacred. In this view of things, comic caricatures are almost unavoidably present in any context over which the sacred presides. The integrative and energizing role of the Feast of Fools is confirmed by the fact that, in spite of its obscene and incongruous excesses, the "profanation" that it acted out was never set in opposition to religious institutions as such; it was integrative and not destructive. The phenomenon of the Festival of Fools, in wide extension and long persistence, bears witness to a cultural situation in which the profane element introduces itself into Christianity so as to ease an integration that would otherwise be much more problematic given the distance separating principles from realities. Such a situation is, for the most part, quite distinct—and in a sense complementary—to the "logic" of "holy fools" as it is manifested in the Christian East. As we have seen, the holy fool could be considered as a kind of sudden and uncompromising irruption of the sacred within the profane, the imbalance of which results to a large extent from the polemical relationship between the spirit and the world: the spirit "breaks" the shell of the world by disrupting its horizontal "common sense" and self-satisfaction. While the Western parody of the sacred makes the latter more accessible from within the profane, the profane thereby entering the sacred to facilitate its integration, Eastern "folly" could be conceptualized as a violent entering of the sacred within the profane, the latter being pulled and dragged into the former by all means available. One way or another, the parodic, the burlesque, and the grotesque function as points of junction reaching extremes.

CHAPTER 10

THE PEOPLE OF BLAME

When dealing with the relationship between spirituality and madness, it is helpful to begin with the straightforward observation that medicine is a response to sickness and that the definition of sickness presupposes an understanding of what is meant by health. No doubt, health may be considered on a variety of levels, beginning with the two distinct planes of the soul and the body that are, in the Islamic *Weltanschauung*, the respective domains of spiritual psychology and medicine. In the context of this present essay, we focus on the former, more specifically on the relationship between the soul (*nafs*) and the spirit (*rûh*) that lies at the core of the Islamic mystical science of the soul. However, it should be emphasized from the outset that physical sickness is, according to Ibn Sina—following Empedocles and Hippocrates—the result of a rupture of equilibrium between the various "humors" of the body.[1] Thus, it cannot be isolated from a wider cosmological system of correspondences between animic and physical realities that presupposes a profound connection between inner states and bodily affections. In Islamic traditional medicine, the four "humors" of the body correspond to the four cosmological elements: "black bile to earth, phlegm to water, blood to air and yellow bile to fire."[2] These correspondences emphasize the "natural" foundation of health as an orderly set of relationships. Any physical disease is therefore fundamentally connected, either directly or indirectly, to a loss of balance that bears witness to a separation from a primordial norm of being. The *Qur'ân* itself refers to the "hypocrites" (*munafiqûn*) as to those who are "sick in their hearts" (*fî qulûbihim maradun*) (33:60). This, in itself, is a clear indication that sickness is a reality that originates in spiritual and animic stratas of reality. Bodily health is, in this view, inseparable from that of the health of the soul.[3] In the perspective of the *Qur'ân*, "health" refers more specifically to a state of integrity or totality[4] that can be identified in a very general sense with the *fitrah*, the primordial norm or the original state of mankind. From a Quranic standpoint, the loss of the *fitrah* amounts to a straying from the *shahâdah*, the Islamic testimony of faith, that reads in Arabic *lâ ilâha ill' Allâh*, literally "no divinity if not the Divinity." In other words, what could be called "ontological sickness" is akin to *shirk*, that is the "association" of other realities to God with all the spiritual and moral consequences that this association involves. In this context, it is important to bear in mind that for Sufi gnostics the *shahâdah* does not simply mean the affirmation of one God as opposed to a plurality of gods—which would ultimately be, as Henry Corbin has pointed out, a kind of idolatry like any other[5]—but also and above all as a testimony that there is only one Reality and that all realities "are" only in so far as they "participate" in this Reality, as the drops of water that form the ocean. Consequently, any fault, vice, or transgression fundamentally amounts to an existential *shirk*, or association, that envisages creatures independently from the Reality that sustains them in their being.

From an epistemological standpoint, the *shahâdah* is considered by many Muslim mystics as an expression of intelligence as such, or as a ray of divine light. It is ultimately linked (*'aql*) or identified with the Spirit (*rûh*) since only that which "is" in some way the One may affirm the metaphysical unicity of the One without contradiction or hypocrisy. As for the central agency of denial of truth, it is the tenebrous soul (*nafs al-ammârah*), divorced from the spirit or disconnected from intelligence, which absolutizes the individual status of man and the passions that ensue from it, thereby severing him from his Creator by claiming an illusory metaphysical independence. All disorders, imbalances, and forms of degeneracy result from this existential error and, in a sense, all sicknesses are manifestations or symbols of it.

The "sick" soul must be restored to spiritual health. In general terms, Sufi mystics have two main prescriptions for the cure, two complementary remedies that are most often referred to as *faqr* and *dhikr*. Some emphasize the latter, others stress the former, but no *mutasawwif* would consider any one of the two as accessory, in one way or another, to the restoration of health. *Dhikr* can be best defined as a sustained and ultimately permanent awareness of God through the methodical invocation of one or several of His Names. As such, *dhikr* is sometimes referred to as a remedy.[6] Since the Name *Allâh* flows from the very verbal and textual substance of the *Qur'ân*, and since the fundamental message of the *Qur'ân* is God, or the primacy of God, many Sufi mystics tend to consider this Name (*al-ism al-a'zim*) as the very essence of the *Qur'ân* and therefore as the heart of the whole Islamic tradition that flows from it. In point of fact, it is important to understand that most Sufis consider the Divine Name not only as a means of reference to God, or a way of remembering Him, but also as a vehicle for His grace. This allows us to understand *dhikr* as the "divine side" of the spiritual way. Although the repetition of the Name of God is obviously contingent, at least initially, upon the efforts of the mystic, it remains nevertheless true that, from the highest point of view, the Divine Name—repeated by the mystic with a right intention and in the correct religious and moral context—holds its spiritual effectiveness from its divine "content," in the same way as the ritual and transformative efficacy of the words of the *Qur'ân* results not only from their meaning and their utterance but also, and above all, from their origin and their divine prototype (*umm al-kitâb*). There is in the *Qur'ân* an element of divine presence without which the religious emphasis on the benefits of its recitation would not be fully intelligible. If one were to define the respective modes of effectiveness of the Divine Name and the *Qur'ân* in terms of spiritual therapeutics, one could assert that the Name *Allâh*, by virtue of its unicity and synthetic simplicity, must be primarily understood as a cure through "centering" and "unifying." It constitutes a kind of negation of the negation—a piercing through the mist of the phenomenal universe, a rending of the existential veil (*hijâb*) that hides the Divine. For its part, the *Qur'ân*, or Quranic recitation, inasmuch as it consists of a multiplicity of verses and words, should be envisaged as a means of reintegration, in the sense that the multiplicity of its form and content addresses the multiplicity of the soul, thereby reintegrating this multiplicity into the unity from which it proceeds.

As for *faqr*, it can be defined as a state of perfect awareness of one's dependence upon God's will. *Faqr* is the state of the one who "has made himself independent of everything but God and who refuses anything that leads him astray from God."[7] The spiritual content of *faqr* can also be approached through reference to the state of *mudtarr* or being in spiritual "need" or "constraint." *Mudtarr* could be best defined as the state of being on an existential edge; this extremity is the catalyst of an awareness of one's powerlessness or loss of control over one's own reality; as Sara Sviri has suggestively put it: "when the seeker gives up all hope of being in control, and yet 'knows'—consciously or in his heart of hearts—that he is vertically aligned with a higher source of power, he knows surrender."[8] In some respect, the station of *faqr* corresponds to the human side of the spiritual work, since all that man can do is, in a sense, to acknowledge his own nothingness. However, *faqr* would be unthinkable without *dhikr*, at least in the sense in which an independence from everything but God presupposes a perfect remembrance of God. As for *dhikr*, its perfection is evidently incompatible with placing any reality on the same level of awareness as that of God, which is another way of saying that it requires *faqr* as its precondition. So, in a certain sense, Sufi psychology presents us with the two sides of the same spiritual reality. At its most elementary level of manifestation, "outer" *faqr* could be defined as a socially bound religious virtue that is exclusively defined in terms of conformity to the *sharî'ah*—the individual submitting himself to God's Law, that is literally *islâm*—whereas "outer" *dhikr* could be defined as the performance of the various obligatory and supererogatory devotional prescriptions. However, these relatively external manifestations of *faqr* and *dhikr* do not take us beyond the realm of the individual self since they are perfectly compatible with a lack of awareness of one's immediate and constant dependence upon God's *kun*, or act of existentiation. Of course, these practices and attitudes presuppose a mode of subservience to God and a rational and emotional recognition of His awesome power; however, they do not involve the deepest spiritual meaning of human existence, which Râbi'ah al-'Adawiyyah has expressed in the oft-quoted Sufi *koan*: "Thine existence is a sin wherewith no other sin can be compared."[9] It is this seemingly absurd predicament that *malâmiyyah* spirituality addresses in a most radical and uncompromising way.

*   *   *

One generally associates *malâmiyyah*[10] spirituality—beyond the reference to a particular *tarîqah*—with a systematic disdain for social norms, a transgressive tendency with respect to customs and conventions, and the cultivation of disruptive attitudes aimed at attracting the blame of others upon oneself. This method is sometimes based by its practitioners on a Quranic passage, which stipulates that "those who strive ardently on the path of God" (*yujâhidûna sabîli Allâh*) "will not fear the blame of anyone who blames" (*lâ yakhâfûn lawmat lâimin*) (5:54). This passage has been interpreted as referring to God's blame, and to men's blame. The *malâmiyyah* do not fear any of these two blames, since they profess to be indifferent to men's blame so as not to have to fear God's blame. Now, although such a vision is undoubtedly founded upon psychological and social realities, it does not do full justice to the profound meaning and the vocational principles of this methodical behavior. The term *malâmiyyah* refers to a variety of movements and individuals. Strictly speaking, the *malâmiyyah* originated with Hamdûn al-Qassâr and his disciples, the Qassâris.[11] Hamdûn is also referred to as one of the *abdâl*, or the hidden saints, the apotropaic figures that are referred to by Massignon as being the pillars of light of the world. These saints—who the Sufi tradition numbers at forty—are the invisible and pure witnesses of God in the world, unknown to the world and sometimes even to themselves. As appears more clearly in the following pages, this principle of unknowing is one of the keys of *malâmiyyah* spirituality.

The *malâmiyyah* inspiration, one of the main trends of the mystical milieu of Nishapur in the third and fourth century of the *hegira*, constitutes a path that is predicated upon the distinction between levels of human subjectivity. It emphasizes the discontinuity between the various levels of the soul, the deepest layer of which is the spirit (*rûh*). In his *Risâlat* on the *malâmî*, Sulamî enumerates four levels of consciousness that he defines as *nafs* (soul), *qalb* (heart), *sirr* (secret), and *rûh* (spirit).[12] These four levels of consciousness are to be understood as forming a hierarchic chain ranging from the lowest to the highest. Although the unity of the human subject is not substantially altered by this fourfold division, the spiritual psychology of the *malâmî* tends to emphasize the discontinuity that permits a differentiation of the various levels of the soul. This discontinuity allows one to understand that a lower level cannot identify with the higher level, for in doing so it reduces the higher level to its own limitations. In other words, the continuity between the various levels of the soul—a continuity without which the very idea of a subjective identity would be unthinkable— can only be envisaged from the standpoint of the highest—or the deepest—level of consciousness, and not the other way round. The spiritual goal of *malâmiyyah* psychology consists in preventing any appropriation of a higher spiritual state of consciousness by a lower one notwithstanding that, strictly speaking,[13] a spiritual mode of consciousness cannot be experienced by the lower soul: any appropriation by the soul amounts in fact to a vanishing of spiritual gleams. Spiritual consciousness pertains to the three highest dimensions: the heart, the secret, and the spirit. These refer to more and more central states of consciousness that are, so to speak, increasingly universal and "divine" and decreasingly individual and human. The science of unknowing that is at the core of *malâmiyyah* spirituality can therefore be defined as a way of placing each reality on its own level: spiritual health consists in preventing a confusion between the various levels. Such a confusion would be deadly since it would amount to a "deification" of the human individual as such, or at least of one of his deeper layers of being. Now, this type of confusion is intrinsically connected, according to Sulamî, to the very notion of inner "consideration" or "vision" of oneself (*nazar*). For the soul, to "see" is in a certain sense to "appro-priate" and therefore to "bring down." Spiritual progress presupposes a measure of "unknowing," and any attempt at monitoring this progress amounts to individualizing what pertains, by definition, to the universal order. *Malâmî* identify this individualized appropriation to the Quranic "dispersed dust" (*habâan manthûran*) (25:23).

The "blame," whether it be inner or outer, is the way par excellence to make such a perilous identification impossible, or at least difficult, by obscuring and troubling the complacent "gaze" upon oneself, keeping in mind that the *malâmî's* work is focused on the lower realms of the soul and does not center on the intellect. Their attitude is also connected to a vigilant distrust toward any kind of self-satisfaction or pleasure that would derive from acts of devotion and virtues. In his *Usûl al-Malâmatiyyât wa-Ghiltât al-Suffiyah*, Sulamî emphasizes this ascetic principle of *malâmiyyah* spirituality in a most radical way:

> They believe (the *malâmî*) that their submission is not in their hands but belongs to destiny, and that they have no choice in performing their actions. They went so far as to say that they were forbidden to find any sweetness in worship and submission because when a man likes some-thing and finds pleasure in it while looking at it with satisfaction this is the sign that he is not in a lofty position. One of them said: "Far from you the pleasure of submission, for it is indeed a deadly poison."[14]

Such an ascetic emphasis illustrates most clearly, once again, that the *malâmiyyah* perspective is, in a certain sense, centered on the low-est levels of the human subjectivity, inasmuch as its starting point, or principle, is the congenital limitations of the concupiscent and indi-vidualistic soul (*nafs*). In this respect, *malâmiyyah* spirituality tends to embody a perspective that may be considered to be at odds with the general climate of Islam. The *Qur'ân* centers its reminder on the use of intelligence as a means of connection with God and it repeatedly appeals to this intelligence in man. Although the deceptiveness of the lower soul is also a major Quranic theme, man is far from being defined by the *Qur'ân* in terms of identification with his *nafs*. The *malâmiyyah* inspiration, by contrast, appears to be less intellective in its principle since, as was seen, it lays strong emphasis on the opacity and distorting power of the soul.

Two fundamental methodical tendencies derive from this perspective: (1) the need to hide the "good"; and (2) the benefits of manifesting the "bad." The imperative of concealment refers, in the general context of Islamic mysticism, to a tendency to place high value upon the hidden, and the covered. *Al-Bâtin* (the Hidden) is one of God's names that is most often referred to by Sufi mystics. Moreover, the very term *majnûn*, as epitomized by the mad lover of the same name, implies in Arabic the idea of concealing and covering. The *majnûn* is a person who is possessed by the *jinn*. But the same root, akin to *junûn*, also pertains to what is covered; so it is also for the *jannat*, the "hidden" garden. However, what differentiates the *malâmiyyah* "covering" from the "mad" mystic's "concealment" is that it is actively and purposefully pursued. Even though some of the behavior of the *malâmiyyah* might externally resemble that of the *majnûn*, the internal intent of the former precludes the element of passivity that is attached to the latter. To the *malâmiyyah* could be applied the verb *tajânna*, to feign madness.[15] Commenting upon the man of blame in his *Mi'râj*, the nineteenth-century *shâdhilî*, Ibn 'Ajîba, defines him as "one who does not manifest anything good outwardly and does not hide anything bad."[16] As we shall see, these two tendencies may give rise to seemingly contradictory types of behavior that are respectively "conformist" and "aberrant." Concerning the first of these tendencies, Sara Sviri defines *malâmiyyah* as follows: "The main aim of the Malâmatiyya is to reach a stage in which all one's psychological and spiritual attainments become totally introverted."[17] This utter occultation finds its spiritual models in the ascetic climate of early Islamic mysticism. The figure of Uways Qaranî[18] is most representative in this respect: Farid-ud-Din 'Attar tells us that "during his life in this world, he (Uways) was hiding from all in order to give himself to acts of worship and obedience."[19] 'Attar also relates that the Prophet had declared at the time of his death that his robe should be given to Uways, a man he had never met in this life. When 'Umar looked for Uways during his stay in Kufa, he asked for a native of Qarn (the home town of Uways) and was answered:

> there was one such man, but he was a mad man, a senseless person who because of his madness does not live among his fellow country men [. . .] He does not mingle with anybody and does not eat nor drink anything that others drink and eat. He does not know sadness nor joy; when others laugh, he weeps, and when they weep he laughs.[20]

We can already perceive here, in the case of an early mystic like Uways, the dual—and seemingly contradictory—spiritual vocation of "obscurity" and "eccentricity." The unassuming figure of Uways[21] is at the same time blatantly discordant within the social context. This discordant status, which is willingly referred to as "madness," is the mark of the irruption of a transcendent, vertical perspective within the world of terrestrial horizontality. It is akin to a negation of the negation: the Spirit "negates" the distorting perception of the soul, her biases and comforts.[22] When Uways finally meets with 'Umar, he tells him that it would be better for him that "nobody (but God) would know him and had knowledge of who he was." This principle of spiritual *incognito* can be considered as a seed of *malâmiyyah* spirituality.[23] However, *malâmiyyah* will tend to apply this principle in a way that amounts to opting for the spiritual "desert" of solitude among men rather than choosing a flight toward the physical "desert" of nature. In this sense, the *malâmiyyah* orientation manifests itself as an apparent involvement in exoteric sciences, in the *sharî'ah* and in *adab*.[24] As Ibn 'Arabî has expressed it: "God has imprisoned their outer states (the *malâmiyyah's*) in the tents of habits and worships of outer actions" (*Futûhât*, I, 141). In this respect, *malâmî* will primarily appear in the forms of rigor and separation. Their outer manifestations are a testimony to the divine Majesty (*jalâl*) that finds a human receptacle in an extreme mode of *'ubudiyyah* or servitude. Thus, we read in Sulamî's *Usûl*:

> When they (the *malâmî*) attained a high degree and were confirmed as the people of proximity, connectedness and gathering, the Truth was jealous of their being unveiled to their other people so that He showed to human beings only their exterior aspect which carries the meaning of separation, so that their state of proximity to the Truth be preserved.[25]

It is important to stress that the *malâmiyyyah* is presented by Sulamî in terms that strongly suggest a vocational way or a spiritual calling—God is the inducing "agent" of the *malâmî* orientation—that precludes any kind of "experimental" choice or individualistic whim.

The early tendency of the *malâmiyyah* to hide their states (*talbîs al-hâl*) may be converted, on the basis of the same spiritual premises, to an open manifestation of states. In the history of Sufism, Shiblî provides a kind of model for such attitudes. In Shiblî's case however, the prime motivation seems to have been one of self-protection. The Sufi who wants to be sheltered against exoteric suspicion can escape legal responsibilities by plunging, or appearing to plunge, into the world of "madness" or manic externalization of spiritual moods.[26] In another sense, this attitude can become a symbol of spiritual consciousness: "madness" representing then the violence of the divine pull on the soul, and "sanity" the cold hardening of the soul. Shiblî is quoted in 'Attar as having declared, along these lines: "May God augment my madness and your sanity, that by reason of that madness I may be admitted nearer and nearer, and because of that sanity you may be driven farther and farther."[27] The very intensity and frequency of the spiritual practice, the *dhikr* foremost among others, can be equated by ordinary tepidness or indifference to the raging fire of madness. Besides its symbolic value, however, the whole methodical meaning of such spectacular exteriorization of higher modes of consciousness is epitomized by the spiritual thrust of Bistâmî's famous utterance to his disciples, "Verily I am God; there is no god but I; therefore serve me." According to 'Attar this scandalous statement was not theopathic, as was Hallâj's "*Ana'l Haqq*," in that it expressed a desire, on the part of Bistâmî, to remove himself from the path of his followers, his intention of not standing in the Divine Light as it were.[28] The Buddhist story that says that, should one meet the Buddha on one's way one should kill him, is very much akin to Bistâmî's spiritual teaching. By appearing to be arrogant Bistâmî reveals the most profound meaning of humility, effacement in the Divine Will, while preventing his person from becoming a subjective idol for his disciples. The problem is not Bistâmî's, if one so put it, but it is potentially that of his disciples. Bistâmî's utterance is like a *koan* for those who have ears to hear, or it is like a scarecrow for those whose understanding is blurred. In that respect, Bistâmî's enigmatic utterance is not without analogy with the *malâmiyyah* moral "techniques" used in order to deflate the ego: to some they are an opening, to others a veil. But even the veil is a benefit, since it solidifies the limited understanding of those who cannot go further, thus preserving this limited understanding as a protective wall against worse possibilities. In other words, the folly of *malâmiyyah* speaks to each and every one his own language, and brings him back to what he is. The "folly" of the *malâmiyyah* is not, however, to be understood as a strictly calculated method, since it implies an element of inspiration, "disposition," or "state" (*hâl*).[29] The mystic is lead to behave in a way that may make no sense to others or even to himself, as if to suggest the unintelligible substance of relativity of this world. As a consequence, Ibn 'Ajîba defines the *malâmî* as one who "hides his taste of sanctity and exteriorizes states that make people flee his company."[30] This type of manifestation will tend to situate the mystic in an apparently transgressive posture toward the *sharî'ah* and in a disruptive situation vis-à-vis the common traditional and societal practices, *adab*. Forms, whether they be psychological, moral, or social, are therefore considered from the standpoint of their inadequacy vis-à-vis spiritual realities. The world of forms, even though they may be traditional, is a kind of scandal that must be "scandalized" in order to suggest "real" normality. It is so that *malâmî* ordinariness can actually result in the cultivation of a bad reputation. According to Muhammad Pârsa, a Naqshbandî figure from the ninth to the tenth century, the fact that the Prophet was called a liar, a madman, and a poet was a kind of veil through which God hid him from the eyes of the world.[31] In the same way, the *malâmî* bases his perspective on the idea that sanctity can only be "abnormal" and shocking in a world that is defined by the law of spiritual gravity. In other words, in a sick world, health can only appear in the guise of illness. Moreover, on a microcosmic level, the spirit appears in all its "poverty" and "sickness" from the standpoint of the soul. Titus Burckhardt illustrates this in terms of the reoccurring mythological theme of the "royal hero who comes back to his kingdom under the guise of a poor stranger, or even of a mountebank or a mendicant."[32] In the same perspective, Sulamî quotes Abû-l-Hasan al-Husrî's comment that "if it were possible that there be a prophet (after Muhammad) in our days, he would be one of them (the *malâmatiyyah*)"[33] A prophet could only be unassumingly hidden or scandalous in times when the world has become a spiritual wasteland. He would be either totally inconspicuous or else so "different" and "marginal" that he would shock even those—and perhaps especially those—who profess to be religious.

*   *   *

The *malâmiyyah* are fundamentally saints "in the world" not to say "worldly saints." As Ibn 'Arabî (*Futûhât*, III, 53) describes them:

> The *Malâmiyyah* do not distinguish themselves in anything from any of the creatures of God, they are those whom one ignores. Their state is the state of ordinary people (*al-'awâm*), and it is for this reason that they have chosen this name for themselves and their disciples: they do not cease to blame their soul on the side of God, and they do not accomplish any action in such a way that their soul would rejoice for it, and they do so in order to be forgiven by God.

The *malâmî* does not escape the world but works within it as a hidden warrior in the "greater *jihâd*." He may have an inclination to solitude and retreat but his destiny consists in being a spiritual presence in the world. Actually, by contrast with usual Sufi practices, the *malâmiyyah* way tends to de-emphasize the role of communal structures, organizations, and collective practices, including *majâlis* and *samâ'* in spiritual life. It could even be said that *malâmiyyah* spirituality is akin to the Sufism "without a name" in the earlier times of Islam, before Sufism became "recognizable" as a set of institutions and specific collective practices. The Naqshbandî and Shâdhilî orders are the most representative examples of this orientation in the world of Sufism, since they tend to place the emphasis on inner *dhikr* and social "inconspicuousness."[34] In this sense, the *malâmî* embodies one of the most fundamental tenets of Islamic spirituality, a spirituality that radiates through the most daily and ordinary presence in the world. The splendor of the *malâmî* is purely inward and does not reveal itself outwardly in a spectacular fashion. The mystic is like the Prophet who "talks to people and goes to the markets." This unassuming way of being is parallel to a distrust toward the more representative methodical supports of Sufism, spiritual retreat (*khalwah*), and spiritual concert (*samâ'*). These practices are held in suspicion by most *malâmî*. It is important to understand, in this respect, that *malâmiyyah* objections to *khalwah* and *samâ'* have nothing to do with the intrinsic value and goals of these methodical elements. They are merely directed at the dangers and abuses of these practices. However, the very fact that *malâmî* would focus on these dangers and abuses is indicative of their propensity toward pessimism when it comes to the human soul. In his *Usûl*, Sulamî criticizes the Sufi disciples "who made the error of living in isolation":

> They delude themselves in thinking that isolation and living in caves, mountains and deserts would secure them from the evil of their *nafs* and that this retreat could allow them to reach the degree of sanctity, because they do not know that the reason for Masters' retreat and isolation was their knowledge and the strength of their states. It is the divine attraction that attached them to Him and made them rich and independent from all that is not Him, so he who cannot be compared to them in terms of inner strength and depth of worship can only simulate isolation, thereby being unfair to himself and harming himself.[35]

In the same way, *samâ'* presupposes spiritual requirements that are not met by most of its Sufi practitioners:

> (They think) that *tasawwuf* is chanting, dancing, music, poetry and attending meetings because they saw sincere souls enjoying *samâ'*; but they erred again because they do not know that every heart that is polluted by worldly things and every soul that carries some laziness and lack of intelligence does not have a right to *samâ'* and should not

attend *samâ'*. Junayd said: "If you see that a disciple likes *samâ'* you can be sure that there is laziness in his soul."[36]

The dangers of *khalwah* and *samâ'* are envisaged from the standpoint of *faqr* or lack thereof. In other words, the *malâmiyyah* assessment is once again predicated upon the distance that separates the soul from the Spirit, man from God. The self-deceptive nature of the soul may reveal itself both in the realm of rigor and in that of beauty and mercy. An ascetic isolation that is neither firmly rooted in *faqr* nor the result of a Divine attraction can only foster presumptuousness or self-glorification. In the same way, a participation in *samâ'* can encourage spiritual passivity and overreliance on external and communal supports when it is not solidly grounded in spiritual vigilance.

*   *   *

In the Sufi tradition, several questions, or objections, have been raised concerning the legitimacy of the *malâmiyyah* way from a mystical point of view. First, the *malâmiyyah* concern with blame seems to imply a focus on the individual in his tenebrous aspect (*al-nafs al-ammârah*), which may be deemed to confine him to a kind of ego-centric regime. Why concentrate on the soul when spirituality pertains to concentrating on God? This "soul-centered" tendency testifies to a path that appears to be much more based on will rather than intelligence, since intelligence would presumably be sufficient to dispel the illusions of the *nafs*. It can even be argued that the *malâmiyyah* focus on the corruption of the soul leads, paradoxically, to a *shirk* by concentrating the methodical attention upon the soul instead of concentrating it upon God. In his *Kashf al-Mahjûb*, al-Hujwîrî has proposed a critique of the *malâmiyyah* that is based upon this very line of reasoning:

> In my opinion, to seek blame is mere ostentation, and ostentation is mere hypocrisy. The ostentatious man purposely acts in such a way as to win popularity, while the *Malâmatî* purposely acts in such a way that the people reject him. Both have their thoughts fixed on mankind and do not pass beyond that sphere.[37]

In other words, the *malâmiyyah* way is deemed to be incompatible with a genuine metaphysics of essential unity, *wahdât al-wujûd*, since it de facto absolutizes the negative singularity of the complacent soul instead of focusing on the essential unity of *wujûd*. We find parallel reservations concerning the *malâmiyyah* in Jâmî's *Nafahât al-Uns*:

> However worthy of esteem and commendable the state of *malâmatî* be, it is nevertheless certain that the veil of the existence of creatures has not been completely lifted for them, and that, for this very reason, they are unable to see clearly the beauty of the doctrine of unity, and to envisage in all its purity the nature of the only Reality. For to hide one's actions and supernatural states from men is to make manifest that one still sees the existence of creatures and one's own existence; something that is irreconcilable with what is meant by the doctrine of unity.[38]

The very notion of hiding presupposes a duality of the veil and the veiled, whereas such a duality is excluded by *wahdât al-wujûd*. Along more strictly theological lines, such an emphasis may be considered incompatible with the theomorphic nature of man as *khalifatullâh* (God's vice-regent) by suggesting a fundamental corruption of the human soul that is more akin to the Christian concept of original sin than to the Islamic notion of an unfaithfulness to the *fitrah*. An extreme mystical depreciation of the self would seem to run contrary to the overall Islamic ideal of inner and outer balance. Second, the *malâmiyyah* way appears to place the mystical "interest" of the spiritual traveler above the collective demands of the religious community, therefore setting a bad example by shocking ordinary people to the point of troubling them in their faith. In other words, it places subjective spiritual benefits above objective collective balance,[39] thereby manifesting a very un-Islamic emphasis on the mystical element at the expense of the religious health of the *ummah*.

These two series of objections are undeniable on their own level. However, the substance of their critique can at least partially be addressed by considering two fundamental dimensions of *malâmiyyah* spirituality: first, the emphasis on inner *dhikr* and its intimate connection with *malâmiyyah* behavior; second, the spiritual and collective benefits of the *malâmiyyah* function of "balancing through imbalance."

To define *malâmiyyah* spirituality too exclusively as an ascetic concentration on the self that loses sight of the real Divine Self amounts to separating the exterior manifestations of *malâmiyyah* spirituality from the inner cultivation of the remembrance of God as concentration on the One. In other words, the emphasis on the fight against the *nafs al-ammârah* cannot be disassociated from *dhikr*. From this point of view, one could say that *dhikr* is an act of intelligence—or that *dhikr* is an identification with the Intellect—whereas *malâmiyyah* ascesis functions on the level of the soul; it could also be said that *dhikr* is a means of union whereas *malâmiyyah* practice is a means of distinction on the basis of this union. In other words, *dhikr* is a way of unveiling the "divine" nature of man while *malâmiyyah* practices aim at preventing a confusion between this "divine" nature and the human accidents.[40] Accordingly, in *malâmiyyah* spirituality, *dhikr* is strongly identified with inwardness, or the deepest zones of the soul, the *sirr* (the secret), or even the *rûh* (the spirit). As opposed to Sufi orders, such as the Mevlevi, which exteriorize *dhikr* through *samâ'*, dance, the vocal repetition or singing of the Name, and sacred litanies, the *malâmiyyah dhikr* is purely silent and hidden. In this perspective, silent *dhikr* is in fact less likely to be appropriated by the lower soul since, in principle, it only minimally involves, if at all, its lower levels.

It is a fact that *malâmiyyah* spirituality cannot be considered as a fundamentally intellective way, inasmuch as it is true that it presupposes some sense of duality. In most instances, it cannot be identified either with the state of the *majdhûb*, the "holy fool" who is enraptured by the love of God. Still, it is no more reducible to a mere path of action, in the sense of a way of observant and attentive conformity to the *sharî'ah*. In fact, whatever might be the level one assigns to the path of blame, the *malâmiyyah* perspective raises the important question of knowing to what extent man *qua* man, or the individual self, can identify with pure intelligence. To the extent that one may assume that some areas of the soul remain relatively unenlightened by the Spirit, one may then conclude that their integration may have to take place in a way that the pure path of intellective discernment and unity might not be able to achieve in and of itself. For certain individuals or in certain circumstances, *malâmiyyah* spirituality—among other schools and methods—tends to address these lower levels of the soul without necessarily being unaware of the intellective perspective of essential unity or of being incompatible with it; and it does so in a way that may have a particular appeal to certain spiritual temperaments, without being universally normative. In principle, the spiritual integration just referred to is effected by and through the transcendent means involved in the *dhikr*, the power of the Divine Name; but in fact, it may be that all kinds of psychic knots hinder the effectiveness of this essential means of realization to such an extent that other, more accidental, means may be needed as an adjuvant to the former. This situation is, *mutatis mutandis*, analogous—but to a much lesser extent given the further distance of the physical realm from the spiritual—to that of a body affected with sickness: the central spiritual means should, in principle, positively affect its recovery, but in fact it is most often quite ineffective in this respect. This ineffectiveness is obviously not to be attributed to a failure on the part of the transcendent means of realization; it is simply the consequence of an abnormal state of affairs that must also be addressed on its own level.

From a collective standpoint, *malâmiyyah* spirituality postulates a distance between worldly values and practices—even though they be religiously informed—and spiritual authenticity or sincerity (*ikhlâs*). As with Shakespeare's Hamlet, *malâmiyyah* spirituality tends to emphasize a "pessimistic" anthropology, and *malâmî* mystics would no doubt agree with the prince of Elsinore that "the time is out of joint" and that it is indeed "a cursed spite" to be "born to set it right" (Act I, v, 215–216), if only in a spiritual sense. Like Hamlet, a typical *malâmî* would have no qualms in confessing: "I am myself indifferent honest, but yet I could accuse me of such things that it were better my mother had not borne me" (Act III, i, 130–134). The oscillation between "invisible conformity" and "shocking madness" is, in a sense, an expression of this keen awareness of the lowest possibilities of man, an intimation of the gravity of his sickness; as such it constitutes a two-pronged method of "humiliation" of the *nafs*. Moreover, this heightened sensibility to human defects and failures is closely related to a mystical awareness of God's perfection and presence. The medieval diagnosis of holy madness as the state of one whose body is in this world while his soul is already in heaven bears witness to this.[41] The tension that results from this dichotomy seems to be mystically crystallized in real or feigned madness. As with Hamlet's feigned madness, there is both an aspect of "sadness" and one of "occultation" in the "foolish" or scandalizing ways of *malâmî*.

In addition, this psycho-spiritual point of view runs parallel with a "negative" assessment of mankind in society. In a mad world that claims to be sane, there is wisdom in madness and madness in wisdom ("Though this be madness, yet there is method in't" *Hamlet*, Act II, ii, 223). Any traditional formal system is an approximate equilibrium that points to a higher degree of Reality that transcends it; it must therefore be broken in some ways and in some instances so as not to close in on itself or become petrified to the point of obstructing access to its spiritual referent. In this respect, the most discordant and shocking aspects of *malâmiyyah* spirituality are intended to provoke an alchemical dissolution that can be the prelude to a higher crystallization. On a spiritual level, this is the principle that consists in "breaking habits," thereby obliging the soul to jump into unknown territory, to lose her bearings and to bring to the fore what had remained unconscious. To behave in a *malâmiyyah* way is not only a manner of attracting upon oneself a moral and social blame that would guard one from self-indulgence and overestimation of self; it is also a way of destroying the false equilibrium of the soul, thereby leading it into a state of uncomfortable helplessness that will result in a clearer awareness of its inner knots and will help objectify its latent contents. This is clearly the goal of a Sufi master like the Shaykh 'Alî al-Jamal who, according to his disciple al-Arabî ad-Darqawî, seems to have taught his disciples how to break their soul's habits through the discomforting means of social and psychological discordance and humiliation.[42] In one of the Shaykh al-Arabî ad-Darqawî's letters, we read about particularly instructive instances of this strategy. 'Alî al-Jamal orders his young disciple to go through town carrying two baskets of prunes on his back. In another instance, we read:

> He (the Shaykh 'Alî al-Jamal) took hold of my *haik* with his noble hands, put it off my head and twisted it several times around my neck.[43]

This "test of what is good" makes the disciple feel "oppressed to the point of death": going about town with two baskets of prunes on one's nape or with one's *haik* twisted around one's neck is likely to attract upon oneself the mockeries of social peers, for—as Titus Burckhardt notes in his commentary on this episode—the real intentions and feelings of most people only appear "under pressure" and once conventional masks have fallen. In that sense, "the blame of mankind is the food of the friends of God."[44] In other words, this method is a way to "raise hell" in others and in oneself, so as to reach a full measure of awareness of unconscious layers and knots in one's soul. In a certain sense, this psycho-spiritual therapy is akin to medical homeopathy, insofar as it cures the inner sickness through an initial exacerbation of its symptoms, "bringing out" the poison of the soul by submitting it to her own "disorders." For instance, being singled out as an "odd number" by passers-by and acquaintances—in a society in which eccentricities are, to say the least, not the norm—is likely to bring out discomfort in the soul, providing one with a golden if bitter opportunity for self-knowledge and self-transcendence. From the standpoint of the *nafs*, the temptation is therefore very strong to put back one's *haik* onto one's head, a temptation that must be resisted. The conclusion of the Shaykh ad-Darqawî: "Woe to the *faqir* [. . .] who sees the form of his own soul [. . .] as it is and does not strangle it until it dies" allows us to catch a glimpse into one of the *malâmiyyah* methodical "strategies." Discordance is a catalyst of egoic crystallization and, consequently, the means of an alchemical transmutation. The disciple is taught how to "see" his soul, which means that he becomes uncomfortably aware of it with a view to objectifying its nature. But this "objectivization" is also a way to "kill" the soul, or rather to neutralize its negative tendencies as *nafs al-ammârah*. To the question of knowing how this "strangulation" of the soul may be achieved, one must respond that the answer lies in the ability of the mystic to resist his soul on the one hand—for this is a prerequisite for objectifying self-knowledge—and in God's power through the *dhikr* on the other hand, for none can put to death but He who gives life. If there be no resistance there would not be any knowledge of the centrifugal tendencies of the soul. However, this resistance is futile if it is not grounded in the transcendent element that is the Divine Name. The Divine Name is a symbolic objectification of the Spirit; it fulfills the function of the Spirit in relation to the soul. Only the Spirit can "kill" the soul, but this "killing" is also an act of "love": *mors* and *amor* are the two faces of the same mystery, and the "objectivization" referred to earlier is in a sense the other side of an "identification"[45] or a "union" in which the Name of God, through the *dhikr*, "kills" the soul within its "embrace," thereby "reviving" it to a truer, deeper, and more abundant life. This is the reintegration of the drop into the Ocean, which is both a mode of extinction and an infinite elation beyond all individual limitations.

This page intentionally left blank

Chapter 11

Fools on a Tightrope

Folklore and literature present us with rich and meaningful manifestations of the archetypes and phenomena that are the concern of this book. How could they not, when their function is precisely to mediate between the world of higher realities and that of the most modest, daily, human experiences? This is an instance of the law that teaches us that "extremes meet," for popular stories, as well as literary and dramatic works of entertainment allude to that which cannot be avoided without bypassing the very meaning of human life. Admittedly, literary and folkloric narratives and heroes reflect these realities in a way that may sometimes appear as very distant and indirect. On a most immediate level, they tend to be relevant in social and moral matters, not to say on the psychological plane. It remains nevertheless true that, in the best instances, treasuries of paradoxical and "foolish" wisdom can be gleaned in the most unexpected quarters of popular and literary culture. *Vox populi vox Dei*: popular wisdom is most often closely akin to sapiential wisdom, although it may couch the highest principles in a plain, familiar, or burlesque language. Our focus on but a few of these figures cannot be justified otherwise than by referring to the unavoidable need to choose, and thereby exclude. The few figures that we have chosen to discuss in light of our general perspective have at any rate the merit of diversity and, so we may hope, complementarity, in enlightening some of the essential aspects of the function of madness, laughter, and trickery in our understanding of reality. While Nasredin Hodja, Till Eulenspiegel, and Arlecchino pertain to an inextricable blend of history, folklore, and popular culture, Panurge and Hamlet are "classic" literary characters who sprang from the imagination of two geniuses of European literature. The inextricable mixture of alleged history and legend that characterizes tricksters like Eulenspiegel and Nasredin Hodja is in itself a fruitful lesson. It teaches us that our characters must be envisaged both as functional "archetypes" and as concrete, often topical, occurrences with which traditional cultures have become more or less familiar.

The figure of Hodja appears to be a literary and popular transformation, in fifteenth century Turkey, of an earlier character associated with a collection of popular Arabic narratives entitled the *Jests of Si Djoha*.[1] These stories go back to the fourth century of the Islamic *hegira*. They were later on transmitted, translated, and transformed throughout the whole of Middle East, while they gained a particular notoriety in Turkey. In fact, Turkey became very much Nasredin's home, and his tomb can be visited, to this day, in the Turkish town of Aqshehir. There, it is said, a hole has been left "in the masonry of the tomb so that he (Hodja) can continue to look out upon the world."[2] This small opening is enough to suggest that Hodja's spirit is still alive and well, and, more profoundly perhaps, that his antics and jokes continue to join together the world of the here-below and that of the hereafter. The popular trickster is not only, if he ever was, an historical character; he is also a human type that a given cultural or ethnic collectivity has enriched and transformed along the centuries. In a sense, this ever-enriched reality challenges any kind of one-sided interpretation, just as it also makes any exhaustive and systematic collection and categorization impossible.[3] Eulenspiegel and Nasredin can take as many forms as the popular imagination, or the individual imagination for that matter, can give to them. Their character and stories may respond to a myriad of questions and concerns. They may also be read as mere exercises in the pure enjoyment of pleasantry. It is interesting to note that, as tradition has it, the Middle Eastern Hodja, or Khoja, (or Hoca for the Turks) was a clerical figure, as indicated by his very name, which means preacher or teacher, while Eulenspiegel was associated with the popular classes and the very type of the low-standing practical joker. However, Hodja himself is not immune to associations with the world of jesters, since, according to some traditions, he is recorded as having served as the court-jester of the famous conqueror Tamerlane or Timur-Leng. As a matter of fact, his disproportionately large turban places him squarely in the category of the clown: one can hardly decide whether it suggests a wide wisdom, a sacerdotal crown, or a minuscule head, as a quantitative compensation. The most famous story to stage Hodja as a typical king's jester tells how Timur-Leng happened to weep, one day, upon being presented a mirror in which he could not escape the glaring fact of his ugliness. Taking a typical contrary stand against the courtiers who tried to divert Timur from his depressing self-image by cracking jokes and laughing merrily, Hodja wept and wept, and wept louder. When asked by the king why he was so utterly saddened by a physical appearance that was, after all, of small direct concern to him, Hodja answered: "If you, my Lord, wept for two hours after seeing yourself in the mirror for but an instant, is it not natural that I, who see you all day long, should weep longer than you?"[4] This wisely candid reflection healed the king from his cries, and sent him laughing heartily. The cruel truth is indeed liberating when it is uttered by a fool, and only the fool can introduce this apparently inconsequential distance that makes one free to laugh at oneself with him. Another telling instance in which Hodja pokes fun at terrestrial powers involves a cogent allusion to the small importance of socioeconomic ranks. Invited at a banquet organized by some wealthy locals, Hodja was copiously ignored by the participants: the "threadbare black gown" that he was wearing did not help much to enhance his worldly visibility. Hodja left the room, but came back a few minutes later wearing a splendid garment that one of the guests had hung in another room. This time around, everybody greeted him with respect, "answer, fur!" was his response.[5] In the world of men, tell me what you wear and I will tell you who you are.

As was mentioned earlier, Hodja the fool is also an *imâm*, or a *mullah*: he might thereby represent the sovereign freedom of the spiritual vis-à-vis temporal rulers and powers. As such, he is a constant reminder of the precariousness of terrestrial elections. In the world of religious mores, Imam Hodja injects an element of prosaic and humorous distance within the domain of religious rules and duties. It must be borne in mind that Nasredin "functions" in the context of a society that is both strictly traditional and actually defined by its adherence to the religious law, the *sharʿiah*. As such, he may sometimes represent, in the face of the rigidity of legal "abstractions," the "commonsensical" intelligence of reality, and even the cunning aspect of mankind in its dealing with God's injunctions. The domain of the Law is that of necessity, but it is in a sense a planimetric necessity that the human mind always has the power to escape from above, or to circumvent by means of its numerous resources. In that sense, the necessity of the Law cannot constrain the freedom of mankind, even if the latter is expressed in its most modest, and sometimes ambiguous, manifestations. After all, the Law is there for man, and not man for the Law. Human intelligence is in principle the best of laws. Hodja embodies this mobility of human intelligence over which no external constraint can keep total control. On the other hand, he also incarnates the shortcomings of man, and the ambiguity of his status as an interlocutor of God, and a representative of His Will. In this respect, one of the most famous stories illustrating Hodja's religious *facetiae* introduces him as an *imâm* about to preach at the mosque on Friday:

> "O Moslems, do you know what I am going to say to you today?" "No," replied they. "And no more do I," said the Khoja; and hastily left the mosque. The next Friday he asked the same question, but this time the congregation answered, "Yes." "If you know, then I needn't tell you," said the Khoja, and again made off. Then next week, when the Khoja asked his usual question, the congregation, thinking to display great cunning, said, "Some of us do, but some of us don't." "Then let those who know tell those who don't," said the Khoja, and once more the congregation were outwitted.[6]

To speak the truth about the truth, in the context of a congregation, is perhaps the most perilous exercise there is. The truth is greater than human weaknesses, and it is also, in another sense, greater than speech. As a character who embodies the comic ambiguity of man's predicament, Hodja is probably quite aware that he is not *himself* on par with the truth that he is expected to utter. He is also too cunning not to know that, here-below, truth is not infrequently the most elusive of all catches. Between the *enormity* of truth, if one may say so, and one's *pettiness*, the only solution is to escape. Hodja's escape is not only clever; it is also quite allusive, and instructive in its very glibness. The jester *imâm* is after all only a man like any other man: why should he know when others do not? When confessing that he has no idea what his sermon will teach the faithful, he reveals either his own laziness or his ignorance. But ignorance is worth more than a pretension to knowledge. After all, there is even a school of theology that is founded upon the primacy of ignorance: it teaches that we can only say what the Truth is not, *via negativa*. Hodja reveals the chasm that separates the Infinite from his own limited *stupidity*; but this stupidity is actually much wiser than it appears to be at first. His astute exit on the second Friday is not without an element of wisdom. After all, if these Muslims are really what they ought to be, that is *good* Muslims, they must—in both senses—already know what the *imâm* is about to tell them. A good sermon is only a reminder, and no more. As for the trick that takes place on the third Friday, it is no less intelligent in the sense that it may be considered as alluding to the community as a collective repository of knowledge. In the context of Islam, truth is not a matter of *magisterium*, since it results from a consensus among the believers. In a sense, Hodja's third exit is a nimble recognition of this fact. One can, of course, object to this commentary by pointing out that the story does not draw its humorous power from its possible theological or social implications, and this is all too obvious. Hodja amuses us because of his supreme ability to make the best out of the least, to escape the consequences of his own deficiency with the wherewithal of his wit. Hodja's comic impact is often the result of an unexpected encounter between the limits of his will and the resources of his wit. In his stories, the precariousness of the human condition is often hinted at by reference to the ridiculous inconsistencies and presumptions of his own will. When carried away by petty successes and high moods Hodja tends to forget that he is also, and first of all, a poor servant of God. Coming back from court where a judicial decision has been taken in his favor, Hodja gloriously announces to his wife that he will sow the next day. As a faithful Muslim woman, she thinks it pious and careful to add to her husband's words the traditional "*in sha' Allâh*" (God willing), which suspends everything human to God's will. Hodja is too confident at that time to be as conscious of metaphysical demands as is his wife, and he answers with a definite "No, willing or unwilling tomorrow I will sow." The next day, a potent thunderstorm takes him down from his donkey on his way to sowing. Upon his return home, he knocks at the door, answering his wife's, "Who is there?" with the humble words, "I am the Hodja, if God will."[7] The *Qur'ân*'s account of the unfaithfulness of men who have invoked God during a storm at sea, and then rebelled against Him when the winds have set back, provides a scriptural intertext for Hodja's story.[8] However, the comical shift that leads Hodja to extend recognition of the primacy of God's will to matters of being and identity, and not only to events and actions, is highly indicative of the tremendous effect that an "act of God" may have upon an insouciant soul. Metaphysically, this abrupt extension amounts to a concrete awareness of one's ontological dependency upon God's Being. If the expression "*in sha' Allâh*" is ordinarily reserved for events or actions that are expected to take place in the future, Hodja's use of the formula is all the more striking, and all the more comical, that it refers here to a matter of identity and to the present. As if Hodja were becoming the burlesque spokesman of the Sufi metaphysical principle, expressed by Ibn 'Arabî and others, according to which the entire creation is renewed into being by God's will at each instant. The extreme distance separating the initial boasting and arrogant insouciance of the Hodja and his quasi-mystical attentiveness to God's presence *in fine* provides a comical shock that is not for nothing in the effectiveness of the point.

The spiritual dimension of Nasredin's stories, as implied by his popularity among Sufis and his recently increased notoriety through Idris Shah's published collections, is neither incompatible with their unassuming and popular style, nor with their wide appeal. As a matter of fact, the highest wisdom can hide in the garb of popular folklore, in which it is often inextricably mixed with elements of a more exclusively entertaining nature. Profound ideas can be subtly couched in the language of jokes, and it was not uncommon for Sufi masters, such as Rumi, to allude to spiritual realities through lively narratives. One excellent example of the spiritual subtlety and depth of some of the Mullah's stories is given in one of Idris Shah's books.[9] On his way to town, Nasredin is frightened at the thought that a group of horsemen coming toward him might be thieves or shady traffickers. In order to escape them, he pretends to be dead by lying down in a nearby cemetery. Realizing that he is still alive, and surprised to find him in such an uncomfortable position, the horsemen ask him what he is doing. His answer is a masterpiece of Hodjaism: "Just because you can ask a question does not mean that there is a straightforward answer to it. [. . .] It all depends upon your viewpoint. If you must know, however: I am here because of you, and you are here because of me." Once again, Nasredin is at his best in drawing the most unexpected, witty, and—it must be said here—philosophical, resources when reduced to his last extremities. The expedient answer is at the same time a wonderfully comical, and metaphysically relevant, statement about the human predicament in general. The disproportion between the level of philosophical universality of the Mullah's answer and the utterly pitiful and ridiculous reality of his situation is not for nothing in the effectiveness of the story. This is not only a funny rationalization of one's weakness, that is, inordinate fear; it is also a splendid realization of the limits of human knowledge and the power of illusion. Nasredin is prompted to tell the truth about himself, here and now, but what he tells is actually the truth about mankind. He hides behind this apparently ridiculous disproportionate answer; but by hiding he also reveals a real understanding of reality, and himself. At the same time, this very indirect answer can be taken as a parody of philosophical discourse, since its degree of nonspecificity and abstraction makes it blatantly irrelevant to the actual expectations of the horsemen. The gist of the joke is that the Mullah says much while seeming to say nothing. What he says, ultimately, is that relativity is tied up with illusions of absoluteness.

Nasredin's unintended humor often capitalizes on a way of disjointing certain elements of ordinary reality, or of defying the purpose of these elements as if they were considered from a completely disconnected point of view that evokes an impression of absurdity. Nasredin's world is a world in which reality and meaning are as if dissociated. In one story, the Mullah's wife is frightened when hearing a big thump in the house. She goes to Nasredin to ask him whether he knows what happened. To this, Hodja replies: "It is just my cloak which fell." "Why was it so noisy?" "Because I was in it at the time."[10] That Nasredin would try to calm down the fears of his wife is not surprising, since his somewhat cowardly nature tends to lead him to avoid trouble. When prompted to clarify the conditions of the event, all he can do is admit to his fall, but he does so in being obliged to reverse the usual relationship between body and cloth, "content" and "container." The idea of being "in" a cloak instead of wearing a cloak turns our worldview topsy-turvy. Again, it sounds as if the predicament in which the Mullah finds himself obliges him to point to a fresh, and apparently absurd, viewpoint on the world of relativity. The comic dissociation of Nasreddin from himself, or at least from his body, his seeming ability to "make an abstraction" of himself, so to speak, is highly representative of a kind of humor that thrives on a sense of inner distance and the nonsensical effects that it produces. A similar account is that of the Mullah losing his donkey in a field. Asked by a neighbor why he is praising God at this seemingly unfortunate time, Hodja candidly replies that his gratitude stems from his not having been on the back of the donkey at the time of his loss, for "if I had been, we should both infallibly have been lost."[11] The oblique spiritual lessons that stem from the episode—the relativity of spatial locations, the extent and limits of one's identification with one's belongings, and so on—draw their burlesque power from their being inferred in the context of circumstances that point to human precariousness and its potential for ridicule. The Mullah speaks the truth when conspicuously placed in the position of a fool. The reversal of usual situations is also comically highlighted in stories where the intended purpose of objects is unexpectedly modified in the course of the narrative. As Hodja is about to go on a trip, a friend of his suggests that he take his sword in case he is threatened by robbers who might be after his donkey. Nasredin accepts to carry the sword. He sees a traveler coming his way and, through fear of having his donkey stolen, he says to the newcomer: "Take my sword, and leave me my donkey!" Upon his return home the Mullah thanks his friend: "You were right, your sword was helpful."[12] The play between intended and actual purpose suggests the limits of human mastery over everyday happenings. By defeating the purpose of his friend's foresight Nasredin once again displaces the meaning of phenomena; his human weakness—here cowardice—reveals a new angle on reality. As with all tricksters, he is a mixture of ridiculous weakness along with an ingenious ability to rebound; he is a human paradox of helplessness and resourcefulness. He can find fresh meaning even for apparent absurdity.

One of the reoccurring features of Hodja's character is his tendency to take statements literally, bringing them to the brink of absurdity. This tendency he shares with a number of clowns and tricksters, including his distant cousin Eulenspiegel. When in bed with his wife at night, he is asked to move over a bit so as to leave her with more room. This prompts him to go for a walk until dawn thinking that he should keep moving over. On a first level, this type of literal understanding can point to the "stupid" aspect of the character; but this "stupidity" can only be the other face of a type of intelligence. By taking his wife's request literally, and bringing his response to the point of burlesque exaggeration, Nasredin may also allude to the pitfalls and ambiguities of language. The verb "to move" can, after all, be understood in more than one way. By taking words at face value to the point of absurdity Nasredin may also bring home the point that one should not do so. This is certainly one of the main functions of the fool. This function lies at the intersection of his two seemingly contradictory characteristics: his foolishness and his wisdom. The intimate relationship between these two aspects of his character, which is the source of much of his comic appeal,[13] can be accounted for in several ways. For one thing, wisdom is much more easily imparted when it proceeds from a man who is, in some respects, a fool: the lesson is likely to be more effective when garbed in the charming form of the amusing ambiguities of human nature. Another characteristic that Hodja shares with many other tricksters is an affinity with topsy-turvy situations. It is said when he was asked why he had expressed the wish to be buried upside down, he answered that the reason was that at the end of the world everything would be topsy-turvy and everybody upside down so that he would be the only one to be the right way up.[14] The fool is the only one to be the right way up, and it is especially so in times of corruption and degeneracy.

Eulenspiegel is a distant cousin of Hodja, but his overall profile is often more akin to the realistic and prosaic cunning of the popular classes than to the subtle and "philosophical" implications of the Mullah. In that sense, Eulenspiegel embodies the crafty irreverence and sharp earthiness of the late Middle Ages and early Renaissance. Notwithstanding this more popular aspect, Eulenspiegel is undoubtedly connected to wisdom. The sixteenth-century iconography shows him riding a horse while holding an owl in his right hand, and a mirror in his left. These two emblems also appear on his grave, as a posthumous testimony to his function. The owl—Athena's bird[15]—is an emblem of wisdom, representing the ability to pierce through the darkness of the night of ignorance and unconsciousness; the mirror plays the role of facilitating self-knowledge. The mirror hides nothing; it is perfectly "plain" in its assessment of the soul's vices and shortcomings. Eulenspiegel shows man his true face as it is reflected in the mirror of his antics. The extraordinary nature and function of Eulenspiegel finds a kind of mythic prelude in the account of his baptism: it is told that the jester was baptized thrice: first at church, then in the puddle in which he fell when being carried by his inebriated godfathers, and finally in the kettle in which the women of the house cleaned him again.[16] This parodic baptism clearly points to a destiny of boisterousness and dirtiness, but it also hints at the ultimately good dimension of his character under the auspices of caring mothers. There is a kind of dialectical complexity in his character, and this foundational baptism spells it out with a sense of burlesque fancy. Eulenspiegel's complexity is clearly illustrated by his very first adventure, which may be deemed to function as a symbolic pointer to the possible meaning of his character. One of the first things that we are told about Eulenspiegel is his passion for walking on a tightrope. In spite of vehement opposition on the part of his mother, Eulenspiegel practiced so ably on his tightrope that he stretched it from the roof of his mother's house to the other side of the Saale river. Symbolically speaking, Eulenspiegel's tightrope feat joins together the imaginary themes of elevation, communication, transgression, and precariousness. The first episodes of the story already show him on higher grounds, and this is no doubt another aspect of his symbolic association with wisdom. The communicative and transgressive aspects of his character are also highlighted by his desire to pass from one place to another, to join roofs and to cross rivers. But the precariousness of his function is no less clearly indicated by his uncomfortable position on the rope: in fact, we are told how his mother "crept secretly anyhow, back in the house, to the lattice-work to which the rope was tied, and sliced the rope in two."[17] What an effective symbol of the trickster's role among his peers! He can see mankind from above and may mock it from the height of his rope, but it is not too late before he can be precipitated to the ground . . .

It has been mentioned that two of Eulenspiegel's characteristics make him a somewhat atypical trickster: his somewhat insensitive, revengeful, and even cruel disposition, and his apparent lack of interest in sexual matters. Sometimes, Eulenspiegel's cruelty stems from a desire for revenge, but sometimes not. One may be puzzled, for example, by his playing dirty scatological tricks on an old man who had given him a ride in his chariot. Eulenspiegel spoils the plums that the man carries to the market with his own droppings.[18] There may or may not be reasons, explicit or implicit, in such heartless tricks, but it is more likely that Eulenspiegel's apparent lack of concern is a manifestation of his purely mental interest in life as a game, or as a playground. The moral consequences of his actions are not taken into account, simply because he is a mind at play, and not a real person. Some of his meanest tricks suggest his flirting with the devilish. One of his adventures presents him telling the cruel "truth" to an old beguine who had asked him about the things he felt "sorry about": one of his regrets was not having "stitched up the asses of all the old women who are past their prime."[19] When the angry beguine parts from him with a "well, the devil protect you!" his answer reveals the truth that "there is no beguine who's really devout when she's angry [. . .] then she is more spiteful than the devil." Eulenspiegel's own devilishness is therefore not incompatible with an ability to unmask the devil in others.

When compared with Hodja's amiable jokes, Eulenspiegel's shrewd deeds appear to be much more offensive, and more subversive of normative ways. Eulenspiegel is something of a rebel, at least a rebel of his own cause. He likes to be thought of as an omnipresent figure of foolery who is engaged in a kind of guerilla warfare against those whom he dislikes. The latter are almost always stingy, arrogant, or egoistic members of the middle class. Once he has played a trick in a place where his reputation has not yet preceded him, he likes to leave traces of his whereabouts by drawing an owl and a mirror over the door and writing the following words below: *hic fuit*—here he was. The anonymity of the inscription implies a desire to impress the popular imagination with the picture of a will-o'-the-wisp, a moving angel of disorder and mischief. As for the graphic, if cryptic, emblem, it indicates quite surely that Eulenspiegel is fully aware of the meaning and implications of his name, and that he is proud to use it as a magic signifier of his pervasive function.

One point that is common to both Hodja and Eulenspiegel, and which clearly distinguishes them from a host of tricksters and buffoons is the little interest that they manifest toward women and sexuality.[20] The reasons for this surprising distinction may be primarily cultural and religious in Hodja's case, as a guardrail against possible abuses, or censure by the law. But this should not be the case for Eulenspiegel, whose indulgence in all kinds of immoral deeds, and scatological feats, would make us expect to find him involved in obscenity and the like. It may be that these characters are identified in one way or another to the mercurial and asexual nature of the mind. The mind in itself, as powerful as its cleverness might be, remains indifferent to the instinctive drive of sexual passions. Its primary domain of manifestation is language—its tricks and its traps—an aspect of reality that is more attuned to play than to passion. In that respect, both Hodja and Till are experts. It has been observed that one of the main aspects of this expertise, at least as far as Eulenspiegel is concerned, is an insistence on telling the truth, directly and literally. In a chapter of Eulenspiegel's stories, the trickster announces to a lady from Sangerhausen that he "practice(s) telling the truth."[21] In this particular instance, the truth is quite plain and frank: as a follow-up to the lady's praises of Eulenspiegel's professed sincerity, the trickster, having noticed that the woman was squinting, goes on shouting to her ears: "Squint-eyed lady, squint-eyed lady, where shall I sit and where shall I put my staff and sack."[22] At other times, Eulenspiegel tells the literal truth while forgetting to specify the context, or other elements, that must enter into the economy of the situation. Having promised to mend his ways upon having decided to enter a monastery, Eulenspiegel commits himself to obey the Prior's orders: the Prior has asked him to count monks as they come to the office in the morning. Eulenspiegel does so, but at night "he ripped a number of steps out of the staircase." All the monks fell, but Eulenspiegel assured the Prior that he had indeed counted them falling.[23] Eulenspiegel's "truth telling" alludes to the dimension of the relativity of the truth: it hints at its social limits, and above all at its dependence upon perspectives or standpoints. By committing himself to the portion of literal truth for which he has opted Eulenspiegel turns the objectivity of reality to his own subjective advantage. He protects his subjective freedom under a layer of perfect obedience to the letter of the law. He also suggests the absurdity that results from a confusion between absolute claims and relative standpoints. In these respects, he is indeed an embodiment of the inner liberty that flows from wisdom.

Like Hodja, and like all tricksters, Eulenspiegel is a character who does not and cannot change. Although he is an agent of change and an ever-mobile seeker of troubles, his own nature is immovable. Throughout his stories, it is made clear again and again that he will not mend his ways, even though he may claim to do so, or promise to do so at the thought that he could draw some advantage from doing so. He is a type, and not a genuine person. In that sense, he is akin to the masks that archaic theater has staged the world over.

As a foundation for many trickster-like characters within the European literary tradition, the Italian *Commedia dell' Arte* has immortalized a number of masks that recapitulate some of the features of the legendary type of the clown and trickster. Among them, Arlecchino occupies a place of choice that is highly suggestive of some of the deeper aspects of our topic. It bears being mentioned, first of all, that Arlecchino's mask was blackened by the fire of hell.[24] His apparent, and legendary, innocence and idealism, which was extolled by the Romantics, is only one part of the story. Arlecchino has approached hell, but he has not been consumed by its fire. In the same way as Charles de Coster's Eulenspiegel is described as having been born with a small black dot on his shoulder—a kind of devilish parody of the miraculous birthmarks of Messengers from Heaven—which the midwife who delivered him interpreted as "the dark mark of the devil's finger,"[25] Arlecchino bears a little horn on his head, a sure indication of his distant kinship with the world of the devil. His very name, derived from the French Harlequin, Herlequin, or Hellequin, refers to a demonic character, a leader of small devils, who was one of the theatrical types found in popular mysteries of the eleventh century. Even if the scholarly etymology of his name has not definitely established a connection with hell, there is little doubt that hell has indeed tempted Arlecchino; but it is also true that he has not identified with it to the point of losing his soul. Like virtually all the characters from the *Commedia dell' Arte*, Arlecchino is both something, and its opposite. Pantalone, for example, has a formidable, indomitable, energy that pertains to his legendary virility, but he may, at the same time, be frightened by a mouse. Similarly, Arlecchino can be a tender and idealistic lover, but he can also be animal-like when it comes to expressing his sexual instincts without restraint. His innocence is that of childlike dreams, or that of animal passions. The multiplicity of moods and aspects that may enter the character has sometimes led critics and actors to assert that Arlecchino can actually be whatever one may want him to be.[26] Anyway, his multicolored garb makes it quite plain that his is the function of serving more than one master. Arlecchino is the prince and the pauper of multiplicity. His character recapitulates all the possible cadences of the human dance.

* * *

Rabelais is a comic demiurge among writers. The very form of his work encapsulates the "monstrous" multiplicity and disproportionate structure that defines clowns and tricksters. Its unmatched verbal fantasy, and virtuosity, brings out the dynamics of creative disorder, tension, and opposition that is so characteristic of the demiurgic realm. As William J. Kennedy has indicated, "Rabelais' world is a universe of words in palpable contestation with one another [. . .] as they rub together, their friction produces endless puns, double entendres, multiple ambiguities, and infinite wordplay."[27] The "esoteric" character of his *Gargantua* and *Pantagruel* is evidently related to this "demiurgic" and burlesque dimension. The prologue of *Gargantua* alludes to this trans-grotesque kernel by referring to an analogy between the form of the work and the *Silènes*, which were—according to the author—little pharmaceutical boxes, the lids of which were ornamented with grotesque and bizarre, often zoomorphic, shapes, while containing also the most precious drugs and balms. This analogy is equally shared, according to Rabelais, with Socrates,[28] whose external features were gross and trivial but whose inner wisdom was most beautiful, and actually a prefiguration of the Gospel.[29] We are therefore warned, from the outset, not only that the dimension of depth must not be confused with the surface, but that the grotesque characteristics of the latter bear a singular and privileged relationship with the substance (the "substantial marrow") of the former. The paradox of that relationship is that it is designed to be both an adjuvant in view of the dissemination of the content, and a mask protecting the latter from indiscreet or ill-prepared readers and listeners. In other words, the comical and often monstrous garb that clothes the content of these seemingly buffoonish stories is akin to what Buddhists would call an *upâya*, or a saving means—a fantastically grotesque but enlightening mirage toward the truth. At the same time, those who are not able, by virtue of some impeding limitations, to jump beyond the burlesque literality of the text, or those whose moralistic or conventional leanings render incapable of not being arrested by the numerous profanities, scatological evocations, and sexual innuendoes that are profusely interspersed throughout the book, will not reach the core of this monstrous heap, their unsupple psychic impediments preventing them from moving back and forth from the metaphysical to the obscene, from the gluttonous to the ethical, thereby disqualifying them for this particular kind of access to the truth.

Rabelais' characters are giants in a world of "dwarves," symbolically speaking. Their extraordinary size bears the hallmark of an exception: among ordinary men the wise man is like a giant. Gigantic dimensions signal the anomaly of knowledge and virtue in a world woven of ignorance and pettiness. The gigantic size of the likes of Gargantua and Pantagruel is both an allusion to their enormously healthy embrace of life, and a pointer to their eminent level of intellectual and spiritual enlightenment. These traits have been attributed to the optimistic anthropological outlook of the early Renaissance. However, they may also characterize an aspiration toward a more essential and "natural" perspective with regard to the relationship between man and God. If the doctors, scholars, monks, and other figures of pseudo-knowledge and bogus piety that are mocked by Rabelais and his gigantic spokesmen are to be identified, at least to a certain point, with the limitations of the late Middle Ages, it does not necessarily mean that Rabelais should exclusively be read as a critique of the medieval Christian perspective as such. Even the program of education spelled out by Gargantua to his son's benefits—in chapter VIII of *Pantagruel*, often highlighted as a *summum* of the spirit of the Renaissance, includes elements that were part and parcel of medieval education, such as the *trivium* and the *quadrivium*,[30] as well as the physical and martial exercises pertaining to knightly instruction. Rabelais's pedagogical program and philosophical ideas could just as readily be understood as aiming at the restoration of a normative way of being as they are often considered in terms of a mere overthrow of the past in the name of a humanistic future. If such a view of Rabelais's giants is not to be rejected, the altitudinous point of view and the inexhaustible vital energy and thirst for freedom that the giants embody should be related to a primordial state of being that the utopia of Thelema, placed under the auspicious lesson of the formula "*Faictz ce que vouldras*" (Do what you want) crystallizes as a contemplative rule of life. Once the content of the will is worthy of and proportionate to the True, the Good, and the Beautiful, there is no more need for any externally constraining rules that would limit the expanse of the human ability to choose the good. This is an allusion to a state of prelapsarian perfection that Rabelais appears to hold out as still accessible to men in principle, if not in fact. In that sense, the relationship between giants and men is to be thought of as being analogous to an unequal confrontation between young, bright, and vibrant heroes close to the source of being, and decrepit old men representative of a decadent life—replete with the automatic and formalistic reflexes of lifeless existence—which has lost contact with the waters of life, in the image of the dried up doctors, bogus scholars, logorrheic judges, and pedantic students whom the giants encounter on so many of their ways.

What is the place and function of the enigmatic Panurge in this confrontation between the giant Pantagruel and those men who have lost touch with the substance of mankind? Panurge is obviously a multidimensional character. As indicated by his very name, he is first of all

Panoûrgos. He is able to do everything. Gérard Defaux has judiciously reminded his readers that the lexicon of Suidas, a reference dictionary or encyclopedia written by an ecclesiastical scholar from Constantinople in the tenth century, defines the *Panoûrgos* as "*qui omnia facit in improbitate*" (he who does everything with dishonesty), "*callidissimus, ac improbissimus, ad quoduis facinus patrandum paratus*" (most cunning and most dishonest, and ready to perform any villainy), and also as "*etiam vir valde prudens et qui omnia novit*" (man of great prudential intelligence and who knows everything).[31] The ambiguity of demiurgic intelligence could not be better expressed than by these few segments of definition. Panurge displays a clear affinity with *to pan*, the all, the universal, the inexhaustible, and also, through more than a pun, the "panic" that he is quite apt to produce among "good people" in the most diverse circumstances. He shares this affinity with his master Pantagruel, whose name may mean "thirsty for everything." While Pantagruel is thirsty for everything, Panurge might embody a perfect complementarity in relation to his master, since he is ready to accomplish everything for which Pantagruel is thirsty. In that sense, Panurge is like the demiurgic assistant of Pantagruel; he acts out, skillfully and amorally, what Pantagruel conceives and embodies, but in a way that is clearly not on par with Pantagruel's noble nature and function. In *Pantagruel*, the good giant is consistently presented as a noble soul, while Panurge is undoubtedly of a much more ambiguous mettle; all the same, the giant never disapproves of Panurge's frequently outrageous behavior. He cherishes the resourcefulness of his companion, and he laughs heartily at his rude antics. Panurge is like the amoral complement of Pantagruel; one would be tempted to write that if Pantagruel is like a god, Panurge is like his demiurge.

Panurge's ambiguous and complex character is revealed as soon as he enters into contact with Pantagruel. Panurge is introduced as an ambiguous young man who both looks like and acts as an aristocrat and a rogue. The giant identifies him from afar—as if he knew his kind very well, or as if he was expecting him, like a master his best disciple—as a man who defies all ordinary norms and notions of decency and consistency. He recognizes in Panurge's physiognomy the traits of someone who was born from a "rich and noble lineage" but who has been "reduced to such misery and indigence that he looks like he has just escaped from a hound" (chapter 9). What Panurge looks like is not what he is, and what he is, is not what he looks like. There is an incongruity between his real nature and what life has led him to be. Heterogeneity is his realm, as it is for most tricksters and jesters. He is *le curieux*, whom Gérard Defaux has convincingly related to Ulysses, the prince of that part of intelligence that applies to the outermost periphery of reality, astuteness, cleverness. This is still intelligence as such, but pertains to its outer shores, so to speak. We could say that the radiating manifestation of intelligence involves two distinct aspects that may be referred respectively to enlightening penetration and to external dissemination. Panurge is the nimble facilitator of dissemination: he actually sows seeds of trouble everywhere he has a chance to do so. Panurge's search, adventures, and curiosity have led him to be a poor wretched outcast. On the periphery of the realm of intelligence he personifies the ups and downs of mere cleverness. The enigma of his character is confirmed and highlighted by his bewildering ability to speak all kinds of idioms in order to answer Pantagruel's simple questions: "Who are you? Where do you come? Where do you go? What are you looking for? And what is your name?" Panurge does not really answer these questions; instead he initiates long discourses in German, Scottish, Basque, Greek, and other languages, in all of which he alludes, more or less directly, to his stomach's urgent need of food. Of course, it would appear to be more expedient, and effective, to ask for food in plain French, but the virtuosity of the polyglot's performance is meaningful in more ways than one. First, it introduces one of the main aspects of his type, that is, an ability to speak all kinds of languages and to wear all kinds of hats. This is an apt symbol of his colorful universality. It is as if Panurge advertises his ability to be all things to all people, in a kind of parodic rendering of St. Paul's "*Omnibus omnia factus sum, ut omnes facerem salvos*" (I have become all things to all so as to save all) (1 Cor. 9:22). Second, this universality is a symbol of the quasi-limitless resourcefulness of the character, one who can dig in his pocket whatever might prettily fit the circumstance. In chapter 16 of *Pantagruel* it is explained that Panurge had no less than twenty-six purses in his pocket: he is the jack-of-all-trades of tricks, thefts, and clever craftsmanship. He uses verjuice to blind the eyes of those he dislikes or steals from, throws little horns or small phallus on people's garments, blows fleas and lice into the collars of the most alluring young women, uses hooks in order to mate men and women, and mirrors to play tricks on people at church. Panurge's instruments respond to each set of circumstances: they offer a symbolic allusion to the quasi-inexhaustible vastness of human techniques, but the burlesque particularity of their utilization lies in the power of the character's imagination, his knack of inventing a comically unintended use for them. His polyglot abilities refer to an analogous characteristic of his: they suggest a capacity to speak all languages in a context in which their incongruity vis-à-vis the situation is a source of powerful comical effect. The apparent lack of relevance of each speech may also indicate that Panurge works with *appearances*; he reproduces language in bits and pieces, as if he were reciting a lesson. Each discourse is like a performance of his ability. However, the burlesque paradox is that each of these discourses alludes to the urgent need of his stomach. The first answer to Pantagruel, spoken in German, indicates that the question calls for a painful answer, without stating what the latter might be. In Italian, Panurge compares himself to an empty bagpipe (*cornamusa*) that cannot be played without being filled. In Danish, Panurge draws an analogy between his fate and that of children and animals, whose needs one must understand without their expressing them, since they are deprived of speech. The other tirades in foreign languages follow an analogous pattern. The content of these tirades indicate clearly enough, when juxtaposed to Pantagruel's question, that the trickster's needs are primarily physical: all other considerations must be postponed. This apparent primacy of the physiological is one of the hallmarks of Rabelais' world. Mikhail Bakhtin has convincingly argued that this aspect of Rabelais' work is to be situated in the context of popular culture, as contrasted with aristocratic culture.[32] On another level, Panurge's answer may reveal the comical absurdity of much of that passes for human communication. Panurge wants to alert Pantagruel to his urgent physiological needs, but he has to do it in an indirect way to keep up with the propriety of the situation: the only solution is to be both direct and indirect at the same time, an uncomfortable strategy that symbolically acts out the predicament of man in society.

Panurge is not only resourceful, he is also given to expediency in all matters. In order to refill his purse, which tends to be empty most of the time, he does not hesitate to steal from churches the coins that have been deposited in trays by the faithful to obtain indulgences. Pretending to give a small coin, he stealthily takes away a dozen.[33] Nothing, therefore, remains immune to his amoral abuses; and this is all the more true of women, and sexual matters. In *Pantagruel*, his relationship with women is characterized by nimble discourse, amorous parody, and disruptive obscenity. His manner of courting a lady from the high society of Paris is interesting in the panoply of arguments and styles that he puts forward. First, he tries to convince the lady to accept his advances in mock philosophical terms by emphasizing the utilitarian benefits of the enterprise.[34] This strategy highlights the profoundly pragmatic dimension of the character: his matter-of-fact discourse cuts to the chase by dispelling appearances and pretensions. One must lay stress on the fact that the lady whom he has decided to woo was chosen primarily on account of her social condition, and because Panurge wanted to build on his already reputable successes as a gifted debater in order to reach a higher status in Paris. The expression "*venir au dessus*" (to come above) that is used by Rabelais to describe Panurge's intention makes it quite plain that the character is using the amorous intercourse to assert a position of eminence. It is suggested by Rabelais that this is in part a result of a foolish tendency to self-aggrandizement on the part of the boastful Panurge. He may well appear, in that sense, as a social opportunist; but one may wonder whether his self-defeating ways of proceeding do not betray a desire to affirm his own particular kind of eminence, a purely disruptive brand, at the expense of prominent characters, rather than ordinary ambition as such. This appears in full light when one considers the second line of courting taken by Panurge, following his being rebuffed by the lady: it is no less than a praise for the ability of his sexual organ. This is obviously no more effective in guaranteeing him access to the lady's mercy. The third discourse is the most interesting: it comprises a parodically emphatic praise for the lady's beauty and virtues, replete with mythological references to Venus, Juno, and Minerva, and theological considerations on the lovers' predestination, but it concludes with a suggestive Rabelaisian verb graphically evoking physical postures of sexual intercourse. As he becomes more and more impertinent, and the lady grows by degrees haughtier and haughtier, his subsequent speeches involve lascivious pastiches of *courtois* poetry and language, such as references to the celestial beauty of the lady, juxtaposed with lewd allusions to the advantages he expects to draw from her. In chapter 22, he goes so far as to write a rondel in the lady's honor. The rondel is filled with conventional and hyperbolic tropes drawn from *courtois* poetry ("eternal suffering," "burnt by the spark of beauty," etc.) while ending up with a request that she allow him to serve as a "cover" to her beauty. Having been once again vehemently rejected by the lady, he does not stop playing practical jokes and dirty tricks on her. All in all, his debasing point of view and his outrageous actions illustrate a fundamental subversion of the language and code involved in the *courtois* and Platonic service of the lady by means of sophisticated and creative obscenity. As a trickster, Panurge undoes the fundamental tenets of the *fin'amors*. He not only manifests the obscene dimension of popular culture that emphasizes caricatural explicitness with respect to physiological functions, but he also deftly juxtaposes this *gaulois* tradition, which he "refines" through an extraordinary verbal virtuosity, to the idealistic register of *courtois* love.

While, as has been amply illustrated, *Pantagruel* shows us Panurge as a nimble trickster, the Third Book (*Tiers-Livre*) stages him as an indecisive fool, and the Fourth Book (*Quart-Livre*) as a cowardly clown. In *Pantagruel*, Panurge is an entertaining prankster whose subversive stands and actions meet with Pantagruel's benevolence because he acts out his opposition to grave, pedantic, and worldly fools, as well as to petrified practices and conventions. Panurge is the nimble servant of truth, although he might not himself even be fully aware of it. He is in full possession of his abilities, most often filled with self-confidence, because he is firmly backed by the wisdom and balance of Pantagruel. In the *Tiers-Livre*, Panurge becomes the central figure, but he is quite far from gaining grounds through this narrative promotion. His resourcefulness comes to a halt on the question of knowing whether he should be married or not. An embarrassment of philosophical and dialectical riches leaves him unable to decide either way. He has to wander from one foolish character to another in order to beg for advice on the matter. From an assisting demiurge in *Pantagruel*, he has become an embodiment of man's uncertainties and doubts; he becomes the fool that Pantagruel must teach, and sometimes correct. Ironically, the last character to appear in his round of consultations is the fool and jester Triboulet. The true fool answers his question by a most sibylline statement: "By God, oh, by God, you wild fool, watch out for the monk! Hey, *Buzançais* bagpipes."[35] Pantagruel deciphers this statement as a clear warning against the dangers of marrying (Panurge is likely to marry a woman as empty as a bagpipe and end up being cuckolded by a monk), whereas Panurge indulges in a self-serving and meandering interpretation that flatters his desire to get married against all reason. As a prelude to this foolishly and absurdly convoluted translation of Triboulet's enigma, Panurge protests that he will not deny the initial part of the fool's statement ("you wild fool!"). In a passage that paradoxically highlights his profound understanding of the world and himself, Panurge founds his reliance on Triboulet's advice on a recognition of his own foolishness:

> Not that I would arrogantly disclaim allegiance to the kingdom of folly. I'm a loyal subject, I admit it. But the whole world is crazy. [. . .] Solomon says that the number of fools is infinite. [. . .] and I'd be a wild fool, yes, if being a fool I didn't consider myself one.[36]

The literary theme of the universality of folly, far from being a reason to caution himself against rash and self-seeking judgment, becomes, with Panurge, a tacit acceptance of his blind rush into foreseeable troubles.

One of the most interesting features of Panurge, which reveals his kinship with other tricksters, is the disproportion between the wealth of his verbal and practical inventiveness, and the actual weaknesses of his character. Panurge is given to ups and downs, as testified by the miserable state of his physical condition upon first encountering Pantagruel. In fact, the hyperbolic profusion of his odd skills and nimble words functions most of the time as a veil upon, or as a distraction from, the not-so-glamorous realities of his life. This sorry truth comes into full light in the Fourth Book. In this volume, Panurge revels in the clownish burlesque of plain denial of what is evident. Panurge's attempts at covering his own weakness and cowardice no longer highlight his astute mind or his clever words, as they might have in the previous books; they plainly reveal his unsubstantial folly. It is highly significant that the Fourth Book concludes on a scene that sees Panurge enthralled in a quasi-mystical state of fear in which he fantasizes being surrounded by devils. Thus, the apprentice sorcerer, presented in *Pantagruel* as a most deceitful strategist and an amoral jack-of-all-trades who would have claimed to trick the devil, makes his final appearance in total psychic disarray, as if he had become the victim of his own cozening duplicity; so much so that fear has led him to a point where he has sullied his own clothes in the presence of all Pantagruel's companions. Confronted with this pitiful evidence of his own cowardice all he can do is deny the reality of his excrement by insisting that far from being what it appears to be, it is in fact precious "saffron from Spain," (*saphran d'Hibernie*) a most precious condiment indeed. One is reminded, in this instance, of Rabelais's warning to his readers in his prologue of *Gargantua* not to be duped by the apparent coarseness of his work. The *substantifique moelle* (St. Jerome's "substantial marrow") must be discovered underneath the grossness and filth of the surface: reading these stories should therefore be understood as a kind of alchemical work by which the pure metal of understanding is extracted from a seemingly rough and disgusting substance. This is the esoteric meaning of Rabelais's work, and it is also the true meaning of genuine folly. However, as Walter Kaiser has emphasized, Panurge is not a true fool in the evangelical sense. His folly is only fueled by natural reason and instinct, and not by a divine inspiration from above.[37] The conclusion of the *Quart-Livre* is, in this respect, a perfectly eloquent evidence of this fact: not only because Panurge is reduced to the bare manifestation of his own concupiscent nature, but also because his pretension at denying the truth by changing excrement

into precious spices is but a grotesque caricature of the true alchemical transmutation that Rabelais has in view.

*   *   *

By contrast with the figures of fools that have just been sketched,
Hamlet brings a tragic profundity to the clown's predicament. As
opposed to Hodja, Eulenspiegel, and Panurge who are *unable* to
change because they are "immovable movers," Hamlet is a character
who undergoes an inner transformation throughout the play. Is
Hamlet a fool, a madman, or a clown? In order to answer this question, one must begin by setting the stage of the tragedy in terms of the
relationship between kingship and folly. As William Willeford has
judiciously noted, the predicament of Denmark at the beginning of
the play lies in its having neither a king nor a king's fool.[38] In a traditional context, the king is like an outer manifestation of the divine,
whereas the fool is a reminder that the manifestation is not the divine
in itself. In a sense, kingly role corresponds to the exoteric, and the
fool's role to the esoteric. The exoteric tends to "absolutize" forms;
the esoteric tends to "break" them. In *Hamlet*, however, the king is
not legitimate, he is a usurper. Being illegitimate, the king cannot
have a fool to tell him the truth since his very situation is predicated
upon falsehood. Hamlet cannot be king since the throne has been
usurped, and he is not yet powerful and decisive enough to restore its
legitimacy. In a sense, he is constrained to be a fool because he cannot
be a king. His meeting with his father's ghost, and the secret that is
divulged to him during this encounter, is the symbol of his kingly
lineage: but this lineage must remain hidden. Hamlet must be a fool
in order to protect the secret of this lineage: thus, he is to be a king in
hiding, a king in spiritual exile. But he was not destined to be a fool,
he was destined to be a king; whence his incapacity to be a genuine
and effective fool, an incapacity that he must palliate through dissim-
ulation and madness. As a king, or as a legitimate heir, he should
assert the truth outwardly; not being able to do so, he must suggest
the truth obliquely, not as a jester who dare tell the truth to the king's
face, but as a mad clown who can only allude to it as to an absent reality.
Two absences meet in the figure of the mad fool that has become
Hamlet's second nature: that of the "exiled" king who must hide
under clownish madness, as Ulysses—upon returning to Ithaca—
disguised his kingly nature in the rags of a beggar; and that of the contemplative who must allude to the hidden truth through the symbols
of his apparent madness.

Hamlet is not a fool, at least in the usual sense, since he displays, throughout the tragedy, a metaphysical and strategic intelligence that sets him above the other protagonists of the play, spiritually speaking. Actually, Hamlet is so little a fool that he is the keenest at perceiving folly and foolishness in others. This is illustrated, for example, by his reference to Polonius as an "old fool," and by his advice to Ophelia to "marry a fool." In fact, Polonius epitomizes the worldly-wise fool, as testified both by his sound advice to his son Laertes and by his undeniable lack of wits. He may be considered, therefore, as Hamlet's opposite, at least insofar as Hamlet embodies "otherworldly" folly. After having killed Ophelia's father, Hamlet calls him an "intruding fool" (III, iv, 38) and "a foolish prating knave" (III, iv, 238). Moreover, Polonius actually plays the role of an entertaining buffoon in virtually all the scenes in which he is present. This is particularly true, of course, in the famous scene (II, ii) in which Polonius tries to find the "truth" about Hamlet's "madness." In this scene, we attend an instructive exchange, or lack thereof, between spiritual "madness" and worldly "folly." Polonius is eminently a "fool" in that he appears to be the only character to believe that Hamlet has actually become mad, this belief being founded on his conviction that his daughter Ophelia is the source of Hamlet's disturbed mind. Scene ii of act II is arguably the most comical scene in the whole play, precisely because it so sharply contrasts the real fool and the pretending one. Polonius relates each and every aspect of Hamlet's "lunacy" back to his daughter with a kind of foolish paternal obsession. Hamlet plays the fool, or the madman, but his repartee springs forth in a wealth of cryptic gibberish and obliquely wise statements. One of the richest and most revealing of these repartees sounds like a piece from an anthology of clowns' reversals: "you yourself, sir, should be old as I am if, like a crab, you could go backward" (II, ii, 220). The undeniable truism that this sentence highlights is set in the symbolic context of backward motion, an allusion that clearly bears the hallmark of the clown's contrariness and absurdity. No statement is therefore more deserving of the celebrated and unintentionally wise aside uttered by Polonius, "though this be madness, yet there is method in't." Not the least comical paradox of the play lies in that this keen, albeit unconscious, recognition of Hamlet's strategy is in fact pronounced by the most foolish and least discerning of all the characters. Hamlet's function as a clownish inverter of conventional language and truth also appears in his comical exchange with the courtier Osric. To the latter's claim that "it is hot," Hamlet retorts that " 'tis very cold." When the courtier thinks it well inspired to admit that "it is indifferent cold," Hamlet is prompted to reply that, actually, "it is very sultry and hot for my complexion" (V, ii, 100–105). The burlesque tone of this seemingly absurd conversation suggests how Hamlet conceives of his standing in life as a radical contradiction to things as they are perceived and distorted in and by the world, a world of human inhumanness in which truth and nobility have no say. Far from being a fool himself, Hamlet shows a capacity to allude to the most profound metaphysical realities, as when he refers to the mysteries that surround man, bearing witness to a sense of the sacred, and a sense of the unfathomable profundity of the real: "There are more things in heaven and earth, Horatio, Than are dreamt of in your philosophy" (I, v, 191–192). This metaphysical acumen makes him able to pierce through the veil of illusion, as evidenced by his acute awareness of worldly limitations: "How weary, stale, flat, and unprofitable Seem to me all the uses of this world" (I, ii, 139–140). Notwithstanding these statements, Hamlet is not a dreamer, as he has sometimes been made out to be, as evidenced by the fact that he displays sharp and penetrating insight, particularly in the domain of psychology, in which he excels. His knowledge of the human soul has no peer in the play. His gift is, in this respect, quasi-mediumistic, as befits a clown. Actually, he almost seems to be endowed with a kind of sixth sense, as when he reads the souls of his friends Rosencrantz and Guildenstern with a razorblade-like intuition of their real purpose: "You were sent for, and there is a kind of confession in your looks, which your modesties have not craft enough to color. I know the good King and Queen have sent you" (II, ii, 294–297). His strategic sense is no less impressive when dealing with the theatrical technicalities and effects designed to awaken his uncle's sense of shame and guilt, thereby uncovering his crime. Finally, he is remarkably perceptive with regard to knowledge of self. He has no illusions concerning himself, nor about human nature, as is clearly testified by the harsh words that he unleashes during his cruel but lucid confrontation with Ophelia: "I am myself indifferent honest, but yet I could accuse me of such things that it were better my mother had not borne me" (III, i, 132–134).

Despite his wide and profound intelligence, Hamlet is keen on playing the fool in order to protect himself, or in order to disarm his enemies. But this foolishness is more akin to mad gaiety or virtuoso verbal nimbleness than to the appearance of naivety. This is the case, for example, when he rushes to take leave from his good friend Horatio, following the appearance of the ghost, in order to keep his own counsel. Wishing to hide his secret from his friend, he indulges in a hurried, and somewhat comical, sequence of truisms and exhortations to part from the company of his dear friends "And so, without more circumstance at all, I hold it fit that we shake hands and part; You, as your business and desires shall point you, For everyman hath business and desire, Such as it is" (I, v, 143–147), thereby dispatching Horatio and preventing him from intruding into his hidden torment. Horatio defines Hamlet's speech in this instance as "wild and whirling words." However, it is also true that these "whirling words" point to the hero's spiritual solitude, as expressed by his need to attend to his own inner work away from his dearest friends.

Hamlet's first encounter with Rosencrantz and Guildenstern (II, ii) also reveals an extraordinary ability to play with language, thereby concealing his bleeding wounds and apprehensions, while giving vent to his repressed good humor and perhaps also veiling his first suspicions of his friends. However, even on this happy occasion, it is clear that his merrymaking and verbal foolery remain in tune with a sharply lucid view of the ills of the world. To Rosencrantz, who claims that "the world's grown honest," Hamlet responds with a dark and ironic joke, "Then is doomsday near!" before flatly denying his friend's assertion, "But your news is not true" (II, ii, 255). This is actually the first signal of the rift between Hamlet and his two friends. After having engaged in a good-natured and witty metaphoric exchange with them about the various parts of Fortune's body, as gifted students who could revel in displaying the keenness of their minds, he comes headfirst to a realization that his friends do not see the world as he does, and he understands thereby that their incapacity to see things as they are cannot but be the symptom of some hypocrisy on their part.

Hamlet's ability to "play the fool" with clever words also appears in an interesting light as he attends, in the company of the court, the play within the play during which he has planned to unmask his uncle's corruption. When Ophelia notices his somewhat elated mood, a mood that is prompted by an impassioned joy to see the king placed face to face with the enormity of his crime so that justice may be done, Hamlet responds at first with a feigned surprise, "who, I?", and then with an exclamation and a question that are not exempt from a taste of bitterness: "O God, your only jig-maker! What should a man do but merry?" (III, ii, 124–125). This question encapsulates the whole meaning of Hamlet's apparent foolery; confronted with a world that is disorderly and evil, and above all oblivious of its own corruption and hypocrisy in dealing with its own evils, the only ironic response is "merriment." It is therefore obvious that Hamlet's sense of absoluteness collides with the realities of the relative world. Such a collision is both a source of despair and an inspiration for clever irony, but it also

paradoxically animates a sense of foolishness and amusement that
is the only cure for the emotional violence of this condition. Verbal
games have, in particular, an important role to play in this subtle war
against the world. They isolate the lonely warrior in a world that is foreign to others. When confronted by his enemies, Hamlet likes to use
"wild and whirling words" like weapons that disorient others, or raise
their apprehensions and concerns. Playing on the ambiguity of words
amounts to keeping fallen men "on the brink" of fear and doubt, like
a clown who revels in unsettling those who "may smile and smile and
be a villain." As the king deplores that "clouds still hang on" him,
Hamlet jumps to an opposite image that both hides and reveals the
real substance of his mood: "Not so, my lord. I am too much i' the
sun" (I, ii, 71). This unexpected and sibylline response can be taken,
as so often with Hamlet's words, in more than one way. To the oft-
mentioned pun on "sun" and "son," one may add the image of the
blinding evidence of the evil of the Danish court and the gravity of its
predicament. Hamlet's melancholy is not a matter of mist and clouds,
it is rather the result of an unbearable certainty, the blinding certainty
that something "is rotten in the state of Denmark" and that "the time
is out of joint." This interpretation of the phrase can be buttressed by
the lines that conclude scene ii of the same act, when Hamlet declares
that "foul deeds will rise, though all the earth o'erwhelm them, to
men's eyes" (I, ii, 281–282). The "sun" of the blinding evidence of
evil cannot be covered for long, or at least not forever. Between the
allusively sibylline and the suggestively incoherent, Hamlet plays the
fool, or the madman, by turning upside down and vertiginously
whirling the daily language of men. It is interesting to note that
Ophelia's fall into unambiguous madness will lead her into becoming
a kind of sublime echo of Hamlet's voice, uttering meaningfully symbolic nonsense like him. In the presence of the king, Ophelia's madness
seems to emulate Hamlet's enigmas, and the literal nonsensicalness of
her words mysteriously alludes to looming and unfathomable dimensions of destiny: "They say the owl was a baker's daughter. Lord, we
know what we are, but know not what we may be" (IV, v, 43–46).

The central question related to Hamlet's "folly" is obviously that of
real madness versus feigned madness. In a sense, the difficulty is symbolically acknowledged by Polonius—a fool who, as such, has to tell
the truth in his own laughable way—when the "perfect knave" asserts
that "Mad call I it (Hamlet's madness); for, to define true madness,
what is't but to be nothing else than mad" (II, ii, 99–100). The
impossibility of defining madness otherwise than through a pleonastic
truism hints at the mystery of Hamlet's state. That Polonius claims to

have discovered the cause of Hamlet's "lunacy" is another example of the receding mystery of this ailment, for we know full well that Hamlet's sickness is not really an amorous *mania*.[39] Coleridge's assessment that Hamlet's deportment is "less than madness and more than feigning"[40] is an important key in this respect. It clearly points to the nonpathological state of the hero while suggesting that madness might be understood in a way that is less medical than metaphysical, or spiritual. The play gives unambiguous evidence of the feigned character of Hamlet's mad behavior. The most explicit of these pieces of evidence springs forth from Hamlet's mouth: "I am but mad north-north-west. When the wind is southerly I know a hawk from a handsaw" (II, ii, 388). This is not only a pleasant, albeit cryptic, allusion to the alleged influence of particular winds upon depressive states, it is also and above all a lucid and symbolic recognition, on the part of the prince, of the feigned psychological state into which he has thrown himself. If "losing the north" might refer to a fall into madness, the reference to the north-northwest direction subtly points to the small gap between true and feigned madness, a small gap that is in fact *everything* in Hamlet's folly. Moreover, by speaking in this way, Hamlet already gives himself away to his friends Rosencrantz and Guildenstern. This probably explains, at least in part, why they are not totally duped by his feigned madness, as testified by their report to the king, when they mention his "crafty madness" as a way to "keep aloof" from them (III, i, 8). The king himself, not without perspicacity, notices that Hamlet's vehement discourse to Ophelia, "though it lacked form a little, Was not like madness" (III, i, 173–174). Accordingly, the king has a clear intuition that Hamlet's madness, whatever might be its causes and its scope, is not of an ordinary kind. "Madness in great ones must not unwatched go" (III, i, 198) is a sentence that bears witness both to Claudius's political foresight, and to a perspicacious sense of the looming mystery of his nephew's imbalance. By contrast, one of the paradoxes of the play rests in the fact that Hamlet is thought to be mad at a time when he perceives reality in the most evident manner, and when he is actually beginning to part from his "madness in craft." During the scene in which he confronts his mother, the appearance of the ghost of his father plunges him into an ecstasy that prompts the queen to think him mad (III, iv, 120). From this there ensues the necessity, for Hamlet, to unveil to his mother the secret of his "crafted" madness (III, iv, 208–210). It is when he perceives messages from the "other world," truer than nature, that Hamlet is thought to be mad, but it is also at this juncture that he must dispel the veil of his strategy to enter into the realm of real communication with his mother. This scene is like a release of his burden, a restoration of the relationship with his mother, and the foundation for his revenge. Martin Lings has written that the discourse of Hamlet to the queen—which can also be interpreted as a discourse addressed to his own soul—reveals "an exalted penetration worthy of a spiritual master who has years of practical experience of the mystic path behind him."[41] From now on, Hamlet has reached a level of lucidity about himself and others that will be the foundation of his spiritual work. He has known himself ("mad in craft") and has perfectly understood the logic of spiritual ascesis: "I must be cruel only to be kind" (III, iv, 199).

Although Hamlet's madness is often political strategy, it is not mere pretense. His state of psychic imbalance and melancholy is undeniable. It is undoubtedly based on a violent reaction to certain aspects of the human predicament. During the scene in which Hamlet voices his bitter rage against mankind before Ophelia, he specifically mentions having been made "mad," thereby pointing in very explicit terms to the profound wound that is harming him. The "it" of "it hath made me mad" (III, i, 156) has a somewhat ambiguous referent: it may seem to refer to women's "jig, amble and lisp," but it is much more likely that it obliquely alludes to the royal adultery, and more generally to the terrestrial evil that this particular instance exemplifies. The madness of Hamlet is a metaphysical and moral ill: the prince can no longer bear with the sharp edges of relative existence, especially as they manifest themselves blatantly through human vices and deceptions. If the world is too small for him it is because his thirst for infinity and perfection cannot be quenched here-below: "the earth [. . .] seems to me a sterile promontory" (II, ii, 314).

*   *   *

The use of theater as a strategic device for revealing the true nature of the guilty is one of the hallmarks of Hamlet's play on the intermediary zone between reality and illusion, of which sanity and madness are both a symbol and a part. One will remember, in this connection, Hamlet's definition of theater as "the abstract and brief chronicles of the time" (II, ii, 532). Theater is indeed more "real" than the world because its level of "abstraction" allows for the communication of a higher "concentration" of the truth, a truth that remains otherwise too diluted, and cannot therefore be as easily perceived in the "real world." Hamlet loves theater because he loves the truth, and because he has a sense for illusion. His cordiality toward the actors is directly evident, and one is under the definite impression that he feels as one of them. This, no doubt, is a result of his disgust with the world, but also a consequence of his feeling marginalized in the world of men. There is much of the sad clown in Hamlet, and the rapidity of his changes of mood testifies to a clownish ability to switch back and forth between extremes of human emotion. There is, in the same context, Hamlet's affinities with clowns and jesters. In a sense he himself plays the role of the king's jester at court, telling the truth in the guise of semi-intelligible puns and apparent nonsense. A major instance of his relationship with the world of jest is the famous scene (V, i) in which he engages the clown at the burial ground. This scene joins together death and laughter by evoking the precariousness of human life and laughter, but it also shows Hamlet being fooled by a fool, an occurrence that is in itself a symbol of the tragicomic predicament of the hero. Hamlet nevertheless manifests a kind of relish in his dealing with this "absolute knave." He feels close to him in some sense, as if his own folly were mirrored in the clown's. Hamlet feels "at home" among fools, and it almost appears as if his contact with fools, actors, and clowns might be his only way to crack the walls of his solitude. As Malcolm A. Nelson has judiciously stated, it is "his grand quest for justice that also leads to his isolation as a fool,"[42] whence the sense of commonality, and almost complicity, that he experiences in his dealings with marginal fools and people of the theater; whence also the utterly idiosyncratic and cryptic meaning of his language, a language of puns and allusions that isolates him from his fellow humans. The affinity of Hamlet with the world of dramatic representations is such, in fact, that his contact with theater awakens and energizes the actor and the joker in him. When attending the play by Ophelia's side, he answers the young woman's question, "what means this, my Lord?" by indulging in a play on words and alliterations, "marry this is miching malicho; it means mischief" (III, ii, 148–149). He also revels in witty and somewhat brisk remarks that point to the ultimate inanity of human passions and actions, as when he defines "nothing" as a "fair thought to lie between maids' legs" (III, ii, 118). When put in contact with actors, or while attending the performance of the play that he has masterminded, Hamlet appears to be in his element, so to speak. This element is more "real" to him than the actual everyday reality, a paradoxical situation that is symbolically expressed in his famous utterance, "The play's the thing." These words resound as highly significant when they are placed in apposition with the "nothing" that tends to come through Hamlet's lips to encapsulate his view of life and the world. Theater is akin to jest: it must appear to be an

illusion in order to point all the more powerfully to reality, just as the
jester must appear especially foolish in order to be all the wiser.
Illusion may obliquely refer to reality within the context of its "illusory
reality," like theater, which is a microcosm in which the content of life
is as if essentialized, or reduced to its archetypes. When the king
expresses his concern to Hamlet that there could be "offenses" in the
play, Hamlet answers through a subtle *double entendre*, "no, no! They
(the actors) do but jest, poison in jest; no offense i' the word" (III, ii,
248). The poison is only theatrical in the sense of being "represented,"
but the real "poison" is in the jest of theater since it is aiming at the
king. As theater, Hamlet's words are neither totally one-sided nor do
they bear a single meaning. Hamlet's uncomfortable position between
two worlds can only find a refuge in the domain that lays on their
boundaries, that is, theater. The supreme paradox is that Hamlet's
passion for sincerity, justice, and truth leads him to embrace a world
of theatrical representations. Hamlet hates appearances, but he works
on them for the sake of truth. He unmasks falsehood and illusions
everywhere they manifest, especially in social hypocrisy, when "one
may smile, and smile, and be a villain (I, v, 115). On a deeper level, he
rejects the appearances taken by social morality. His acute and painful
self-knowledge is not merciful to other characters' presumptions,
inconsistencies, and psychic recoiling or blind spots. When the queen
remonstrates with him on account of his brooding over his deceased
father ("why seems it so particular with thee?"), Hamlet responds
with words that make his search for and love of sincerity and reality
quite plain, "Seems, madam? Nay, it is. I know not 'seems.'" (I, ii, 81).
The initial situation of Hamlet at the court of his deceased father is
indicative of, and analogous to, his living in a world in which God's
traces have been erased, and in which everybody lives under the pretentious lie of being able to go about being human without Him. This
is the self-deceptive delusion that Dom Aelred Graham has judiciously
related to the Hindu notion of *Mâyâ*.[43] The all too famous "To be or
not be?" is, in a sense, like a complement to the statement about
"seems." Hamlet cannot live in the world of "seems," he can only be
or not be. The real paradox though, is that he is obliged to mask himself in the name of sincerity. In a sense his suffering stems from an
inability to be himself in the context of human society. He is obliged
to find refuge in theater to connect with reality. Moreover, this quest
of reality within illusion set against the background of an illusion of
reality is also akin to a keen awareness that life is a comedy in which all
human individuals are playing a role. There is undoubtedly a sense in
which Hamlet manifests an intuition of the only Self that lies beneath

the myriad of human masks. The chasm between the terrestrial precariousness of human individuals and the glory of the consciousness that inhabits them is perhaps expressed in the famous lines in which Hamlet attests to his disillusionment about mankind: "What a piece of work is man! How noble in reason! How infinite in faculties! [. . .] in apprehension how like a god! [. . .] And yet to me what is this quintessence of dust?" (II, ii, 115–117).

As Frithjof Schuon has pointed out, Hamlet has pierced the veil of illusion of *Mâyâ*, but he has not gained a sure footing in the world of the Absolute.[44] Symbolically speaking, he is immersed in the world of Ecclesiastes, having realized the *vanitas vanitatum*,[45] but he has no concrete access to the world of the Psalms, the blessed realm of the relationship with God that is predicated upon a sense of His presence. Hamlet's whole perspective bears the mark of this imbalance. Madness, whether it be melancholy and depression or feigned lunacy, is the symptom of this uneven and unstable position. In a sense, therefore, there is no other possible outcome for Hamlet but to die, since the world in which he lives cannot be envisaged by him in light of truth and being. The sacrifice of Hamlet is initiated in melancholy and madness, and it is perfected in a heroic death. It is interesting to note that, preceding the duel with Laertes that will mark his death, Hamlet asks for forgiveness from his opponent: this is like a precondition to his spiritual recovery, a penance preceding the reception of the holy host. At this crucial moment, Hamlet refers to a duality within himself: he denies ever having wronged Laertes of his own accord, but recognizes that if wrong there was, it was on account of his madness. "His madness is poor Hamlet's enemy" (V, ii, 240): such are the final words that Hamlet utters to refer to the tragic schism within himself. Referring to this madness, objectifying it in such clear terms, Hamlet avers that he has finally been able to cure himself from it. But what is this "madness" to which Hamlet refers *in fine*? It can neither be simply a psychic imbalance akin to melancholy and dreaminess, nor can it be *a fortiori* the feigning of madness. On a most immediate level, in asking Laertes for forgiveness, Hamlet must allude to the two deaths that have struck Laertes because of Hamlet's actions: his father's and his sister's. Hamlet is responsible for these deaths inasmuch as they were provoked by his rash emotional and physical violence. The "madness" of Hamlet is, in that sense, none other than his passion, a passion that is characterized by a blend of disgust, bitterness, and anger. This is the wound of his soul, the evil from which he must be purified and redeemed. Considered from this standpoint, Hamlet's death is the ultimate consequence of his entering into the cycle of passional actions and reactions. His passivity vis-à-vis this cycle is in fact profoundly connected to the one-sided contemplativity that was mentioned earlier. Hamlet's inability to integrate action into contemplation, his lack of contentment with being God's hand as it were, leaves him with the only recourse of rushing into passional and violent outbursts that are both the symptoms of his soul's sickness and his tragic pitfall. Still, the final scene of the play instructs us clearly that Hamlet has reached the status of a posthumous hero. In his retrospective eulogy, Fortinbras, the higher alter ego of the Danish prince, declares, "he (Hamlet) was likely, had he been put on, To have proved most royally" (V, ii, 429–430). In other words, it is attested by one of his peers that Hamlet had the substance of a king even though the accidents of his destiny, and the shortcomings of his unredeemed soul, prevented him from actualizing the fruits of this royal substance in this life. It might be that the obstructions and delays of destiny on Hamlet's way to his true self testify to the mystery of a heterogeneous nature that combines, in a somewhat unresolved tension, the detachment of the contemplative and the aggressive and noble passion of the warrior. Hamlet is neither completely a priest—even though he wears the dark garb and shares the disillusion of one who has rended the veil of cosmic illusion—nor integrally a warrior, even though his highly subjective way of envisaging ideals and principles is imbued with the impulsive generosity of a fighter. This dual nature, or this inability to fully actualize one point of view, bears witness, more generally, to the ambiguities of the human predicament, as it is suspended between two worlds, on the tightrope of terrestrial existence. But there is another sense in which Hamlet's limitations and lack of integration, as manifested in rashness and indiscretion, are not merely spiritual stains to be purged as a preparation for something better. From a demiurgic point of view, these shortcomings and failures have knit the very fabric of his and others' destiny, a fate that despite its disappointing unevenness and sharp sufferings has served the "greater glory of God." In the scene that follows the episode of his violent confrontation with Laertes, Hamlet asserts his awareness of a demiurgic alchemy of providence:

> And praised be rashness for it; let us know,
> Our indiscretion sometime serves us well
> When our deep plots do pall; and that should learn us
> There's a divinity that shapes our ends,
> Rough-hew them how we will. (V, ii, 8–12)

It is significant that, at this juncture, Horatio echoes his friend and master's new trust in Divine Providence with a "that is most certain" that cuts so sharply from the indecisions and ambiguities that have, so far, plagued Hamlet's resolution.

Hamlet is the prince of the *via negationis*. As James L. Calderwood has insightfully suggested, *Hamlet* is a play in which negation and absence occupy a central role.[46] They are to be found in the language, the psychology, and the philosophical implications of the play. The *via negativa* approaches the mystery exclusively through negation because it recognizes the transcendence and the infinite distance that separates our world from the absoluteness of the Divine. The *via affirmationis*, by contrast, affirms the Divine through analogies: the King of Heaven is also "representable" in and through the terrestrial king. Now *Hamlet* is a play in which the central character cannot perceive or embody the Absolute, enmeshed as he is in the worrisome uncertainties of the relative. His rejection of terrestrial love, "we will have no more marriage," avers his inability to embrace what is arguably the affirmation *nec plus ultra* of the way of participation, immanence, and analogy, that is, human love. Similarly, Hamlet's repeated uncertainties about death and the beyond, "to' sleep—perchance to dream," also indicate that he is lost indeed in the midst of a sort of *noche oscura*. All he can say is not say anything in the ordinary language of men, whence his amazing and cryptic statements, his allusive puns and his frail prophecies; all he can do is but play the fool, acting instead of being; he substitutes apparent absence with presence, seeming absurdity with meaning, feigned madness with sanity. His absent-mindedness, isolation, and puns are like exercises in negative theology. This is why he cannot be king, whereas Fortinbras will ultimately be king, since he is a kind of solar theophany whose very name suggests vigor and power. Hamlet's actions can only be "negative," he kills and he is killed, but the restoration cannot be his own doing. The destructive dimension of Hamlet is purifying, but it is not intimately connected to his own rebirth as a king, even though it paves the ground for a rebuilding of the kingdom of Denmark. In a sense, Hamlet's death expresses the archetype of the prince's initiation into kingship, "the prince dies that the king may be born of him."[47] However, Hamlet has been too contaminated, as it were, by the evil of the kingdom to be reborn himself as a king. In *Hamlet*, the princely clown can be no more than the sacrificial witness of a terrifying transcendence that is out of reach of human gestures and words. Clowning bears witness to the gap that lies between this world and the hereafter, the mixed and the good.

CHAPTER 12

EPILOGUE: CRACKS OF LIGHT

Cracks of light: these words allude to a variety of phenomena on several levels of reality. The word "crack" may first of all refer to a flaw, or a split in the wall of being; but the word can also suggest an unsoundness of mind, a sudden noise, and a narrow opening. The world of relativity is a realm of flawed qualities, at least when envisaged from the standpoint of existential limitations. In this domain, splits are everywhere inasmuch as relativity means separation. As the process of creative and demiurgic manifestation unfolds, the archetypical purity of qualities becomes gradually altered by the flaws and breaks of evil and nothingness. Lurianic Kabbalah tells of a symbolic "breaking of the divine vases" in order to allude to this mysterious entry into the world of dissimilitude. The essence remains the essence, and its core qualitative sap remains fundamentally no less real below than it is above, but the thickening veil of existentiation makes it increasingly difficult to reach its pristine message. From a certain point of view *Mâyâ* is, and cannot but be, flawed; this flaw being nothing other than the trace of its being "relatively" unfaithful to *Âtman*. Demiurgic tricksters take this unfaithfulness to the limits of seeming absurdity; they take upon themselves to act out—or rather, they are sacrificed to the metaphysical necessity of acting out—the dimension of unintelligibility that is entailed in the externalization of the Infinite; they proceed to unleash this "scandal" by acting up and falling down.

From another standpoint the thickening of the veil amounts to a rising up of walls that obfuscate the only Light. In banging head first into these walls, sacred clowns and holy fools are merrily but painfully involved in a cosmological or psychological widening of the cracks of *Mâyâ*. They point to them, symbolically act them out, often widen them purposefully for the sake of letting the Light be.

How can the Hindu Advaitin consider the world as both real and unreal? How can Christians be both "in this world" and "not of this world"? We have suggested that the answers to these questions are intimately connected to a sense of play and folly. Shiva plays with the forms that he constantly affirms and negates. As the clown of Sanskrit drama, the *Vidūsaka*, he is more involved in the process than in the stases that mark this process.[1] He espouses and explodes becoming in praise of Being; he bears witness both to the reality and to the unreality of the world through his maddening dance. Analogously, Christian holy fools bring the Word to the world through a staccato negation of worldly values in and by which they deny themselves, or—from the reverse standpoint—a denial of themselves by means of negating worldly ways.

The demiurgic and the clownish have to do with the instant, like the flash-like Shiva and the burlesque and precipitous fall from the roof ceremoniously staged by Hopi clowns. In a sense, the instant is now; in another sense, it is coming. Demiurgic gods and tricksters, sacred clowns, holy fools, and the resounding thunder of laughter—all are situated on the vertical axis of shock and suddenness. On this axis, laughter is unexpectedly and oddly akin to tears, and only a superficial understanding of both the comic and the pathetic can oppose them within a lame antithesis. Commenting upon Abraham's laughter at God's pronouncement of his impending fatherhood, Louis Massignon writes:

> [. . .] Abraham's perfect laughter, henceforth ready for everything, axial in relation to the divine source, [. . .] (is) still also the source of the serene tears of his supreme sacrifice: "*hinayni*" (*adsum*).[2]

In this higher mode, we have seen that laughter is a mode of presence, a thundering affirmation—and negation—which means "here I am." True laughter, as true tears, is a mode of poverty, or humility, vis-à-vis the instant of the Divine. But laughter is also the signal of the forthcoming judgment. As we have suggested on numerous occasions, demiurges, clowns, and fools are, in a sense, spokesmen of the "apocalypse." They are astonishing agents, or rather broken instruments, of the sudden unveiling of Reality. Their eschatological function has undoubtedly to do with an acceleration of history, as is already suggested by their ability to spin the wheel of becoming. The dissemination of being that is entailed by the unfolding of manifestation is both their curse and their *raison d'être*. They exhaust possibilities until the divine basket is emptied. Besides, they help to shatter the world of dreams through their lightning-like feats and their explosive jokes. Their function is one of spiritual presence, an abrupt but ultimately merciful reminder that, "He who laughs last, laughs best."

NOTES

INTRODUCTION

1. *Le paradoxe du monothéisme*, Paris, L'Herne,1992.
2. "This contact between the Divine and the human is, by reason of its elusiveness, a mystery, and even the mystery par excellence, for we touch God 'everywhere and nowhere,' as Pascal would say. God is quite close to us, infinitely close, but we are far from Him; He is incarnate in a given symbol, but we risk grasping only the husk, retaining only the shadow. Idolatry, which divinizes the shadow as such, and atheism, which denies God by reason of His intangibility—but it is we who are 'absent,' not God—reduce to absurdity the two aspects of symbolism: identity, which is unitive, and analogy, which is separative, but parallel." Frithjof Schuon, *Stations of Wisdom*, Bloomington: World Wisdom, 1995, p.70.
3. "'Mediation' [. . .] is always achieved by introducing a third category which is 'abnormal' or 'anomalous' in terms of ordinary 'rational' categories. Thus myths are full of fabulous monsters, incarnate gods, virgin mothers. This middle ground is abnormal, non-natural, holy." Edmund Leach, "Genesis as Myth," *Discovery*, 23, 30–35, May 1962.
4. Translated by W.F. Trotter, "Car enfin qu'est-ce que l'homme dans la nature? Un néant à l'égard de l'infini, un tout à l'égard du néant, un milieu entre rien et tout." *Pensées*, II: *Misère de l'homme sans Dieu*, 72. Translated by W.F. Trotter. "L'homme n'est ni ange ni bête, et le malheur veut que qui veut faire l'ange fait la bête." *Pensées*, VI: *Les philosophes*, 358. Dover Publications, 2003.
5. *Lame Deer, Seeker of Visions*, by John Fire/Lame Deer and Richard Erdoies, New York: Touchstone, 1972, p.79.
6. "This book contains many facts that Indians, until recently, had avoided divulging because they thought, with reason, that these things are too sacred to be communicated to just anybody; nowadays, the few old sages who still live among them say that as the end of the cycle is approaching, when men have become everywhere incapable of understanding and above all of realizing the truths that were revealed to them in the origin—together with the consequence of disorder and chaos in all domains—it is allowed and even preferable to bring this knowledge into full light; for truth defends itself against profanation by its own nature, and it is possible that thus it may reach those who are qualified

to penetrate it deeply and capable, thanks to it, to strengthen the bridge that must be built to lead out of this dark age." Translation of Frithjof Schuon's "Avant-propos," in Héhaka Sapa, *Les rites secrets des indiens sioux*, collected and annotated by Joseph Epes Brown, translated by Frithjof Schuon and René Allar, Paris: Payot, 1975, p.5.

7. Barry Holstun Lopez, *Giving Birth to Thunder, Sleeping with His Daughter: Coyote Builds North America*, New York: Perennial, 1990.

1 *MÂYÂ* AND THE DIVINE TREASURE

1. This "before" is to be interpreted as a symbol of metaphysical primacy, and not of chronological anteriority.

2. Cf. Henry Corbin, *Alone with the Alone: Creative Imagination in the Sufism of Ibn Arabî*, translated by Ralph Manheim, Princeton: Princeton University Press, 1998. The Greek term *kenôsis* ("emptying") refers to the theological commentary of Phil. 2:6–8: "Who being in the form of God, thought it not robbery to be equal with God: But emptied [*ekenosen*] himself, taking the form of a servant, being made in the likeness of men, and in habit found as man." It primarily symbolizes the "ontological humiliation," lowering, or emptying, of God taking flesh for the Redemption of mankind. But it may be more generally applied, in mystical theology, to God's "letting be" of His exclusive Reality for the sake of the "being" of other-than-Himself. In the Kabbalah of Isaac Luria, the Infinite contracts (*tsimtsum*) and withdraws to allow the Creation to be. It is from this "withdrawal" that evil springs forth through the *qelippot* (literally "shells," singular *qelippa*) in which the divine Light becomes entrapped after the breaking of the divine vases from which manifestation emanates.

3. This notion, as also the concept of "subject–object consciousness," was forged by Franklin Merrell-Wolff in his *Pathways through to Space*, New York: Julian Press, 1973.

4. Swami Prabhavananda, *Spiritual Heritage of India*, Madras: Sri Ramakrishna Math, 1977, p.43.

5. Ibid., p.288.

6. Cf. *Pathways through to Space*, New York, 1973, pp.148–150.

7. *Brahmasutrabhâsya*, II, 1, 33, translated by George Thibaut, Oxford, 1890.

8. *Holy Laughter*, edited by M. Conrad Hyers, New York: Seabury Press, 1969, pp.24–25.

9. Cf. Titus Burckhardt, *Introduction to Sufism*, San Francisco, 1995, pp.65–66.

10. "The idea of *mâyâ*, the world as the magical display of the gods, describes a world that is enchanting, topsy-turvy, and ephemeral. The world born of *mâyâ* is at once a stage created by the gods upon which they may strut, a toy for their amusement, and a mirage through and

by which they may dazzle. As a by-product of divine display, the world as the play of the gods or the magic of the gods is a fleeting, albeit dazzling, creation that lacks ultimate reality." David R. Kinsley, "Creation as Play in Hindu Spirituality," *Studies in Religion/Sciences Religieuses*, 4.2, 1974/5, p.113.

11. Eknath Easwaran, "Three in One: Spirit, Matter, and Mâyâ," *Parabola Magazine*, 14.4, 1989, p.27.

12. "L'homme de l'Occident est un homme essentiellement tragique parce que la négativité est chez lui originaire et non dérivée. Sa croyance à la réalité de l'ego nous paraît expliquer ce par quoi il se distingue fondamentalement de l'homme asiatique traditionnel." Georges Vallin, "Le Tragique de l'Occident à la lumière du non-dualisme asiatique," *Revue philosophique de la France et de l'étranger*, 165, 1975, p.280.

["Western man is essentially tragic because, with him, negativity is original and not derivative. We think that his belief in the reality of the ego is the explicatory principle of his fundamental difference from the traditional mankind of Asia."]

2   AMBIGUITY OF THE DEMIURGE

1. Frithjof Schuon, *Logic and Transcendence*, London, 1975, p.152.

2. Ibid., p.154.

3. The Infinite is faceless because it transcends and encompasses all faces: "And Allâh's is the East and the West, therefore, whither you turn, thither is Allâh's face; surely Allah is Amplegiving, Knowing" (*Qur'ân* 2:115).

4. Frithjof Schuon, *Survey of Metaphysics and Esoterism*, Bloomington: World Wisdom, 1986, p.23.

5. "To the extent that the God of Genesis is all-powerful in His creation, matter is a passive substrate; to the extent, however, that He is not responsible for evil in the world, matter is a factor of recalcitrance, though its role is reduced to a minimum and it shares the function of recalcitrance with human souls, which can turn in their freedom of choice to corruption." Gretchen Reydams-Schils, *Demiurge and Providence, Stoic and Platonist Readings of Plato's Timaeus*, Turnhout, Brepols 1999, p.150.

6. [*houtô dê pan hoson ên horaton paralabôn ouch hêsuchian agon alla kinoumenon plêmmelôs kai ataktôs, eis taxin auto êgagen ek tês ataxias, hêgêsamenos ekeino toutou pantôs ameinon*]. Cf. The Perseus Digital Library, Gregory Crane, Editor-In-Chief, Tufts University, www. perseus.tufts.edu. Text based on the following books: Plato. Plato in Twelve Volumes, Vol. 4 translated by Harold North Fowler. Cambridge, MA; London, 1977. Plato. Plato in Twelve Volumes, Vol. 7 translated by R.G. Bury. Cambridge, MA; London, 1966. Plato. Plato in Twelve Volumes, Vol. 8 translated by W.R.M. Lamb. Cambridge, MA; London, 1955. Plato. Plato in Twelve Volumes, Vol. 9

translated by W.R.M. Lamb. Cambridge, MA; London: William Heinemann Ltd., 1925.

7. [*agathos ên, agathôi de oudeis peri oudenos oudepote engignetai phthonos: toutou d' ektos ôn panta hoti malista eboulêthê genesthai paraplêsia heautôi*].

8. *Purusha* and *Prakrti* refer strictly speaking to the level of Being, thereby transcending the realm of the Demiurge, but what happens "above" is analogous to what happens "below." Moreover, as the Demiurge can sometimes be understood in the widest sense as a dimension of Being itself.

9. "The Demiurge is no separate power or Independent Divinity, but merely a part or faculty of the World Soul, his apparent independence being due solely to the mythical form of the exposition." Ibid., p.10.

10. "In [. . .] the demiurgic Shiva of the *Trimûrti* [. . .] it is not always easy to make a clear separation between principial necessity and demoniacal initiative; or between the wrath of Heaven and this or that malefic caprice of the *samsâra*." Frithjof Schuon, *Having a Center*, Bloomington, World Wisdom, 1990, p.67.

11. The black and white checkered textile that is the emblem of Shiva in Bali, the uses of which stem from devotion to magic, is a direct expression of this ambiguity.

12. Another passage of the *Qur'ân* states: "Remember how the unbelievers plotted against thee, to keep thee in bonds, or slay thee, or get thee out (of thy home). They plot and plan, and Allah too plans; but the best of planners is Allah" (8:30).

13. Cf. René Guénon, "Le Démiurge," *Mélanges*, Paris, Gallimard, 1976, p.13.

14. Ibid., p.25.

15. Moreover, the King James version illustrates the two aspects of the matter by specifying "for thy sake" and "to thee," thereby indicating that the "malefic" aspect of nature is not primordial but postlapsarian in origin.

16. Robert Ambelain, *La Notion gnostique du Démiurge*, Paris, Adyar 1959, pp.102–103.

17. "Thus *bereshit bara Elohim* (usually 'in the beginning God created') is interpreted mystically to refer to the first three *Sefirot*: through the medium (the prefix *be*) of *Hokhmah* (called *reshit*), the first *Sefirah*—the force hidden within the third person singular of the word *bara*—produced by an act of emanation the third *Sefirah* (*Binah*), which is also called *Elohim*." Gershom Scholem, *Kabbalah*, New York: Dorset Press, 1974, p.110.

18. Leo Schaya, *L'Homme et l'Absolu selon la Kabbale*, Paris: Dervy-Livres 1977, p.44.

19. Ibid., p.162.

20. Scholem, *Kabbalah*, p.110.

21. It goes without saying that this divine unfolding using the Kabbalistic symbolic distinction between grammatical persons refers to a totally different point of view than that which is involved in the Sufi interpretation of the *hadîth qudsî* that we used as an opening pointer.

22. Frithjof Schuon, *To Have a Center*, Bloomington, Indiana: World Wisdom, 1990, p.102.

23. "Cependant, nous savons que la notion d'un démiurge aux ordres de Iaweh était familière à certaines sectes juives de la période de Saadia, sectes dont les doctrines demeurèrent pendant fort longtemps à la limite extrême du judaïsme rabbinique orthodoxe, et ce sont elles qui, certainement, inspirèrent les docteurs gnostiques non-juifs." *La notion gnostique*, p.43.

24. Frithof Schuon, *Roots of the Human Condition*, Bloomington: World Wisdom, 2002, p.71.

25. "Quand nous trouvons chez Saint Jean l'expression 'Prince du Monde', ou plus exactement 'Archonte du Monde', nous entendons qu'il s'agit du Diable, *et l'habitude nous cache la singularité de l'expression*! C'est bien le Diable, en effet, mais non pas tel que nous le concevons, non pas un Esprit qui sortirait accidentellement de l'Enfer pour jouer sur terre quelque mauvais tour aux humains. C'est un diable qui est, avant tout, le Prince du Monde. Il est le symbole, l'action, la loi, de l'Univers. C'est, si l'on veut, le Dieu du Monde" (Simone Pétrement, *Le Dualisme chez Platon, les gnostiques et les manichéens*, Paris, PUF 1947, VI, 1).

26. Frithjof Schuon defines this "Supreme Angel" as "the projection of the Absolute in the relative," by contrast with the "Personal God" who corresponds to the "prefiguration of the relative in the Absolute." *Le jeu des masques*, Lausanne, 1992, p.12.

27. Gershom Scholem, *Kabbalah*, New York: Dorset Press, 1974, p.377. This vision induced Elisha ben Avuyah to postulate a form of dualism *in divinis*.

28. Schaya, *L'Homme et l'Absolu selon la Kabbale*, p.78.

29. David J. Halperin, "Sabbatai Zevi, Metatron, and Mehmed: Myth and History in Seventeenth-Century Judaism" in *The Seductiveness of Jewish Myth*, edited by S. Daniel Breslauer, Albany: State University of New York Press, p.282.

30. David J. Halperin sees Metatron as "a Johnny-come-lately in the heavenly realms," ibid., p.279.

31. Halperin, "Sabbatai Zevi," p.272.

32. Cf. Scholem, *Kabbalah*, p.379.

33. Ibid., p.380.

34. Cf. A.K. Coomaraswamy, "Kwâjâ Khadir et la Fontaine de Vie," *Etudes Traditionnelles*, Paris, août–septembre 1938, no.224–225, pp.310–311.

35. Ibid., p.311.

36. Cf. Albert Abecassis, "Le Prophète Elie dans la tradition juive," *Connaissance des Religions*, Vol. IV, no. 1–2, 1988, p.141.
37. Leo Schaya, "The Mission of Elias," *Studies in Comparative Religion*, Bedfont, England, 14–15 (1980–1983), pp.159–167.
38. The *Tikkun* refers, in Lurianic Kabbalah, to the spiritual work of man as he strives to remedy, on the level of Creation, the breaking of the Sephirotic vases which were to receive the emanation of Perfection. This symbolic metaphysical statement accounts, in its own suggestive way, to the "incomplete" and imperfect nature of *Mâyâ*.

3   Dionysus, Shiva, Osiris

1. Walter F. Otto, *Dionysus, Myth and Cult*, Bloomington: Indiana University Press, 1965, pp.65–73.
2. Plutarch, *Peri Isidos kai Osiridos, Isis and Osiris*, Plutarch's de Iside et Osiride, edited by J. Gwyn Griffiths, Cardiff: University of Woles Press, 1970, 355b.
3. Simone Weil, *Waiting for God*, New York, 2000, p.28.
4. "As a true god he symbolizes an entire world whose spirit reappears in ever new forms and unites in an eternal unity the sublime with the simple, the human with the animal, the vegetative and the elemental." Walter Otto, *Dionysus*, p.202.
5. Ibid., p.203.
6. Ibid., p.74.
7. "I had no desire to give my daughter to this person, who has broken all rules of civility. Because of not observing the required rules and regulations, he is impure, but I was obliged to hand over my daughter to him just as one teaches the messages of the Vedas to a sudra. He lives in filthy places like crematoriums, and his companions are the ghosts and demons. Naked like a madman, sometimes laughing and sometimes crying, he smears crematorium ashes all over his body. He does not bathe regularly, and he ornaments his body with a garland of skulls and bones. Therefore only in name is he Siva, or auspicious; actually, he is the most mad and inauspicious creature. Thus he is very dear to crazy beings in the gross mode of ignorance, and he is their leader." *Bhâgavata Purâna*, IV,13–15, translation Swami Prabhupâda.
8. Ibid., IV, 21–22.
9. René Guénon: "Shiva est appelé Pashupati, le 'Seigneur des êtres liés', parce que c'est par son action 'transformatrice' qu'ils sont 'délivrés' <Shiva is called Pashupati, the 'Lord of bonded beings,' because it is through his 'transforming' action that they are 'delivered.'>." *L'Homme et son devenir selon le Vedanta*, Paris: Editions Traditionnelles, 1974, note 1, p.180.
10. Wendy O'Flaherty, *Asceticism and Eroticism in the Mythology of Siva*, London: Oxford University Press, 1973, p.171.

11. David Smith, *The Dance of Siva: Religion, Art and Poetry in South India*, Cambridge: Cambridge University Press, 1996, p.105.

12. "The contrast between the erotic and the ascetic tradition in the character and mythology of Siva is not the kind of 'conjunction of opposites' with which it has so often been confused. *Tapas* (asceticism) and *kâma* (desire) are not diametrically opposed like black and white, or heat and cold, where the complete presence of one automatically implies the absence of the other." *Asceticism and Eroticism in the Mythology of Siva*, London, 1973, p.35.

13. *Pâshupata Sutra*, 3, 6–19.

14. O'Flaherty, *Asceticism and Eroticism*, p.36.

15. Paul Eduardo Muller-Ortega, *The Triadic Heart of Siva*, Albany, New York: State University of New York Press, 1989, p.139.

16. Ibid., p.138.

17. Alain Daniélou, *Shiva et Dionysos*, Paris, 1979, p.64.

18. In his *Commentary* of *Ecclesiastes*, Lorinus mentions that "the original Hebrew word is a particle addressed to Laughter: 'You are mad'; or, 'You cause madness'; or, 'you are driven mad'. It derives from *halal*, from which is formed *Hallelujah*, which is a most happy chant fringing on madness—a madness which is spiritual and holy." Screech, *Laughter at the Foot of the Cross*, Boulder, Colorado, 1997, p.76.

19. "She learnt that Osiris, confusing her with their common sister, had by mistake an amorous relationship with the latter" (Plutarch, 356f). Other versions of the myth involve the responsibility of Nephthys in this state of affairs: "During her mourning Isis was told that her sister Nephthys had fallen in love with Osiris and tricked him into her bed." Robert A. Armour, *Gods and Myths of Ancient Egypt*, Cairo/New York: American University in Cairo Press, 2001, p.57.

20. R.T. Rundle Clark, *Myth and Symbol in Ancient Egypt*, New York: Grove Press, 1960. Cf. Armour, *Gods and Myths*, p.69.

21. Ananda K. Coomaraswamy, *Hinduism and Buddhism*, edited by Keshavaram N. Iengar and Rama P. Coomaraswamy, New Delhi, 1999.

22. "Here we have (only) proposed to emphasize that the Dragon, or Giant—by whatever name, whether we call him Ahi, Vrtra, Soma, Prajâpati or Purusa, or Osiris or Dionysos or Ymir—is always himself the Sacrifice, the sacrificial victim; and that the Sacrificer, whether divine or human, is always himself this victim, or else has made no real sacrifice." Ananda K. Coomaraswamy, *The Door in the Sky*, Princeton, NJ: Princeton University Press, 1997, p.101.

23. Priya Hemenway, *Hindu Gods: The Spirit of the Divine*, San Francisco: Chronicle Books, 2003, p.32.

24. "The name of that divinity was Theuth, and it was he who first discovered number and calculation, geometry and astronomy, as well as the games of checkers and dice, and, above all else, writing." (274c) Plato, *Complete Works*, edited by John M. Cooper,

Indianapolis-Cambridge: Hackett, 1997, Alexander Nehamas and Paul Woodruff translation, p.551.

25. Arthur, Cotterell, *A Dictionary of World Mythology*, Oxford: Oxford University Press, 1986, p.73.

26. Thoth is "the deity who defends and restores harmony in the cosmos" but "there are certain allusions to a demoniacal trait in his nature." C.J. Bleeker, *Hathor and Thoth: Two Key Figures of the Ancient Egyptian Religion*, Leiden: Brill 1973, p.117.

27. "First and foremost, Ganapati is a physical embodiment of the great Upanisadic *mahâvâkya tat tvam asi* (that thou art). He combines the two seemingly incongruous parts, an elephant's head and a human body, in one form. Thus, like the *mahâvâkya* that unifies two seemingly incongruous parts, That (*tat*) and Thou (*tvam*), so does Ganesa. He is a physical embodiment of the infinite and the finite, of the immortal and the mortal, of the large and the small, of the manifest and the unmanifest." John A. Grimes, *Ganapati: Song of the Self*, Albany, NY: State University of New York Press, 1995, p.73.

28. C.J. Bleeker notes, for example, that "in spite of the charitable assistance lent by Thoth to gods and mortals, he remains a deity insofar as his behavior is occasionally contrary to what human rationality and ethics would expect." *Hathor and Thoth*, p.132.

29. Grimes, *Ganapati*, p.1. As in this funerary proclamation: "I see to it that Re is at peace with Osiris (lord of the netherworld) and Osiris and Re, I ensure that he (Re) can enter the secret cave to revive the heart of the weary at heart (Osiris)." Bleeker, *Hathor and Thoth*, p.120.

30. The latter being manifested, within immanence, by central figures such as Shiva, Dionysus, and Osiris.

31. Thoth is the promoter of peace, defined as "the one who signifies the peace of the gods" (Bleeker, *Hathor and Thoth*, p.118), but he is also the guardian of laws and as such an embodiment of rigorous justice. Ganesha removes obstacles, but he is also the one who guards Shiva and fights to protect his father during his sleep.

4   DIVINE TROUBLEMAKERS

1. "In the cosmogony of the Iroquois, according to Mr. J.N.B. Hewitt, Yoskehâ', or Otêñtoññi̇̀a,—the former name means 'it is the dear little sprout,' and the latter has about the same signification,—is the personification of the reproductive, rejuvenating force of nature, as opposed to Tawískarà, his brother, who exemplifies chiefly 'the destructiveness of frost, hail, and ice, often holding for months in its stiffening, solidifying, deadening embrace the rivers, lakes, and ponds, the sap of the trees, plants, and vegetation of the land.' [...] He taught men the art of firemaking, so that they could have, when needful, new fire." Alexander Chamberlain, "The Mythology and Folklore of

Invention," *Journal of American Folklore*, X, April–June 1897, no.XXXVII, pp.91–92.

2. "Further indication that Kami embraces the conception of divine spirit is shown by the common use in Shinto mythology of the expression *mitama*, which means august or divine jewel or spirit, and is applied to the Kami. The Kami are explained in Shinto as having Ara-Mitama, 'Rough Divine Spirit,' the spirit of creative action, and Nigi-Mitama, 'Gentle Divine Spirit,' the balancing counterpart. Motoori Norinaga warns against the mistaken idea that some Kami are Ara-Mitama and others Nigi-Mitama, and he asserts they are different manifestations of the same spirit." J.W.T. Mason, *The Meaning of Shinto*, New York, 1935, p.61.

3. "So as they then swore to each other from the opposite banks of the Tranquil River of Heaven, the august names of the deities that were born from the mist of her breath when, having first begged His-Swift-Impetuous-Male-Augustness (Susano) to hand her the ten-grasp saber which was girded on him, and broken it into three fragments, and with the jewels making a jingling sound, having brandished and washed them in the True-Pool-Well of Heaven, and having crunchingly crunched them, the Heaven-Shining-Great deity (Amaterasu) blew them away, were Her Augustness Torrent-Mist-Princess, another august name for whom is Her Augustness Princess-of-the-Island-of-the-Offing; next Her Augustness Lovely-Island-Princess another august name for whom is Her Augustness Good-Princess; next Her Augustness Princess-of-the-Torrent. The august name of the deity that was born from the mist of his breath when, having begged the Heaven-Shining-Great-August deity to hand him the augustly complete string of curved jewels eight feet long—of five hundred jewels—that was twisted in the left august bunch of her hair, and with the jewels making a jingling sound having brandished and washed them in the True-Pool-Well of Heaven, and having crunchingly crunched them, His-Swift-Impetuous-Male-Augustness blew them away, was His Augustness Truly-Conqueror-I-Conqueror-Conquering-Swift-Heavenly-Great-Great-Ears. The august name of the deity that was born from the mist of his breath when again, having begged her to hand him the jewels that were twisted in the right august bunch of her hair, and having crunchingly crunched them, he blew them away, was His Augustness Ame-no-hohi. The august name of the deity that was born from the mist of his breath when again, having begged her to hand him the jewels that were twisted in her august head-dress, and having crunchingly crunched them, he blew them away, was His Augustness Prince-Lord-of-Heaven. The august name of the deity that was born from the mist of his breath when again, having begged her to hand him the jewels that were twisted on her left august arm, and having crunchingly crunched them, he blew them away, was His Augustness Prince-Lord-of-Life. The august name of the deity that was born from the mist

of his breath when again, having begged her to hand him the jewels that were twisted on her right august arm, and having crunchingly crunched them, he blew them away was His-Wondrous-Augustness-of-Kumanu." *Kojiki or Records of Ancient Matters,* Kobe: J.L. Thompson, 1932.

4. "Then His-Swift-Impetuous-Male-Augustness said to the Heaven-Shining-Great-August deity: 'Owing to the sincerity of my intentions I have, in begetting children, gotten delicate females. Judging from this I have undoubtedly gained the victory.' With these words, and impetuous with victory, he broke down the divisions of the rice-fields laid out by the Heaven-Shining-Great-August deity filled up the ditches, and moreover strewed excrements in the palace where she partook of the great food. So, though he did thus, the Heaven-Shining-Great-August deity upbraided him not, but said: 'What looks like excrements must be something that His Augustness mine elder brother has vomited through drunkenness. Again, as to his breaking down the divisions of the rice-fields and filling up the ditches, it must be because be grudges the land they occupy that His Augustness mine elder brother acts thus.' But notwithstanding these apologetic words, he still continued his evil acts, and was more and more violent." Ibid.

5. Ibid., p.131.

6. Frithjof Schuon, "Mythology of Shinto," *in Treasures of Buddhism,* Bloomington: World Wisdom, 1993, p.193.

7. Snorri Sturluson, *Edda,* London, 1987, p.157.

8. Georges Dumézil, *Loki,* Paris, 1986, p.12.

9. Ibid., p.128.

10. Bricriu rejoices in acting in such a way that "kings, princes, great heroes and young warriors engage in quarreling, so that they kill each other." Ibid., pp.206–207.

11. Sturluson, *Edda,* p.58.

12. Dumézil, *Loki,* p.220.

13. Ibid., pp.37–38.

14. This ability to change into a female character to deceive and trick by playing on the ambiguities of reality is also illustrated in the further episode of the story, in which the gods beg all beings to help them draw Baldr out of Hell. All of them answer their request by crying on Baldr's fate; only a giant female refuses, saying "I will cry on Baldr's cremation with dry tears." She happens to be Loki in one of his metamorphoses. The fate of Baldr is thus tragically sealed. Cf. Ibid., p.39.

15. Garth Fowden, *The Egyptian Hermes,* Cambridge: Cambridge University Press, 1986, p.22.

16. Lewis Hyde, *Trickster Makes This World,* New York, 1998, p.318.

17. Norman O.Brown, *Hermes the Thief, the Evolution of a Myth,* Madison, WI: University of Wisconsin Press, 1947, pp.6–8.

18. Ibid., p.46.

19. Ibid., p.86.

20. Ibid.

21. Jane Harrison, "Pandora's Box," in *Journal of Hellenic Studies*, 20, 1900, pp.99–114.
22. Hyde, *Trickster Makes This World*, p.210.
23. Brown, *Hermes the Thief*, p.96.

5 COYOTE AND KIN

1. Barre Toelken, in Barry Holstun Lopez, *Giving Birth to Thunder, Sleeping with His Daughter: Coyote Builds North America*, New York: Perennial, 1990, p.xiii.
2. Swami Ramdas,*In the Vision of God*, vol. 1, San Diego: Blue Dove Press 1995, p.97.
3. Foreword, Barry Holstun Lopez, *Giving Birth to Thunder, Sleeping with His Daughter: Coyote Builds North America*, Kansas City, 1977, p.xii.
4. Ibid.
5. In some myths "Supernaturals, men, and animals lived together at this time, and death was unknown." Alfonso Ortiz, *The Tewa World*, Chicago: University of Chicago Press, 1969, p.13.
6. In a sense, the "fixing" of the directions of space that is often staged in Amerindian cosmogonic myths signals the emergence of "space" as we know it; and it is always the work of a demiurgic trickster of some kind.
7. *American Indian Trickster Tales*, selected and edited by Richard Erdoes and Alfonso Ortiz, New York, 1998, p.74.
8. Diana Ferguson, *Native American Myths*, London: Collins and Brown, 2001, pp.31–34.
9. "How People Were Made," in *American Indian Trickster Tales*, ed. Erdoes and Ortiz, New York, 1998, p.12.
10. Erdoes and Ortiz, pp.4–6.
11. Ibid., pp.6–7.
12. John Fire\Lame Deer and Richard Erdoes, *Lame Deer, Seeker of Visions*, edited by John Fire\Lame Deer, New York, 1972.
13. Ibid., p.12.
14. Lopez, *Giving Birth to Thunder*, p.118.
15. Erdoes and Ortiz, *Trickster Tales*, pp.69–71.
16. Even though this might no doubt be missed by most readers, the duality in question has a profound meaning since it hints at the universal nature of the sexual organ. On the one hand, the penis means individual concupiscence; on the other hand it is a reflection of the universality of the Self.
17. Lopez, *Giving Birth to Thunder*, p.70.
18. Mourning Dove, *Coyote Stories*, Lincoln: University of Nebraska Press, 1990, p.23.
19. Ibid., p.7.
20. "The twins may be perceived as representatives of a cleft in the composite nature of the culture hero, as personifications of two

tendencies, one productive and the other destructive. Let us note that the relationship between the high god and the culture hero is directly reminiscent of the twin relationship."Ake Hultkrantz, *Native Religions of North America*, Waveland Press, 1997, pp.38–39.

21. Lopez, *Giving Birth to Thunder*, p.180.
22. Lewis Hyde, *Trickster Makes this World: Mischief, Myth, and Art*, New York, 1998, p.4.
23. Cf. Joseph Campbell, *The Hero with a Thousand Faces*, Princeton: Princeton University Press, 1968, p.44.
24. Ibid.
25. Harold Scheub, *A Dictionary of African Mythology*, Oxford: Oxford University Press, 2000, p.118.
26. "The decisive act is never more-or-less, maybe-so-maybe-no. It is either/or. It is the yea or the nay. When one acts, one is *in extremis* in the sense that one places one's very life—or some portion of it—on the line. Herein lies that proverbial 'point of no return' which clowns always precipitously move beyond with their antics." Tom Boyd, "Clowns, Innocent Outsiders," *Journal of Popular Culture*, 22.3, 1988, p.108.
27. Swami Ramdas, *In the Vision of God*, vol. 2, San Diego, 1994, p.23.

6   Reading the Trickster's Footsteps

1. *Black Elk Speaks*, as told to John G. Neihardt, Lincoln and London: University of Nebraska Press, 1979, p.189.
2. MacLinscott Ricketts, "The North American Indian Trickster," *History of Religion*, 5, 1966, p.346.
3. Franchot Ballinger, "Living Sideways: Social Themes and Social Relationships in Native Trickster Tales,"*American Indian Quarterly*, 13.1, 1989, pp.15–30.
4. Ibid., p.28.
5. Joseph Epes Brown, "The Wisdom of the Contrary," *Parabola Magazine*, 4.1, 1979, p.61.
6. Brown, "The Wisdom of the Contrary," p.55.
7. Gerald Vizenor, "Trickster Discourse," *American Indian Quarterly*, 14.3, 1990, pp.285–286.

7   Thundering Clowns

1. This being said, it is undoubtedly true that the clown has an affinity with childhood: this affinity is primarily expressed in the directness of his ways, whether in expressing his desires or in telling the truth. As many cultures have indicated, "truth comes out of children's mouths."
2. "In the days before the invaders came...we had clowns. Not clowns like you see now, with round red noses and baggy costumes. Our

clowns wore all kinds of stuff. Anything they felt like, they wore. And they didn't just come out once in a while to act silly and make people laugh, our clowns were with us all the time, as important to the village as the chief, or the shaman, or the dancers, or the poets." Anne Cameron, *Daughters of Copper Woman*, Vancouver: Press Gang Publishers, 1981, p.109.

3. Alfonso Ortiz, *The Tewa World*, Chicago, 1969.

4. John Fire, Lame Deer and Richard Erdoes, *Lame Deer*, New York, 1972, p.240.

5. Peggy Andreas, "Path of the Sacred Clown," in *Towards 2012: Culture Language*, The Unlimited Dream Company, 1997, p.3.

6. "*Wakiniyan* is a material god whose substance is visible only when He so wills. His properties are *wakan* and anti-natural. He abides in His lodge on the top of the mountain at the edge of the world where the Sun goes down to the region under the world. He is many, but they are as only one; He is shapeless, but he has wings with four joints each; He has no feet, yet He has huge talons; He has no head, yet has a huge beak with rows of teeth in it, like the teeth of a wolf: His voice is the thunder clap and rolling clouds; He has an eye and its glance is lightning. In a great cedar tree beside His lodge He has His nest made of dry bones, and in it is an enormous egg from which His young issue. He devours His young and they each become one of his many Selves. He had issue by the Rock and it was Iktomi, the oldest son of the Rock. He flies in the domain of the Sky, hidden in a robe of clouds, and if one of mankind sees His substance he is thereby made a *heyoka*, and must ever afterwards speak and act in clownishly and anti-natural manner. Yet, if He so wills, He may appear to mankind in the form of a [...] man, and if so, He is then the God, Heyoka. One who looks upon the God, Heyoka, is not thereby made a *heyoka*. The potency of the Winged God cannot be imparted to anything. His functions are to cleanse the world from filth and to fight the Monsters who defile the waters and to cause all increase by growth from the ground. The acceptable manner of addressing Him is by taunt and vilification, the opposite of the intent of the address. He may be visualized as a bird whose wings have four joints. His symbol is a zigzag red line forked at each end. His *akicita* (messengers or police) are the dog, swallow, snowbird, night hawk, lizard, frog, and dragon fly, and if either of these is seen in a vision the one to whom it appears is thereby made a *heyoka*." J.R. Walker, *Anthropological Papers of the American Museum of Natural History*, 16, pp.83–84, 1917.

7. "(The clown) has power. It comes from the thunder-beings, not the animals or the earth. In our Indian belief a clown has more power than the atom bomb. This power could blow off the dome of the Capitol." Fire and Erdoes, *Lame Deer*, p.236.

8. "The clown walks along the line of dancers, and gets in their way. He dances out of order and out of time. He peers foolishly at different

persons. He sits on the ground, his hands clasped across his knees, and rocks his body to and fro. He joins regularly in the dance toward the close of a figure, and when the others have retired, he remains going through his steps, pretending to be oblivious of their departure; then, feigning to discover their absence, he follows them on a full run." "Navaho Night Chant," Washington Matthews, *The Journal of American Folklore*, 1901, p.16.

9. "Part of the duty of the Miwok clown is to keep people awake. The Cahuilla Paha or 'funny man' also is supposed to do this and he accomplished it by throwing water on the people or by dropping live coals down their backs. This recalls the Huichol clown who torments people with 'botherations' and prevents their sleeping by shaking his rattle near their ears or hooking their clothing with his rattle." Julian Haynes Steward, *The Clown in Native North America*, New York & London: Garland Publishing, 1991, p.83.

10. Peggy Andreas, *Towards 2012 part III: Culture/Language*, 1997, "It's a little more difficult to spot a young clown than it is to spot a young warrior. Those who describe a child as being 'too sensitive' need to be aware that the little one may be a Sacred Clown in the making. The child may be shy, or she may be a temperamental show-off, sometimes both in different situations. In any case, a young clown is an explorer in the world of emotions."

11. "For the Hopi, the Underworld is the antithesis of the normal world: when it is winter here it is summer there; whoever is ugly here is handsome there; here, beings are solid and unchangeable while there, the body is insubstantial and mutable. Every attribute is reversed, which may account for the clowns saying the opposite of what they mean, for their association with the dead, and for their coming over the clouds to the villages." Barton Wright, *Clowns of the Hopi: Tradition Keepers and Delight Makers*, Flagstaff, Arizona: Northland Publishing, 1994, p.4.

12. "I am joking, but if I had a *heyoka* dream now which I would have to reenact, the thunderbeing would place something in that dream that I'd be ashamed of. Ashamed to do in public, ashamed to own up to it. Something that's going to want me not to perform this act. And that is what's going to torment me. Having had that dream, getting up in the morning, at once I would hear this noise in the ground, just under my feet, that rumble of thunder. I'd know that before the day ends that thunder will come through and hit me, unless I perform the dream. I'm scared, I hide in the cellar, I cry, I ask for help, but there is no remedy until I have performed this act. Only this can free me. Maybe by doing it, I'll receive some power, but most people would just as soon forget about it." Fire and Erdoes, *Lame Deer*, p.242.

13. "As a consequence, there is an inordinate fear on the part of the individual of having one's shortcomings exposed to village scrutiny through the activities of the clowns. The fact that no one, regardless of age or station, is immune from these vignettes of ridicule further

strengthens this aspect. The result is that the clown is the ultimate keeper of tradition." Wright, *Clowns of the Hopi*, p.3.

14. "The Plains Cree clowns performed partly in imitation of the important soldiers' lodge, and the Plains Ojibway imitated the buffalo police society. A favorite stunt of the Arapaho clowns too was to mimic and burlesque people." Steward, *The Clown*, p.78.

15. "(The old wise people) know that a *heyoka* protects the people from lightning and storms and that his capers, which make people laugh, are holy." Fire and Erdoes, *Lame Deer*, p.237.

16. John G. Neihardt, *Black Elk Speaks*, Lincoln and London, 1979, p.189.

17. "In one of their major ceremonies, Heyoka Kaga 'clown making, ceremony,' they plunged their hands into boiling-hot water in an effort to retrieve choice bits of dog meat, and complained of the coldness of water." William K. Powers, *Oglala Religion*, Lincoln: University of Nebraska Press, 1982, p.57.

18. Robert H. Lowie, "Plains Indian Age-Societies," *Anthropological Papers of the American Museum of Natural History*, 11, 1916, p.859.

19. "The Cheyenne Contrary or Inverted Warriors [...] comprised several young men who stood in dread fear of thunder. These men were formed to behave in a contrary manner at all times but they were a far cry from clowns. They formed a small band of braves of great importance in battle. They dressed in old clothes, might never use a bed, might not joke or have a good time, must always do and say things by contraries, and were required to live alone and preserve the utmost dignity. Such a mode of life was far from enjoyable. Moreover, these men were expected to be brave to the point of foolhardiness in war. Longevity among them consequently was rare and there were few in any tribe." Steward, *The Clown*, p.129.

20. "The directions moved from place to place over the world so the Wind told the Four Winds to mark the directions so that each of them would know where he belonged. He told them that the North Wind, as the oldest, ought to have the first direction, which must be farthest from the Sun. He told them to put a great pile of stones at each direction so that it would be forever marked. When they were going to the edge of the world to mark the directions, the wizard met them. Because the North Wind was surly and a coward he took from him the birthright of the oldest and gave it to the West wind. Then he made it cloudy so that the Sun could not be seen, and guided them to the edge of the world. A little bird told them to set up a pile of stones there. They did so. When the Sun was leaving the world He passed very near them. Then they knew that that was the direction of the West Wind and that it would always be considered the first. Then the Four Winds traveled together until they came to the place where the Sun was furthest from them. There they saw the tipi of the wizard and he invited them inside. They all went inside except the North Wind who said that his tipi should be where the tipi of the wizard stood and that he was afraid of

the wizard. Then he told a magpie to sit on the poles of the tipi and befoul the wizard when he came through the door. When magpie did this the wizard said that because of this it should befoul its nest forever. So to this time magpies befoul their nests. Then he told the North Wind that because he had told the magpie to do a nasty thing, he should be his messenger forever and that the wizard would take the first place in the name of the direction of the North Wind. This is why the direction of the North Wind is called Waziyata." J.R. Walker, *The Sun Dance and Other Ceremonies of the Oglala Division of the Teton Dakota*, The American Museum of Natural History, New York, 1917, p.172.

21. "[...] the Indian tradition [...] (establishes) a symbolical link between the West Wind, bearer of thunder and rain, and the Rock which is an angelic or semi-divine personification of a cosmic Aspect of *Wakan-Tanka*; [...] in the rock are united the same complementary aspects as in the thunderstorm: the terrible aspect by reason of its destructive hardness (the rock is, for the Indians, a symbol of destruction—hence his stone weapons of which the connection with thunderbolts is obvious), and the aspect of Grace through its giving birth to springs which, like the rain, quench the thirst of the land." Frithjof Schuon, *The Feathered Sun*, Bloomington, 1990, p.56.

22. The Winged God is not without analogy to Shiva who "is also described as the Great Fear, the upraised thunderbolt whose anger makes even the gods afraid." Priya Hemenway, *Hindu Gods: The Spirit of the Divine*, San Francisco, 2003, p.32.

23. Ake Hultkrantz, *Native Religions of North America*, Long Grove, Illinois: Waveland Press, 1997, p.76.

24. Ibid.

25. Karl H. Schlesier, *The Wolves of Heaven*, Norman: The University of Oklahoma Press, 1987, pp.13–16.

26. "The clowns represent ourselves. They do all the things we do. They act like children. [...] The kachinas do not take notice of the clowns. The kachinas are always the same. They represent unchanging laws—eternity." Laura Thompson, *Culture in Crisis: A Study of the Hopi Indians*, New York: Harper, 1950, p.130.

27. Louis Dumont, *Homo Hierarchicus: The Caste System and Its Implications*, Chicago: University of Chicago Press, 1970.

28. Schlesier, *Wolves of Heaven*, p.41.

29. Ortiz, *Tewa*, p.169.

30. Ibid., p.170.

31. "[...] in East Lancashire in the week before Easter groups of boys dressed as girls and girls dressed as boys went around accompanied by the 'fool' or 'tosspot' and asked for presents of eggs." William Willeford, *The Fool and His Scepter: A study in Clowns and Jesters and their Audience*, Evanston: Northwestern University Press, 1969, p.86.

32. Stewart, *The Clown.*

33. "The first group consists of those themes of humor in which sacred and vitally important ceremonies and sometimes persons are ridiculed and burlesqued." Ibid., p.71.

34. Ibid., p.72.

35. Ibid., p.91.

36. Paul V.A. Williams, "Exú: the Master and the Slave in Afro-Brazilian Religion" in *The Fool and the Trickster. Studies in Honour of Enid Welsford*, edited by Paul V.A. Williams, Ipswich, UK: Rowman and Littlefield, 1979, p.118.

37. Lewis Hyde, *Trickster Makes This World*, New York, 1998.

38. "Since Sulfur represents the essential pole in its natural refraction, it can be said to be active in passive mode, while Quicksilver, in view of the dynamic character of Nature, can be said to be passive in active mode. The relation of the two primordial forces to each other is thus similar to that of man and woman in sexual union." Titus Burckhardt, *Alchemy*, Louisville, 1997, p.124.

39. Steward, *The Clown*, p.71.

40. M. Willson Disher, *Clowns and Pantomimes,* London, p.9.

41. "The Piptuyakyamu usually accomplish this satire in the most obscene fashion possible. Some of the lampooned groups include Navajos, white schoolteachers, white storekeepers, Plains Indians, and Anglo photographers. These buffoons dress accordingly, exaggerating actions for a humorous effect." Elizabeth Hoffman Nelson, "Clowns of the Hopi," in *Fools and Jesters in Literature, Art, and History*, Westport, Connecticut: Greenwood Press, 1998, p.253.

42. Stephen E. Feraca, *Wakinyan, Lakota Religion in the Twentieth Century*, Lincoln and London: University of Oklahoma Press, 1998, p.50.

43. Massignon considers Abraham's reception of the Angels at Mamre as the spiritual archetype of this inner attitude vis-à-vis the foreign host. Cf. Louis Massignon, *Les trois prières d'Abraham*, Paris: Le Cerf, 1997.

8   SPIRITUAL LAUGHTER

1. Uzume is the Shinto goddess of happiness and joy. Her name means "whirling."

2. "Laughter is a divine gift, and a precious safety-valve." Marco Pallis, *A Buddhist Spectrum*, Bloomington: World Wisdom, 2003, p.199.

3. John Morreall, *Taking Laughter Seriously*, Albany: State University of New York Press, 1983.

4. Henri Bergson, *Le Rire*, Paris: PUF, 1930, p.4.

5. Cf. Screech, M.A., *Laughter at the Foot of the Cross*, Boulder, Colorado: Penguin, 1997, p.59. "[. . .] as soon as charity prevails the laughter is over. Or is it vice versa? Does laughter banish pity, or pity banish laughter? The two seem incompatible." Ibid., p.307.

6. "Can we then define the man who jokes well as the one who says nothing unbecoming a well-bred man, or as one who does not give pain in
his jokes, or even as one who gives delight to his listeners? Or is that
definition itself indefinable, since different things are hateful or pleasant to different people? The kind of jokes he will listen to will be the
same, for the kind of jokes a person can put up with are also the kind
he seems to make. There are, then, jokes he will not make, for a joke is
a kind of abuse. There are some kinds of abuse which lawgivers forbid;
perhaps they should have forbidden certain kinds of jokes."
Nichomachean Ethics, Book IV, ch. 8 quoted in John Morreall, *The
Philosophy of Laughter and Humor*, Albany: State University of
New York Press, 1987, p.15.

7. Plato's case in relation to humor is highly ambivalent depending on the
context in which the matter is approached. Socratic irony is undoubtedly akin to Taoist humor as it constantly mocks conventional assump-
tions and ignorance; however the *Republic* presents a picture that is
much closer to the Aristotelian ethics in that it emphasizes the dangers
of laughter and sets rigorous rules for its integration. Cf. Plato,
Republic, 388e.

8. Such a disassociation seems to be central in the phenomenon of holy
laughter such as it is envisaged, for instance, by Frithjof Schuon in a
private correspondence: "It is very likely that in the case of the saints
that you referred to < . . . those who spent most of their life laughing
and telling jokes> there is indeed a disassociation between the spiritual
element and the psychic element, as well as a paradox that is intended
by dint of profundity . . ." ("Il est très probable que dans le cas des
saints dont vous parlez il y ait précisément dissociation de l'élément
spirituel et de l'élément psychique, et paradoxe voulu à force de pro-
fondeur.") (Letter to Martin Lings, May 1, 1940).

9. Swami Rajeswarananda, *Thus Spake Ramana*, Tiruvannamalai: Sri
Ramanashramam, p.111. The Book of Genesis presents occurrences
of laughter that are akin to such a swift removal of limitations:
Abraham's laughter at his hearing God's promise of a son (XVII, 17)
should be understood as a sudden understanding of the disproportion between "human impossibility" and "Divine All-Possibility," so
to speak. Such laughter involves an abrupt shift of metaphysical level.

10. In *Mystics, Masters, Saints and Sages: Stories of Enlightenment*, Robert
Ullmann and Judyth Reichenberg-Ullmann, Edmonds, Washington:
Condri Press, 2001, p.76.

11. Rinzai Zen Master Yasuda-Tenzan-Roshi, in Lucien Stryk, *Encounter
with Zen*, Chicago, Athens, and London: Swallow Press, 1981,
pp.124–125.

12. "When a man laughs, he gives way to his own body and thus foregoes
unity with it and control over it." Jamees Spencer Churchill and
Marjorie Grene, *Laughing and Crying*, Evanston: Northwestern
University Press, 1970, p.142.

13. This is the spirit of childlike playing: "We discover with a laugh that things need not at all be as they are and as we have been told they have to be." Jürgen Moltmann, *Theology of Play*, New York: Harper and Row, 1972, p.13.

14. John C.H. Wu, *The Golden Age of Zen. Zen Masters of the T'ang Dynasty*, Bloomington: World Wisdom, 2003, p.88.

15. "Unanswerableness, through (various) mutually exclusive possibilities of response, sets up resistance against a rebuff by the problematical situation, i.e., the tension which is released in laughter." Churchill and Grene, *Laughing and Crying*, p.142.

16. Coleman Barks, *Delicious Laughter*, translation of excerpts from Rûmî's *Mathnawi*, Athens, Georgia: Maypop Books, 1990, p.18.

17. The *Hilaria* were celebrated in honor of Cybele at the vernal equinox whereas the *Lupercalia* were held in honor of Lupercalus in mid-February—Lupercus is identified with Faunus and Pan. The Dionysiac and Panic inspiration is akin to the Lakota *heyoka* in many of its modalities, including its "subversive," "manic," and sexual powers. Cybele as Goddess of Nature is associated with the triumph of life.

18. In his articles "Lupercales" and "Rire" (cf. *Dictionnaire critique de l'ésotérisme*, edited by Jean Servier, Paris: PUF, 1998), Joël Thomas judiciously notes that the laughter of the young men who were touched by the bloody sacrificial knife during the festival of the month of lustration (February) "reproduced mystically the first victory of the forces of life over those of death" (p.1109). To laugh is in this sense to overcome death through a consciousness of the precariousness of existence.

19. Bergson, *Le Rire*, p.18.

20. *Abhinavagupta's Conception of Humor*, chapter 6, p.6, http://www.svabhinava.org/HumorPhD/

21. "These states (Mâ's) often included *attahâsî*, or 'laughing like thunder,' as described by six devotees and mentioned by several others. Swami Gitananda referred to it as 'the laughter that goes on at all eight levels' and said: 'When I saw Mâ, the first thing that struck me was her *attahâsî*. Such joyful laughter reverberates out of all the pores of Mâ's body. The laughter and supreme bliss was coming out of her, radiating unlike any human being. I felt both wonderment and joy. I wondered to see such a person. No human being can laugh like this.'" Lisa L. Hallstrom, *Mother of Bliss*, Oxford University Press, 2000, p.111.

9 FOOLS FOR CHRIST'S SAKE

1. "The difficulty of asserting overconfidently that the folly of the *saloi* is feigned or simulated is that it assumes as absolute some already available definition of what madness and sanity are." John Saward, *Perfect Fools: Folly for Christ's Sake in Catholic and Orthodox Spirituality*, Oxford: Oxford University Press, 1980, p.26.

2. "The idea of God laughing at us, however, is incomplete. God and his prophets would be just plain nasty if all they did was double up with laughter every time some poor pompous fool made an ass of himself. The fact is, however, that this isn't so. A deeper look into the Scriptures indicates that God not only laughs at us, but also with us, and this makes all the difference." John E. Benson, "The Divine Sense of Humor," *Dialog*, vol. 22, no. 3 (1983), pp.191–197, 194.

3. Let us note that the word "slaughter" is much more frequently used, in the King James version of the Old Testament, than the word "laughter," a fact that is indicative of a certain spiritual perspective, or focus.

4. Ugolino di Santa Maria, *The Little Flowers of St. Francis of Assisi*, edited and adapted from a translation by W. Heywood, New York: Vintage Books, 1998, p.14.

5. The point here is not that human conventions are necessary or unavoidable; it is that they can act as a veil upon things as they truly are.

6. In Palladius's *Lausiac History*. Cf. Kari Vogt, "La Moniale folle du monastère des Tabbenésiotes: une interprétation du chapitre 34 de l'Historia Lausiaca de Pallade," *Symbolae Osloenses* 62 (1987), 95–108.

7. Cf. Derek Krueger, *Symeon the Holy Fool*, Berkeley: University of California Press, 1996, p.58.

8. Ibid., p.58.

9. Cf. Lennart Rydén, *Bemerkungen zum Leben des heiligen Narren Symeon von Leontios von Neapolis*, Uppsala: Almgvist and Wiksell, 1970; A.J. Festugière, *Vie de Syméon le Fou et Vie de Jean de Chypre*, Paris: Geuthner, 1974.

10. The contemporary philosopher and mystic Franklin Merrell-Wolff has remarkably captured the spiritual pitfalls of the large city, and even more so the modern city: "I find the jazz-like discordance of the city has an analogous (distressing) effect, intensified to a degree that is positively destructive. Not only does the maze of lights, sounds, and motions have this force, but, in even larger measure, the non-integrated mass of thoughts, feelings, and desires produces the same result. It is, in a measure, dangerous." *Pathways through to Space*, New York: Julian Press, 1973, p.48.

11. Ibid., p.149.

12. "But if you receive strength entirely from God, brother, so that whatever the forms, words, or actions the body makes, your mind and your heart remain unmoved and untroubled and in no way are defiled or harmed by them, truly I rejoice in your salvation, if only you would pray to God, so that he won't separate us from each other in the world to come." Ibid., p.149.

13. Ibid., pp.111–125.

14. Krueger, *Symeon the Fool*, p.161.

15. "The Comic Profanation of the Sacred" in *Holy Laughter*, edited by M. Conrad Hyers, New York: Seabury Press, 1969, p.13.

16. "Christ taught in figures nearly all the time, and everyone knows that no figure is to be accepted in its entirety." Hyers, *Holy Laughter*, p.168.

17. Harry Emerson Fordick, *The Manhood of the Master*, New York: Association Press, 1958, p.16.

18. This is also true of Mary insofar as she is considered in her "divine" dimension. "Doubtless Mary should be classed with those great mystics who did not laugh because they had risen above their humanity, but most human beings who never laugh have fallen below it." M.A. Screech, *Laughter at the Foot of the Cross*, Boulder, Colorado, 1997, p.1.

19. Baudelaire, *The Essence of Laughter and Other Essays, Journals and Letters*, edited by Peter Quennell, New York: Meridien Books, 1956, p.112.

20. John Morreall, *Taking Laughter Seriously*, Albany: State University of New York Press, 1983, p.126.

21. "(Christ's) divinity, too, would make him a completely serious person, for the Christian God could have no sense of humor. He knows fully every thing and every event in the past, present, and future, and so nothing that happened could surprise him. He could not discover something he did not already know about, nor could he adopt a new way of looking at anything. For these reasons, and because he is a changeless being, nothing that happened could amuse God; he could not experience the psychological shift that is behind laughter. He would *recognize* incongruities, but as the failures of things to be what he intended them to be—not as events which delight by jolting one's picture of the world, but as violations of his divine plan for the world." Morreall, *Taking Laughter Seriously*, p.126.

22. Reinhold Niebuhr, "Humor and Faith," in *Holy Laughter: Essays on Religion in the Cosmic Perspective*, edited by M. Conrad Hyers, New York, 1969, p.137.

23. Nicodemus of the Holy Mountain, *A Handbook of Spiritual Counsel*, translated by Pater A. Chamberas, New York: Paulist 1989, pp.114–115.

24. Meister Eckhart, *Selected Writings*, London: Penguin, 1994, p.186.

25. "Therefore I shall now name it in a nobler manner than I have ever done before, and yet it mocks such reverence and the manner and is far above them. It is free of all names and is devoid of all forms, quite empty and free in himself." Ibid., p.163.

26. "So entirely one and simple is this citadel, and so far above all particular manner and all powers is this single oneness, that no power or manner can ever look into it, not even God himself. In full truth and as truly as God lives: God himself will never look in there even for a moment, nor has he ever done so in so far as he exists in the manner and individual nature of his Persons." Ibid., pp.163–164.

27. This is, in essence, the penetration of the mystery of play. St. Clement of Alexandria mentions Isaac's playing with his wife Rebecca as a

marriage of "laughter" with "perseverance." Isaac means "laughter" (*gelôs*) and Rebecca "perseverance" (*hypomenê*). *Gelôs* is a sense of the infinite creativeness of God, *hypomenê* a disposition of awe before his supreme transcendence. Cf. Hugo Rahner, *Man at Play or Did You ever Practice Eutrapelia?* London, 1965, p.44.

28. Ibid., p.153.

29. "God does not seek his own interests but in all his works he is untrammeled and free and acts from pure love. The same is true of that person who is united with God. They too are unfettered and free in all their works, performing them for God alone, not seeking their own interests; and God works in them." Ibid., p.154.

30. Morreall, *Taking Laughter Seriously*, p.125.

31. Screech, *Laughter at the Foot*, p.73.

32. St. Gregory Palamas, *To the Most Reverend Nun Xenia*, *The Philokalia*, vol. 4, edited by Palmer, Sherrard, and Ware; London: Faber and Faber, p.313.

33. Cf. Chapter five, "Diogenes in Late Antiquity," in Krueger, *Simeon the Holy Fool*.

34. Ibid., pp.78–89.

35. "I admire also the scorn of Diogenes for all human good without exception [. . .]" Ibid., p.80.

36. These include eating in public places and defecating where he wanted.

37. Ibid., p.153.

38. The term "strategy" is not without its ransom since it tends to blur the aspect of "inspiration" or "vocation" that is essentially involved in the fool's way. This strategy is more a divine strategy than a human planning.

39. Ibid., p.154.

40. Ibid., p.154.

41. Ibid., p.159.

42. Ibid.

43. "The dialectic of the sacred and the comic" *Holy Laughter*, edited by M. Conrad Hyers, p.237.

44. *Life of Symeon the Fool*, p.155.

45. Such is the case when he is falsely accused by a slave to have engrossed her. She cannot deliver her child before she has admitted to the calumny. Still, while some people from the house of the girl realize that Symeon is a saint, others come to the conclusion that he prophesied thanks to the devil. See Ibid., p.156.

46. Harvey Cox, *The Feast of Fools: A Theological Essay on Festivity and Fantasy*, Cambridge: Harvard University Press, 1969.

47. Ibid., p.141. The Feast of Fools is one of these manifestations, but it was never fully integrated within the Church outlook, at least officially.

48. Ibid., p.142.

49. "In light of this description of play it becomes clear that in several ways prayer and play are strikingly similar. Both are acts of disciplined fantasy.

In both we 'yield to a kind of magic.' Neither prayer nor play is limited or circumscribed by the 'inconvenient world of fact.' Both go beyond it." Cox, *The Feast of Fools*, p.147.

50. "Hugo Rahner [. . .] believes that the Hebrew word in the book of Proverbs which describes the activity of the logos can better be described as 'dance.' It is the same word used in *II Samuel* 6:5 and 6:21 to describe David's notorious dance before the ark of the Lord." Ibid., p.151.

51. Cf. Irina Goraïnoff, *Les fols en Christ dan la tradition orthodoxe*, Paris: Desclee de Brouwer, 1983, pp.90–91.

52. "The simulated, or theatrical, nature of holy folly is problematic. It clearly connects the hagiographical phenomenon in some way to the profane; it is surely significant that the profane fool disappears from the courts of Europe at precisely the time when the holy fool becomes rarer in the Christian community." John Saward, *Perfect Fools: Folly for Christ's Sake in Catholic and Orthodox Spirituality*, Oxford: Oxford University Press, 1980, p.26.

53. For an interesting account of the relationships between Irish and Eastern forms of Christianity, see "Folly from East to Far West" in Saward, *Perfect Fools*, pp.31–47.

54. This could also be said of some sectors of Flemish Christianity; we think, for example, of Ruysbroek or Hadewijch.

55. "[. . .] the fool for Christ's sake is protected above all by his childlikeness, his purity and simplicity of heart. Spiritual infancy cannot be simply equated with holy folly but is its constant companion." Saward, *Perfect Fools*, p.30.

56. Goraïnoff, *Les Fols*, p.140.

57. Saward, *Perfect Fools*, p.99.

58. Cf. Goraïnoff, *Les Fols*, pp.93–94.

59. "The Reformation also abolished the holidays, games, and safety valves of that society (medieval society). This led to the establishment of the Puritan society of penny pinchers and to the industrial workaday world among the very people who had at first insisted on believing that men are justified by faith alone." Jürgen Moltmann, *Theology of Play*, New York, 1972, p.11.

60. "The Rise and Function of the Holy Man in Late Antiquity," *Journal of Roman Studies*, lxi, (1971), p.92.

61. "[. . .] folly for Christ's sake is always *eschatological*. The holy fool proclaims the conflict between this present world and the world to come." Saward, *Perfect Fools*, p.27.

62. Goraïnoff, *Les Fols*, p.184.

63. Ibid., p.104.

64. Ibid., p.169.

65. Ibid., p.141.

66. Saward, *Perfect Fools*, p.25.

67. The spiritual relationship between "drunkenness" and "nakedness" is alluded to in Genesis 10:21 where Noah is uncovered after becoming drunk.

68. Cf. John Chryssavgis, *In the Heart of the Desert*, Bloomington: World Wisdom, 2003, pp.83–84.

69. Goraïnoff, *Les Fols*, p.139.

70. Ibid., p.81.

71. Meriol Trevor, *Apostle of Rome: A Life of Philip Neri 1515–1595*, London: Macmillan, 1966, p.5.

72. L. Ponnelle and L. Bordet, *St. Philip Neri and the Roman Society of His Time*, London: Sheed and Ward, 1932, p.59ff.

73. See Saward, *Perfect Fools*, p.98.

74. Trevor, *Apostle of Rome*, p.151.

75. Ibid.

76. Eleonora Mazza reports that he prophesied the advent of the revolution in the context of his chastisement of the decadence of the clergy and the influence of the *Encyclopédistes*. Cf. J. Mantenay, *St. Benoît Labre (1748–1783)*, Paris, 1908, p.78.

77. Saward, *Perfect Fools*, p.197.

78. Ibid., p.164.

79. François Gaquère, *Le saint pauvre de Jésus-Christ, Benoît-Joseph Labre, 1748–1783*, Avignon: Aubanel Père, 1954, p.280.

80. When the people of Fabriano, in Italy, begin to recognize him as a saint, Benoît left the town without any further ado. Cf. Mantenay, *St. Benoît Labre*, p.33.

81. Ibid., p.54.

82. Gaquère, *Le saint pauvre*, p.270.

83. Troubles and temptations assailed him in his cell, so that he had to leave the monastery and live as a wanderer and a pilgrim. Cf. Mantenay, *St. Benoît Labre*, pp.15–19.

84. This appears clearly in a letter from Benoît to his parents, following his departure from the Chartreuse monastery in which he had hoped to become a monk: "I am informing you that the Chartreux having judged that I am not fit for their life, I left the monastery on the second day of October. I consider this as an order from the divine providence that calls me to a more perfect state." Ibid., p.20.

85. This principle of "occultation" of the saint has been expressed by a contemporary mystic in its deepest non-dualistic implications:

> My God, bury me and hide me
> under the savage appearance of an obscure soul,
> so that neither myself nor others
> be conscious of the Treasure that I am. (Jean-Marie Tresflin, *Alone with the Alone in the Name*, Louisville: Fons Vitae, 2005)

86. Gaquère, *Le saint peuvre*, p.273.

87. Mantenay, *St. Benoît Labre*, p.83.

88. Jim Forest, "Holy Foolishness," *Parabola Magazine* 19.4 (1994): 22–28.
89. Saward, *Perfect Fools*, p.212.
90. Cf. Sandra Billington, " 'Suffer Fools Gladly': The Fool in Medieval England and the Play *Mankind*," in *The Fool and the Trickster*, edited by Paul V.A. Williams, Ipswich: Rowman and Littlefield, 1979, pp.36–37.
91. "In the Middle Ages, the feast of fools on New Year's Day gave rise to excesses of buffoonery which verged on sacrilege. A layman dressed up as a bishop gave the benediction and derisively proclaimed indulgences; people ate on the altar and played soldiers' game on it; the pseudobishop indulged in all manner of witticisms. Abuses like this show up a certain characteristic lack of equilibrium in the European mentality which has the tendency to descend from one extreme to the other. It is true that the carnivalesque parodies have as their purpose the exhausting of the dangerous lower psychic possibilities, but the fact that this is necessary and above all the excesses to which it gives rise prove the existence of a latent contradiction in the collective soul." Frithjof Schuon, *Logic and Transcendence*, London: Perennial Books, 1975, note 7, p.157.
92. This is validated, for example, by the comical role of San Pedro, as a kind of burlesque counterpart of Christ, in Yaqui storytelling. San Pedro plays the role of a mimetic and foolish trickster, as illustrated by the following story: "One time San Pedro and Jesucristo were walking along, and Jesucristo sent San Pedro up to a nearby house to get a cooked chicken. On the way back Pedro ate one leg of the chicken. When Jesucristo saw what San Pedro had brought back he asked, 'Why has this chicken but one leg?' 'It never had another leg,' answered Pedro. 'All of the chickens around this part of the country have but one leg, Sir.' The two proceeded and came to a big tree under which were sleeping many chickens. All of the chickens had one leg tucked up out of sight under their feathers. Pedro pointed to them and said, 'You see! All of the chickens have but one leg a piece.' Jesucristo took a small rock and threw it at one of the chickens. It woke up and stood on both feet. 'Oh,' said Pedro, 'A miracle!' He then took a large rock and threw it to awaken the rest of the chickens. 'You see,' he said, 'I can perform miracles, too.' Ruth W. Giddings, *Yaqui Myths and Legends*, Tucson, AZ: University of Arizona Press, 1959, p.46.
93. This is symbolically verified, or confirmed, by the crucifixion of St. Peter upside down.
94. Urs von Balthasar, *Elucidations*, London: S.P.C.K 1975, p.103.
95. "The slave might rail at his master, intoxicate himself like his betters, sit down at table with them, and not even a word of reproof would be administered to him. Nay, more, masters actually changed places with their slaves, who gave their orders and laid down the law as if they were indeed invested with all the dignity of the consulship, the praetorship,

and the bench." James Frazer, *The Golden Bough*, New York: Mentor Books, 1959, p.642.

96. This is an excerpt from considerations on festive excesses during these times by a doctor in Sorbonne. It is quoted in Maurice Lever, *Le sceptre et la marotte*, Paris: Fayard, 1983, p.17.

97. Maurice Lever has rightfully reminded us of the fact that the French *crétin* (imbecile) is directly derived from *chrétien*.

10   THE PEOPLE OF BLAME

1. As indicated by Michael W. Dols in *Majnûn: The Madman in Medieval Islamic Society*, Oxford: Oxford University Press, 1992 and Seyyed Hossein Nasr in his *Science and Civilization in Islam*, Harvard University Press, 1968, chapter VII.

2. "The Hippocratic doctors borrowed the concept of the four elements of nature—air, earth, fire, and water—and considered them to be the essential elements of the human body. These elements corresponded, in theory, to the four humors that were believed to be produced in various organs of the body: blood, black bile, yellow bile, and phlegm. [. . .] The doctor, in various ways, was supposed to manipulate these humors by their qualities in order to maintain a humoral equilibrium, which was the meaning of health, or rectify their disequilibrium, which was illness." Dols, *Majnûn*, p.18.

3. "[. . .] The Qur'an could not have embraced a notion of the soul as being healthy and the body being sick or vice versa. Hence it is said of Saul, for example, 'We gave him amplitude in body and in knowledge' " (2:246). Fazlur Rahman, *Health and Medicine in the Islamic Tradition*, New York: Crossroad, 1987, p.21.

4. Let us recall that the English "health" derives from the Old English "hâl" that connotes wholeness.

5. Cf. Henry Corbin, *Le paradoxe du monothéisme*, Paris, 1980.

6. "The heart is healed by the permanent remembrance of God." Al-Hakîm at-Tirmidhî, quoted in Sara Sviri, *The Taste of Hidden Things*, The Golden Sufi Center: Inverness, California, 1997, p.124.

7. Jean-Louis Michon, *Le soufi marocain Ibn 'Ajîba et son Mi'râj*, Paris, 1973, p.263.

8. Sara Sviri, *The Taste of Hidden Things*, The Golden Sufi Center: Inverness California, 1997, p.34.

9. See Martin Lings, *What is Sufism?* Cambridge: Cambridge: University Press, 1993, p.97.

10. We use the term *malâmiyyah* as opposed to *malâmatîah* in accordance with Ibn 'Arabî's preference for the first of these denominations, Cf. *Futûhât*, 16/2.

11. "The importance of the *malâmatî* trend in Khurâsânian Sufism, constituting an evolutionary development of the pure asceticism of the

earlier generation, goes back to the precedence of Hamdûn Qassâr (d. 271/884), a master of Nîshâpûr, who put his stamp on the Sufi practice of the region, and stressed the importance of sincerity, declaring, 'God's knowledge of you is better than people's.'" Terry Graham, "Abû Sa'îd ibn Abî 'l-Khayr and the School of Khurâsân" in *The Heritage of Sufism, volume I,* edited by Leonard Lewisohn, Oxford: One World, 1999, p.128.

12. Cf. Roger Deladrière, "Les premiers malâmatiyyah" in *Melâmis-Bayrâmis: Etudes sur trois mouvements mystiques musulmans,* edited by Nathalie Clayer, Alexandre Popovic and Thierry Zarcone, Istanbul: Les Editions Isis, p.10.

13. Islamic mysticism presents a variety of classifications of the various levels of consciousness, not all of them being in agreement with Sulamî's. According to Ibn 'Ajîba, *al-rûh* is the place where the epiphanies of the Kingship (*al-malakût*) occur, whereas *al-sirr* refers on a higher plane to the level of the All-Powerful (*al-jabarût*). The latter refers to the Divine infinitude whereas the former pertains to the realm of intelligible archetypes (*asrâr al-ma'ânî*). Let us remember, in this respect, that Shî'ite gnosis equates *malakût* with the intermediary or animic realm, whereas *jabarût* refers to the angelic and archetypical level of reality. Cf. Henry Corbin, *Temple and Contemplation,* London: Kpi, 1986, p.192.

14. Muhammad Ibn al-Husayn Sulamî, *Usûl al-Malâmatiyyat wa-Ghiltât al-Suffiyyah,* Cairo, 1985, p.106, the English version from which I quote is an unpublished translation by Amira El-Zein.

15. Dols, *Majnûn,* p.352.

16. Cf. Michon, *Le soufi,* p.57.

17. Sara Sviri, "Hakîm Tirmidhî and the Malâmatî Movement in Early Sufism," in *The Heritage of Sufism,* edited by Leonard Lewisohn, One World: Oxford, 1999. p.599.

18. In his *Kitâb 'Uqalâ's al-majânin,* an-Naysâbûrî ranks Uways among four of the best-known "wise fools" with Majnûn, Sa'dûn and Buhlûl. Cf. Dols, *Majnûn,* p.355.

19. Cf. *Le mémorial des saints,* translated by Pavet de Courteille, Paris: Le Seuil, 1976, p.28.

20. Ibid., p.29.

21. Uways is also, and quite tellingly, the "patron" of Sufis who do not have a living master: "The Sufi tradition has distinguished a special group of seekers: those whose *sole* link with the teaching is through Khidr himself. There are those rare Sufis who do not have a teacher in the flesh. [. . .] They have been given a special name: *uwaysiyyûn.*" Sviri, *The Taste of Hidden Things,* p.98.

22. This "madness" is also related to the function of the American Indian "contrary," Sioux *heyoka,* or Hopi *kochare,* or the "gray one" of the Apaches, who embodies the apparently senseless reversal of terrestrial and social norms of behavior.

23. It is interesting to note that Uways al-Qaranî is both a norm and a shocking exception in the world of early Islam. He is a shocking exception insofar as his asocial perspective and ascetic disposition took him away from the communal establishment of the *ummah* that is, in a sense, the very identity of Islam. Still, at the same time, Uways is referred to in at least two *ahadîth* that make of him the spiritual pole of the community. Two interesting facts must be commented upon in this context: first, the Prophet declared that on the Day of Judgment and later in Paradise, God will give the form of Uways to 70,000 angels so that nobody could know, even in the hereafter, who the actual Uways is. This hyperbolic and symbolic manifestation of anonymity is quite suggestive of the principle of "invisibility" that presides over the *malâmiyyah* way. Second, when referring to Uways in connection with 'Umar, 'Attar carefully avoids any expression that would seem to give precedence to Uways over 'Umar: "You should know that Uways al-Qaranî was not superior to 'Umar, but that he was a man of detachment vis-à-vis things of this world. 'Umar, as for him, was an accomplished perfection in all his works" (ibid., p.31). 'Umar's perfection is defined in terms of presence and action in the world of men, whereas Uways' perfection is understood in terms of separation from the world. Given its emphasis on equilibrium between the two worlds, Islam cannot extol Uways' virtues to the point of "otherworldliness." Moreover, the Prophet's robe is no doubt a different kind of investiture than the line of succession in the *khalifat*: it points to a spiritual authority like the *khirkah* (or coat) of the Sufi Shaykh; but this type of investiture and eminence must remain hidden.

24. This apparent involvement can also be a way of attracting upon oneself the blame of the religious "elite" of Sufis who may consider themselves of a different stuff than the common faithful.

25. Sulamî, *Usûl*, p.141, translated by Amira El-Zein.

26. "Ash-Shiblî's conduct was often that of the conventional madman, which relieved him of responsibility for his mystical claims." Dols, *Majnûn*, p.385.

27. Ibid., p.386.

28. Ibid., p.380.

29. We read for example in the letters of the Shaykh ad-Darqawî as he was one day wearing three prayer caps on his head, for "such was my disposition" at the time (*Letters of a Sufi Master*, the Shaykh ad-Darqawî that he was al-'Arabî ad-Darqawî, London: Perennial Books, 1987, 2nd edition, see #53).

30. Ibid., p.263.

31. Such an association of prophecy with madness has nothing extraordinary about it. In the *Qur'ân*, for instance, Pharaoh accuses Moses of being struck with madness (51:39).

32. Cf. "Le retour d'Ulysse" in *Symboles*, Milano: Arche, 1980, p.39.

33. Cf. Roger Deladrière, "Les premiers Malâmatiyyah," p.13.

34. "Other features of early Naqshbandî practice were also linked to the concern for sobriety and anonymity implied by the choice of silent

dhikr. [. . .] As with the Shâdhiliyya, all these features are highly reminiscent of the Malâmatî movement of Nîshâpûr, and it may be suggested that Bahâ' al-Dîn Naqshband was an heir to the traditions of the Malâmatiyya although not in a formal, initiatic sense." Alexander Knysh, *Islamic Mysticism, A Short History*, Boston: Brill, 2000, p.221.

35. *Tabaqât*, p.182.
36. Ibid., p.184.
37. *The Kashf al-Mahjub*, Ali bin Uthman al-Hujwiri, translated by Reynold A. Nicholson, p.67.
38. Abd-ar Rahmân al-Jâmî, *Kitâb nafahât al-uns*, Paris: Michel Allard, 1977, pp.102–103.
39. This point of view has been expressed by Frithjof Schuon in his chapter "Sincerity: What it Is and what it Is Not" in *Esoterism As Principle and as Way*, Bedfont, Middlesex: Perennial Books, 1981, pp.123–127.
40. The purely gnostic way of knowledge would simply consider these accidents as "unreal." As Ghazalî puts it: "Each thing hath two faces, a face of its own and a face of its Lord; in respect of its face it is nothingness, and in respect of the Face of God it is Being." *Mishkat al-Anwâr*, quoted in Martin Lings, *A Sufi Saint of the Twentieth Century: Shaikh Ahmad Al-'Alawi*, Cambridge: Cambridge University Press, 1993, p.169. The *malâmiyyah* applies this discernment on the level of the will and the soul.
41. "(In the Middle Ages) [. . .] madness might be explained by the fact that the weakened body of the medically insane allowed the soul partially to escape." Dols, *Majnûn*, p.369.
42. This does not necessarily point to the prideful nature of the disciple, for it may also function on a more impersonal level as the morally neutral shock of the Zen "warning stick."
43. *Letters of a Sufi Master*, the Shaykh al-'Arabî ad-Darqawî, London: Perennial Books, 1987, 2nd edition, p.33.
44. Quoted in Dols, *Majnûn*, p.380.
45. This is accomplished through the alchemical "blending" of the psychic "matter" and the spiritual "form," the "emotions," and the *dhikr.*

11   FOOLS ON A TIGHTROPE

1. Enid Welsford, *The Fool: His Social and Literary History*, London: Fabuand Faber, 1935, p.29.
2. Sir Harry Luke, *An Eastern Chequerboard*, London: L. Dickson, 1934, p.117.
3. "(Hodja) has been the dominant figure of humor and satire in Turkey since the 13th century. His anecdotes and tales represent the solutions that the collective imagination of the Turks has brought to bear upon life's diverse and complex problems. As such, they defy being indexed and categorized. Any attempt to do so is bound to serve an editor's

subjective preferences rather than reflect scholarly criteria or help the readers." Aziz Nesin, *The Tales of Nasrettin Hoca*, Istanbul: Dost Yayinlari, 1988, p.11.

4. Luke, *Eastern chequerboard*, p.118.
5. Ibid., p.141.
6. Welsford, *The Fool*, p.31.
7. Ibid., p.135.
8. "He it is Who makes you travel by land and sea; until when you are in the ships, and they sail on with them in a pleasant breeze, and they rejoice, a violent wind overtakes them and the billows surge in on them from all sides, and they become certain that they are encompassed about, they pray to Allah, being sincere to Him in obedience: If Thou dost deliver us from this, we will most certainly be of the grateful ones. But when He delivers them, lo! they are unjustly rebellious in the earth. O men! your rebellion is against your own souls—(10:22–23) (translated by M.H. Shakir).
9. Idris Shah, *The Exploits of the Incomparable Mullah Nasrudin*, London: Cape, 1983.
10. Ibid., p.62.
11. Luke, *Eastern chequerboard*, p.127.
12. Shah, *The Exploits*, p.80.
13. "[. . .] Khoja's peculiar charm lies in the fact that he is as foolish as he is wise, that in all his doings buffoonery alternates with shrewdness, simplicity with guile." Luke, *Eastern Chequerboard*, p.123.
14. Nesin, *The Tales of Nasrettin Hoca*, p.59.
15. Athena is the protector of another famous trickster, Ulysses.
16. *A Pleasant Vintage of Till Eulenspiegel*, translated from the edition of 1515, edited by Paul Oppenheimer, Middletown: Wesleyan University Press, 1972, p.5.
17. *Till Eulenspiegel, His Adventures*, edited by Paul Oppenheimer, New York and London: Garland, 1991, p.8.
18. Ibid., p.220.
19. Ibid., p.227.
20. There are, to be fair, a few stories that point to some interest in the feminine on the part of Hodja. After all, he is married. "Hoca is preaching at the mosque, declaring that it is sinful for women to wear make-up. Someone in the audience points out that Hoca's wife wears make-up. 'But, says Hoca, it looks good on the hussy.'" Nesin, *The Tales of Nasrettin Hoca*, p.47.
21. Oppenheimer, *Till Eulenspiegel*, p.73.
22. Ibid.
23. Ibid., p.222.
24. We are grateful to Giovanni Vitello, who has trained in the Italian tradition of acting, for sharing with us the conclusions of his direct experience of Arlecchino's multifaceted psyche.
25. Charles de Coster, *La légende d'Ulenspiegel*, Bruxelles: Labor, 1983, p.17.

26. " 'Arlequin,' said Gherardi, 'has no marked character; he is whatever one wishes him to be.' Originally he was the serving man in the Commedia dell' arte. When the Italians turned parodists, he represented all manner of men." Maurice Willson Disher, Clowns and Pantomimes, New York: B. Blom, 1968, p.251.
27. *Fools and Jesters in Literature, Art, and History*, edited by Vicki K. Janik, Westport, London: Greenwood Press, 1998, p.371.
28. "Alcibiades en un dialogue de Platon, intitulé Le banquet, louant son precepteur Socrates sans controverse prince des philosophes: entre aultres paroles le dict estre semblable es Silènes. Silènes estoyent iadis petites boites telles que voyons de present es bouticqs des apothecaires, pinctes au dessus de figures ioyeuses et frivoles, comme de Harpies, Satyres, oysons bridez, lievres cornuz, canes bastées, boucqs volans, cerfz limonniers, & aultres telles pinctures contrefaictes à plaisir pour exciter le monde à rire. Quel fut Silène maistre du bon Bacchus. Mais au dedans l'on reservoit les fines drogues, comme Baulme, Ambre gris, Amomon, Musc, zivette, pierreries, et aultres choses precieuses. Tel disoit estre Socrates: parce que le voyans au dehors, & l'estimans par l'exteriore apparence, n'en eussiez donné un coupeau d'oignon: tant laid il estoit de corps & ridicule en son maintien, le nez pointu, le reguard d'un taureau: le visaige d'un fol: simple en meurs, rusticq en vestemens, pauvre de fortune, infortuné en femmes, inepte à tous offices de la republicque: tousiours riant, tousiours beuvant à un chascun, tousiours se guabelant, tousiours dissimulant son divin sçavoir."

[Alcibiades, in that dialogue of Plato's which is entitled The Banquet, Whilst he was setting forth the praises of his schoolmaster Socrates (without all question the price of philosophers), amongst other discourses to that purpose, said that he resembled the Silenes. Silenes of old were little boxes, like those we now may see in the shops of apothecaries, painted on the outside with wanton toyish figures, as harpies, satyrs, bridled geese, horned hares, saddled ducks, flying goats, thiller harts, and other such-like counterfeited pictures at discretion, to excite people unto laughter, as Silenus himself, who was the foster-father of good Bacchus, was wont to do; but within those capricious caskets were carefully preserved and kept many rich jewels and fine drugs, such as balm, ambergris, amomon, musk, civet, with several kinds of precious stones, and other things of great price. Just such another thing was Socrates. For to have eyed his outside, and esteemed of him, by his exterior appearance, you would not have given the peel of an onion for him, so deformed he was in body, and ridiculous in his gesture. He had a sharp pointed nose, with the look of a bull, and countenance of a fool: he was in his carriage simple, boorish in his apparel, in fortune poor, unhappy in his wives, unfit for all offices in the commonwealth, always laughing, tippling, and merrily carousing to everyone, with continual gibes and jeers, the better by those means to conceal his divine knowledge.]

Francis Rabelais, *Five Books of the Lives, Heroic Deeds and Saying of Gargantua and his son Pantagruel* by Sue Asscher and David Widger, Project Gutenberg's Gargantua and Pantagruel, 2004, http://www.gutenberg.org

29. "Socrates was not only a teacher of wisdom: he was for many a paragon who helped prepare the way for the Gospel. Yet Socrates enjoyed a laugh. Socrates enjoyed a drink. Socrates had a sense of fun. He was laughed at too. He showed by his good example that worldly fools kill what is spiritual and good. They also laugh at it." Screech, *Laughter at the Foot of the Cross*, Penguin, 1997, p.127.

30. The *trivium* comprised grammar, logic, and rhetoric. The *quadrivium* included geometry, arithmetic, music, and astronomy.

31. Gérard Defaux, *Le curieux, le glorieux et la sagesse du monde dans la première moitié du XVIe siècle*, Lexington, 1982, p.134.

32. See Mikhail Bakhtin, "The Language of the Marketplace in Rabelais," *Rabelais and his World*, translated by Helene Iswolsky, Bloomington: Indiana University Press, 1984.

33. *Gargantua and Pantagruel*, chapter 17.

34. "It would be useful for the whole Republic, pleasant for us, honorable for your lineage and necessary for me," ibid., chapter 21.

35. Ibid., p.358.

36. Ibid., p.360.

37. "Even when we first meet him, we are aware that he (Panurge) is incapable of becoming the Fool in Christ because, paradoxically, he is not foolish enough." Walter Kaiser, *Praisers of Folly: Erasmus, Rabelais, Shakespeare*, London: Harvard University Press, 1964, p.127.

38. "Just as the kingdom lacks an adequate king, so it lacks anyone in whom folly assumes a redeeming form." William Willeford, *The Fool and His Scepter*, Eronston, Illinois: Northwestern University Press, 1969, p.194.

39. Ophelia's description of Hamlet's "mad" gestures and attitudes is interpreted for what it is not (II, i, 86–94). Hamlet's puzzling and bizarre parting from Ophelia's love is not a result of love as such, but the consequence of the conflict between Hamlet's inability to "believe" in this world and the embrace of life that love must of necessity involve. Hamlet can no longer love Ophelia because he cannot love life.

40. Vicki Janik, editor, *Fools and Jesters in Literature, Art and History*, Westport, Connecticut, 1998, p.232.

41. Martin Lings, *The Secret of Shakespeare*, New York: Inner Traditions International, 1984, p.36.

42. *Fools and Jesters in Literature, Art, and History*, edited by Vicki K. Janik, Westport, London, 1998, p.235.

43. Chief among the obstacles to this fundamental enlightenment is the situation indicated by Hamlet's words, "Seems, madam? Nay, it is;

I know not seems." Dom Aelred Graham, *Zen Catholicism*, New York: Crossroad, 1963, p.97.

44. "This is what the tragedy of Hamlet expresses: facts and actions, and the exigencies of action were inescapable, but Shakespeare's hero saw through it all, he saw only principles and ideas; he plunged into things as into a morass; their very vanity, or their unreality, prevented him from acting, dissolved his action. [. . .] The contemplativity of Hamlet had unmasked the world, but it was not yet fixed in God; it was as it were suspended between two planes of reality." Frithjof Schuon, *Light on the Ancient Worlds*, Bloomington: World Wisdom, 1984, p.57.

45. This aspect of his sensibility is quite expressively manifested in his words to the king who had just inquired about Polonius's whereabouts: "(He is) at supper. [. . .] A certain convocation of politic worms are e'en at him. Your worm is your only emperor for diet. We fat all creatures else to fat us, and we fat ourselves for maggots. Your fat king and your lean beggar is but variable service—two dishes, but to one table. That's the end" (IV, 22–27).

46. "I have sought to demonstrate that Hamlet is extraordinarily given to *via negativa*." James L. Calderwood, *To Be and Not To Be, Negation and Metadrama in Hamlet*, New York: Columbia University Press, 1983, p.189.

47. Ananda K. Coomaraswamy, *The Door in the Sky*, Princeton, NJ: Princeton University Press, 1997, p.80.

12 Epilogue: Cracks of Light

1. "(Clowns) are subject to constant movement within themselves, an oscillation between opposing attributes and attitudes; they are thus never wholly formed, always in the process of becoming, and transcending, themselves." David Dean Shulman, *The King and the Clown in South Indian Myth and Poetry*, Princeton: Princeton University Press, 1985, p.208.

2. "[. . .] le rire parfait, préparé désormais à tout, d'Abraham, axial à la source divine, et qui est tout de même la source des larmes sereines de son sacrifice suprême: '*hinayni*' (*adsum*)." "La syntaxe intérieure des langues sémitiques et le mode de recueillement qu'elles inspirent," *Etudes Carmélitaines*, 49, p.47.

This page intentionally left blank

BIBLIOGRAPHY

Ahstrom, Birger. (1980). "Raven Flies with the Summer Birds: Raven Myths and Trickster Stories North of Mexico." *The Alaska Seminar.* Uppsala 84–107.

Ambelain, Robert. (1959). *La Notion Gnostique du Démiurge dans les écritures et les traditions judéo-chrétiennes.* Paris: Adyar.

Armour, Robert A. (2001). *Gods and Myths of Ancient Egypt,* Cairo/ New York: American University in Cairo Press.

Aspinall, Dana E. (2002). *The Taming of the Shrew: Critical Essays.* New York: Routledge.

Bakhtin, Mikhail. (1984). *Rabelais and His World,* trans. Helene Iswolsky, Bloomington: Indiana University Press.

Barnhart, Bruno and Joseph Wong (Eds). (2001). *Purity of Heart and Contemplation: A Monastic Dialogue between Christian and Asian Traditions.* New York: Continuum.

Basso, Ellen B. (1987). *In Favor of Deceit: A Study of Tricksters in an Amazonian Society.* Tucson: University of Arizona Press.

Beane, Wendell Charles. (1977). *Myth, Cult and Symbols in Sákta Hinduism: A Study of the Indian Mother Goddess.* Leiden: Brill.

Belo, Jane. (1949). *Bali: Rangda and Barong.* New York: The American Ethnological Society and J.J. Augustin Publisher.

Bergson, Henri. (1930). *Le rire: essai sur la signification du comique.* Paris: PUF.

Betty, L. Stafford. (1976). "Aurobindo's Concept of Lila and the Problem of Evil." *International Philosophical Quarterly,* 16: 315–329.

Bhattacharyya, Narenda Nath and Nirmal Jain (Eds.). (1974). *History of the Sákta Religion.* New Delhi: Munshiram Manoharlal Publishers.

Black Elk, Wallace H. (1991). *Black Elk: The Sacred Ways of a Lakota.* San Francisco: Harper.

Black Elk Speaks, as told to John G. Neihardt. (1979). Lincoln and London: University of Nebraska Press.

Bleeker, C.J. (1973). *Hathor and Thoth: Two Key Figures of the Ancient Egyptian Religion.* Leiden: Brill.

Boucquey, Thierry. (1991). *Mirages de la farce, fête des fous: Bruegel et Molière.* Amsterdam/Philadelphia: John Benjamins Publishing Company.

Bowen, Barbara C. (1998). *Enter Rabelais, Laughing.* Nashville: Vanderbilt University Press.

Boyer, Régis and Eveline Lot-Falck. (1974). *Les religions de l'Europe du Nord.* Paris: Fayard-Denoël.

Brooks, Douglas Renfrew. (1992). *Auspicious Wisdom: The Texts and Traditions of Srîvidyâ Sâkta Tantrism in South India.* Albany: State University of New York Press.

Brown, Norman O. (1947). *Hermes the Thief. The evolution of a myth.* Madison: University of Wisconsin Press.

Burckhardt, Titus. (1980). "Le retour d'Ulysse," *Symboles.* Milano: Arche.

Burckhardt, Titus. (1995). *Introduction to Sufism.* San Francisco: Thorsons.

Calderwood, James L. (1983). *To Be and Not To Be, Negation and Metadrama in Hamlet.* New York: Columbia University Press.

Cameron, Anne. (1981). *Daughters of Copper Woman.* Vancouver: Press Gang Publishers.

Campbell, Joseph. (1968). *The Hero with a thousand faces.* Princeton: Princeton University Press.

Christen, Kimberly A. (1998). *Clowns and Tricksters: An Encyclopedia of Tradition and Culture.* Denver: ABC-Clio.

Chryssavgis, John. (2003). *In the Heart of the Desert.* Bloomington: World Wisdom.

Collins, Michael J. (1997). *Shakespeare's Sweet Thunder: Essays on the Early Comedies.* Newark: University of Delaware Press.

Coomaraswamy, Ananda K. (1997). *The Door in the Sky,* Princeton: Princeton University Press.

Corbin, Henry. (1998). *Alone with the Alone: Creative Imagination in the Sufism of Ibn Arabî,* trans. Ralph Manheim. Princeton: Princeton University Press.

Corbin, Henry. (1981). *Le paradoxe du monothéisme.* Paris: L'Herne.

Coster, Charles de. (1983). *La légende d'Ulenspiegel.* Bruxelles: Labor.

Cotterell, Arthur. (1986). *A Dictionary of World Mythology.* Oxford: Oxford University Press.

Cox, Harvey. (1969). *The feast of fools: A Theological Essay on Festivity and Fantasy.* Cambridge: Harvard University Press.

Daniélou, Alain. (1979). *Shiva et Dionysos: la religion de la nature et de l'Eros: de la préhistoire à l'avenir.* Paris: Fayard.

Das, Prafulla Kumar. (1964). "Lila as the creation of Love." *Visva Bharati Quarterly* 29: 62–75.

Davidson, Hilda Roderick Ellis. (1964). *Gods and Myths of Northern Europe.* Baltimore: Penguin Books.

Davidson, Hilda Roderick Ellis. (1969). *Scandinavian Mythology.* London/New York: Hamlyn.

Davies, Stevie. (1995). *William Shakespeare, The Taming of the Shrew.* New York: Penguin.

Davis, Hadland F. (1992). *Myths and Legends of Japan.* New York: Dover Publications.

Defaux, Gérard. (1982). *Le curieux, le glorieux et la sagesse du monde dans la première moitié du XVIe siècle: l'exemple de Panurge (Ulysse, Démosthène, Empédocle)*. Lexington, KY: French Forum.

Defaux, Gérard. (1997). *Rabelais agonistes: du rieur au prophète: études sur Pantagruel, Gargantua, le Quart livre*. Genève: Droz.

Devanandan, Paul David. (1950). *The Concept of Mâyâ: An Essay in Historical Survey of the Hindu Theory of the World, with Special Reference to the Vedânta*. London: Lutterworth Press.

Dols, Michael W. (1992). *Majnûn: The Madman in Medieval Islamic Society*. Oxford: Clarendon Press.

Dooling, D.M. (Ed.). (2000). *The Sons of the Wind: The Sacred Stories of the Lakota*. Norman: University of Oklahoma Press.

Dumézil, Georges. (1959). *Les dieux des Germains: Essai sur la formation de la religion scandinave*. Paris: Presses Universitaires de France.

Dumézil, Georges. (1986). *Loki*. Paris: Flammarion.

Dumont, Louis. (1970). *Homo hierarchicus: The Caste System and Its Implications*. Chicago: University of Chicago Press.

Dundas, Marjorie (Ed.). (2002). *Riddling Tales from Around the World*. Jackson: University Press of Mississippi.

Easwaran, Eknath. (1989). "Three in One: Spirit, Matter, and Mâyâ," *Parabola Magazine*, 14.4.

Eliot, Alexander. (1990). *The Universal Myths: Heroes, Gods, Tricksters, and Others*. New York: Plume Books.

Erdoes, Richard and Alfonso Ortiz (Eds.). (1999). *American Indian Trickster Tales*. New York: Penguin Books.

Feraca, Stephen E. (1998). *Wakiniyan, Lakota Religion in the Twentieth Century*. Lincoln: University of Nebraska Press.

Ferguson, Diana. (2001). *Native American Myths*. London: Collins and Brown.

Festugière, A.J. (1974). *Vie de syméon le Fou et vie de Jean de Chypre*. Paris: Geuthner.

Fickett, Harold. (1983). *The Holy Fool*. Wheaton, IL: Crossway Books.

Fire, John/Lame Deer and Erdoes, Richard. (1972). *Lame Deer, Seeker of Visions*, by John Fire/Lame Deer. New York: Simon and Schuster.

Fled Bricrend: The Feast of Bricriu: An Early Gaelic Saga Transcribed. Trans. George Henderson. (1899). London: Irish Texts Society/D. Nutt.

Forde, Daryll (Ed.). (1999). *African Worlds: Studies in the Cosmological Ideas and Social Values of African Peoples*. Piscataway, NJ: Transaction Publishers.

Fowden, Garth. (1986). *The Egyptian Hermes*. Cambridge: Cambridge University Press.

Gaquère, François. (1947). *Le saint pauvre de Jésus-Christ, Benoît-Joseph Labre, 1748–1783*. Avignon: Editions Aubanel Père.

Garner, Alan. (1975). *The Guizer: A Book of Fools*. London: Hamish Hamilton.

Gauna, Max. (1996). *The Rabelaisian Mythologies*. Cranbury, NJ: Associated University Presses.

Giddings, Ruth W. (1959). *Yaqui Myths and Legends*. Tucson, AZ: University of Arizona Press.

Goraïnoff, Irina. (1983). *Les fols en christ dans la tradition orthodoxe.* Paris: Desclee de Brouwer.

Graham, Dom Aelred. (1994). *Zen Catholicism.* New York: Crossroad.

Griaule, Marcel. (1970). *Conversations with Ogotemmêli: An Introduction to Dogon Religious Ideas.* New York: Oxford University Press.

Grimes, John A. (1995). *Ganapati: Song of the Self.* Albany: State University of New York Press.

Guénon, René. (1974). *L' Homme et son devenis selon le Vedanta.* Paris: Editions Traditionnelles.

Guénon, René. (1976). "Le Démiurge," *Mélanges.* Paris: Gallimard.

Hemenway, Priya. (2003). *Hindu Gods: The Spirit of the Divine.* San Francisco: Chronicle Books.

Hillman, Richard. (1992). *Shakespearean Subversions: The Trickster and the Play-text.* New York: Routledge.

Hoffacker, Charles. (1998) "Holy Fools." *Weavings* 13.4: 32–38.

Huizinga, Johan. (1950). *Homo Ludens: A Study of the Play Element in Culture.* New York: Roy Publishers.

Hultkrantz, Ake. (1997). *Native Religions of North America.* Long Grove, IL: Waveland Press.

Hyde, Lewis. (1999). *Trickster Makes This World: Mischief, Myth, and Art.* New York: North Point Press.

Hyers, Conrad. (1996). *The Spirituality of Comedy: Comic Heroism in a Tragic World.* New Brunswick: Transaction Publishers.

Hyers, Conrad M. (Ed.). (1969). *Holy Laughter: Essays on Religion in the Cosmic Perspective.* New York: Seabury Press.

Hynes, William J. and William G. Doty. (1993). *Mythical Trickster Figures: Contours, Contexts, and Criticisms.* Tuscaloosa: University of Alabama Press.

Janik, Vicki K. (Ed.). (1998). *Fools and Jesters in Literature, Art, and History: A Bio-bibliographical Sourcebook.* Westport, CT: Greenwood Press.

Kaiser, Walter Jacob. (1963). *Praisers of Folly: Erasmus, Rabelais, Shakespeare.* Cambridge: Harvard University Press.

Kauffmann, Friedrich. (1978). *Northern Mythology.* Trans. M. Steele Smith. Norwood, PA: Norwood Editions.

Kidwell, Clara Sue, et al. (2001). *A Native American Theology.* Maryknoll, NY: Orbis Books.

Kinser, Sam. (1990). *Rabelais's Carnival: Text, Context, Metatext.* Berkeley: University of California Press.

Kinsley, David R. (1974/5). "Creation as Play in Hindu Spirituality," *Studies in Religion/Sciences Religieuses,* 4.2.

Kinsley, David R. (1975). *Kâlî and Krishna: Dark Visions of the Terrible and the Sublime in Hindu Mythology.* Berkeley: University of California Press.

Kinsley, David R. (1979). *The Divine Player: A Study of Krsna Lila.* Delhi: Motilal Banarsidass.

Knysh, Alexander. (2000). *Islamic Mysticism, A Short History.* Boston: Brill.

Kumar, Pushpendra. (1974). *Sakti Cult in Ancient India, with Special Reference to the Puranic Literature.* Varanasi: Bhartiya Publishing House.

Kundu, Nundo Lall. (1983). *Non-dualism in Saiva and Sakta Philosophy.* Calcutta: Firma KLM Pvt.

Leach, Edmund. (1969). *Genesis as Myth and other Essays,* London: Jonathan Cape.

Lefcourt, Herbert M. (2001). *Humor: The Psychology of Living Buoyantly.* New York: Kluwer Academic/Plenum Publishers.

Lever, Maurice. (1983). *Le sceptre et la marotte.* Paris: Fayard.

Lindow, John. (2001). *Handbook of Norse Mythology.* Santa Barbara: ABC-Clio.

Lings, Martin. (1984). *The Secret of Shakespeare.* New York: Inner Traditions International.

Lopez, Barry. (1990). *Giving Birth to Thunder, Sleeping With His Daughter: Coyote Builds North America.* New York: Perennial.

Luke, Sir Harry. (1934). *An Eastern Chequerboard.* London: L. Dickson.

Mantenay, J. (1908). *St. Benoît Labre (1748–1783).* Paris.

Marshall, Bonnie C. and Mihailovich, Vasa D. (Ed.). (2001). *Tales from the Heart of the Balkans.* Englewood, CO: Libraries Unlimited.

Massignon, Louis. (1997). *Les trois Prières d'Abraham.* Paris: Le Cerf.

Merrell-Wolff, Franklin. (1973). *Pathways through to Space.* New York: Julian Press.

Moltmann, Jürgen. (1972). *Theology of Play.* New York: Harper and Row.

Morreall, John. (1999). *Comedy, Tragedy, and Religion.* Albany: State University of New York Press.

Motz, Lotte. (1997). *The Faces of the Goddess.* New York: Oxford University Press.

Mourning Dove. (1990). *Coyote Stories.* Lincoln: University of Nebraska Press.

Muller-Ortega, Paul Eduardo. (1989). *The Triadic Heart of Śiva.* Albany: State University of New York Press.

Nemoianu, Virgil and Robert Royal (Eds). (1992). *Play, Literature, Religion: Essays in Cultural Intertextuality.* Albany: State University of New York Press.

Nesin, Aziz. (1988). *The Tales of Nasrettin Hoca.* Istanbul: Dost Yayinlari.

O'Flaherty, Wendy. (1973). *Asceticism and Eroticism in the Mythology of Siva.* London: Oxford University Press.

O'Neil, Louis Thomas. (1980). *Mâyâ in Sankara: Measuring the Immeasurable.* Columbia, MO: South Asia Books.

Olson, Carl. (1990). *The Mysterious Play of Kâlî: An Interpretive Study of Ramakrishna.* Atlanta, GA: Scholars Press.

Oppenheimer, Paul (Ed.). (1972). *A Pleasant Vintage of Till Eulenspiegel,* translated from the edition of 1515. Middletown: Wesleyan University Press.

Ortiz, Alfonso. (1972). *The Tewa World Space, Time, Being and Becoming in a Pueblo Society.* Chicago: University of Chicago Press.

Otto, Beatrice K. (2001). *Fools Are Everywhere: The Court Jester Around the World.* Chicago: University of Chicago Press.

Otto, Walter F. (1965). *Dionysus, Myth and Cult.* Bloomington: Indiana University Press.

Page, Raymond Ian. (1993). *Norse Myths.* Austin: University of Texas Press.

Pallis, Marco. (2003). *A Buddhist Spectrum.* Bloomington: World Wisdom.

Peiffer, Katrina Schimmoeller. (2000). *Coyote at Large: Humor in American Nature Writing.* Salt Lake City: University of Utah Press.

Pelton, Robert D. (1980). *The Trickster in West Africa: A Study of Mythic Irony and Sacred Delight.* Berkeley: University of California Press.

Pétrement, Simone. (1947). *Le Dualisme chez Platon, les gnostiques et les manichéens.* Paris: PUF.

Ponnelle, L. and Bordet, L. (1932). *St. Philip Neri and the Roman Society of His Time.* London: Sheed and Ward.

Powers, William K. (1982). *Oglala Religion.* Lincoln: University of Nebraska Press.

Prabhavananda, Swami. (1963). *The Spiritual Heritage of India.* Garden City, NY: Doubleday.

Pyle, Sandra J. (1998). *Mirth and Morality of Shakespeare's Holy Fools.* Lewiston, NY: The Edwin Mellen Press.

Quennell, Peter. (Ed). (1956). *The Essence of Laughter and other Essays, Journals and Letters.* New York: Meridian Books.

Rabelais, François. (1990). *Gargantua and Pantagruel,* ed. and trans. Burton Raffel. New York: W.W. Norton.

Radin, Paul. (1969). *The Trickster: A Study in American Indian Mythology.* New York: Greenwood Press.

Ragland, Mary E. (1976). *Rabelais and Panurge: A Psychological Approach to Literary Character.* Amsterdam: Rodopi.

Rahner, Hugo. (1967). *Man at Play,* translated by Brian Battershaw and Edward Quinn. New York: Herder and Herder.

Ramdas, Swami. (1994). *In the Vision of God,* volume 2. San Diego: Blue Dove Press.

Reydams-Schils, Gretchen. (1999). *Demiurge and Providence, Stoic and Platonist Readings of Plato's Timaeus.* Turnhout: Brepols.

Rooth, Anna Birgitta. (1961). *Loki in Scandinavian Mythology.* Lund: C.W.K. Gleerup.

Rûmî, Jalâl al-Dîn. (1990). *Delicious Laughter: Rambunctious Teaching Stories from the Mathnawi,* Coleman Barks (translator). Athens, CA: Maypop Books.

Rundle Clark, R.T. (1960). *Myth and Symbol in Ancient Egypt.* NewYork: Grove Press.

Rydén, Lennart. (1970). *Bemerkungen zum Leben des heiligen Narren Symeon von Leontios von Neapolis,* Uppsala: Almqvist and Wiksell.

Saward, John. (1980). *Perfect Fools: Folly for Christ's Sake in Catholic and Orthodox Spirituality.* New York: Oxford University Press.

Sax, Williams S. (1995). *The Gods at Play: Lîlâ in South Asia.* New York: Oxford University Press.

Schaya, Leo. (1977). *L'Homme et l'Absolu selon la Kabbale.* Paris: Dervy-Livres.

Scheub, Harold. (2000). *A Dictionary of African Mythology: The Mythmaker as Storyteller*. New York: Oxford University Press.

Schlesier, Karl H. (1987). *The Wolves of Heaven*. Norman: University of Oklahoma Press.

Scholem, Gershom. (1978). *Kabbalah*. New York: Meridian.

Schuon, Frithjof. (1984). *Light on the Ancient Worlds*. Bloomington: World Wisdom.

Schuon, Frithjof. (1986). *Survey of Metaphysics and Esoterism*. Bloomington: World Wisdom.

Schuon, Frithjof. (2002). *Roots of the Human Condition*. Bloomington: World Wisdom.

Screech, M.A. (1997). *Laughter at the Foot of the Cross*. Boulder, Colorado: Penguin.

Seaburg, William R. and Pamela T. Amoss (Eds.). (2000). *Badger and Coyote Were Neighbors: Melville Jacobs on Northwest Indian Myths and Tales*. Corvallis, OR: Oregon State University Press.

Sédar, Léopold et al. (1965). *La belle histoire de Leuk-le-Lièvre*. London: Harrap.

Sen Gupta, Sudhir Ranjan. (1977). *Mother Cult*. Calcutta: Firma KLM Private Ltd.

Servier, Jean (Ed). (1998). *Dictionnaire critique de l'ésotérisme*. Paris: PUF.

Shah, Idries. (1966). *The Exploits of the Incomparable Mullah Nasrudin*. London: Cape.

Shulman, David Dean. (1985). *The King and the Clown in South Indian Myth and Poetry*. Princeton: Princeton University Press.

Smith, David. (1996). *The Dance of Siva: Religion, Art and Poetry in South India*. Cambridge: Cambridge University Press.

Steward, Julian Haynes. (1991). *The Clown in Native North America*. New York & London: Garland Publishing.

Stoesz, Willis (Ed.). (2000). *The Living Way: Stories of Kurozumi Munetada, a Shinto Founder*. Trans. Sumio Kamiya. Walnut Creek, CA: AltaMira Press.

Stryk, Lucien. (1981). *Encounter with Zen: Writings on poetry and Zen*. Chicago: Swallow Press.

Sturluson, Snorri. (1991). *Edda*. New York: Oxford University Press.

Sulamî, Muhammad Ibn al-Husayn. (1985). *Usûl al-Malâmatiyyat wa-Ghiltât al-Suffiyyah*. Cairo: Matba'at al-Irshâd.

Sundararajan, K.R. (1996). "Experiencing the World: A Comparative Study of Lila and Satori." In *East–West Encounters in Philosophy and Religion*, ed. Ninian Smart. Long Beach.

Swain, Barbara. (1932). *Fools and Folly During the Middle Ages and the Renaissance*. New York: Columbia University Press.

Thompson, Laura. (1950). *Culture in Crisis: A Study of the Hopi Indians*, New York: Harper.

Till Eulenspiegel, His Adventures, ed. Paul Oppenheimer. (1991). New York and London: Garland.

Trevor, Meriol. (1966). *Apostle of Rome: A Life of Philip Neri, 1515–1595.* London: Macmillan.

Turville-Petre, Gabriel. (1964). *Myth and Religion of the North: The Religion of Ancient Scandinavia.* New York: Holt, Rinehart and Winston.

Ugolino di Santa Maria. (1998). *The Little Flowers of St. Francis of Assisi,* W. Heywood (translator), New York: Vintage Books.

Ullmann, Robert and Reichenberg-Ullmann, Judyth. (2001). *Mystics, Masters, Saints and Sages: Stories of Enlightenment.* Edmonds, Washington: Conari Press.

Vallin, Georges. (1975). "Le Tragique de l'Occident à la lumière du non-dualisme asiatique," *Revue philosophique de la France et de l'étranger,* volume 165, pp. 275–288.

Verene, Donald P. (1995). "Folly as Philosophical Idea." In *Being Human in the Ultimate.* Amsterdam: Rodopi, 243–257.

Videbaek, Bente A. (1996). *The Stage Clown in Shakespeare's Theatre.* Westport, CT: Greenwood Press.

Vizenor, Gerald. (1990). "Trickster Discourse," *American Indian Quarterly,* 14.3.

Walker, James R. (1983). *Lakota Myth.* Lincoln: University of Nebroska Press.

Welsch, Roger. (1981). *Omaha Indian Myths and Trickster Tales.* Chicago: Swallow.

Welsford, Enid. (1935). *The Fool: His Social and Literary History,* London: Faber and Faber.

Wiget, Andrew (Ed.). (1996). *Handbook of Native American Literature.* New York: Garland.

Willeford, William. (1969). *The Fool and His Scepter: A Study in Clowns and Jesters and Their Audience,* Evanston: Northwestern University Press.

Williams, Paul V.A. (Ed.). (1979). *The Fool and the Trickster: Studies in Honour of Enid Welsford.* Totowa, NJ: Rowman and Littlefield.

Wright, Barton. (1994). *Clowns of the Hopi: Tradition Keepers and Delight Makers,* Flagstaff, Arizona: Northland Publishing.

INDEX

9 781403 970152